Developing countries and the WTO: Policy approaches

Edited by Gary P. Sampson and W. Bradnee Chambers

United Nations University Press

TOKYO · NEW YORK · PARIS

United Nations University Press
United Nations University, 53-70, Jingumae 5-chome,
Shibuya-ku, Tokyo 150-8925, Japan
Tel: +81-3-3499-2811   Fax: +81-3-3406-7345
E-mail: sales@hq.unu.edu   general enquiries: press@hq.unu.edu
http://www.unu.edu

United Nations University Office at the United Nations, New York
2 United Nations Plaza, Room DC2-2062, New York, NY 10017, USA
Tel: +1-212-963-6387   Fax: +1-212-371-9454
E-mail: unuona@ony.unu.edu

United Nations University Press is the publishing division of the United Nations University.

Cover design by Joyce C. Weston

Printed in Hong Kong

ISBN 987-92-808-1153-7

Library of Congress Cataloging-in-Publication Data

Developing countries and the WTO : policy approaches / edited by Gary P. Sampson and W. Bradnee Chambers.
    p.   cm.
  Includes bibliographical references and index.
  ISBN 978-9280811537 (pbk.)
  1. Developing countries—Commercial policy. 2. World Trade Organization—Developing countries. I. Sampson, Gary P. II. Chambers, W. Bradnee.
HF1413.D285   2008
382'.92091724—dc22   2008007214

Developing countries and the WTO

Contents

Figures

Tables

Contributors

George Akpan is an Assistant Professor of Law at the University of New South Wales Asia Business and Humanities School. He obtained a PhD in Law from the National University of Singapore. Prof. Akpan is a Barrister and Solicitor of the Supreme Court of Nigeria. Until recently, he was a JSPS-UNU Postdoctoral Fellow at the United Nations University Institute of Advanced Studies, Japan. He is also a Visiting Scholar at the WTO Centre, Aoyama Gakuin University, Shibuya, Japan.

Kym Anderson is a Professor of Economics and Foundation Executive Director of the Centre for International Economic Studies (CIES) at the University of Adelaide in Australia, but since mid-2004 he has been on extended leave at the World Bank's Development Research Group in Washington DC as Lead Economist (Trade Policy). He spent 1990–92 as deputy to the director of the Research Division of the GATT (now WTO) Secretariat in Geneva, and subsequently became the first economist to serve on a series of dispute settlement panels at the World Trade Organization.

W. Bradnee Chambers is the Senior Programme Officer at the United Nations University Institute of Advanced Studies, Japan. He is specialized in public international law and international relations and works on environmental treaty and international economic legal issues. Before working at UNU-IAS, he worked at the Transnational Corporation Division of UNCTAD (Geneva).

Graham Dutfield is the Herchel Smith Senior Research Fellow at Queen Mary, University of London. He was formerly Academic Director of the UNCTAD-ICTSD Capacity-building Project on Intellectual

Property Rights and Development. He has served as a consultant or commissioned report author for several governments, international organisations, United Nations agencies and non-governmental organisations, including the governments of Germany, Brazil, Singapore and the United Kingdom, the European Commission, the World Health Organization, the World Intellectual Property Organization, and the Rockefeller Foundation.

Ken Heydon is an economic consultant, a Visiting Fellow at the London School of Economics, and a Visiting Lecturer at Sciences-Po in Paris. Until 2006, he was Deputy Director for Trade at the Organisation for Economic Co-operation and Development. Prior to that, he was the Deputy Director-General of the Office of National Assessments in Canberra, providing advice to the Prime Minister on international economic, political and strategic developments.

Sam Laird is currently the Inter-Regional Adviser for UNCTAD's Division on International Trade in Goods and Services, and Commodities. He is also a Special Professor of International Economics at the University of Nottingham, UK, and Visiting Professor at Sciences-Po, Paris. Previously, he has worked at the World Trade Organization, the World Bank, and for the Australian Government as a research economist in the areas of trade and industrial policy.

Will Martin is a Lead Economist with the World Bank's Trade and

Development Research Group. He has been a member of the GTAP Advisory Board since its inception in 1994. His areas of expertise include agriculture, textiles and apparel, and services trade policy, with a special focus on East Asia. He was a contributor to World Bank studies of the East Asian Crisis and Recovery (1998–2000), as well as a major contributor to the China 2020 studies.

Constantine Michalopoulos is a Special Economic Advisor at the World Trade Organization on secondment from the World Bank.

Nora Neufeld is a Legal Affairs Officer, Trade and Finance, in the Trade Facilitation Division at the World Trade Organization.

Jens Pössel studied law at Christian-Albrechts-University Kiel, Germany, and the University of Hamburg, Germany, specialising in public international and European integration law. He has worked in the field of human rights since 2004, leading the Cuba/Haiti-Coordination Group of Amnesty International's German section. During his postgraduate legal studies at the University of Stellenbosch, South Africa, Jens Pössel specialised in international human rights and trade law. He is currently writing his articles in Germany.

Gary P. Sampson is a Professor of International Economic Governance at the United Nations University Institute of Advanced Studies, Japan, and John Gough Professor of the Practice of International Trade at the Melbourne Business School, Melbourne University. He was

Director of the services negotiations at the GATT for Uruguay Round.

Magda Shahin is Egypt's Assistant Foreign Minister for International Economic Affairs and earlier served as her country's Ambassador to Greece and its chief trade negotiator. She is also a Professor of Economics at the American University in Cairo.

Manickan Supperamaniam is Malaysia's former Ambassador to the World Trade Organization and an Adjunct Professor in the Department of Economics at the International Islamic University of Malaysia.

Acknowledgements

In the absence of a successful conclusion to the Doha Development Agenda, it is not surprising that developing countries see their vision of a truly development-oriented, rules-based WTO trading system drifting away. However, as the outcome of the Doha Development Agenda falls short of their expectations, this should not be taken as a signal to lower expectations for the future. On the contrary, it calls for coordinated and well-informed initiatives to reverse the apparent neglect of their concerns in the Doha negotiations. This then raises the question of what are the important issues for developing countries in the trade negotiations, and what are the alternatives before them if something other than the very short term is under consideration.

For this reason, it seemed that a constructive and timely exercise would be to invite world-experts in those areas of major concern to developing countries to propose both ambitious and realistic policy reforms. For this exercise, it was necessary to identify a selection of priority areas of concern to developing countries. The next step was to invite world-experts to review chosen issues from a policy perspective and advance a number of ambitious but realistic policy proposals.

In carrying out this exercise, there were many sources from which to draw ideas. For example, some priorities were identified in the discussions associated with the joint initiatives of the Institute of Advanced Studies and WTO in their regional training course for academics from developing countries. These courses have now been conducted in Tokyo, Kuala Lumpur, Cape Town and Arusha. Indeed, Chapter 10, which reviews the relationship between the World Trade Organization and human rights, was written by a junior participant in the course designed for SADAC countries and held in Cape Town.

While there have been contributions in terms of advice and ideas from colleagues too numerous to mention, some individuals must be singled out in this context. Both Jorge Vigano and Serafino Marchese of the WTO Secretariat were particularly helpful in offering useful suggestions with respect to the structure of the book, and commenting on a number of the individual chapters. Gregory Sampson of the International Trade Centre played an important role in reviewing the entire volume, and making numerous useful suggestions. It is also important to mention Professor Hamid Zakri, Director of the Institute of Advanced Studies, for his continued support at all stages of this initiative.

The objective of this book is not only to make a useful contribution to the policy debate relating to the WTO and developing countries, it is also to provide a useful and educative text for those that would like to know more about the issues confronting developing countries and possible means of dealing with them. We hope the book has achieved both objectives.

Abbreviations

AB	Appellate Body
ABI	Argentina, Brazil and India
ABS	access and benefit sharing
AC	Andean Community
ACP	African, Caribbean and Pacific
AFT	aid for trade
AFTA	ASEAN FTA
AGOA	African Growth and Opportunities Act
AIDS	Acquired Immunodeficiency Syndrome
ALADI	Latin American Integration Association
AMS	Aggregate Measure of Support
AoA	Agreement on Agriculture
APEC	Asia-Pacific Economic Cooperation
ASEAN	Association of Southeast Asian Nations
BOP	balance of payments
BSE	bovine spongiform encephalopathy
CAFTA	US-Central American FTA
CARICOM	Caribbean Community and Common Market
CBD	Convention on Biological Diversity
CEEC	Central and East European country
CG	Core Group
CGE	computable general equilibrium
CIF	cost, insurance and freight
COMESA	Common Market for Eastern and Southern Africa

CSME	Caribbean Single Market and Economy
CTD	Committee on Trade and Development
DDA	Doha Development Agenda
DIA	Development Impact Assessment
DSB	Dispute Settlement Body
DSU	Dispute Settlement Understanding
EAC	East African Community
EAs	Europe Agreements
EC	European Community
ECA	East and Central Africa
ECCAS	Economic Community of Central African States
EFTA	European Free Trade Association
EPA	economic partnership agreement
EPZ	export processing zone
EU	European Union
FAO	Food and Agriculture Organization
FDI	foreign direct investment
FTA	free trade agreement
GA	General Assembly
GATS	General Agreement on Trade in Services
GATT	General Agreement on Tariffs and Trade
GDP	gross domestic product
GI	geographical indication
GNP	gross national product
GSP	Generalized System of Preferences
GTAP	Global Trade Analysis Project
HIV	human immunodeficiency virus
ICCPR	International Covenant on Civil and Political Rights
ICESCR	International Covenant on Economic, Social and Cultural Rights
ICJ	International Court of Justice
IF	Integrated Framework for Trade Related Assistance for the LDCs
ILO	International Labour Organization
IMF	International Monetary Fund
IP	intellectual property
IPP	IP protection
IPR	IP rights
ITC	International Trade Centre
LAC	Latin America and the Caribbean
LDC	least-developed country; less-developed country
LLDC	least-less-developed country
MDC	more-developed country

MDG	Millennium Development Goal
MERCOSUR	Southern Common Market
MFN	most-favoured nation
MTS	multilateral trading system
NAFTA	North American Free Trade Agreement
NAMA	non-agricultural market access
NFIDC	net food-importing developing country
NG	Negotiating Group
NGO	non-governmental organization
NTB	non-tariff barrier
OECD	Organisation for Economic Co-operation and Development
PICTA	Pacific Island Countries Trade Agreement
R&D	research and development
RTA	regional trade agreement
SACU	Southern African Customs Union
SADC	South African Development Community
SAFTA	South Asian Free Trade Area
SDT	special and differential treatment
SME	small and medium-sized enterprise
SPS	Sanitary and Phytosanitary Agreement
SSA	Sub-Saharan Africa
TA	trade assistance
TACB	technical assistance and capacity building
TB	tuberculosis
TBT	Technical Barriers to Trade Agreement
TF	Trade Facilitation
TK	traditional knowledge
TNC	transnational corporation
TPR	Trade Policy Review Mechanism
TRIM	trade-related investment measure
TRIPS	Trade-Related Intellectual Property Rights
TRQ	Tariff Rate Quota
UDHR	Universal Declaration of Human Rights
UN	United Nations
UNCTAD	UN Conference on Trade and Development
UNDG	UN Development Group
UNDP	UN Development Programme
UNESCO	UN Educational, Scientific and Cultural Organization
UNHCHR	UN High Commissioner for Human Rights
US	United States
US-DR-CAFTA	US-Dominican Republic-Central America FTA
VCLT	Vienna Convention on the Law of Treaties

WCA	West and Central Africa
WCO	World Customs Organization
WHO	World Health Organization
WIPO	World Intellectual Property Organization
WTF	World Trade Fund
WTO	World Trade Organization

1

Introduction and overview

W. Bradnee Chambers and Gary P. Sampson

With a well-accepted – albeit controversial – link between trade and development, it follows that achieving the objective of a well-functioning trading system is an integral part of the process of trade-led development. The goal of a world trading system centred on the World Trade Organization (WTO) is for multilaterally agreed law, coupled with the progressive liberalization of trade, to the basis for international trade relations. The goal is to ensure respect for the interests of all trading partners – large and small. This should come through trading arrangements built on non-discrimination, and agreed rules that apply equitably to countries of all sizes and levels of development. As rules mean little if not effectively enforced, any rules-based system should be backstopped with an effective dispute settlement mechanism. To promote international trade and the interests of developing countries, the system should be coupled with a global forum for the discussion and negotiation of trade issues, and the progressive removal of tariff and non-tariff barriers to trade.

The goal of the Doha Development Agenda (DDA) has been to improve the existing system to achieve this result. However, to create and maintain such a system there must be a collective sense that market access for trade in services, agricultural and non-agricultural goods is in the interest of each country. There must also be a sense that the system provides the necessary legal flexibility for each country to pursue and implement its own national priorities. Additionally, the system must be sufficiently robust to withstand systemic and other challenges. Finally, the

Developing countries and the WTO: Policy approaches, Sampson and Chambers (eds),
United Nations University Press, 2008, ISBN 978-92-808-1153-7

processes that underpin the system must be seen to be both efficient and equitable.

The objective of this book is to investigate each of these aspects of the multilateral trading system as they relate to developing countries and the policy options before them.

At the most fundamental level, the characteristics of a development-oriented rules-based trading system are not easy to define. The question of what is an effective development policy has itself been a moving target. The vast development literature of the last half-century has vacillated between extremes with respect to what is the appropriate development strategy for developing countries. In the early years of the General Agreement on Tariffs and Trade (GATT), economic development was seen to come through industrialization via import substitution. Emphasis was on manufactured exports of developing countries coupled with considerable legal flexibility through high levels of protection in the absence of reciprocal respect to tariff concessions. This legal flexibility constituted the core of *special and differential treatment*, with its withdrawal *graduation*.

By the time of the Uruguay Round negotiations, perceptions had changed as to what were the most appropriate policies to foster economic development. Import substitution fell out of favour. In fact, the legal flexibilities offered to developing countries were seen by many as not only ineffective, but also counterproductive. Part of this new policy prescription was a change in approach. Developing countries should adopt broadly the same liberalization policies as developed countries, which required a different domestic policy space, market access priorities and legal flexibility. The objective of increasing participation of developing countries in world trade came to be increasingly measured in terms of the extent of adoption of legal obligations and liberalization commitments of developing countries in their own markets.

It is against this backdrop that this book addresses key policy issues of developing countries within the global trading system. The intent is to examine a cross-section of critical issues facing developing countries, with the objective of offering policy prescriptions that are both ambitious and realistic. The intent is not to be comprehensive in the sense of covering all issues of importance to developing countries. It is, rather, to analyse a selection of issues in each of the areas that are identified in this book as being of importance to them. There is a necessary overlap between the sections. Market access in manufactured goods (Part I) cannot be de-linked from special provisions for developing countries (Part II), nor can the legal flexibility (Part II) be divorced from process matters (Part IV).

Part I of this book addresses questions related to improving the market access of developing countries in services, agricultural and non-agricultural goods. Cotton is examined as a special case. What priorities should be assigned to opening markets in each of these areas, and what obligations should developing countries undertake themselves? The answer is that each country is different and treating developing countries in a generic sense in terms of their priorities and the legal flexibilities offered to them is no longer – if it ever was – appropriate.

In chapter 2, Kym Anderson and Will Martin address a number of key questions for policy makers, including the relative importance of liberalizing agricultural products, non-agricultural goods and services in developed versus developing countries; should market access, domestic support or export subsidies be the focus of attention in agriculture for developing country negotiators; and should "sensitive" or "special" agricultural products be subject to lesser reform?

Their results indicate that liberalizing merchandise trade in the DDA negotiations has the potential for a disproportionately high share of the gains to be available for developing countries, and for agricultural policy reform to be much more important as a source of global welfare gains than reform of the non-agricultural sectors. This follows from the greater degree of trade distortion in agriculture, and points to the market access pillar being the most important source of potential welfare gain.

But realizing potential gains will not be easy. While it is in agriculture that the greatest cuts in bound tariffs and subsidies are required, the political sensitivity of farm support programmes complicates reaching agreement. Because of high tariffs on many products, a compromise agreement with the exclusions sought for "sensitive" and "special" farm products would significantly decrease the gains from reform. With South-South trade expansion potentially contributing to half the benefits to developing countries from further reform, now that developing countries are trading much more with each other, the major beneficiaries of such reforms would be within their own region.

The authors note that expanding non-agriculture market access at the same time as reforming agriculture would increase the prospects for a successful conclusion to the DDA. For developing countries, much of that would come from decreasing barriers to textile and clothing trade.

In chapter 3, Magda Shahin draws attention to the strategic nature of the cotton trade and its importance for four least-developed countries, Burkina Faso, Benin, Mali and Chad. In response to the very considerable decline in world cotton prices in recent years, the four countries launched the "cotton initiative" in the run-up to the Fifth WTO Ministerial Conference in Cancun. The initiative was aimed at removing trade-distorting subsidies and obtaining compensation for losses incurred while subsides were being phased out.

The United States – a major producer and exporter of subsidized cotton – had shown neither interest nor willingness to address the cotton initiative. It called upon the countries to diversify their farm production, and benefit from the US African Growth and Opportunities Act (AGOA) by eliminating tariffs on textiles and garments, and drawing on US development assistance.

On their side, the four countries proposed a mechanism for phasing out support for cotton production with a view to its total elimination. There were to be transitional measures offering financial competition to offset the income the countries were losing. Two decisions were to be taken at the Cancun Ministerial meeting in September 2003, but the proposal failed with the rest of the Cancun agenda.

In the July 2004 WTO Framework Agreement (July Package) the African countries won a major concession from the United States to prioritize the cotton issue as a separate sectoral initiative. In addition, Brazil's WTO dispute settlement case against the US cotton subsidies lent impetus to the debate. Consequently, the African countries were determined to reach some kind of agreement at the sixth ministerial meeting in Hong Kong. It was in fact agreed that the elimination of cotton subsidies would be accelerated and that cotton imports from the four countries would be free of duty or quotas. Ministers also agreed to emphasize the phase-out of trade-distorting domestic subsidies.

According to Shahin, the WTO decision should encourage developing countries to continue their struggle to make the WTO a fairer place. The cotton initiative remains a practical manifestation of DDA objectives. As the only specific interest of African cotton-producing countries, the elimination of subsidies is a critical test of whether the DDA can deliver on development and poverty reduction. She says it would be unfortunate if the elements agreed on in Hong Kong are not implemented as long as the Doha round remains in a state of flux.

In chapter 4, Sam Laird sets out how the current DDA Work Programme provides the basis for negotiation on non-agricultural market access (NAMA) by means of "a non-linear formula applied on a line by line basis". Given the mandate of the DDA to reduce or eliminate tariffs, in particular on products of export interest to developing countries, it is perhaps inevitable that negotiations focus on "harmonizing" formula approaches. In particular, the discussion has focused on variations of a Swiss formula. Numerous formulae for NAMA-related tariff-cuts have been proposed since negotiations started.

The second broad approach is based on a proposal by Argentina, Brazil and India for a coefficient to be based on each country's current national tariff average, possibly multiplied by another factor that could be linked to flexibilities or to credit for past unilateral reforms. The African Group has proposed incorporating a "correction coefficient" in this formula linked to the treatment of non-reciprocal preferences, while the African Caribbean and Pacific Group has called for a "vulnerability index" to identify products eligible for special treatment.

With so many possible coefficients and many questions over the treatment of non-formula issues, it is difficult to evaluate the various proposals. However, one general conclusion is that, at the technical level, analysis of the main proposals shows that, regardless of the approach taken, aggregate global trade and welfare is mostly affected by the level of exemptions taken by developed countries. In this respect, a further consideration is that while the more ambitious scenarios offer greater export possibilities and welfare gains, they involve increased imports and greater inter-sectoral shifts in production and employment with losses of tariff revenue. Therefore, they face greater resistance.

A number of developing countries have expressed concern over the erosion of their preferences following most-favoured nation (MFN) tariff reductions. The effects of the erosion, while estimated to be minor in aggregate, are more likely to be affected by the level of ambition rather than the precise formula. Laird believes that, to some extent, improvement in the scope and operation of existing preference schemes, including simpler administration and rules of origin, could help offset some losses.

While developing countries generally accept that trade liberalization is beneficial, at least in the long term, many are concerned about adjustment costs, as well as potential losses from preference erosion and a decline in tariff-based revenues. Success in implementing the eventual agreement on the new commitments depends critically on developing countries' being able to generate a supply response that takes advantage of market opportunities. To do this, many counties will need to build physical and institutional infrastructure, especially for transport. This need can be met only by substantial financial flows that go beyond the remit of the WTO. In this sense the Aid for Trade Initiative as described in chapter 12 is of special importance.

In chapter 5, Gary Sampson points out that the General Agreement on Trade in Services (GATS) holds the potential to greatly expand trade in services and profoundly change international patterns of investment and production consumption. As ongoing negotiations have been folded into the DDA, significant future liberalization of trade in services looks bleak at best.

Sampson notes that, against this backdrop, it is perhaps timely to reflect on some of the broader consideration of policy relevance with respect to GATS. In particular, GATS provides the policy space that developing countries consider absent in other WTO agreements. As there is considerable flexibility for developing countries to pursue their own development paths, these options should be carefully reviewed in the light of each country's development strategy.

Developing countries were successful in making development an integral part of GATS. The most important policy challenge facing them now is how best to exploit the opportunities presented in GATS. GATS provides a framework within which developing countries can promote domestic policy reform. On the market access front, as is formally recognized, developing countries should receive recognition for liberalization taken autonomously.

A principle criticism of GATS is that the foreign provision of many services could constitute an encroachment of national sovereignty and be at variance with domestic development priorities. Commitments with respect to government services supplied on a commercial basis in the area of education and health services are frequently singled out. Developing countries have not, however, engaged in a privatization of public healthcare or education systems. Indeed they have enforced the same standards on foreign suppliers as on nationals for the protection of the public. Furthermore, when developing countries provide access to their markets for Foreign Service suppliers, they are free to attach conditions aimed at their participation in trade in services.

The vast majority of measures that affect trade in services arise from domestic regulations. As the degree of sophistication of the nature of services provision increases with technological advancement, so does the concern of the public for health, the environment and safety. Consequently, the regulation of services trade and production will become increasingly complex. There is thus need for effective disciplines on the domestic regulation of services activities so as to ensure that they do not "constitute unnecessary barriers to trade".

Part II asks, if each developing country is unique, with a need to implement its own appropriate development strategy, what meaning can be given to commitment not to treat un-equals equally in the WTO legal system? What form should legal flexibilities take for the multilateral trading system to be truly supportive of economic development? In the DDA, the increase in participation of developing countries has become increasingly synonymous with developing countries forgoing legal flexibility and undertaking more commitments in the context of trade liberalization. The validity of this approach raises the question of what is the appropriate development strategy for each developing country.

In chapter 6, Constantine Michalopoulos notes that, while special and differential treatment (SDT) for developing countries has long been accepted and WTO agreements contain a large number of provisions for SDT, developing countries have felt that the provisions have not been properly implemented and more flexibility – more "policy space" – is required to permit the implementation of their development strategies.

The DDA called for a review of WTO SDT provisions with the objective of "strengthening them and making them more precise, effective and operational". Despite extensive negotiations in the context of the DDA, there is little agreement on the type of measures required.

Many developing countries regard SDT provisions as meaningless, while many developed countries regard them as bad economics and outdated. A fundamental premise of SDT is that developing countries are intrinsically disadvantaged in their participation in international trade and therefore multilateral agreements must account for this weakness when specifying their rights and obligations. A related premise is that trade policies that maximize sustainable development in developing countries differ from those in developed economies, and policy disciplines applying to developed economies need not necessarily apply to developing countries. A final premise is that it is in the interest of developed countries to assist developing countries in their fuller integration and participation in the international trading system.

Based on these premises, provisions in WTO agreements fall into two broad categories: positive action by developed-country members and exceptions to rules and obligations. In the DDA, developing countries have made numerous proposals both addressing the principle of SDT and with respect to sector-specific provisions.

In broad measure, there are two main problems with the present system of SDT. First, there is no consensus on whether developing countries should be subject to different trade rules. Second, the system has encouraged a "pretend" culture in the WTO. According to Michalopoulos, developing countries pretend that they are the same except for the least developed countries (LDCs), while the developed countries pretend that they provide meaningful SDT to all developing countries. Underlying both premises is the fact that the WTO is not primarily a development institution, but one in which trade policies are formulated by trade ministers primarily beholden to domestic producers.

If there is to be country-specific SDT, country differentiation requires agreement on the criteria used to define eligibility for SDT. At the moment, the WTO recognizes 50 LDCs, of which 32 are WTO members. For the rest, vast differences in institutional capacity and degree of integration in the world markets remain ignored if a generic approach is adopted. A policy is needed that more narrowly defines which countries are eligible for SDT and the nature and conditions under which legal flexibility can be resorted to.

Michalopoulos's recommendations include: a regular review of SDT implementation by utilizing the Trade Policy Review Mechanism (TPR); detailed guidelines regarding the commitments sought from acceding members; and enhancing the capacity of the Secretariat to provide technical assistance.

For Manickan Supperamaniam in chapter 7, the concept of SDT is a fundamental element of the multilateral trading system and has increasingly defined the nature of developing country participation in the trading system. SDT has evolved to include preferential market access, a longer tariff phase-out period and flexibilities on implementing GATT/WTO disciplines and rules, as well as offers by developed countries to provide technical assistance and capacity building to facilitate implementation of GATT/WTO agreements. At the same time, it has changed from providing flexibilities and spaces for development policy based on economic criteria, to time-limited derogations from the rules with more favourable treatment regarding tariff and subsidy reduction commitments and more generous thresholds in the application of market defence measures.

WTO agreements contain approximately 155 provisions on SDT aimed at enabling developing countries to avail themselves of the rights provided while observing their obligations. According to Supperamaniam, experience has shown that these SDT provisions have failed to even remotely achieve their objectives in terms of integrating developing countries into the multilateral trading system and improving their trading conditions. The reasons for these shortcomings are: they only recognize the interests of developing countries in very general terms; merely provide for a longer time frame for implementation; or provide for some form of technical assistance.

Developing countries succeeded in putting SDT in the DDA as an implementation component of the development dimension to correct the inequities and imbalances of the international trading system. Numerous developing-country proposals call for making SDT provisions mandatory rather than best-endeavour commitments. Supperamaniam believes that decisions on these proposals have been somewhat desultory and no headway has been made so far despite intense negotiations and several extended deadlines.

There are two serious problems with the current WTO approach to SDT. First, there is a fundamental flaw in the presumption that developing countries are equipped to take on obligations similar to developed countries. Second, it is false to argue that developing countries should liberalize on the same basis as developed countries, ignoring the real differences in adjustment capacity and developmental needs.

There are strong reasons why favourable treatment for developing countries should be maintained and further enhanced in the WTO. One of the very clear arguments for SDT relates to a wide range of level-playing-field issues, whether it is in terms of size of economies, trade share, industrial capacity or poverty issues or the size and capacity of enterprises. Furthermore, because the WTO constrains domestic policy choices necessary to make strategic liberalization possible, SDT has a crucial role in providing development space in respect to certain instruments and obligations.

The focus of the Doha work programme on development necessitates that efforts are made to mainstream development considerations into existing WTO rules and emerging disciplines. Potential problems will arise from the outcome of the Doha regulations and other elements of the work programme in terms of the costs of current and emerging WTO agreements.

Part III recognizes that challenges to the efficacy of the multilateral trading system can come in many forms, and provides three examples. First, the recent proliferation of preferential trading arrangements has potentially fragmented the rules-based trading system built on the founding-stone of non-discrimination. Second, should the trading system be the vehicle for the implementation of non-commercial goals and social standards such as environmental protection, labour standards and human rights? Could it become a vehicle whereby social values are used as a form of disguised protection? Finally, WTO agreements could be seen to be imbalanced and lead to a loss of confidence in the system itself. Trade-related intellectual property protection is reviewed in this context.

In chapter 8, Graham Dutfield sees a number of complications when dealing in the WTO with rulemaking in the area of intellectual property (IP). Because of the enormous diversity in terms of economic circumstances, there are necessarily quite disparate interests involved. Furthermore, intellectual property rights are designed with certain assumptions as to what should be eligible for protection. In developing countries, creativity may be common, but not easily described or communicated in ways that lend it to IP protection. Examples given by the author include curare, batik, myths and the dance "lambada", which flow out of developing countries unprotected by intellectual property rights, while Prozac, Levis, John Grisham novels and the movie *Lambada!* flow in – protected by a suite of intellectual property laws, which in turn are backed by trade sanctions. A further difficulty is that the sophisticated and aggressive intellectual property forum management and other political strategies employed by the United States and the European Union seem to undermine WTO multilateralism. Increasingly, developing countries are pressured outside the WTO forum to raise their IP standards well above those required by the WTO Agreement on Trade-Related Intellectual Property Rights (TRIPS) to become what is commonly dubbed "TRIPS plus".

Dutfield notes that the current conventional wisdom is that the world's most successful nations are those best at producing, acquiring, deploying and controlling valuable knowledge. Knowledge, especially new knowledge unavailable to one's rivals, is key to international competitiveness and therefore to national prosperity. Those who accept such a view tend to assume, first, that knowledge-based economies are nowadays wealthier, almost by definition, than traditional or natural resource-based ones. Second, that wealth-creating knowledge of the kind that turns economies into knowledge-based ones comes almost exclusively out of universities, corporate laboratories and film, music, art and design studios, and not out of such unlikely places as peasant farmers' fields and indigenous communities. Third, this transformation requires the availability of high US- or European-style standards of intellectual property protection and enforcement. In short, rich countries have such standards, poor countries do not. Therefore, to be like rich countries, poor countries must adopt these standards; the "magic of the marketplace" will presumably conjure up the rest.

Dutfield's overall conclusion is that well-designed IP systems can benefit national economies just as poorly designed ones can harm them. But how does one go about designing and negotiating an appropriate IP system or fine-tuning an existing one? The economic and social impact of IP reform is very hard to predict reliably, especially in the long-term. This is particularly the case for developing countries. This is a real handicap in the present situation, where countries are pressured to negotiate and implement new multilateral trade rules and bilateral or regional free trade or investment agreements, and to respond to powerful stakeholder groups – often foreign ones – demanding changes to national regimes that may not serve the interests of their citizens and other domestic stakeholders. Such difficulties in measuring impacts make it difficult for governments and their representatives to know what negotiating position to adopt on IP, how best to handle complex trade issue-linkage bargains, and how far they should accommodate the demands of international business interests clamouring for change to domestic IP rules.

According to Ernst-Ulrich Petersmann in chapter 9, WTO law suffers from the same ambivalence as WTO politics. Idealists claim that "member-driven governance" serves the "public interest". Realists counter that consumer welfare, human rights and other constitutional safeguards of citizen interests are neither mentioned nor effectively protected in WTO law. WTO negotiations are driven by producer interests, bureaucratic and political interests; citizens, their human rights and consumer welfare are treated as marginal objects of benevolent governance, resulting in widespread alienation of citizens and democratic distrust vis-à-vis intergovernmental power politics in the WTO.

The author poses a number of questions: how should the "development objectives" of the WTO and "special and differential treatment" be defined in WTO law and policies? Here there is a need for democratic legitimacy based on respect for human rights and "principles of justice". Are human rights legitimate criteria for differentiating SDT among developing countries? What about differentiating WTO technical assistance programs, such as trade-facilitation for combating corruption in customs administration?

Petersmann concludes that, similar to the focus of human rights on empowering individuals and people and protecting their rights against domestic abuses by their own governments, WTO law should focus on empowering private economic actors and consumers by protecting their rights against welfare-reducing abuses of trade-policy powers at national and international levels. He points to the DDA, where WTO Members "recognize ... the need for all our peoples to benefit from the increased opportunities and welfare gains that the multilateral trading system generates". This suggests that citizen interests – in order to reduce poverty and the welfare-reducing protectionism of governments more effectively – must be legally protected more effectively by defining the WTO objective of "sustainable development" in terms of human rights and by empowering "WTO citizens" as legal subjects and democratic owners of the WTO legal system. As governments and WTO dispute-settlement bodies are legally required to interpret international treaties "in conformity with principles of justice" as defined also by universal human rights, WTO Members should recognize for the world trading system what the World Bank has long since recognized for its development assistance.

In chapter 10, Jens Pössel notes that the multilateral rules-based trading system has made a significant contribution to world economic growth and stability over the past 50 years. It has correspondingly established extensive authority within the field of international economic affairs. It now focuses on far more than trade, and has extended its reach to issues that are central to sustainable development. WTO rules now have a potential impact on almost all sectors of society and law. From both an economic and a social perspective, stable and rules-based societies constitute a necessary condition for sustainable development, a well-functioning world economy and a multilateral trading system.

Given the frequency of reference to sustainable development in WTO texts, including ministerial declarations, it is clear that, from the legal perspective, the goal of sustainable development is one of the main objectives of the WTO. In light of this, Pössel explores the human rights dimension of the term "sustainable development" within the context of the WTO, along with the legal basis for a human rights approach to sustainable development. The direct link between trade, sustainable development and human rights comes through the right to non-discrimination, the right to work, the right to food and the right to health, all of which can be directly affected by international trade. Moreover, their realization forms part of the economic or social development process.

The chapter concludes that sustainable development, besides environmental protection, essentially means nothing else but the effective realization of particular human rights associated to the economic and social development process. The globalization of human rights and of economic integration offers mutually beneficial synergies, that is, protection and enjoyment of human rights depend also on economic resources and on integration law opening markets, reducing discrimination and enabling a welfare-increasing division of labour. Therefore, it is vital that WTO Member States consider the human rights dimension of their respective trade policies.

In chapter 11, Ken Haydon notes that, in recent years, there has been a proliferation of preferential regional trade agreements (RTAs). Of the 200-plus RTAs notified to the WTO in the last decade, one quarter have been made since the failed WTO Ministerial Conference in Cancun in September 2003. Furthermore, the share of world trade accounted for by RTAs has grown from 40 per cent to over half of global trade in the last five years. The so-called "new-regionalism" is characterized by a new concern with respect to domestic regulations when compared to more conventional tariff-based preferential agreements.

There are several reasons for this growth. Preferential RTAs are perhaps viewed by both government and business as offering quicker gains to market access than can be achieved through the process of multilateral negotiation. Regional agreements also offer the opportunity to address issues that have been deliberately excluded from multilateral negotiations – notably the two so-called Singapore Issues, investment and competition, which have been dropped from the DDA. What are the implications of this deeper integration for developing countries both as parties and non-parties to the agreements concerned?

Haydon notes that the proliferation of RTAs – both plurilateral and bilateral – increasingly involves agreements between countries at markedly different stages of development. In recognition of these differences, RTAs commonly contain special and differential-type provisions that seek to benefit the less advanced partner. However, while RTA provisions often go beyond those found in the WTO, and while there may be lessons for the evolving debate on aid-for-trade, care is needed in seeking to draw on RTA experiences. Of the two broad types of special and differential treatment, there is one – flexibility in liberalization commitments – that is widely applied in regional agreements. It is, however, of questionable value insofar as it weakens the commitment to market opening. Another – financial and technical assistance – is seen as being broadly beneficial but is implemented in regional accords at a level well below its potential.

Moreover, even where developing countries may benefit from SDT-type provisions in RTAs, such benefit needs to be set against the negative aspects of regionalism. These include increased transaction costs for business and pressure to address trade-related concerns such as core labour standards or protection of the environment. While regional agreements can complement the multilateral trading system, they can never be a substitute for it. Complementarity would be fostered by donor support for regional efforts at capacity building and by a strengthened commitment, by all countries, to open markets and strengthened rules of trade.

Part IV looks at two very practical process-related issues of importance for developing countries – how to ensure that the dispute settlement system functions in such a way as to adequately preserve their rights, and what means to facilitate trade will enable developing countries to take full advantage in a practicable sense of the opportunities offered by the multilateral trading system.

In chapter 12, George Akpan explores developing countries and reform of the Dispute Settlement Understanding (DSU). He looks at how the present system affects the participation of developing countries, and how reforms could improve their participation in the Dispute Settlement Body (DSB). Many proposals have been made. One relates to the introduction of permanent panellists, similar to that of the Appellate Body. The present ad hoc system, he says, is a carry-over from the old GATT days. Although this proposal has received little support among members, he believes much can be said in support of the idea. Some developing countries are opposed, as they feel that it will lead to increased judicialization of the system and remove flexibility that they might have in regulatory solutions to meet their peculiar circumstances.

Other procedure-related proposals include the consultation process, where some have proposed the period required for consultations should be decreased from the present 60 days to 30 days to speed up the process. Others call for the enhancement of third-party participation in the consultation process. The current rules recognize that a Member with substantial trade interests can request consultation and join in the process as a third party. In Akpan's view, developing countries should support proposals to increase participation in general, as this provides them the opportunity to learn more about substantive and systemic issues. In the case of non-compliance, he proposes that the right to retaliate should be reformed, and used only as a last resort to force compliance with the ruling of the panel or Appellate Body.

Many other proposals on the table are systemic in nature: on the issue of transparency of WTO dispute settlements systems; to strengthen SDT provisions of the DSU for developing country Members; and facilitating the access of developing countries to the dispute settlement system in general.

According to Akpan, many developing countries joined the WTO in the expectation that it would help them to address their development challenges through trade. To achieve this they need to be able to participate in the system effectively – including using the dispute settlement mechanism to defend their trade interests. It is not suggested in the chapter that the rules are biased against developing countries, rather the argument is that, given the peculiarity of developing countries, specific arrangements should be introduced to facilitate participation of developing countries in dispute-settlement proceedings.

According to Nora Neufeld in chapter 13, Trade Facilitation (TF) negotiations were slow to start due to developing countries' reluctance to engage in what they saw as an already ambitious multilateral round. This view was strengthened by the parallel attempt to launch negotiations on three other Singapore issues.

Traditionally, due to developing-country resistance, TF work has taken place in customs or other market-access-related WTO bodies. However, the resistance to rulemaking for TF was overcome in the July Package, where negotiations to make commerce more efficient through the rationalization of procedures, documentation and information flows were foreseen. The first two years of TF negotiations showed that they could deliver substantive improvements to the current trading regime. They produced a promising set of proposed rules. On the table when the Round was suspended was a framework for the elimination of the remaining barriers in the non-tariff field. This would involve rules to significantly change trading realities on the ground.

TF negotiations have been successful for a number of reasons. There is no doubt that TF has a direct link to economic growth. Trade Facilitation is increasingly believed to have the potential to make global liberalization a tool for development by allowing for enhanced participation in international trade, lower trade transaction costs, strengthening of a country's tax and revenue base and ensuring better resource allocation. In this context, the Washington consensus has gradually been replaced by a line of thinking to promote a trade liberalization model that centres on poverty eradication and that bridges gaps in development. For this, a constructive approach to trade facilitation is crucial.

According to Neufeld, the TF negotiations are among the best prepared areas of the DDA. A Work Plan, adopted at the start of negotiations, encapsulated the shared sense of a need for a balanced advancement. Never before had developing countries engaged so actively in making proposals. Perhaps this success is related to the technical nature of the subject, enabling negotiators to focus on relatively uncontroversial substance with political considerations kept at a low-key level.

However, progress in the TF negotiations should not hide the fact that problems need to be addressed. Substantive advances in discussing detailed proposals do not equal agreement on final outcomes. There are wider systemic challenges – especially with regards to positioning within the total outcome of the DDA, and related risks of hostage-taking and the overall fate of the Round.

Neufeld concludes that failure to conclude the TF negotiations would mean failure to realize their trade enhancement and cost-reduction potential – a failure to deliver on the very promises that led to the initiation of the DDA in the first place. It would not only destroy a decade of intense work with tangible advances, but would also put an end to what many see as a new way of constructive cooperation between the developed and developing world.

Part I
Market access

2

Why developing countries need agricultural policy reform to succeed under Doha

Kym Anderson and Will Martin*

Trade-policy reform is of increasing importance to developing countries, given the ever-expanding opportunities globalization forces offer for them to trade their way out of poverty. While hopes were initially high that the WTO's Trade Ministerial held in Hong Kong in December 2005 would reach agreement on the modalities for liberalization under the Doha Development Agenda (DDA), these hopes had to be revised downward prior to the Ministerial. The subsequent suspension of negotiations seven months later has lowered expectations even further. One of the key contributing factors to this impasse has been the frustration many developing countries feel because of the unwillingness of developed countries to reform their agricultural-support policies.

This chapter seeks to explain why the DDA agricultural negotiations are important for developing countries, expose the stumbling blocks to bringing them to a successful conclusion and explore the possible consequences of various choices developing countries might make from the viewpoint of how they could help or hamper the negotiations. In the process, the chapter addresses a number of key questions for trade policy makers, including:

• What is the relative importance of liberalizing agricultural products, non-agricultural goods and services?
• What is the relative importance of liberalizing trade in developed versus developing countries? (Is it enough for developing countries to obtain gains in market access to high-income countries, or do large

Developing countries and the WTO: Policy approaches, Sampson and Chambers (eds), United Nations University Press, 2008, ISBN 978-92-808-1153-7

gains to developing countries require liberalization also of their own barriers?)

- Within the controversial agricultural sector, which of the three "pillars" – market access, domestic support or export subsidies – should be the focus of attention for developing country negotiators?
- Within the agricultural market access "pillar", how helpful would it be to allow some agricultural products to be subject to lesser reform because they are "sensitive" or "special"? (Is this a low-cost way to obtain a political agreement, or does it amount to throwing the baby out with the bathwater?)

All of these questions are critical to assessing the consequences of a Round outcome, and all are empirical and so cannot be answered on the basis of economic theory or a priori reasoning alone. Detailed information on the structure of production, trade, protection and existing WTO commitments is needed, together with a global economy-wide simulation model. This chapter summarizes empirical results from such modeling exercises as an attempt to provide answers to the above questions. Because it is important to understand the way in which results are obtained, we begin by explaining the modeling methodology and data used in this analysis. We then examine what that modeling suggests about the costs of current policies (which from a modeling viewpoint is the same as the benefits from fully removing those policies), before reporting results from various partial reform scenarios that might be considered by negotiators as they contemplate ways to get back together to complete the Doha Agenda.

The model used to assess effects of trade-related policy reform

The model used for this analysis is the World Bank's global, dynamic computable general equilibrium (CGE) model, known as Linkage (van der Mensbrugghe 2005). It is a relatively straightforward CGE model but with some characteristics that distinguish it from standard comparative static models such as the Global Trade Analysis Project (GTAP) model. A key difference is that it is recursive dynamic, so it begins with 2001 as its base year and can be solved annually through to 2015. The dynamics are driven by exogenous population and labour supply growth, savings-driven capital accumulation, and labour-augmenting technological progress (as assumed for the World Bank's Global Economic Prospects exercise in 2004). In any given year, factor stocks are fixed. Producers minimize costs subject to constant returns to scale in production technology; consumers maximize utility; and all markets, including the market for labour, are cleared with flexible prices.

There are three types of production structures in the model. Crop sectors reflect the substitution possibility between extensive and intensive farming. Livestock sectors reflect the substitution possibility between pasture and intensive feeding. All other sectors reflect the standard capital-labour substitution (with two types of labour, skilled and unskilled). There is a single representative household for each modeled region, allocating income to consumption using the extended linear expenditure system. Trade is modeled using a nested Armington structure in which aggregate import demand is the outcome of allocating domestic absorption between domestic goods and aggregate imports, and then aggregate import demand is allocated across source countries to determine the bilateral trade flows.

The model covers six sources of protection. The most important involves the bilateral tariffs. There are also bilateral export subsidies. Domestically, there are subsidies only to agricultural production, where they apply to intermediate goods, outputs and payments to capital and land.

Three closure rules are used. First, government fiscal balances are fixed in any given year. The fiscal objective is met by changing the level of lump-sum taxes on households. This implies that losses of tariff revenues are replaced by higher direct taxes on households. Second, the current account balance is fixed. Given that other external financial flows are fixed, this implies that ex ante changes to the trade balance are reflected in ex post changes to the real exchange rate. For example, if import tariffs are reduced, the propensity to import increases. Additional imports are financed by increasing export revenues, which is typically achieved by a real exchange rate depreciation. Third, investment in the model is driven by savings. With fixed public and foreign saving, investment is driven by two factors: changes in the savings behaviour of households, and changes in the unit cost of investment. The latter can play an important role in a dynamic model if imported capital goods are taxed. Because the capital account is exogenous, rates of return across countries can differ over time and across simulations. The model solves only for relative prices. The *numéraire*, or price anchor, in the model is given by the export price index of manufactured exports from high-income countries. This price is fixed at unity in the base year and throughout the projection period to 2015.

The newest version of the Linkage model is based on the latest release of the GTAP database (Version 6 – see http://www.gtap.org). The detailed database on bilateral protection integrates, at the tariff line level, trade preferences, specific tariffs and a partial evaluation of non-tariff barriers such as tariff rate quotas. Tariffs are lower in the new GTAP database than they were in the previous version because of the inclusion of bilateral trade preferences and of major trade reforms between 1997 and 2001. These included the continued implementation of the Uruguay Round Agreement, especially the elimination of quotas on textile and clothing trade, and China's progress toward WTO accession. Together, these reforms boosted trade's share of world GDP (gross domestic product) from 44 per cent to 46 per cent during those four years.

The version of the Linkage model used for this study is a 27-region, 25-sector aggregation of the GTAP database. There is a heavy emphasis on agriculture and food, which account for 13 of the 25 sectors, and a focus on the largest commodity exporters and importers.

The model's subsidies and import protection database

The main source of protection resides in tariffs or border barriers, although some countries – notably, high-income countries – also have significant agricultural production and export subsidies. The average import tariff for agriculture and food is 16.0 per cent for high-income countries and 17.7 per cent for developing countries, while for manufactures other than textiles and clothing it is 8.3 per cent for developing countries and just 1.3 per cent for high-income countries (table 2.1). The averages of course obscure large variations across countries and commodities. For example, if high-income countries put tariffs on temperate zone farm products at a prohibitive 100 per cent but set tariffs on tropical products such as coffee at zero, the import-weighted average agricultural tariff could be quite low. Commodity averages also obscure bilateral differences. India, for example, has an average tariff on agriculture and food of 82 per cent on imports from East Asia, but only 20 per cent on imports from Sub-Saharan Africa. For high-income countries, agricultural tariffs on goods from low-income countries are lower than on imports from high- and middle-income countries. In other sectors, however, there is less evidence of preferences at this level of aggregation. Imports of textiles and clothing – indeed, of all merchandise – from low-income countries face a higher average tariff in high-income countries than do imports from middle- or high-income countries.

The relative importance of policies in different sectors

Negotiators have only limited amounts of negotiating capital, and would like to be able to allocate it in ways that promise the greatest potential

Table 2.1 Import-weighted average applied tariffs, by sector and region, 2001

Importing region	Agriculture, processed food	Textiles, clothing	Other manufacturing	All goods
High-income countries	16.0%	7.5%	1.3%	2.9%
Developing countries[a]	17.7	17.0	8.3	9.9
	(14.2)	(14.3)	(7.1)	(8.4)
Middle-income	16.5	16.8	7.3	8.9
Low-income	22.2	17.9	14.5	15.9
Developing countries by region				
East Asia and the Pacific	26.3	17.8	8.6	10.5
of which China	37.6	19.4	11.3	13.6
South Asia	33.9	20.1	22.2	23.5
Europe & Central Asia	14.8	10.7	4.1	6.0
Middle East & North Africa	14.1	27.1	7.2	9.8
Sub-Saharan Africa	18.2	23.7	10.5	12.6
Latin America & Caribbean	10.3	11.3	7.1	7.7
World total	16.7	10.2	3.5	5.2

[a] The selected Sub-Saharan African countries (for which national modules are available in the Linkage model) include Botswana, Madagascar, Malawi, Mozambique, Tanzania, Uganda, Zambia, Zimbabwe. *Source:* Authors' World Bank Linkage model simulations
Source: Authors' compilations from the GTAP database Version 6.05.
Numbers in parentheses are the averages at the start of 2005 following WTO accessions including China; the completion of Uruguay Round implementation including the end of textile quotas under the Multifibre Arrangement; and the eastward enlargement of the European Union to 25 members.

gains to their countries. However, identifying where the greatest gains might be obtained is difficult, since this depends on the actions taken not only by the country itself but also by its trading partners. Table 2.2 shows that, overall, developing countries would gain disproportionately when expressed as a percentage of GDP. The second pair of columns in that table shows the income effects of changes in the international terms of trade for each country. For some developing countries the terms of trade effect is negative, reducing somewhat the gains from improved efficiency of domestic resource use (especially in China and India). A comparison of columns 4 ("other countries") and 5 ("own plus other countries") of table 2.2 reveals that it is mainly own-country reform that is lowering developing countries' terms of trade.

From the total estimated potential gains of US$287 billion per year from full global trade reform, those results suggest that 63 per cent would be obtainable from the abolition of tariffs, domestic support and export subsidies in the agricultural sector (table 2.3). This result is striking given

Table 2.2 Impacts on real income from removing all global merchandise trade distortions (including agricultural subsidies), without and with own-country participation, by country/region, 2015

	Real income gain p.a. (US$billion)		That due just to change in terms of trade (US$billion)		Total gain as % of baseline income
	From other countries' reforms	From own + others' reforms	From other countries' reforms	From own + others' reforms	From own + others' reforms
Australia and New Zealand	6.2	6.1	4.4	3.5	1.0
EU 25 plus EFTA	40.6	65.2	29.7	0.5	0.6
United States	21.6	16.2	18.8	10.7	0.1
Canada	1.7	3.8	1.2	-0.3	0.4
Japan	17.4	54.6	13.7	7.5	1.1
Korea and Taiwan	17.0	44.6	10.0	0.4	3.5
Hong Kong and Singapore	8.7	11.2	6.6	7.9	2.6
Argentina	4.0	4.9	1.9	1.2	1.2
Bangladesh	0.0	0.1	-0.1	-1.1	0.2
Brazil	11.8	9.9	7.4	4.6	1.5
China	16.6	5.6	12.5	-8.3	0.2
India	3.9	3.4	1.3	-9.4	0.4
Indonesia	3.6	1.9	1.5	0.2	0.7
Thailand	9.8	7.7	3.9	0.7	3.8
Viet Nam	2.4	3.0	1.5	-0.2	5.2
Russia	-1.0	2.7	0.2	-2.7	0.6
Mexico	-1.2	3.6	0.9	-3.6	0.4
South Africa	1.1	1.3	0.7	0.0	0.9
Turkey	2.1	3.3	1.3	0.2	1.3
Rest of South Asia	1.9	1.0	0.7	-0.8	0.5
Rest of East Asia	2.8	5.3	1.8	-0.9	1.9

Rest of LAC	11.8	10.3	5.3	0.0	1.2
Rest of ECA	0.8	1.0	0.7	−1.6	0.3
Middle East and North Africa	5.4	14.0	3.3	−6.4	1.2
Selected SSA countries[a]	1.1	1.0	0.8	0.5	1.5
Rest of Sub-Saharan Africa	1.0	2.5	0.9	−2.3	1.1
Rest of the World	3.2	3.4	1.5	0.1	1.5
High-income countries		201.6		30.3	0.6
WTO Developing countries		141.5		−21.4	1.2
Developing countries (World Bank def'n)		85.7		−29.7	0.8
Middle-income countries		69.5		−16.7	0.8
Low-income countries		16.2		−12.9	0.8
East Asia and Pacific		23.5		−8.5	0.7
South Asia		4.5		−11.2	0.4
Europe and Central Asia		7.0		−4.0	0.7
Middle East and North Africa		14.0		−6.4	1.2
Sub-Saharan Africa		4.8		−1.8	1.1
Latin America and the Caribbean		28.7		2.2	1.0
World total		287.3		0.6	0.7

Source: Authors' World Bank Linkage model simulations (changes relative to the baseline, in 2001 dollars and per cent)
[a]The selected Sub-Saharan African countries (for which national modules are available in the Linkage Model) include Botswana, Madagascar, Malawi, Mozambique, Tanzania, Uganda, Zambia, Zimbabwe.

Table 2.3 Potential gains to the world from full global goods trade reform

Liberalization by:	Agriculture and food	Non-agricultural goods	Total
High-income countries	135	24	159 (55%)
Developing countries	47	81	128 (45%)
All countries	182 (63%)	105 (37%)	287 (100%)

Source: Anderson and Martin (2006, table 12.6)
(US$billion per year, and percentage contribution to global total)

the relatively small share (less than 9 per cent) of agriculture and processed food in global production and trade, but not surprising when it is
recognized that world agricultural trade is extremely distorted in both developed and developing countries. From a policy perspective, it suggests
that the importance attached to agriculture in these negotiations is highly
appropriate. Of these total global gains, 55 per cent are estimated to
come from liberalization by high-income countries and a still-sizeable 45
per cent from developing countries.

Table 2.4 presents the same decomposition of potential welfare gains
as does table 2.3 for what are frequently termed the developing countries
– the low- and middle-income countries identified by the World Bank.
This group differs from the self-identified developing members of the
WTO in that it excludes the high-income economies of Hong Kong,
Singapore, the Republic of Korea and Taiwan (China). The importance
of agriculture is again highlighted by the fact that an estimated 63 per cent
of the gains to developing countries also accrue from agricultural trade

Table 2.4 Potential gains to developing countries from global goods trade reform

Liberalization by:	Agriculture and food	Non-agricultural goods	Total
High-income countries	26	17	43 (50%)
Developing countries	28	17	43 (50%)
All countries' policies	54 (63%)	32 (37%)	86 (100%)

Source: Anderson and Martin (2006, table 12.6)
(US$billion per year, and percentage contribution to global total)

reform. Furthermore, a little over half of these gains arise from agricultural trade reforms by developing countries themselves: they benefit both by expanded South-South trade and through the efficiency gains resulting from own-country trade reform. Another important policy conclusion from this table is that developing countries' own reforms, in both agricultural and non-agricultural trade, provide half their total benefits, so that the traditional GATT practice (at least prior to the Uruguay Round ending in 1994) of allowing developing countries to exclude themselves from multilateral disciplines halves their potential to benefit from participation in the negotiations.

The relative importance of policies within the agricultural sector

Within the agricultural negotiations, important decisions must be made on the allocation of resources between the three "pillars" of the negotiations – disciplines on market access (tariffs), domestic support (domestic subsidies) and export competition (export subsidies). Table 2.5 gives the estimated impacts of each reform on the welfare of high-income and developing countries. A striking feature of that table is the overwhelming importance of tariff reductions under the market access pillar. Domestic and export subsidies are almost trivial by comparison, contributing only 5 per cent and 2 per cent, respectively, of the global gains from agricultural reform.

This result, which proved very controversial despite being consistent with results obtained in earlier modeling studies,[1] led Anderson, Martin and Valenzuela (2006) to drill down to explain its origins. The key factors determining the result turn out to be that border measures provide the overwhelming amount of support to agriculture (US$402 billion out of a total of US$499 billion in global agricultural support); that the rates of

Table 2.5 Benefits of agricultural trade reform due to each of the three pillars

Policy measure: Benefiting region:	Tariffs	Domestic subsidies	Export subsidies	All
Developing countries	106	2	−8	100
High-income countries	89	6	5	100
World	93	5	2	100

Source: Anderson, Martin and Valenzuela (2006)
(Per cent of total gains from full global agricultural reform)

protection provided by border measures are much more variable than those provided by domestic support; that tariffs and export subsidies distort both production and consumption while domestic subsidies distort only production; and that export subsidies provide a second-best global welfare gain by offsetting the strong anti-trade bias of most agricultural trade distortions. While the widely used OECD measures of agricultural support suggest that subsidies paid by treasuries contributed roughly 40 per cent of OECD agricultural assistance, these measures cover only primary agriculture in the OECD countries. When the measure is broadened to cover processed agricultural products and all protection provided to agriculture in developing countries, Anderson, Martin and Valenzuela find that the contribution of border measures such as import tariffs and export subsidies to overall transfers to agriculture rises to over 80 per cent.

These results help in understanding key stumbling blocks in the agricultural negotiations. Domestic support is particularly important in the United States, where it accounts for nearly two-thirds of all support to farmers (compared with barely 40 per cent in Europe and less than 10 per cent in Japan and Korea), whereas export subsidies are mostly provided by Western Europe where market access barriers also are prominent. Thus, the United States is not willing to lower its farm supports unless (1) the European Union not only eliminates export subsidies but also provides substantially greater access to its lucrative markets for farm products – which is where the greatest gains in global and developing country welfare could come from, according to the results in table 2.4 – and (2) large developing countries also provide greater access to US farm products. Since neither finds such reform easy to offer in the current political climate (not least because of upcoming presidential elections in France and the United States), the required leadership to revive the DDA is lacking. US politicians in particular would vote for a DDA agreement only if they could be convinced that they will lose less political support from cutting US farm subsidies than they would gain in political support from securing greater market access for their farmers and agribusiness.

To get better insights into the likely effects of the types of *partial* reforms that are being contemplated by negotiators, careful additional modeling is required, as reported in the next section.

What might Doha partial reforms deliver?

With the above full-liberalization results in mind, what might have been gained from partial reform along the lines considered in the Doha Round

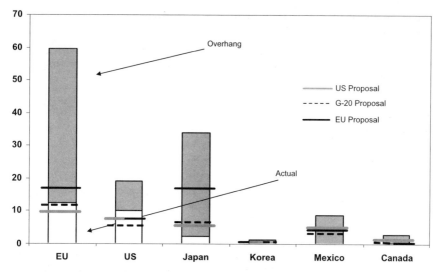

Figure 2.1 Domestic support commitments, actual in 2001, WTO-bound and under various reform proposals (US$billion)
Source: Anderson and Martin (2006)

negotiations? Much about the shape of a potential Doha agreement can be discerned from the tentative agreements reached by WTO members on 1 August 2004 and at the December 2005 Trade Ministerial Meeting in Hong Kong. These provide for protection to be cut from the existing *bound* tariff and subsidy rates – a decision with extremely important implications for the degree of liberalization actually achieved because of the large gaps (binding overhang) between *applied* rates and the legal bindings (commitments) made by member countries at the WTO. This binding overhang is observed in high-income countries (see figure 2.1 for domestic support overhang), but it is even more so for tariffs in many developing countries. Yet under "special and differential treatment" provisions, any cuts in protection will be at least one-third smaller in developing countries and could be zero in least-developed countries. Within agriculture, the highest tariffs and levels of domestic support are to be cut at higher rates under so-called tiered formulas, and export subsidies are to be abolished.

Some parameters

Except in the case of export subsidies, where there is agreement on abolition by 2013, there remains considerable disagreement between WTO

Table 2.6 Proposed cuts in tariff (market access) protection and Doha scenarios examined

	Top Tariff Cut (%)	Sensitive Products (%)	EU/US AMS cut (%)
US proposal	90	1	83/60
EU proposal	60	8	70/60
G-20 proposal	75		80/70
Reform scenario of Anderson, Martin and van der Mensbrugghe (2006)	75	0–5	75/75

Source: Author compilations from EC (2005), G-20 (2005), and United States (2005).

members about the depth of the proposed cuts. This is evident from table 2.6, which shows some key elements of the market access proposals put forward by the United States (United States 2005), the European Commission (EC 2005), and the G-20 group of developing countries (G-20 2005). While the United States sought cuts of 90 per cent in the highest agricultural tariffs, and the G-20 sought cuts of 75 per cent in these tariffs, the European Union has been unwilling to cut these tariffs by more than 60 per cent. Another key parameter is the treatment of "sensitive" products, which the United States sought to limit to 1 per cent of all tariff lines, while the European Union sought 8 per cent of tariff lines. As is evident from the final row of table 2.6, the scenarios examined in this study fit well within the range of the proposals that were under discussion up to July 2006. Under the domestic support pillar, the United States sought an 83 per cent cut in Europe's Aggregate Measure of Support (AMS), while proposing a 60 per cent cut in its own; Europe sought cuts of 70 per cent and 60 per cent, respectively; and the G-20 proposed cuts of 80 per cent and 70 per cent (see figure 2.1).

One issue that has emerged as critical is the approach taken to dealing with the "sensitive" products, for which greater flexibility is to be allowed in all countries, and the "special" products, for which even greater flexibility is to be tolerated in developing countries. These products are to be self-selected by each WTO member, although subject to a number of constraints including the number of tariff lines, the depth of cut for these products, and whether Tariff Rate Quotas (TRQs) must be expanded on these products. However, most of the focus in the debate has been on the number of tariff lines affected. Hence, Martin and Anderson (2006) examine the sensitivity of the outcome for one key region – the

European Union – by assessing the impact of increases in the number of sensitive products on the depth of cut achieved in average applied tariffs.

The Martin and Anderson (2006) analysis was undertaken using the MAcMaps database (Bouët et al. 2004). For simplicity and for clarity, the tariffs to be treated as sensitive were assumed to be subject to no effective reduction in applied tariffs. While the WTO's framework agreement requires that market access be expanded on these goods, many proposals envisage doing this through the expansion of TRQs, a form of liberalization that has frequently proved ineffective in the past (de Gorter and Kliauga 2006). For this analysis, it is assumed that countries take into account the height of the initial bound tariff and hence the implied tariff cut; the extent of the gap between bound and applied tariffs (binding overhang) and hence the required reduction in applied tariffs; and the importance of each product as an import. This leads to a simple criterion for selecting products based on the resulting loss of tariff revenues. However, a more sophisticated analysis based on the likely political-economy determinants of reductions in protection (Jean et al. 2005) reaches broadly similar conclusions.

Figure 2.2 shows that a truly slippery slope can be involved when countries are allowed to self-select the products to be exempted from tariff-reduction disciplines. With no products allowed to be exempted, the tiered formula used in our analysis results in a reduction of 40 per cent in the trade-weighted-average applied tariff. As the percentage of tariff

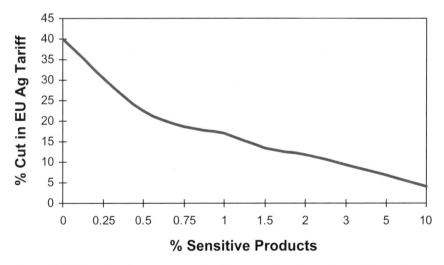

Figure 2.2 The reduction in average tariffs versus the share of sensitive products
Source: Martin and Anderson (2006)

lines allowed to be excluded rises from zero, however, the size of the cut in the average tariff falls very rapidly. With 1 per cent of tariff lines excluded, the reduction in the average tariff falls by more than half, to under 20 per cent. With 8 per cent of tariff lines excluded, the reduction in the average tariff falls to around 5 per cent of its initial level. The key problem illustrated by this example is a consequence of the ability to select the tariff lines to be excluded: some tariff lines refer to products that are trivial in terms of production and trade, or will be subject to little liberalization, while others are hugely important. If discretionary "sensitive" products are to be allowed, disciplining them by the number of products is likely to be ineffective. Instead, disciplines are likely to be needed on the required depth of cut in these products, through the imposition of overall tariff caps, or by restricting the use of these products to a certain percentage of imports (see Jean et al. 2005).

Another striking feature of our analysis is the extent of the effective "overhang" in WTO members' domestic support commitments. In its ambition to discipline domestic subsidies, the Uruguay Round agreement on agriculture includes assistance provided through administered domestic prices, as well as through subsidies paid by treasuries. This ignores the fact that administered prices must be supported by border measures if they are to be sustainable, and therefore counts this support under both the market access and domestic support pillars. Worse, from the point of view of reform, it opened up a possibility of evading future disciplines. The support provided by administered market prices in the past now appears in countries' commitments on domestic support. If the form of protection is changed away from an administered price – even without changing the level of protection provided – then the current measure of support may be greatly reduced relative to the fixed ceiling without any reduction in the actual support provided.

A consequence of the flexibility described above, and under-utilization of countries' existing ceilings, is large gaps between current ceilings on assistance and the levels to which these ceilings need to be cut before actual domestic support must be reduced. The extent of this "overhang" is illustrated by the shaded sections of the columns in figure 2.1, which show the gaps between commitments and actual protection provided for a number of major economies once allowance is made for the possibility of reducing reported support by moving away from administered prices, without necessarily changing the average level of protection.

The US, EU and G-20 proposals for reductions in AMS result in the new commitment levels shown by the cross-bars in figure 2.1. The height of the columns shows current commitments, while the shaded part shows the extent of reduction possible without reducing actual subsidies. As is clear from the diagram, only the deeper reductions proposed by the

United States and the G-20 would require reductions in actual protection in the European Union. The United States has relatively less of a buffer from commitment overhang and so would need to reduce actual support under any of the three proposals, most notably under the G-20 proposal for a 70 per cent cut. However, virtually no other country would need to reduce its domestic support – partly because so much of most countries, AMS comes from market price support, and partly because developing countries would make smaller cuts in their domestic support.

Some scenarios embracing the above parameters

A number of scenarios are considered initially for agricultural and food products in isolation of non-agricultural tariff cuts, before incorporating also some non-agricultural market access. Throughout this section, the WTO usage of the term "developing countries" applies when allocating special and differential treatment (SDT) in the form of lesser commitments to reform, which means Hong Kong, Korea, Singapore and Taiwan are all able to enjoy SDT despite their high-income status.

The experiments begin for Scenario 1 with a progressive or tiered reduction formula with marginal agricultural tariff rate reductions of 45 per cent, 70 per cent and 75 per cent within each of the three bands defined initially by the Harbinson (WTO 2003) inflection points of tariff rates of 15 per cent and 90 per cent for developed countries (that is, for low agricultural tariffs the marginal rate of reduction is 45 per cent, for medium-level tariffs it is 70 per cent and for the highest tariffs it is 75 per cent), and for developing countries the reductions are 35 per cent, 40 per cent, 50 per cent and 60 per cent within each of their four bands (except least-developed countries are not required to undertake any reduction commitments). Even these large cuts to bound tariffs (which are about half way between those proposed by the United States and the European Union in late 2005 in the lead-up to the Hong Kong Ministerial meeting) would lead to the average applied tariffs on agricultural and food products in 2015 being only one-third lower globally (10.0 per cent instead of 15.2 per cent) and 12.5 per cent instead of 14.2 per cent for developing countries.

Scenario 2 examines the consequences of including "Sensitive" farm products as allowed for in the July Framework, with developed countries allowed to treat 2 per cent of their HS6 agricultural tariff lines as sensitive and, we assume, subject to just a 15 per cent tariff cut, and double those proportions of products for both developing and least-developed countries, in part to incorporate also their demand for "Special" products treatment.[2] This would lead to the average agricultural tariff falling only to 13.5 per cent in both high-income and developing countries.

Scenario 3 considers the effects of adding to Scenario 2 a tariff cap of 200 per cent such that any product with a bound tariff in excess of that limit will be subjected to a reduction down to that cap rate, which leads to average cuts in agricultural tariffs of 18 per cent for both developed and developing countries. This would lead to the average agricultural tariff falling in 2015 considerably more for high-income countries (to 11.5 per cent) and but only very slightly more (to 13.3 per cent) for developing countries.

Scenario 4 adds to Scenario 1 the cuts in non-agricultural tariff bindings of 50 per cent in developed countries, 33 per cent in developing countries, and zero in least-developed countries. That lowers the average tariff on all merchandise from 2.9 per cent in the baseline to 1.6 per cent for high-income countries and from 8.4 per cent to 7.5 per cent for developing countries.

Finally, Scenario 5 makes developing (including least-developed) countries full participants in the round, undertaking the same reductions in bound (but not necessarily applied) tariffs as the developed countries in Scenario 4. That lowers the average tariff on all merchandise for developing countries from 8.4 per cent to 6.8 per cent instead of to 7.5 per cent, a cut of almost one-fifth in this case instead of just one-ninth as in Scenario 4.

Estimated welfare and trade effects of those scenarios as of 2015

The welfare consequences of implementing these various reforms over the 2005–2010 period and allowing the global economy to adjust to 2015 are summarized in table 2.7(a) in dollar terms and in table 2.7(b) as percentage changes in real income in 2015.

Column 1 of table 2.7(a) suggests that agricultural liberalization using the harmonizing formula (Scenario 1) would generate a global gain of US$75 billion even without the inclusion of non-agricultural tariff reform. But almost all those benefits accrue to the reforming high-income economies (with whom we include protective Korea and Taiwan as well as Hong Kong and Singapore in this and subsequent tables), such that low- and middle-income countries would gain only US$9 billion. This is largely because their tariff-binding overhang is so great as to lead to almost no cuts in their applied tariffs.

Were countries allowed to have lesser cuts for even just 2 per cent of their farm products they declare to be "Sensitive" (and another 2 per cent in developing countries for their "Special" farm products), those global gains would shrink to just US$18 billion and developing countries as a group would be worse off (Scenario 2). If such exceptions are to be

Table 2.7 Change in real income in alternative Doha scenarios, 2015

	(a) Dollar change					(b) Percentage change				
	Scen. 1	Scen. 2	Scen. 3	Scen. 4	Scen. 5	Scen. 1	Scen. 2	Scen. 3	Scen. 4	Scen. 5
Australia & New Zealand	2.0	1.1	1.2	2.4	2.8	0.35	0.20	0.20	0.42	0.48
EU 25 plus EFTA	29.5	10.7	10.9	31.4	35.7	0.29	0.11	0.11	0.31	0.36
United States	3.0	2.3	2.1	4.9	6.6	0.02	0.02	0.01	0.03	0.05
Canada	1.4	0.5	0.4	0.9	1.0	0.15	0.05	0.05	0.10	0.11
Japan	18.9	1.8	12.9	23.7	25.4	0.38	0.04	0.26	0.48	0.51
Korea & Taiwan	10.9	1.7	15.9	15.0	22.6	0.86	0.13	1.26	1.19	1.79
Hong Kong & Singapore	-0.1	-0.1	-0.2	1.5	2.2	-0.02	-0.03	-0.04	0.35	0.52
High-income countries	65.6	18.1	43.2	79.9	96.4	0.20	0.06	0.13	0.25	0.30
WTO Dev. countries	19.7	1.2	16.8	32.6	47.7	0.17	0.01	0.14	0.27	0.40
Developing countries (WB)	9.0	-0.4	1.1	16.1	22.9	0.09	0.00	0.01	0.16	0.22
Middle-income countries	8.0	-0.5	1.0	12.5	17.1	0.10	-0.01	0.01	0.15	0.21
Low-income countries	1.0	0.1	0.0	3.6	5.9	0.05	0.01	0.00	0.18	0.30
World total	74.5	17.7	44.3	96.1	119.3	0.18	0.04	0.10	0.23	0.28

Source: Anderson and Martin (2006).
(2001 US$billion and percentage changes from baseline)

made, it would be important to exploit the opportunity – provided for in the Ministerial Declaration – to put a cap on bound tariffs. Scenario 3 shows that even a cap as high as 200 per cent would restore at least half of the welfare gain forgone by allowing such exceptional treatment for "Sensitive" and "Special" farm products.

The final two scenarios add non-agricultural tariff cuts to the agricultural reforms in the preceding scenarios. In Scenario 4, lesser cuts are provided for developing countries' non-agricultural tariffs, as is the case for all the preceding agricultural-cut scenarios. Even so, the gain to developing countries doubles by adding these non-farm reforms, relative to Scenario 1 where only agriculture is cut, contributing one-third of the extra boost to global welfare (US$7.1 billion out of the US$21.6 billion difference between the global gains from Scenarios 1 and 4). In Scenario 5, the developing (including least-developed) countries fully engage in the reform process, forgoing the lesser cuts provided for in Scenarios 1 through 4. That boosts their own and global welfare substantially, because their cuts in bound tariffs lead to considerably larger cuts in applied tariffs. Nonetheless, the global average merchandise tariff hardly changes if there were only agricultural reform, whereas it falls by almost one-third or 1.5 percentage points when manufacturing is included in the reform package.

Retaining lesser cuts for developing countries as in Scenario 4 would yield a global gain of US$96 billion from Doha merchandise liberalization, which is a sizable one-third of what is on the table (the potential welfare gain from full liberalization of US$287 billion, reported in table 2.2). But for developing countries the gain would be only US$16 billion, which is less than one-fifth of that group's potential gain shown in table 2.2 of US$86 billion. If developing countries forgo the option of reforming less than developed countries, their gain would rise by 42 per cent, or an extra US$7 billion.

How big would be the consequences of partial reform for farm output and employment growth over the Doha implementation period post-2004? If there were completely free trade, farm output would decline (instead of growing slightly) in just the European Union and Japan while growing slower in a few other highly protective countries – but, for most countries/regions, farming activities would expand. The Doha Scenario 4 would involve much less reform than a move to free trade, and hence a much slower loss of farm output for the European Union and Japan – but also less output growth than under free trade for the vast majority of countries where farm output would be greater. For most of the protective economies, Doha Scenario 4 would simply slow the growth of farm output a little over the coming decade.

The farm employment picture is somewhat different. Typically, economic growth leads to declines in not only the relative importance of agriculture but also in absolute numbers employed in farming once a country reaches middle-income status. Thus it is not surprising that numerous middle- and high-income countries are projected to lose farm jobs over the next decade in our baseline scenario. For the most protected farm sectors, that rate of farm employment decline would more than double if the world were to move to completely free trade but it would increase only slightly under Doha Scenario 4. For most developing economies, though, farm employment would grow a little faster under that Doha scenario as compared with the baseline, allowing them to absorb more workers on their farms (Anderson, Martin and van der Mensbrugge 2006, table 12.17).

A summary of the effects on economic welfare of these scenarios as compared with full liberalization is provided in figure 2.3. Clearly, the more exceptions are made, the less distance the world will move toward realizing the potential gains from opening up our national economies.

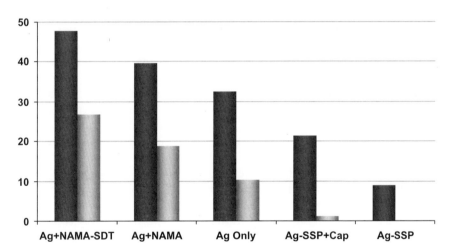

Figure 2.3 Welfare gains from Doha partial-reform scenarios as a percentage of gain from global reform, high-income and developing countries, 2015
Source: Authors' World Bank Linkage model simulations
Ag + NAMA − SDT = Doha Scenario 5: full participation by developing countries
Ag + NAMA = Doha Scenario 4: same as Doha 5 but includes SDT for DCs
Ag Only = Doha Scenario 1: same as Doha 4 but without NAMA reform
Ag − SSP + Cap = Doha Scenario 3: same as Doha 1 but with exemptions for Sensitive and Special Products and a tariff cap of 200%
Ag − SSP = Doha Scenario 2: same as Doha 3 but no tariff cap

Summary and conclusions

The results presented above on the cost of current trade and farm subsidy policies show that liberalizing merchandise trade under Doha has the potential for (1) a disproportionately high share of the gains to be available for developing countries (relative to their share of the global economy), and (2) agricultural policy reform to be much more important as a source of welfare gains to the world, and to developing countries, than reform of the much bigger non-agricultural merchandise sector. This reflects the much higher and more variable distortions in agriculture. Within the agricultural sector, the market access pillar is much more important as a source of potential welfare gain than the two subsidy pillars.

When we turn to partial reforms consistent with the negotiating framework that has been developing in the Doha negotiations, we find substantially smaller potential gains, particularly for developing countries, not least because developing countries have large gaps between their bound commitments and their applied rates of protection, and because they plan to make smaller reductions than high-income countries in their own WTO commitments. Despite this, these proposals could result in worthwhile gains, particularly if they were implemented toward the more ambitious end of the range of possible scenarios under consideration.

But to realize that potential gain, it is in agriculture that by far the greatest cuts in bound tariffs and subsidies are required. However, the political sensitivity of farm support programs ensures that reaching agreement on such reform will not be easy. Even if a compromise agreement is reached, allowing lesser cuts for even just a few "Sensitive" and "Special" farm products would reduce hugely the gains from reform, given the tariff peaks currently in place. Expanding non-agricultural market access at the same time as reforming agriculture would increase the prospects for a successful conclusion to the DDA. For developing countries, much of that would come from reducing barriers to textile and clothing trade.

With South-South trade expansion potentially contributing half the benefits to developing countries from further reform, now that developing countries are trading much more with each other, the major beneficiaries of such reforms would be within their own region. This is especially so in East Asia, where fragmentation of the production process is at its greatest. We hope the political will can be mustered to ensure the Doha round does indeed exploit its potential to make a major contribution to development.

Notes

* The authors are grateful for funding from the UK Department of International Development. The views expressed are the authors' alone and not necessarily those of the funder.
1. See, for example, USDA (2001) and OECD (2006).
2. As described above and in Jean et al. (2005), "Sensitive" farm products are chosen for each country by taking into account the importance of the product, the height of its existing tariff, and the gap between its bound and applied tariffs in that country.

REFERENCES

Anderson, K., and W. Martin, eds (2006) *Agricultural Trade Reform and the Doha Development Agenda*, London: Palgrave Macmillan, and Washington, DC: World Bank.

Anderson, K., W. Martin and E. Valenzuela (2006) "The Relative Importance of Global Agricultural Subsidies and Market Access", *World Trade Review* 5(3): 357–376, November.

Anderson, K., W. Martin and D. van der Mensbrugghe (2006) "Market and Welfare Implications of Doha Reform Scenarios", in K. Anderson and W. Martin, eds, *Agricultural Trade Reform and the Doha Development Agenda*, London: Palgrave Macmillan, and Washington DC: World Bank, pp. 333–400.

Bouët, A., Y. Decreux, L. Fontaigné, S. Jean and D. Laborde (2004) "A Consistent, *Ad Valorem* Equivalent Measure of Applied Protection across the World: The MAcMaps-HS-6 Database", Paris: Centre des Etudes Prospectives et d'Informations Internationales (CEPII).

de Gorter, H., and E. Kliauga (2006) "Reducing Tariffs versus Expanding Tariff Rate Quotas", in K. Anderson and W. Martin, eds, *Agricultural Trade Reform and the Doha Development Agenda*, London: Palgrave Macmillan, and Washington DC: World Bank, pp. 117–160.

EC (2005) "Making Hong Kong a Success: Europe's Contribution", Brussels: European Commission, October 28.

G-20 (2005) "G-20 Proposal on Market Access", mimeo, Geneva, October 12.

Jean, D., D. Laborde and W. Martin (2005) "Rules and Flexibility in Trade Negotiations: The Case of Sensitive Agricultural Products in the WTO", mimeo, Washington DC: World Bank.

Martin, W. and K. Anderson (2006) "The Doha Agenda Negotiations on Agriculture: What Could They Deliver?" *American Journal of Agricultural Economics* 88(5): 1211–1218, December.

OECD (2006) *Agricultural Policy and Trade Reform: Potential Effects at Global, National and Household Levels*, Paris: Organization for Economic Cooperation and Development.

United States (2005) "U.S. Proposal for Bold Reform in Global Agriculture Trade", Facts on Doha Round, available from http://www.ustr.gov.

USDA (2001) *Agricultural Policy Reform in the WTO: The Road Ahead*, Economic Research Service, Agricultural Economic Report 802, Washington, DC: US Department of Agriculture.

van der Mensbrugghe, D. (2005) "Linkage Model Technical Reference Document: Version 6.0", Washington, DC: World Bank Development Prospects Group, January.

WTO (2003) "Negotiations on Agriculture: First Draft of Modalities for the Further Commitments", TN/AG/W/1/Rev.1, Geneva: World Trade Organization, 19 March (The Harbinson Draft).

3

The cotton initiative

Magda Shahin

Cotton is a strategic crop for many developing countries, especially for the four least developed countries in West and Central Africa (Burkina Faso, Benin, Mali and Chad), which succeeded to attract worldwide interest in their fight against trade-distorting subsidies by the United States. Despaired by the decline of some 40 per cent in world cotton prices between 1997 and 2002, they launched jointly what came to be known as the "cotton initiative" in the run-up to the WTO Fifth Ministerial Conference in Cancun. The timing and framework of the initiative were carefully chosen and rightly fitting. The initiative was placed squarely within the framework of the WTO/Doha Development Agenda.[1] As for the timing, it was meant to draw the attention of the Ministers in their first ministerial after the launching of the so-called Doha Round to review progress in the DDA. To date, the cotton initiative has raised more questions than presenting us with viable solutions. Plagued with extreme poverty and malnutrition, these four countries are fighting against a structural trade problem inherent in the multilateral trading system, that of cotton subsidies.[2] However, little interest for a durable and adequate solution has been shown so far. This paper will address briefly the different stages the initiative has gone through. This is mainly for the purpose of pointing to the strengths and weaknesses of such an initiative, procedurally as well as in terms of substance all along its evolution. The landmark victory of Brazil over the United States in its dispute at the WTO and the agreement reached in the last ministerial in Hong Kong (December

Developing countries and the WTO: Policy approaches, Sampson and Chambers (eds),
United Nations University Press, 2008, ISBN 978-92-808-1153-7

2005) were important stepping stones but have definitely not helped solve the issue for the African countries.

Was it a blessing or a curse to have the cotton initiative as part of the agricultural negotiating framework? Would such a course of action help bring the initiative forward or lead to a deviation from the original objective of the co-sponsors? Why have we deviated so much from the initial submission, when – at a time – the cotton initiative was considered to be among the "make or break" of the Cancun conference? What went wrong? How much does the cotton initiative remind us of the Uruguay Round decision on net food-importing developing countries (NFIDCs)? Will it encounter the same fate? Is the cotton initiative operational? What if Brazil had not gone to litigation and won its case timely against the United States for "Subsidies of Upland Cotton"[3] prior to the sixth Ministerial in Hong Kong (December 2005), could the African countries have been able to reach any understanding with the United States in Hong Kong? This is certainly highly doubtful. Yet today, with the Hong Kong outcome vanished into thin air as a result of the suspension of the Doha negotiations and the US manoeuvres regarding its compliance with the Dispute Settlement Body (DSB) rulings, the African countries are back to square one. Lastly, this chapter will also look into possible options – if any – remaining for the African countries in this regard. What should be done to avert the worst of seeing the cotton initiative dying out?

The logic behind the initiative

In June 2003 in Geneva, not far from Evian, where the heads of state of the G-8 were holding their summit, four West African countries, Burkina Faso, Mali, Benin and Chad put forward a sectoral initiative at the WTO to eliminate cotton subsidies. Without sufficient prior coordination with other developing-country groupings, the theory of conspiracy was resonant. Some were pointing the finger at the invisible hand of France, whose main purpose was to embarrass the United States, while diverting attention from the EU agricultural subsidies, at a time when the G-8 was grappling with agricultural subsidies within the preparations for Cancun. Others felt that the four West African countries were prodded and encouraged by non-governmental organizations, especially Oxfam. In the view of many, however, there were more pertinent and valid reasons for such a step.

For the fourth consecutive year, prices were below their long-term average of 72 US cents per pound, reaching the bottom in 2001/02 of 42 US cents per pound (Oxfam 2002). Such a collapse has caused havoc to the

already very fragile economies of these countries and generated substantive losses in their hard currency earnings due to the quasi-total dependence of the West African countries on their cotton exports. In fact,
from 1999/2000 to 2001/02, they had increased their production by 14
per cent, but export earnings fell by 31 per cent. As over 90 per cent of
the cotton produced in the West and Central Africa (WCA) countries is
for export, cotton accounts for up to 75 per cent of the export earnings
and is thus vital for the poverty reduction strategies in the countries of
the four co-sponsors (Goreux 2004).

One would think that the use of the initiative as a litmus test for the
credibility of the Doha Development Agenda might not have been initially a priority goal for the co-sponsors. They launched the initiative for
a dual purpose: the phase-out of subsidies and compensating their recipients for their incurred losses until the completion of the phase-out (WTO
2003b). Little interest was then given to the initiative, as it was left open
to the Ministers to address it. Tabling the initiative, however, under the
title of "Poverty Reduction: Sectoral Initiative in Favor of Cotton", the
four co-sponsors managed to place the initiative on the WTO agenda at
the Cancun ministerial conference in September 2003. It was transmitted
to the heart of the DDA, whose main objectives are poverty reduction
and sustainable development, and was considered as a "make or break"
issue at the ministerial, testing the validity of Doha as a development
round.

The four West African countries like to perceive their initiative more
along the lines of the African initiative for medicines, which was brought
up in Doha and a solution was forced two months prior to Cancun. It was
after strenuous efforts that the developing countries, spearheaded by the
African group, succeeded in the fourth ministerial in Doha to adopt a
ministerial declaration on "Trade-Related Intellectual Property Rights
and Public Health", which in essence gives precedence to public health
over the TRIPS agreement. In other words, the declaration recognizes
that the TRIPS agreement is but one facet of the wider national and international actions to address the public health problems, pandemics as
well as epidemics. Furthermore, the declaration gives its members the
right to determine on which grounds to grant compulsory licensing and
finally emphasizes the promotion of medicines for all, which implicitly
means providing the medicines at affordable prices.

The four African countries dreamt of achieving similar success in regard to their cotton initiative. To my mind, not only do the circumstances
differ, but the substance of the two initiatives is far apart. Not only was
the case of medicines presented by the African group as a whole, and
not an initiative representing only the interest of four African countries,
but also the former attracted strong support from countries such as Brazil

and India, which the cotton initiative lacks to some extent. In addition, at the Doha Conference, taking place after 11 September 2001, Robert Zoellick, the US trade representative, was seeking political solidarity and support for the United States in its fight against terrorism, making the US position more flexible and forthcoming. Thus, the negotiators were able to pull out clearer language from the United States, language less open to various interpretations. This is not to undermine the vitality of the cotton initiative to its proponents, only to bring about the differences surrounding the two initiatives, which make them incomparable with one another.

The United States has shown neither interest nor willingness to address the cotton initiative in a substantive and serious manner. Instead, and to the surprise of many, it called upon these countries to diversify their farm production out of cotton,[4] thus benefiting from the US proposal within the framework of the Africa Growth and Opportunity Act (AGOA) to eliminate tariffs on textiles and garments as well as from the development assistance the United States provides to the African countries in question. One is reminded of Marie-Antoinette when she proposed to the Parisian people, who were lamenting the lack of bread as their minimum condition for livelihood, to eat cake instead. The more logical question to be put to the United States is, wouldn't it be easier – in the framework of globalization and trade liberalization – for its cotton growers to shift to other crops instead of producing at a net loss to the United States?[5] Should it not be more legitimate for the US to reform its policies, where subsidies of the amount of US$3 billion-plus per year is lavished on 25,000 cotton farmers (Williams and Jonquiùres 2003), while 10 million cotton farmers in West and Central African countries are estimated to be losing as much as $1 billion annually in foreign earnings (Williams and Jonquiùres 2003). In the United States, the cost of producing 1 kg of cotton is 50 per cent higher than in the Western and Central African countries. Cotton producers in the WCA region are among the most competitive in the world.[6]

In addition, trying to lure some African countries by giving them preference under the AGOA scheme to import cheap, subsidized US cotton in return for helping them establish and develop value-added export products in textiles and garment sectors cannot be a substitute for removing trade-distorting subsidies. It is incumbent upon the United States to reform, which should be in the end in its own interest and in the interest of its consumers. AGOA cannot be considered as a panacea for all of the United States' sins and can certainly not compensate for US subsidies. Be it preferences through the AGOA or technical assistance packages in the framework of the WTO or additional financial and technical assistance from other competent organizations and specialized agencies, it is no sub-stitute for trade reform on the part of the United States. The gains gener-ated by reform are several times more than those generated by technical assistance packages. Let there be no doubt that the idea of diversifying from cotton in the United States is for its own good. Empirical studies by the World Bank and highly knowledgeable and specialized economists such as Kym Anderson and others have clearly indicated that two-thirds of the gains from agricultural reform in the United States, especially in cotton, will actually accrue to the United States. Furthermore, it is a well-known fact that it is easier in general for developed countries, let alone the United States, to diversify into other agricultural crops and/or other industries than for developing countries to do so because of the rel-ative ease of educating, adapting to new technology and moving around farmers and labour. As for the recognized non-trade objectives of a crop related to its relative importance to food production and/or rural devel-opment and poverty alleviation, cotton is certainly classified as a "special product"[7] for developing countries in general and the WCA countries in particular. This is certainly not the case for the United States and other subsidizing industrialized countries. Hence, other agricultural products in the latter can easily replace cotton production (WTO 2003c: para. 34). Also, cotton constitutes only a minor component of total US merchandise trade, whereas for the four West African countries cotton occupies a stra-tegic position in the development of policies and poverty reduction pro-grams. Cotton accounts for 5 per cent to 10 per cent of GDP, more than one-third of total export receipts and over two-thirds of the value of agri-cultural exports (WTO 2003c: para. 1).

In contrast to the United States viewing the cotton initiative within trade liberalization of textiles and clothing and at best as an integral part of the agricultural negotiations,[8] the initiative had gathered momen-tum among developing-countries groupings. Many developing countries felt frustrated as a result of all the manoeuvres and twisted interpreta-tions of the Doha mandate in the run up for Cancun. Strengthened in their position, the four co-sponsors refused to budge. They insisted on a stand-alone agreement on cotton. They were hesitant to combine cotton with the agriculture negotiations, dealing with it under the broader head-ing of agricultural negotiations encompassing all three pillars of the Agreement, namely, market access, domestic support and export compe-tition. This would only mean that the cotton issue will be pushed to the back burner and find its fate linked with the slow and tedious negotia-tions on each of the three pillars of the agreement on agriculture.

On 16 May 2003, Burkina Faso, on behalf of Benin, Mali and Chad, presented the WTO's Agriculture Committee Special Session with a new

proposal for cotton titled "Poverty Reduction: Sectoral Initiative in Favor of Cotton" (WTO 2003c). The initiative called for two decisions to be taken at the Cancun ministerial meeting in September 2003:
- The establishment of a mechanism for phasing out support for cotton production with a view to its total elimination, and
- The establishment of transitional measures for LDCs: "until cotton production support measures have been completely eliminated, cotton producers in LDCs should be offered financial compensation to offset the income they are losing, as an integral part of the rights and obligations resulting from the DDA".

Without much ado, the proposal failed with the rest of the Cancun agenda. However, it is of note that the Cancun revised text was devoid of any mention of eliminating cotton subsidies or of compensation to the West African countries, which to them was even more disappointing.

An example of manoeuvring: Make it a development issue

In spite of the failure of Cancun, a rightful solution had to be found to the cotton initiative. The WTO, within the framework of its technical assistance programs, organized a workshop between 23 and 25 March 2004 in Cotonou, Benin, to address the issue in a more substantive manner. It was in Cotonou where the issue took all of a sudden more of a developmental twist at the expense of the trade-distorting subsidies. But why would a WTO workshop on cotton highlight the development dimensions when the issue was more of establishing a level playing field in cotton trade and less of developmental assistance (ICTSD 2004)? It is not difficult to imagine that, on the one hand, the subsidizing countries had felt that the promise of additional aid would satisfy the co-sponsors, combined with strong diplomatic pressure they could even push West and Central African governments to drop their demands for urgent reforms of agricultural subsidies. On the other hand, this would have also allowed the WTO to pour cold water on a hot issue and to let the grass grow.

Such manoeuvring is not the first of its kind. One can draw on a similar case not a long time ago when intractable negotiations were held prior to the conclusion of the Uruguay Round regarding the possible negative effects of the agricultural reform program on the net food-importing developing countries. The successful conclusion of a ministerial decision[9] on the issue was more than fulfilling for the countries in question. However, their apparent success has proven not long after to be illusory rather than real.

Though the decision committed the developed countries to provide the NFIDCs with broadly three different types of assistance, food aid, tech-

nical and financial assistance and short-term financing facilities,[10] to date
it has had no effects whatsoever on any type of assistance. The decision
does not lack in substantive requests; however, it is completely devoid of
any issue that is qualified to be addressed in the WTO. The fact that the
decision was made as an integral part of the agriculture negotiations did
not bring it closer to implementation. The decision remained a political
showcase with no teeth, which demonstrated, in part, bad faith from the
very beginning to operationalize its content. With so many caveats, the
decision was prone to failure from the very beginning. Drafted in a best
endeavour clause and with no clear definition as to who were the beneficiaries, it was never designed to be truly implemented. At a subsequent
stage, more than 100 developing countries described themselves as
NFIDCs to benefit from the decision. Furthermore, linking the short-
term facilities with other independent institutions, such as the IMF and
the World Bank, has placed the WTO in the most comfortable position
of disassociating itself from any responsibility of implementation. While
the decision on NFIDCs was envisaged as containing mechanisms for
across-the-board solution, the complexities encountered for its implementation were such that every country suffering from any possible negative effect from the reform program had to find its own way through the
donors and the Multilateral Financial Institutions. For each and every net
food-importing country to prove to its donors that it was affected by the
rise in prices caused by the agricultural reform program has proven practically impossible.

By the same token, there was an inherent risk in diverting the cotton
initiative from a systemic issue into a development one of additional aid
or compensation that will have to be proven separately. Succeeding in
such manoeuvring would simply mean dragging the issue outside the
framework of the WTO and the DDA, as financial compensations fall
outside of the WTO mandate.

Though trying to draw some comparisons with previous initiatives, so
as to avoid any pitfalls of the past, the success of the cotton initiative is
too vital to be measured or guided by what happened to other initiatives.
The WCA have in fact succeeded to work with other African and developing countries on more imaginative solutions by focusing themselves in
Hong Kong on the distorting trade effects of the cotton subsidies. A word
of caution is nevertheless necessary at this point; African countries have
to resist any attempts to divert the issue as to transfer any solution for the
cotton problem beyond the WTO borders. It is also important that
studies pertaining to the effects of American and European cotton subsidies on the WCA countries should emanate from the WTO secretariat.
The work of the panel and Appellate Body regarding the Brazil case
should be a good basis for a study to be conducted within the WTO.

Studies of international cotton committees and independent economists and NGOs, in particular an Oxfam briefing paper on the impact of US cotton subsidies on Africa, are all very valuable but serve as no guidance to the United States or the European Union in the WTO.

The July Package trade-off: A case of constructive ambiguity

The July 2004 Framework Agreement,[11] which helped establish a road map for different areas of the negotiations, managed to bring the Doha round back on track after the debacle of Cancun. This paved the way early enough to allow for extensive preparations to take place prior to the next WTO ministerial, which was held in December 2005 in Hong Kong.

The agreement reached on cotton in the July package, as one of the five selected priority issues, was a prototype for trade-offs where in appearance all parties came out satisfied. For having to give in on pursuing the negotiations on cotton as an integral part of the larger agriculture negotiations, the African countries were able to pull out a major concession from the United States, that of prioritizing the cotton issue independently from other sectoral initiatives. Singling out cotton was something of a novelty. Though falling short of making reference to "early harvest", the decision by the General Council adopting the July Package stipulates that cotton will be addressed ambitiously, expeditiously and specifically within the agriculture negotiations. The complementarity of the trade and development aspects was also stressed.

Juxtaposing the concessions made by the Africans to that made by the United States, the result, at its face value, would be in favour of the Africans 3 to 1. In line with the prioritization of cotton and the exceptional way of handling it, a sub-committee was established upon request of the Africans, to meet periodically to report to the Special Session of the Committee on Agriculture. Yet, the effectiveness of the sub-committee was questioned from the very beginning as its meetings were to be held in the backrooms with so many other meetings taking place at the same time in parallel. Furthermore, the danger was bigger for the issue to lose its specific character as the subsidizing powers had every incentive to dilute the question within the overall negotiations. Another approach would be to hide behind "beautiful promises" the fact that subsidizing members were not in a position to offer a concrete response to the Cancun initiative. African countries' only option was to continue to fight for specific and urgent measures, linking them to the trade distortions caused by subsidies and the precarious situation of their cotton growers. The future will tell whether the WTO is capable of taking into consideration the vital development interests of those of its members that are among the most disadvantaged of the world. In this respect, cotton presents a crucial challenge to the multilateral trading system (Keim 2004).

Though clarifications in the July Package were not made for cotton as to be considered part of the single Undertaking, unlike the Trade Facilitation issue, one would assume that as part of the agriculture negotiations it is a foregone conclusion to address cotton within the framework of the final package. This, however, is double-edged and highly debatable not only in the light of singling out cotton to be dealt with in an exceptional manner (ambitiously, expeditiously and specifically) but more so in the light of the suspension of the Doha round. It is of no interest to the African countries to have cotton as an integral part of the final package, as we are going to see.

Following the July package, the sub-committee on cotton was established on 19 November 2004 and held its first meeting on 16 February 2005. Little progress has been made since then on the cotton issue. Even if it is improbable that the WTO could ignore cotton in the future, there is a clear danger – as said earlier – of the issue losing its specific character.

The first meeting of the sub-committee in February focused on organizational issues relating to the future work. Members highlighted the importance of cotton for their economies, and their desire to see speedy and substantial results from their work program. It should also provide regular updates on the cotton-related developmental implications of the talks, in order to support coherence between the trade and development aspects of cotton. However, they could not agree on whether the sub-committee should address "other" subjects, including broader textile-related issues such as industrial market access and trade facilitation. The United States favoured a broader agenda, potentially covering progress in other areas of negotiations related to cotton such as industrial market access (because of textiles) and rules discussions on subsidies and trade remedies. The United States suggested that the sub-committee could also study a range of trade-distorting policies affecting cotton, such as market access barriers, agricultural subsidies and government policies that benefit synthetics.

The US proposal did not receive broad support from other Members, several of which opposed dealing with such subjects, arguing that the sub-committee was part of the agriculture negotiations and should therefore remain focused on its mandate. They felt that the main problems that needed to be addressed in the sub-committee were export subsidies and domestic support for cotton. Members should agree upon modalities for this sector by July 2005 in preparation for Hong Kong (ICTSD 2005).

Litigation or negotiations

Drawing on the Brazilian case of subsidized upland cotton against the
United States is with a view to opening up more venues for the African
countries in their future course of action. This section will assess the
available options for the African countries, particularly in light of the
lack of enthusiasm shown so far to deal adequately with the cotton initiative. The section will further look into whether litigation is a valid option
for the African countries and, if so, its right timing.

Affected by the subsidies on cotton, Brazil had challenged in September 2002, sometime before the tabling of the African countries of their
initiative, the subsidies by the United States to upland cotton as prohibited and actionable subsidies. Brazil had requested for consultations on
the grounds of its interest being seriously injured due to reduction in
export prices and a loss in world market share on the basis of two main
factors:

1. The United States had doubled the level of subsidies it provided in
   2001 to its farmers compared with 1992, so that cotton subsidy was
   not covered by the immunity granted under the Peace Clause[12] of the
   WTO's Agreement on Agriculture. This clause protected countries
   using subsidies from being challenged under other WTO agreements,
   as long as the level of domestic support for a commodity remained at
   or below 1992 levels.
2. The use of export subsidies for cotton without including them in the
   list of subsidies notified by the United States to the WTO under the
   Agreement on Agriculture. Central to other legal challenge were direct payments to US farmers under the 1996 and 2002 Farm Bills, as
   well as payments under emergency supplemental appropriation bills.[13]

The consultations having ended unsatisfactorily, as the United States
refused to budge, Brazil did not shy away from requesting the establishment of a Panel, which was established in accordance with Article 6 of
the DSU[14] to examine the matter, referred to the DSB by Brazil (WTO
2003d). The US government argued that direct payments were de-
coupled and not linked to current production, therefore they were not
trade distorting and should not have been counted when compared to
1992 levels of support. The Panel and the Appellate Body examined the
matter subsequently, where both found the US cotton subsidies to be in
violation of the WTO rules and that some US de-coupled payments did
provide an incentive for production, and thus were trade distorting.
Hence, they were causing serious prejudice to the interests of Brazil as a
result of continued depressed cotton prices. The decision in favour of
Brazil had apparently accepted the principle that it is possible to calcu-
late the damage from subsidies even if they were formally de-coupled

(Gillson et al. 2003). The panel ruled that the subsidies did not qualify for exemption from WTO challenges under the exemption of the "Peace Clause", which terminated in January 2004. The Panel also found the US in the wrong in its Export Credit Guarantee Programs, as they also give US exporters a clear advantage over competitors (Oxfam 2002: chapter 4).

According to the "Bargaining Power Theory", when negotiations fail or stop, dispute settlement procedures start. In the negotiations, bargaining power in favour of the stronger is dominant. In the dispute settlement, power becomes irrelevant as the legal considerations become then the dominant factors. The Dispute Settlement is supposed to be fair and legal, thus disfavouring power politics to the benefit of the weakest partner and safeguarding their rights. The United States wants negotiations, not litigation, to manipulate the situation. African countries opted for negotiations because they want to prove a systemic issue or they cannot do otherwise. Brazil has opted to challenge the United States on cotton and the European Union in its sugar regime to help negotiations proceed in a fairer manner without power politics, and force the two giants to change their policies. It was only Benin and Chad out of the four West African countries that ventured into the Brazil–US cotton dispute as a third party. How big was their disappointment when they felt that their participation, efforts and money spent were all of little use, if any. A hard lesson was to be drawn from the case for African cotton producing members in particular and participation as third parties in general. Upon assertion of the United States that it was only the interests of Brazil as a complaining party which were at issue, disregarding the vested interests of Chad and Benin as third parties, both the panel and Appellate Body sided with the United States and did not see the plight of the cotton producers of Benin and Chad as an issue in question here (Munyuki 2005). That can only mean that whatever measures the United States will take with respect to removing the subsidies at issue or removing their adverse effects relate only to Brazil, not to Benin or Chad or any other African country producer of cotton.

Litigation is double-edged, not only for the African countries but also – and moreso – for the WTO as a negotiating and rulemaking body. No one can contest that it is the inalienable right of each and every Member in the WTO to have recourse to the WTO Dispute Settlement Understanding (DSU) to settling their disputes. The DSU is also considered as the jewel of the crown in the WTO. Difficulties in negotiations, however, should not be used as a pretext for excessive usage of the DSU to compensate for the difficult process of decision making in the organization on the basis of consensus. Having constant recourse to the DSU as a "judicial lawmaking mechanism" might undermine its usefulness in the long run and render the WTO as a negotiating forum obsolete. It is true that the use of litigation as substitutive or analogous to negotiations should be avoided, on one hand. On the other hand, negotiations should be conducted in good faith without attempts of exploitation of the weaker partners. The African countries have proven the rightfulness of their case. Brazil winning its dispute against the United States on subsidized cotton has added sustainability and strength to the case. There should be nothing to obstruct a clear and fair solution to the problem in line with WTO rules and principles, which developed and developing countries alike have pledged their faithfulness to.

The cotton case is clearly indicative of power politics and a double standard, as the United States has shown neither interest nor willingness to address the cotton initiative in a substantive and serious manner. It is true that African countries have opted for negotiations, as they lack the financial and technical capabilities and are susceptible to any political implications and fear mostly any cutting of their development assistance or preferential market access as a result of their going to litigation. But it is also true that African countries wanted to prove their systemic interest in the WTO as a negotiating forum and one that should safeguard the rights of the weak. Though supported by the majority of WTO membership, the United States has simply refused to give in to what has proven to be the legitimate right of the African countries and did not shy away from manipulating the situation and protracting the negotiations to no avail.

Financial compensation is outside the scope of the WTO and retaliation is not an option

Compensation is due to the African countries for their loss in export earnings because of trade-distorting subsidies. But it is well-known that compensation is not an easy option in the WTO, as it must be reached through litigation. Financial compensations fall outside of the WTO mandate. In principle, compensation in the WTO is through two instruments. First of all, supplementary concessions are offered for other products. This mechanism cannot apply to cotton-producing LDCs because they only have a few other export products and, in most cases, these already receive preferential access. Second, customs tariffs are increased on imports (WTO 2003b). This is also of little use to the cotton-producing African countries, as it will backfire on their consumers. Also, the African countries may not be importing sufficiently from the United States to offset their loss in cotton exports. A case in point is Ecuador in the Banana Dispute, which had found it difficult to apply increased tariffs on its imports from the European Union.[15] These two instruments are therefore counter-productive for cotton-producing LDCs.

Retaliatory actions are not within the reach of the four African countries. They have virtually no option to retaliate against the United States for two reasons: (1) the negative impact on the economy of the four African countries and (2) the little effect – if any – it will have on the economy of the United States. It is worthwhile to remember that the DSU is in the first place about compliance with obligations, not retaliation (Mavroidis 2000).

Though the option of litigation remains an open and valid option for the African countries, it seems reasonable not to choose it at present. At no rate should the United States push the African countries to the edge and force them to have recourse to the DSU, which would undermine in a flagrant manner the negotiating process the African countries were willing enough to conduct in the WTO. The question then is, would the United States, after having lost its case with Brazil, strive for a fair solution to the cotton problem?

For the African countries, the WTO final ruling against the US cotton subsidies in early March 2005 came as a blessing. This decision meant that the United States was to have 15 months to change its cotton-subsidy policy so as to fall within WTO obligations or face retaliatory trade measures. Such a ruling undoubtedly strengthened the African position and one could assume that the matter was even settled. Yet, nothing was further from the truth, as all options remained widely open:

1. The United States refused to abide by the DSB ruling. Fifteen months after the March 2005 DSB decision against the United States, the WTO opened a formal investigation into whether the United States had complied with the ruling to eliminate its illegal subsidies paid to American cotton growers.[16] In fact, on 28 September 2006 Brazil won a decision by the DSB to set up a "compliance panel" in the continuing dispute over US subsidies to its cotton growers. If the panel proves that the United States has violated its obligations again, Brazil could ask for permission to impose retaliatory sanctions against US goods. Thus the option of continuing to subsidize cotton to the detriment of the African countries and causing "serious prejudice" by distorting market prices is still there.

2. The African countries have chosen from the very beginning the option of negotiations rather than litigation for reasons stated above; this does not undermine their right to make full use of the WTO DSU. The African countries are entitled to draw on the assistance of the Legal Advisory Center in Geneva, which was established in the first place to reinstate the rights of the developing and LDCs in accordance with the multilateral trade rules and principles.

3. Pressure for reducing subsidies should not be relaxed. The United States would not lose in the process of reducing its cotton subsidies because the losses suffered by special powerful lobby groups would be more than offset by taxpayers' savings (Goreux 2004). In fact, the American consumer is forced to pay twice, in terms of taxes for the coverage of subsidies, and in terms of higher domestic prices for cotton, as well as for value-added textiles and garments.

Hong Kong Ministerial

The best remaining option was to urge the US administration, in light of the results of its dispute with Brazil, to bring its cotton subsidies in conformity with the WTO regulations and principles. African countries were determined to reach some kind of agreement in the sixth ministerial in Hong Kong. They were confident of a worldwide support to pressure the United States into a negotiated settlement in the framework of the Doha Development Round. The African countries went to Hong Kong seeking an "early harvest" for the cotton initiative. A number of salient points were made clear in the ministerial:

1. Solutions for the cotton initiative were to be looked for solely within the framework of the WTO. Possibilities to negotiate recommendations in the WTO that could be addressed or implemented elsewhere were as good as useless and fictitious. Such an assertion was drawn on the basis of the major difficulties encountered when attempts were made to implement the NFIDCs Uruguay Round decision, which remains to date non-functional.
2. Options such as establishing a trust fund or setting up a cotton consultative group for Africa (Goreux 2004) chaired by the four co-sponsors and assisted by the World Bank does not fall within the mandate of the WTO and thus should be avoided within the framework of multilateral trade negotiations.
3. It is of utmost importance for further negotiations that the co-sponsors succeed in raising interest in the cotton initiative and look for the solidarity of their respective groupings to force an adequate solution across the board. The African group stood firm behind the four West African countries in Hong Kong. They were adamant that a solution should lie in addressing the trade aspects, export and domestic subsidies for cotton, while not neglecting, as referred to in the July Package, the development aspects of the initiative. The complementarity between the trade and development aspects should be implemented by leveling the playing field in the world market prices for cotton and reducing the trade-distorting effect of cotton subsidies as an efficient

way to put trade at the service of development and reduce poverty in Africa.

4. It is true that litigation to prove serious injury within the WTO DSU remains the sole venue to attain contractual compensation. The point, however, was made that African countries were not seeking a tailor-made solution for each and every country suffering from subsidized cotton but the initiative was addressing the issue of harmful subsidies to cotton that distort trade as a systemic one. Drawing on the Brazil–US dispute was enough of a moral and legal guidance to the negotiations in Hong Kong.

At the 11th hour of the ministerial conference in Hong Kong, an agreement on cotton – though modest compared to the original African request – was reached. For cotton export subsidies the elimination is accelerated to the end of 2006. In addition, cotton exports from least-developed countries will be allowed into developed countries without duty or quotas from the start of the period for implementing the new agriculture agreement. Ministers have also agreed to aim to cut trade-distorting domestic subsidies on cotton by more than would normally apply under the new agreement, and to do so more quickly (WTO 2005a: para. 11,12).

Conclusion

It would be interesting to put the outcome of the Hong Kong ministerial and the July Package into context, following Brazil's landmark victory in the WTO dispute settlement case against US cotton subsidies on 28 April 2004. The WTO decision against the United States should encourage developing countries to continue their struggle to make the WTO a fairer place while working also for the interest of the developing countries. African countries had rejoiced over the results they achieved in Hong Kong. Brazil thought that having won its case straight against the United States in the panel and subsequently the Appellate Body, things would fall in place. Today, the Hong Kong results have become but a mirage and Brazil, as we have seen above, requested a "compliance panel".

Nevertheless the cotton initiative remains a practical manifestation of the Doha developmental objectives. As the only specific interest of WCA cotton-producing countries in the Round, the elimination of subsidies for cotton production and export is the critical test of whether the Doha Round can deliver on development and poverty reduction. The WCA countries fighting for the respect of the principles of free trade and fair competition in the global trade in cotton cannot be simply disregarded because of the unsuitability of their requests for the stronger trading partner. Such a situation negates the ultimate objectives of both the Uruguay Round and the Doha Development Round, which were to build a fairer and market-oriented trading system where the rule of law prevails over power politics, as well as to help integrate the developing countries better into such a system. At no time have we been further from achieving these "divine" goals than we are today.

The WTO should not become an organization that allows countries to get away with things unless challenged in the DSU and then trying to protract procedures to the maximum extent possible. WTO is about negotiating rights and obligations in good faith based on the principles universally agreed upon and adopted at the Uruguay Round. The African countries have shown from the outset that they are for negotiations. They have exerted immense efforts and gone a long way to reach some results in Hong Kong. Having agreed to devote this Round to the developing countries and LDCs, let the cotton initiative be the test proving that we are on the right track and truly within the framework of a development round.

At the beginning we raised a number of questions, answers were given throughout this chapter, as we have gone a long way since the cotton initiative was first put on the table. The outstanding questions regarding the initiative today are certainly of a different character:

- What if the Doha Round is suspended until after the US presidential election in November 2008, and the granting of the Trade Promotion Authority to the new administration occurs not before the beginning of 2009, which is very likely to happen?
- What if the Doha Round takes a different turn, which might extend the negotiations for a few extra years to reach a final package, which again is not improbable?
- Are the African farmers to continue to endure losses, at a time it is well known that they are better qualified and among the most competitive in the world?

It would be unfortunate if none of the elements agreed upon regarding the cotton initiative in Hong Kong are implemented as long as the Doha Round remains in a state of flux. Taking into account certain premises, a fair and equitable solution for the cotton problem should be considered along the following lines:

1. Litigation remains as good as a non-option for the African countries, they simply cannot afford it. Remaining on the margin of the trading system, the African countries, like many developing countries and the bulk of LDCs, have little to gain from going to litigation. In fact they have much to lose even if they win the dispute and largely expose the wrongdoing of the stronger partner. In contrast, Brazil can and will use retaliation against the United States, which WTO authorization is

expected for some US$4 billion in additional levies on US merchandise if Washington is found to be at fault again.

2. African countries cannot await the end of the negotiations of the Doha round for a solution of their cotton problem to figure in the so-called final package. The four LDCs cannot be held hostage to the proportionate horse-trading on agriculture, on one hand, and market access for services and industrial goods, on the other hand, between developed countries and major developing ones, notably Brazil and India. Solutions along the line of the Hong Kong outcome and in line with the recommendations of the July Package to deal with the cotton initiative "expeditiously" should be expected as soon as possible.

3. It is true that the July Framework recognized – and rightly so – the complementarity between the trade and development components of the cotton problem. Yet, it is unfortunate to observe what the four countries experience as one component is merely discrediting the other. It is encouraging and a source of pleasure for the Director General to report progress on the total value of cotton development assistance commitments (WTO 2005b). He emphasizes the specific commitments toward the cotton sector of Benin are approximately US$53 million, of Burkina Faso are US$93 million, of Chad are US$52 million and of Mali are US$78 million. This demonstrates the willingness of the development community to help low-income members address the difficulties they face. Yet, it is unfortunate to note that during the 2004/2005 season alone, WCA countries recorded a loss of over US$400 million (WTO 2005c). This makes the solution for the trade dimensions of the cotton problem all the more compelling. What would be the use of reporting progress on development assistance to the cotton producers, if their trade situation is deteriorating drastically?

4. As a sign of good faith in the ongoing multilateral trade negotiations, the United States has to recognize that cotton is a strategic crop for development and poverty reduction in those four African countries as well as in many developing countries and LDCs. The United States should be well disposed to help the four WCA countries not only within the framework of the AGOA program but in terms of complying foremost with its WTO obligations. It is incumbent upon the United States to validate its repeated calls for negotiations in the WTO to have precedence over litigation. Negotiations should accomplish something in order to uphold the system and prove its fairness and not be exploited in favour of the stronger.

5. Solutions to the cotton problem should be applied by all subsidizing members, as non-conforming WTO subsidies are not only given by the United States but also by the European Union and China, which

are of an estimated sum at US$6 billion in 2001/2002, which corresponded in value terms to all global exports during that year.[17] As said, the four cotton-producing WCA countries see their initiative as a testimony of the rightfulness and implementation of the Doha developmental objectives and their only *raison d'être* in the framework of the negotiations.

6. It is hard to perceive with the plight of the four African LDCs that any developed country would venture to circumvent WTO disciplines by re-classifying cotton subsidies from one box to another, mainly from the amber to the green box. This is certainly quite complex and not as harmless as said, as the green-box support within the framework of the EU Common Agricultural Policy has proven to help farmers to produce and export at a lesser cost.[18] The United States should avoid in the case of cotton a repetition of such apparent restructuring of agricultural support policy.

Under all assumptions, the world community expects a final and fair solution to the cotton problem, which would redress the world price of cotton to increase the income of those LDCs most dependent on cotton for their foreign exchange earnings.

Notes

1. Due to the controversy that arose in the WTO Third Ministerial Conference (30 November–3 December 1999) in Seattle for the launching of a new round of trade negotiations and cognizant of the fact that developing countries were experiencing a negotiation fatigue, WTO Member states agreed in the fourth Ministerial in Doha (9–13 November 2001) to hail the new trade negotiations as the "Doha Development Agenda" (DDA). It is obvious today that the DDA has defied its purpose and is called "par excellence" the Doha Round, which is the ninth round of negotiations.
2. Almost half of the direct domestic support received by cotton producers is given by the United States. It was estimated in 2003 American cotton producers received a total of US$3.7 billion. Moreover, the US gives direct aid for cotton exports. The European Union gives producers in Spain and Greece around US$980 million through a ceiling price support mechanism. In 2001/02, Spanish cotton producers received support corresponding to 180 per cent of global prices and Greek producers 160 per cent, compared with 60 per cent for American producers. These are the highest subsidies in the world per kilo of cotton (Gillson et al. 2003).
3. DS 267 US – Subsidies on Upland Cotton. The term "upland cotton" means raw upland cotton as well as the primary processed forms of such cotton including upland cotton lint and cottonseed. The focus of Brazil's claims relate to upland cotton (WTO 2003a).
4. This hard-line stance reflects the political realities in the US Congress: the chairman of the Senate agriculture committee is a close ally of the cotton farmers (*Economist* 2003).
5. The value of subsidies provided to the cotton barons of Texas and elsewhere in 2001 exceeded the market value of output by around 30 per cent. In other words, cotton was produced at a net cost to the United States (Oxfam 2002).

6. "Préjudices causés par les subventions aux filières cotonnières de l'AOC" (Goreux 2004: para. 14).
7. The Committee on Agriculture recognizes the principle of "special products" for developing countries. These products are deemed to be "special" by reason of their importance for "food security, rural development and/or livelihood security".
8. The United States has much to gain in integrating cotton as an agricultural crop within the framework of the agricultural subsidies' negotiations, and little to lose. The logic behind the US argument was not difficult to detect. We may refer briefly to such arguments as: (1) not to be singled out as a violator of WTO obligations; (2) to buy time, knowing that the European Union will delay the negotiations on agricultural subsidies to the maximum extent possible, and knowing also that there is a potential risk of the whole round failing because of agricultural subsidies; and (3) to include cotton within the overall package of eliminating agricultural subsidies, which at best will be gradual and probably even elusive through some kind of imaginative formula to be designed specifically for agricultural subsidies.
9. Uruguay Round Ministerial Decisions and Declarations: "Decision on Measures Concerning the Possible Negative Effects of the Reform Program on Least-Developed and Net Food-Importing Developing Countries".
10. 1. Improve food aid via:
    • Reviewing the level of food aid and
    • Providing an increasing share on grant terms;
    2. Full consideration to requests for technical and financial assistance to improve agricultural productivity and infrastructure.
    3. Short-term financing facilities from international financial institutions to be provided under "existing facilities, or such facilities as may be established, in the context of adjustment programs".
11. The July Package, a very fragile and mostly incomplete framework, was meant in the first place to secure a continuation of the negotiations on the DDA, which had encountered a very severe blow in the Fifth Ministerial in Cancun (10–14 September 2003). The so-called Big Five (Australia, Brazil, the European Community, India and the United States) putting together a minimal agreement on agriculture helped bring about the July Package, which focused on the basic issues of contention, notably agriculture, non-agriculture market access, services, trade facilitation and the cotton initiative (For reference, please see: http://www.wto.org/english/tratop_e/dda_e/draft_text_gc_dg _31july04_e.htm)
12. The Peace Clause, under article 13 titled "Due Restraint", was included in the Uruguay Round mainly at the insistence of the European Union and the United States. This clause protected countries using agricultural subsidies from being challenged under other WTO Agreements, as long as the level of domestic support for a commodity remained at or below 1992 levels. It was terminated according to the Agreement on 1 January 2004.
13. The 1996 Farm Bill marked an important stage in US subsidy policy by introducing direct payments to producers, which were de-coupled from production. The Act, which encompasses all agriculture including cotton, aimed to spend US$47 billion between 1996 and 2002, with US$35 billion as direct payments to farmers. In 2002, the United States introduced the 2002–2008 Farm Bill. As a result, government assistance will increase from 32 per cent of average farmer income under the 1996 Farm Law to 45 per cent under the new Law (Gillson et al. 2003).
14. Article 6 of the Agreement on the "Understanding on Rules and Procedures Governing the Settlement of Disputes", titled "Establishment of Panels", stipulates that a panel shall be established at the latest at the DSB meeting following that at which the request

first appears as an item on the DSB's agenda, unless at that meeting the DSB decides by consensus not to establish a panel.

15. Ecuador was entitled to suspend concessions to the European Union of the amount of US$202 million. Ecuador's imports from the European Union, however, did not exceed US$61 million on a yearly basis. Nevertheless having won the dispute case against the European Union, Ecuador was able to negotiate a successful settlement.

16. After blocking Brazil's request for the establishment of a panel in early September 2006 for the WTO to investigate US compliance, Washington cannot veto the request a second time. This gives the United States an extra three months for the issuance of the results of the investigations.

17. Estimated American subsidies for cotton producers amount to US$3.7 billion in 2003 according to the International Cotton Advisory Committee (ICAC) and the US$1.2 billion support by China in addition to the US$980 million by the European Union to Spain and Greece, hence a round figure of close to US$6 billion (WTO 2003c: para. 16).

18. May 2004: During the Uruguay Round negotiators separated domestic policies judged to have no direct effect on agricultural trade (green box), from those that did have clear trade and production-distorting effects (amber box). Direct payments could be moved to the green box provided that they were "de-coupled" from production. This provided freedom to increase domestic assistance levels (Gillson et al. 2003).

REFERENCES

Economist (2003) "Special Report: The Doha Round", 20–26 September.

Gillson, I., C. Poulton, K. Balcombe and S. Page (2003) "Understanding the Impact of Cotton Subsidies on Developing Countries", Working Paper TN/AG/GEN/4, Geneva: WTO.

Goreux, L. (2004) "Cotton after Cancun", Washington D.C.: World Bank, available from http://www.oecd.org/dataoecd/38/48/30751318.pdf.

ICTSD (2004) "Agriculture Negotiations at the WTO: The Cotton Initiative", Quarterly Intelligence Report No. 11, International Center for Trade and Sustainable Development, June.

ICTSD (2005) "Technical Negotiations Reveal No Progress on Key Doha Round Issues", *Bridges* 9(4).

Keim, N. (2004) "Will Cotton Survive Endless WTO Debate?" *Bridges* 1, January.

Mavroidis, P. (2000) "Remedies in the WTO Legal System: Between a Rock and a Hard Place", *European Journal of International Law* 11(4): 763–813.

Munyuki, E. (2005) "Brazil vs USA: Whither Africa?" *SEATINI* 8(4), available from http://www.seatini.org/bulletins/8.4.php.

Oxfam (2002) "Cultivating Poverty: The Impact of US Cotton Subsidies on Africa", available from http://www.oxfam.org.uk/what_we_do/issues/trade/bp30_cotton.htm.

Williams, F., and G. Jonquiùres (2003) "The US Fights Plea by Africans on Cotton Subsidies", *Financial Times*, September 11.

WTO (2003a) "United States – Subsidies on Upland Cotton – Constitution of the Panel Established at the Request of Brazil – Note by the Secretariat", WT/DS267/15, 23 May.

WTO (2003b) "Poverty Reduction: Sectoral Initiative in Favor of Cotton – Joint proposal by Benin, Burkina Faso, Chad and Mali", WT/MIN(03)/W/2, 15 August.

WTO (2003c) "Poverty Reduction: Sectoral Initiative in Favor of Cotton – Joint Proposal by Benin, Burkina Faso, Chad and Mali", in the WTO Committee on Agriculture (Special Session), TN/AG/GEN/4, 16 May.

WTO (2003d) "United States – Subsidies on Upland Cotton – Request for the Establishment of a Panel by Brazil", WT/DS267/7, 7 February.

WTO (2005a) "Ministerial Conference – Sixth Session – Hong Kong, 13–18 December 2005 – Doha Work Programme – Ministerial Declaration – Adopted on 18 December 2005", WT/MIN(05)/DEC, 18 December.

WTO (2005b) "Implementation of the Development Assistance Aspects of the Cotton-Related Decisions in the July Package"; Second Periodic Report by the Director General, WT/GC/97, 21 November.

WTO (2005c) "Ministerial Conference – Sixth Session – Hong Kong, 13–18 December 2005 – Chad – Statement by HE Mrs Odjimbeye Soukate Ngarmbatina – Minister of Commerce and Handicrafts", WT/MIN(05)/ST/40, 15 December.

4

The WTO non-agricultural market access negotiations: Opportunities and challenges for developing countries

Sam Laird*

The current WTO negotiations on non-agricultural market access have potentially important consequences for developing countries. In the aggregate, there is likely to be expanded trade and increased general economic welfare, but there are also likely to be wide variations across sectors and countries, with some net losses. In some cases, there are also likely to be negative consequences for production, employment and revenues. Some of these potentially negative outcomes may need to be addressed with "aid for trade", including social safety nets, and extended transition periods, while the normal growth of trade would also be expected to provide a cushion. But there are also uncertainties about the implications of forgoing certain policy options as the WTO rules are tightened and developing countries commit to further liberalization. Moreover, it is not certain how "aid for trade" would address the supply side constraints that are the key to lifting productive capacities, especially in the poorest countries.[1]

Depending on the specific scenarios for the WTO negotiations as well as technical assumptions in the modeling, annual aggregate global gains in agriculture and non-agricultural products (including fish) of about US\$70 billion to US\$150 billion have been estimated by the World Bank and UNCTAD (more later), while liberalizing trade in services could be even more important, especially if agreement were reached to facilitate the temporary movement of labour.[2] This is remarkably modest, amounting to significantly less than 0.5 per cent of global GDP, but these aggregate estimates conceal some important sectoral gains and losses in

Developing countries and the WTO: Policy approaches, Sampson and Chambers (eds), United Nations University Press, 2008, ISBN 978-92-808-1153-7

individual countries. Moreover, these comparative static results do not give any clue as to the short-term effects during the adjustment process. Obviously, much depends on the "ambition" (i.e., the agreed extent of the liberalization) of the negotiations, the implications of other trade and competition instruments and on policies to facilitate adjustment. At least as important is the global economic environment: it is generally easier to adjust in a healthy growth environment, such as has been experienced in recent years.

This chapter looks at the Doha mandate in non-agricultural market access (NAMA) and the current state of the WTO negotiations, in particular some key proposals being considered before the negotiations were "suspended" in August 2006. We analyse various scenarios and their implications for trade, welfare, output, employment, revenues and preferences, as well as the distributional effects across countries and sectors. We note the expanded opportunities but also possible adjustment problems related to balance of payments and pressures for structural change, as well as possible revenue and preference losses. These suggest the need for a careful adjustment package to help developing countries realize gains possible from WTO negotiations.

Doha Declaration

In November 2001 WTO Ministers agreed, in the part of the Ministerial Declaration relating to non-agricultural market access, "by modalities to be agreed, to reduce or as appropriate eliminate tariffs, including the reduction or elimination of tariff peaks, high tariffs, and tariff escalation, as well as non-tariff barriers, in particular on products of export interest to developing countries. Product coverage shall be comprehensive and without a priori exclusions" (Doha Ministerial Declaration: para. 16). Full account was to be taken of the special needs and interests of developing and least-developed country participants, "including through less than full reciprocity in reduction commitments, in accordance with the relevant provisions of Article XXVIII bis of GATT 1994". Ministers also agreed that the modalities to be agreed would include "appropriate studies and capacity building measures to assist the least-developed countries to participate effectively in the negotiations".[3]

The significance of the agreement was that the negotiations were to tackle some serious problems facing developing countries in their trade: tariffs, including tariff peaks, which are biased against their trade, and tariff escalation that hinders their attempts to industrialize. For example, as table 4.1 shows, even taking account of unilateral and regional preferences, developing countries face higher weighted average tariffs than

Table 4.1 Import-weighted average applied tariffs (including preferences) by development status

Source	Developed	Developing	Least-developed
Developed	2.1%	9.2%	11.1%
Developing	3.9	7.2	14.4
Least-developed	3.1	7.2	8.3
Total	2.9	8.1	13.6

Source: Laird, de Córdoba and Vanzetti (2004).
Computed from UNCTAD TRAINS database.

Table 4.2 Peaks in bound and applied tariffs as share of total tariff lines

Scenario	Bound	Applied
Developed countries	8.2%	9.9%
Developing countries	0.4	3.5
Least-developed countries	0.4	0.7

Source: Laird, de Córdoba and Vanzetti (2004).
Computed from UNCTAD TRAINS database.

developed countries (including in other developing countries). Table 4.2 indicates that tariff peaks are more pronounced in developed countries, mostly on items that come from developing countries. Table 4.3 shows the presence of tariff escalation – higher protection on processed goods – that makes it more difficult to export goods with greater value added.

The notion of "less than full reciprocity", based on Article XXVIII *bis* of the GATT, was added to the GATT text after the 1954/55 Review Session in order to provide flexibility for developing countries to assist their economic development. The idea was that developing countries would not need to reduce their tariffs in a negotiation to the same extent as the developed countries. Article XVIII, added at the same time, covered

Table 4.3 Tariff escalation: Trade-weighted applied tariffs by stage of processing

	Primary	Intermediate	Final
Developed	0.4%	3.0%	3.4%
Developing	6.0	9.1	8.0
Least-developed	6.9	18.0	12.0

Source: Laird, de Córdoba and Vanzetti (2004).
Computed from UNCTAD TRAINS database.

other measures of government assistance to economic development, including for balance of payments reasons. In effect, these amendments to the original GATT, stemming in part from the Havana Charter, were recognition of the role that trade measures might have in fostering economic development. This is the legal basis for the demand of developing countries that they be granted flexibility, or "policy space", in their trade policies to promote their industrial development, as discussed further below.

All told, the part of the Doha Declaration concerning non-agricultural tariffs met important criteria for determining whether the Doha Work Programme would produce a "development round", but of course much would depend on the negotiated outcome and eventual implementation.

As a final point on the Doha Declaration, it is important to note that the Doha meeting took place in the immediate aftermath of the attack on the New York World Trade Center ("9/11"). The concern that the world economy and globalization needed a boost therefore helped to produce the pressures that brought about the Doha agreements.

July 2004 Package

Largely because of disagreement over the package on agriculture, WTO Ministers were unable to reach agreement on progress in negotiations at the September 2003 meeting in Cancun, Mexico. The WTO General Council, however, reached an important decision on the Doha Work Programme on 1 August 2004. This "July Package" (WTO Document WT/L/ 579 of 2 August 2004) has since provided the basis for negotiations on non-agricultural market access.

The framework for establishing modalities in market access for non-agricultural products is in Annex B of the July Package. The framework contains "the initial elements for future work on modalities by the Negotiating Group on Market Access". These include the following:

1. Elements for decisions on a formula for tariff reductions;
2. Provisions for increasing binding coverage and setting the level of newly bound tariff rates;[4]
3. Sectoral elimination of tariffs on products of export interest to developing countries;
4. Supplementary modalities ("zero-for-zero", sectoral harmonization and request and offer);[5]
5. The possible elimination of low duties;
6. Provisions for exemption from tariff cuts by least-developed countries;
7. Special provisions to take account of commitments by recently acceded countries;

8. The need to intensify work on non-tariff barriers (NTBs);
9. The need to take account of challenges faced by non-reciprocal preference beneficiaries and countries that are highly dependent on tariff
   revenues;
10. The need to address the issue of environmental goods; and
11. The need for appropriate studies and capacity-building measures.

While the package helped restore momentum to the Doha Round negotiations, it also left many questions unanswered. At the time of suspension of the negotiations in August 2006, a formula had yet to be selected,
consensus on participation in sectoral elimination was lacking, and provisions for special and differential treatment were yet to be clarified.

Much of the package repeats text that had failed to achieve acceptance
in Cancun. One new element was the phrase in a new paragraph stating
that the framework "contains the initial elements for future work on modalities" by the NAMA negotiating group. For some developing countries, the reference to "initial elements" meant that the modalities issue
was still wide open, that all options remained possible. Developed countries may have disagreed with that interpretation, but a number of new
proposals have been tabled in 2005.

One important area of early agreement was the decision to adopt a
formula approach for the main negotiations, supplemented by other approaches as outlined in the text. Using a formula to determine the tariff-
cutting commitments of individual WTO members is intended to simplify
negotiations, avoiding bilateral request-and-offer negotiations among
each pair of 148 members on as many as 10,000 or more tariff lines in
each case. A formula approach was first used in the Kennedy Round (linear cuts) and in the Tokyo Round (the "Swiss" formula) but the Uruguay
Round returned to request-and-offer, supplemented by zero-for-zero cuts
among a critical mass of participants on about 10 product groups and
later on information technology goods (the "ITA Agreement").

The July 2004 Framework provides for further work on tariff reductions by means of "a non-linear formula applied on a line by line basis".
Given the mandate of the Doha Declaration to reduce or eliminate tariffs, including tariff peaks,[6] high tariffs and tariff escalation – in particular
on products of export interest to developing countries – it is perhaps inevitable that negotiations focus on formula approaches to cut high rates
more than proportionately, that is to say, "harmonizing" approaches. In
particular, discussion has focused on variations of a Swiss formula. Some
developing countries, however, view harmonizing approaches as counter
to the Doha requirement of allowing them less than full reciprocity.
Some of these countries feel that they need flexibility or "policy space"
to use tariffs for industrial development,[7] to mitigate the impact of liberalization on output and employment in key sectors and to avoid resorting

to alternative WTO measures, such as anti-dumping. Another problem is that some of the proposed variations lack transparency in that it is relatively difficult for any country to compute what it has to do and to assess what others are doing (i.e., it is difficult to compute the balance of concessions). This may be criticized as being unnecessarily burdensome, since, from an economic perspective, it is possible to tailor more-transparent approaches to achieve very similar results for trade, welfare, output, employment and revenues.

Beyond the formula component, the Framework also foresees the possibility of more ambitious tariff cuts and elimination in certain sectors, including those of interest to developing countries ("sectoral initiatives"), and some negotiations to achieve a critical mass in a few sectors. If such a critical mass of key players – importers and exports – were achieved in any sector, MFN treatment would also be accorded to other WTO members as free riders. On the other hand, the idea of obligatory participation in a series of key sectors said to be of export interest to developing countries, originally proposed by the first NAMA Group Chairman, Ambassador Pierre-Louis Girard of Switzerland, no longer seems to be being discussed.

The Framework also proposes increasing the binding coverage in non-agricultural products. (All WTO members bound all agricultural tariffs in the Uruguay Round.) Some developing countries still have a high proportion of unbound tariffs, and, in the Framework, it is proposed that members bind any currently unbound rate at [two] times the MFN applied rate for that product. (Square brackets indicate draft text that is not agreed.)

Some flexibility is provided for countries that have a very low binding coverage. Thus, paragraph 6 of the Framework states that members with a binding coverage of less than [35 per cent] would be exempt from making tariff reductions. Instead, they would bind [100 per cent] tariff lines at the average tariffs for all developing countries. The text does not state, however, which average would be used. Here, the issue is whether this would be the simple or trade-weighted average (as was used in earlier GATT negotiations on industrial tariffs). Since the simple average is about 28 per cent and the weighted average 12 per cent, the choice is significant.

LDCs would be exempt from tariff reductions. This does not imply that they will have a free round, as has been argued: LDCs and some other members are likely to experience preference erosion as MFN rates are reduced while the lower or even zero preferential rate applicable to LDCs stays the same (not being subject to WTO multilateral negotiations). Moreover, they are "expected to substantially increase their level of binding commitments". Developed countries and others "who so decide" are called on to grant autonomous duty-free and quota-free access in NAMA for LDCs. There is no implication that such treatment would be bound, as some LDCs have been requesting.

LDCs can also be affected in other ways. For example, Tanzania and Uganda are LDCs but they are in a customs union, the East African Community (EAC) with Kenya, which is not an LDC. Kenya is likely to have to make cuts in its tariff, that is, in the common external tariff of the EAC, thereby reducing the tariffs of Tanzania and Uganda. Moreover, the LDCs are also likely to be affected by changing terms of trade. This movement could well be negative if food import prices rise as a result of the elimination of export subsidies in agriculture.

What is on the table? – The main proposals

Numerous formulae for NAMA-related tariff-cuts have been proposed since negotiations started. The initial US proposal was to eliminate all tariffs on non-agricultural products after 2015, in effect a proposal for global free trade in these products. This US proposal apart, all other proposals have specifically targeted high tariffs and, implicitly, tariff escalation. Some, such as China's initial proposal, are based on non-linear formulae; others, such as those by India and Korea, take linear approaches that vary according to a range of initial values to produce an overall nonlinear effect; and still others combine these two approaches (e.g., the initial EU proposal, the phase-in stages of the initial US proposal).[8] India's initial proposal included higher linear tariff cuts by developed countries, while capping rates at three times each country's national average to produce a net non-linear impact.

In his draft text for the Cancun Ministerial Meeting, the first Chairman of the NAMA negotiating group, Ambassador Girard, put forward a proposal whose formula component was based on China's initial proposal. This has been the focus of debate for some time.[9] This proposal also underlies a proposal made jointly by Argentina, Brazil and India (ABI) in 2005. The basis of this proposal is the Swiss formula of the earlier Tokyo Round, $T_1 = (a \times T_0)/(a + T_0)$, where T_0 is the initial rate, T_1 the final rate and a is a fixed, negotiated coefficient (14 in the Tokyo Round), which comes from the maximum rate for all countries applying the formula.

However, in the Cancun text, instead of a fixed coefficient, a, which becomes the maximum rate, the coefficient is based on each country's own initial average rate, t_a. This could also be multiplied by another factor (B), greater or less than unity, depending on the development status of the country. If B is greater (less) than unity the outcome is lesser (greater) tariff cuts. The formula is given by:

$$T_1 = \frac{B \times t_a \times T_0}{B \times t_a + T_0}$$

where t_a is the national (weighted) average of the base rates, T_0 the initial rate for an individual tariff line, T_1 the final rate for that line and B is a multiplicative coefficient that can be used to raise or lower the final maximum rate, that is, to moderate the level of ambition.

Discussion of formulae stagnated until March 2005, when a series of proposals and counterproposals were tabled. These proposals energized negotiations, refocusing them on two broad approaches. One approach uses a "simple Swiss" formula with the possibility of a separate, higher rate for developing countries. However, developed countries would link the use of a higher coefficient to the non-use or lesser use of flexibilities under paragraph 8 of the July 2004 text. Pakistan, following the "simple Swiss" approach, has suggested that the developed country coefficient be 6 while the developing country coefficient be 30 (this is similar to the un-weighted average of all developing countries' bound rates, 27 per cent), and flexibilities under paragraph 8 would also be available to developing countries. The European Community has countered that the coefficient should be 10 for developed and "advanced" developing countries but with some flexibilities for the latter, while other developing countries would apply a coefficient of 15.

The second broad approach is based on the ABI proposal. The coefficient would be based on each country's current national average, possibly multiplied by another factor that could be linked to flexibilities or to credit for past unilateral reforms. The African Group has proposed incorporating a "correction coefficient" in the ABI formula linked to the treatment of non-reciprocal preferences, while the ACP Group of States has called for a "vulnerability index" to identify products eligible for special treatment.

The simple Swiss approach, with dual coefficients, implies harmonization of rates across countries; the ABI approach, with variations, would focus on harmonization within countries and take greater account of initial patterns of protection in each country and, in some variations, of other factors.

At the time of suspension of the negotiations in mid-2006, none of the technical details or parameters, or how these should be determined, had been agreed. Some proposals link developing countries' depth of cuts to options for flexibilities (e.g., the deeper the cut, the greater the flexibility in binding coverage and levels). Other issues include: how to determine the level at which bindings should be made on previously unbound tariff lines (and whether these should also be cut), the extent of binding coverage (e.g., share of tariff lines or trade), the methodology for establishing base rates or final bound rates and the conversion of specific rates to an ad valorem or percentage format. The possibility of eliminating tariffs, voluntarily or otherwise, in sectors of export interest to developing countries or even cutting tariff rates to zero (zero-for-zero) among a critical mass of key countries was also being discussed. Discussions on non-tariff barriers were inconclusive, although this issue was also being handled in the negotiations on WTO rules.

Scenarios

With so many possible coefficients, whether or not modulated according to criteria that are not yet agreed, and many questions also remaining to be resolved over the treatment of non-formula issues, it is difficult to evaluate the various proposals. However, it is possible to make some

Table 4.4 Changes in developed countries' weighted average industrial tariffs

	Bound weighted averages			Applied weighted averages	
	Before	After		Before	After
		Initial coverage	Final coverage		
Simple Swiss	3.4%			3%	
Ambitious		0.5%	0.5%		0.5%
Moderate		0.5	0.5		0.5
Flexible		1.4	1.4		1.3
ABI	3.4			3	
Ambitious		0.7	0.7		0.6
Moderate		0.5	0.5		0.4
Flexible		0.8	0.9		0.8
Capped	3.4			3	
Ambitious		0.8	0.8		0.8
Moderate		0.8	0.8		0.8
Flexible		1.6	1.6		1.5
Free trade		0	0		0

Source: de Córdoba and Vanzetti (2006).
Derived from UNCTAD TRAINS database.

Table 4.5 Changes in developing countries' weighted average industrial tariffs

	Bound weighted averages			Applied weighted averages	
	Before	After		Before	After
		Initial coverage	Final coverage		
Simple Swiss	12.5%			8.0%	
Ambitious		2.6%	3.4%		2.5%
Moderate		4.0	6.4		4.0
Flexible		5.9	9.2		5.2
ABI	12.5			8.0	
Ambitious		3.9	5.0		3.3
Moderate		9.4	15.3		6.1
Flexible		10.4	17.1		6.3
Capped	12.5			8.0	
Ambitious		4.4	5.7		3.8
Moderate		7.0	9.2		5.9
Flexible		8.2	10.5		6.2
Free trade		0	0		0

Source: de Córdoba and Vanzetti (2006).
Derived from UNCTAD TRAINS database.

judgements about the package in general, depending on whether WTO members decide to pursue a more ambitious approach, with greater liberalization, or a more conservative, less liberalizing approach. Making some assumptions about how these issues might be resolved, it is then possible to recompute bound and applied tariffs under different scenarios to assess the range of possible outcomes.

Tables 4.4 and 4.5 present estimates by de Córdoba and Vanzetti (2006) of likely tariff changes based on scenarios that include the application of the simple Swiss and ABI approaches, as well as a differentiated linear approach (50 per cent for developed countries and 33 per cent for developing) with a cap on tariffs at three times the national average of individual countries.[10] These scenarios correspond more or less to the proposals, with a range of assumptions about undefined elements based on discussions with WTO delegates in Geneva. In each case, the respective formulae are applied with increasing flexibility or a lesser degree of ambition (liberalization). The most ambitious or more liberalizing approaches include sectoral elimination and low Swiss-type coefficients (equivalent to weighted average applied rates for the developed and developing countries, respectively). The moderate scenario allows for developing countries to opt out of sectoral elimination, while the least ambitious or more flexible approach excludes sectoral elimination and allows doubling of coefficients (approximately similar to Pakistan's proposal). In the ABI approach, the most ambitious approach applies a unitary B coefficient for all countries, while less ambitious approaches increase the B coefficient to 3 and then to 5 for developing countries and reduce it to 0.5 for developed countries.

One significant finding of this analysis is that the impact on developed countries' tariff averages is fairly similar regardless of approach. For example, one analysis shows that developed-country weighted average rates on non-agricultural products would decline from 3.4 per cent to 0.5–1.6 per cent, depending on the scenario (table 4.4). (The "Final coverage" column shows the average when unbound rates are bound according to the Framework text and included in the average.) Applying the same formula to individual tariff lines reveals that even high individual rates would be substantially reduced to a relatively narrow spread: an initial tariff of, say, 20 per cent in a developed country would be reduced to between 3 and 5 per cent, depending on the scenario.

In contrast, the approach to tariff-cutting, including possible sectoral elimination, makes a big difference to developing countries' tariffs. For example, the average weighted bound industrial tariffs of developing countries could be reduced from 12.5 per cent to between 2.6 and 10.4 per cent, depending on the scenarios (table 4.5). Applied rates would fall from 8 per cent to between 2.5 and 6.3 per cent. For individual countries and sectors the changes could be much more. These averages are based on the same, currently bound tariff lines; bringing new products within the binding coverage would affect these results overall and for individual countries, as may be observed in the column "Final coverage".

In either case, within the range of likely outcomes, the level of ambition or liberalization matters more for assessing the final average rates than the precise formula.

Implications for trade, welfare, output, employment, revenues and preferences

Computing the likely effects of proposals on tariffs permits the use of various economic models to deduce the possible economic consequences of different approaches. Detailed studies of such consequences have been carried out by UNCTAD using GTAP and the World Bank using the Linkage model.[11] The studies use different assumptions but show considerable similarity in outcomes over a range of scenarios.

Perhaps the most detailed treatment of industrial tariffs (but one that allows for liberalization in all sectors) is that by de Cordóba and Vanzetti (2006), who estimate global annual welfare gains from liberalization in non-agricultural products to be about US$93.7 billion to US$134.7 billion per year, or more than US$200 billion under free trade. A range of complex scenarios is explored, including alternative formulae, binding assumptions, sectoral elimination and free trade. Anderson, Martin and van der Mensbrugghe (2005) simulate 50 per cent tariff cuts by developed countries, 33 per cent by developing countries generally and LDCs zero per cent, as well as more complex scenarios in agriculture. They estimate global welfare gains of US$17.7 billion to US$119.3 billion, including agriculture, with NAMA accounting for US$21.6 billion to US$44.8 billion in the more ambitious scenarios (and more than US$100 billion under free trade). In both sets of estimates, developing countries accrue about one-third of total gains.

In order to make a range of estimates of possible effects of various scenarios, it is necessary to make some assumptions about the application of the formulae as well as the treatment of a number of issues not covered by the formulae. As an illustration, table 4.6 shows the detailed scenarios used by de Córdoba and Vanzetti (2006), in their study, while table 4.7 summarizes the computed long-term, comparative static welfare gains under their scenarios, as well as the percentage changes computed for exports and domestic output (value added). As noted, the global welfare gains range from US$94 billion to US$208 billion under "free trade", but US$135 billion under an ambitious liberalizing scenario for the current negotiations. The computed effect on exports ranges from 2.6 per cent to 7.7 per cent under free trade or 4.6 per cent under an ambitious application of the "simple" Swiss formula. Finally, the effects on global output range from 0.18 per cent to 0.48 per cent under free trade or 0.28 per cent under the ambitious Swiss formulation. Charts 4.1 and 4.2 provide the aggregate welfare and export results for developing countries, somewhat more than half of the global gains.

De Córdoba and Vanzetti (2006) also compute a decline in global tariff revenue of 21 to 50 per cent, depending on the scenario (chart 4.3). The significance of this decline in tariff revenues depends on the extent to which such trade taxes contribute to overall government revenues. In some small African, Caribbean and Pacific countries, trade taxes can amount to as much as 70 per cent of government revenues. In some such cases it may be possible to replace tariffs with direct sales taxes that would essentially tax the same goods, most of which are imported (with few consequences for trade), but in other cases the shift to alternative revenue sources could take some time.

Table 4.6 Possible scenarios

Scenario	Description	Formula	Binding	Sectoral elimination	Elimination of low nuisance tariffs	Coefficients
Free trade	Zero tariffs on all non-agricultural goods		100%			
Swiss formula	Ambitious	$T_1 = \dfrac{(a \times T_0)}{(a + T_0)}$	100% for all countries Developed = twice the applied rate Developing = twice the applied rate "Paragraph 6" = simple average of bound tariffs for all developing countries (29.4%)	Yes	All tariffs below 2% reduced to zero	Based on average weighted industrial bound tariff by country grouping Developed = 3.4% Developing = 12.5%
	Moderate	$T_1 = \dfrac{(a \times T_0)}{(a + T_0)}$	Developed = 100% Developing and "Paragraph 6" countries = 95% Developed = twice the applied rate Developing = twice the applied rate or twice the simple average of bound tariffs for developing countries ($29.4\% \times 2 = 58.8\%$) "Paragraph 6" = twice the applied rate or twice the simple average of bound tariffs for developing countries ($29.4\% \times 2 = 58.8\%$)	Developed: yes Developing: no	Developed countries only: All tariffs below 2% reduced to zero	Based on average weighted industrial tariff by country grouping Developed = 3.4% Developing = 12.5%

Note: Least-developed countries are exempt from formula reductions and sectoral eliminations

Table 4.7 Global welfare, trade and output under alternative scenarios

	Free trade	Swiss ambitious	Swiss moderate	Swiss flexible	WTO ambitious	WTO moderate	WTO flexible	Capped ambitious	Capped moderate	Capped flexible
Welfare (US$b)	208	135	122	108	128	103	99	123	104	94
Exports (%)	7.69	4.62	3.93	2.93	4.34	3.22	2.92	4.11	3.19	2.48
Output (%)	0.48	0.28	0.24	0.21	0.27	0.20	0.19	0.25	0.20	0.18

Source: GTAP simulations

On the other hand, in some cases, trade expands so much in response to tariff cuts that revenue can even increase (Fisher 2006). Moreover, if exports expand as a result of improved market access, one can expect that some of the increased income will be spent on imports, again boosting revenue. Thus, under some assumptions, even a few African, Asian, Central American and Caribbean countries could experience a modest increase in tariff revenue. However, declines in excess of 80 per cent are

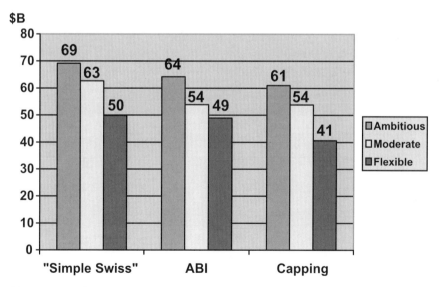

Chart 4.1 Estimated welfare gains for developing countries under various scenarios

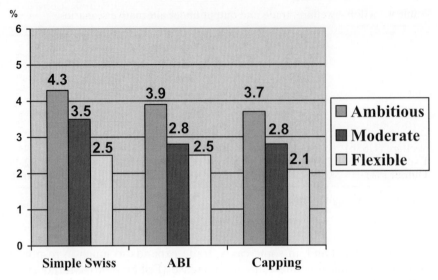

Chart 4.2 Estimated export expansion by developing countries under various scenarios

predicted for China and the United States, while developing countries as a whole are estimated to experience a decline in tariff revenues of about 44 per cent.

The detailed results for industrial value added by sector and by region under the scenario of an ambitious application of the "simple Swiss" formula are shown in table 4.8. As may be noted, while the large majority of the predicted changes are quite modest, the results also encompass large

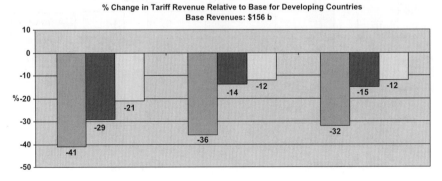

Chart 4.3 Implications for developing country tariff revenue

negative and large positive effects for individual sectors and regions. The greatest expansion occurs in apparel in Malawi (+86.4 per cent from a very small base), followed by the Philippines (+56 per cent). The region covering "Rest of South Asia" (i.e., excluding India) experiences the largest losses in the automotive sector (−36.2 per cent), but also experiences one of the larger gains in apparel (+31.9 per cent).

A number of studies show relatively minor welfare and/or trade losses in sub-Saharan African countries and other countries that are major beneficiaries of preferences, as well as some countries that participate in regional trade agreements (e.g., Mexico with the United States, Turkey with the European Union). In large-scale modeling exercises that use broad groups of countries and products, these losses are very small, but other work shows that they could be significant for specific exports of some countries.

Adjustment issues – a need for caution

The various modeling exercises carried out by the international organizations are useful in comparing the possible outcomes of complex scenarios where effects are not obvious. Most of these models, however, are based on static analysis that provides a "before and after" comparison of the application of policy shocks, rather than giving a firm prediction of the path from an initial situation to the situation after policies change or shocks are experienced. What can be said is that structural changes estimated to occur in the long-term are likely to be greater than in the short term. Structural unemployment, however, may be greater in the short term than in the long term as those displaced by increased imports find alternative employment in expanding sectors.

In addition, it will be normal for imports to respond more quickly than exports to changes in trade policy expected as a result of WTO negotiations. Thus, while the aggregate results on welfare and employment presented in various analytical studies raise little concern, some problems may arise, such as: large increases in imports in some developing countries, leading to possible balance of payments problems; large declines in the output of some sectors in some countries, with consequent unemployment; and large tariff revenue losses.

In a major analysis of developing countries' labour markets following trade liberalization and other forms of globalization, Rama (2003) surveys more than 100 papers and concludes that
• Wages grow faster in economies that integrate with the global economy, although they may fall in the short run. Openness tends to

Table 4.8 Change in output relative to base: Swiss ambitious (%)

	European Union 25	USA	Japan	Canada	Rest OECD	High Income Asia	China and Hong Kong	India	Brazil	Mexico
Unskilled labour	0.0	0.0	0.0	0.0	0.0	0.0	6.0	2.2	0.7	1.0
Unprocessed agriculture	−0.4	2.7	−0.9	1.9	−0.2	−1.1	−5.4	0.7	10.6	0.2
Processed agriculture	−0.5	0.0	−0.8	0.4	4.8	−0.5	4.9	1.2	0.8	−0.1
Fisheries and forestry	0.1	0.4	−0.4	0.5	1.2	−0.4	3.1	0.5	−0.3	0.0
Coal, oil, gas and other minerals	1.2	0.2	0.9	−0.1	−1.2	−1.1	2.9	−6.1	−0.2	0.7
Petroleum and coal products	0.4	0.1	−0.4	0.4	0.2	1.6	1.1	3.4	0.3	0.2
Lumber	0.4	−0.1	−1.4	0.0	0.0	−2.7	5.9	0.0	−0.2	1.1
Paper products	0.1	0.2	−0.2	0.6	0.2	−0.9	2.3	−1.4	−0.4	0.7
Textiles	−1.3	−9.3	11.2	−17.9	−10.5	17.4	11.3	8.3	−5.9	−15.0
Apparel	−6.6	−9.9	−7.2	−19.3	−10.9	13.5	21.3	38.1	−1.9	−20.3
Leather	−4.7	−15.9	−29.8	−20.6	−1.4	23.5	16.7	6.2	−1.1	−11.2
Chemical, rubber & plastics	0.0	0.0	0.5	−0.4	0.1	1.5	−0.2	−1.6	−1.8	−0.4
Iron & steel	0.6	0.1	1.6	0.2	−0.4	−2.2	0.7	−3.8	−2.2	2.6
Non-ferrous metals	0.4	0.8	0.5	0.5	−1.1	−1.1	0.2	−1.5	−6.9	4.6
Non-metallic manufactures	−0.5	1.0	−0.2	1.5	1.9	−3.4	−0.6	−25.3	−0.4	4.7
Fabricated metal products	0.2	0.1	0.4	−0.2	−0.6	−0.9	3.4	2.4	−3.2	1.6
Other manufactures	1.1	0.4	−0.7	0.7	0.2	−1.3	3.8	−1.5	−2.9	−4.6
Motor vehicles	0.3	−0.1	3.0	0.7	−2.5	1.2	−7.8	−4.6	−3.6	4.1
Transport equipment	−3.0	1.0	1.6	3.5	−0.3	0.6	4.9	−0.1	−1.2	0.4
Electronic equipment	−0.8	0.4	−1.2	2.2	−1.3	−0.1	9.8	0.1	−1.8	10.3
Construction	0.1	0.0	0.1	0.0	0.4	1.4	3.2	2.0	0.8	0.3
Transport	0.4	0.1	0.1	0.4	0.4	0.1	3.1	1.5	0.3	0.4
Business services	−0.4	−0.1	−0.4	−0.1	−0.5	−2.0	1.1	1.0	−0.2	−0.3
Services and other activities	0.1	0.0	0.1	−0.1	0.0	0.0	2.3	0.2	0.2	0.1

Source: GTAP simulation

Bangladesh	Philippines	Malawi	Zambia	Bulgaria	Rest South Asia	South East Asia	Central America and Caribbean	Andean Pact	Agentina, Chile and Uruguay	Middle East and North Africa	Sub-Saharan Africa	All other regions
0.0	1.5	2.7	0.2	1.3	2.1	3.6	3.1	0.8	0.6	2.3	1.6	1.4
0.1	−0.3	−0.9	0.4	0.8	0.4	0.2	1.3	1.9	8.5	1.4	1.0	0.8
0.3	0.3	−3.1	0.2	1.0	0.3	1.1	0.6	1.2	−2.2	0.9	1.4	1.2
0.1	0.4	3.8	0.2	0.7	1.0	1.1	0.5	0.3	−0.6	0.5	1.2	0.7
−0.1	−4.2	−6.5	−0.1	1.2	−2.2	−2.8	−4.6	0.4	−3.6	0.9	−0.3	0.3
−0.3	0.3	−0.6	−0.5	1.3	−7.3	0.3	0.4	1.8	0.3	1.4	−0.5	0.8
0.1	−4.2	−1.2	1.2	0.5	−2.5	−0.2	−4.5	−0.6	−5.4	−1.1	1.4	−0.1
0.5	−0.7	−3.1	−0.3	0.6	−1.7	−0.2	−0.3	0.2	−2.3	−1.4	0.4	0.4
−0.8	19.8	39.2	−9.7	−5.6	8.4	6.8	25.1	−7.2	−8.1	−12.6	−6.9	−3.2
4.3	56.0	86.4	−1.1	−5.5	31.9	18.1	17.5	3.0	−6.1	12.6	−2.4	−1.3
−13.5	1.1	−13.6	−6.9	2.0	−5.4	25.4	0.8	−7.2	−9.1	−8.5	−13.6	−4.3
−1.4	−0.3	−2.6	−0.1	0.3	−4.8	5.0	−0.5	0.5	−1.6	3.2	0.9	0.4
0.2	−1.9	−12.1	0.4	1.3	−11.8	−2.9	−3.4	0.0	−3.0	2.9	3.0	0.9
−2.3	3.8	−10.4	6.1	1.0	−8.1	1.8	−5.8	−4.7	−3.9	0.2	1.0	0.9
−0.9	−6.3	−17.0	−1.8	1.2	−12.5	−5.1	−7.3	7.7	−8.0	6.2	9.9	1.4
−0.4	−4.3	−3.9	0.2	0.5	−3.3	−2.0	−2.6	−1.0	−3.0	−2.8	−0.5	0.7
0.3	−2.3	1.7	17.3	0.7	−6.7	−1.4	−5.4	−3.1	−1.8	−2.1	0.3	−1.1
2.4	−6.6	−4.9	1.1	1.0	−36.2	−5.6	−0.6	−9.3	9.7	1.2	1.9	−0.3
0.2	19.2	−13.6	−0.8	1.2	−11.0	4.7	−1.5	1.1	−4.9	1.8	3.3	2.2
−1.0	−4.6	−8.5	−0.3	0.4	−14.0	0.7	−4.3	−10.3	−13.2	5.5	−1.4	−1.8
0.0	−0.1	−0.8	0.2	0.5	2.2	3.4	−0.7	0.5	1.0	1.0	0.7	0.5
0.0	−0.4	2.8	0.4	1.1	0.9	1.2	0.9	0.5	0.2	1.2	1.3	1.0
−1.1	−2.0	−2.5	−0.7	0.6	−2.2	−1.4	−0.7	−0.5	−0.6	−0.1	−0.9	−0.3
0.0	0.4	1.2	−0.1	1.1	0.9	1.2	1.3	0.3	0.6	0.3	0.8	0.7

increase returns to skilled labour and women, thus increasing inequality but narrowing the gender gap. Both of these effects have social consequences;

- Unemployment tends to be higher after liberalization, but in the long run is no higher in open economies; and
- The major threats to labour come from financial crises rather than competition from abroad.

If these observations are correct, developing countries' policies should aim to improve education and macroeconomic stability while furthering integration into the world economy. Some labour market policies, such as income support and unemployment insurance, have proved beneficial in some countries.

Recent studies based on national experiences with trade reforms over the last 10 to 15 years have also indicated the need for some caution in implementing further trade policy reforms in the context of the WTO negotiation. For example, a recent evaluation of trade lending operations by the World Bank's Independent Evaluation Group shows that a number of mistakes were made in implementing trade reforms (box 4.1).

Moreover, a recent study (of a number of developing and transition economies) concludes that in designing trade and related policies it is

Box 4.1 Economic growth in the 1990s – Learning from a decade of reform: Quotations from the World Bank report

- "Growth-oriented action, for example, on technological catch-up, or encouragement of risk taking for faster accumulation may be needed." (10)
- "There are many ways of achieving macroeconomic stability, openness, and domestic liberalization." (12)
- "Different policies can have the same effect, and the same policy can have different effects, depending on the context." (13)
- "Like that of policies, the effect of institutions depends on the context." (13)
- "The role of activist industrial policies is still controversial but is likely to have been important." (83)
- "The available evidence suggests that restrictions on short-term capital flows may have a role to play in the pursuit of outcomes-based macroeconomic stability in developing countries." (116)

Source: World Bank (2006). Box from UNCTAD's Trade and Development Report 2006, UN Geneva and New York.

necessary to take greater account of the level of development, the quality of institutions, resource endowments and the availability of resources to support reforms (Laird and de Córdoba 2006). "Despite years of experience with reform programmes, there is no recipe for monotonically increasing levels of welfare; reforms are tools/instruments, and serious mistakes are still being made with regard to timing, sequencing, implementation and inclusion of all relevant essential elements". It also notes that little account seems to have been taken of adjustment costs in the design of liberalization programmes, other than to provide balance-of-payments support as countries undertake reforms "while waiting for a supply response that does not always arrive". This study also highlights important negative effects on unemployment after reforms – often continuing for a number of years, consistent with Rama (2003). The study also places considerable emphasis on the importance of expenditure on transport-related physical infrastructure in generating a supply-side response, which it says is perhaps the greatest weakness in the land-locked African countries.

Conclusions and recommendations

The current WTO trade negotiations present both challenges and opportunities for the developing countries. There are opportunities in that the more ambitious scenarios seem to offer greater export possibilities and welfare gains, but there are challenges in so much as the more ambitious scenarios also imply increased imports, greater inter-sectoral shifts in production and employment, and further losses of tariff revenue. The negotiations also offer opportunities to correct imbalances that have resulted from the uneven evolution of rules and commitments in previous negotiations; these have left both a systemic bias in the multilateral trading system as well as higher barriers against developing countries' key exports.

In the past, the GATT moved faster on areas that were relatively easy to tackle. It liberalized areas of export interest to the developed countries and, despite early moves to create provisions in favour of developing countries, subsequently tightened rules on the application of subsidies, balance-of-payments (BOP) measures, infant-industry support, trade-related aspects of intellectual property rights (TRIPS) and trade-related investment measures (TRIMs), while providing lacunae or exemptions of one form or another on agriculture and textiles and clothing. This left a bias in protection against developing countries' exports, manifest through high rates on their exports, tariff peaks and tariff escalations, which the WTO Doha Work Programme sets out to address.

However, despite a considerable amount of work, there are a number of complex technical issues that need to be resolved, and, more importantly, there are also a number of key development issues that will need to be addressed in a broad politico-economic framework.

At a technical level, analysis of the main proposals shows that, regardless of the approach developed countries take, aggregate global trade and welfare is affected more by the level of ambition than any specific formula. Developing countries are seeking deep cuts in tariffs on products that they export to address what they see as long-standing biases against their attempts to diversify and expand their industrial sectors, providing a more secure and stable base for their longer term development needs. In this regard, the various formulae under consideration can certainly address the issues of tariff peaks and tariff escalation. However, in their offensive agenda, developing countries will also be concerned that no unexpected exceptions be made to the formulae to protect sensitive sectors in developed countries, despite the Doha Declaration's provision that there are to be no a priori exceptions. That the value of tariff concessions may be undermined by abuse of the Sanitary and Phytosanitary Measures (SPS) and the Agreement on Technical Barriers to Trade (TBT), anti-dumping, and safeguard measures, as well as conditions of market entry, will also be a concern. Work on WTO rules and non-tariff barriers is therefore a necessary complement to the work on tariffs to ensure that the benefits of the negotiations are realized, but little progress has been made in this area (Fisher 2006).

A number of countries, including LDCs and African, Caribbean and Pacific countries, have expressed concern that some of their exports will be affected as preferences erode under the expected MFN reductions. The effects of erosion are estimated to be minor in the aggregate, but key exports of some countries could be severely affected. But again, the size of loss from preference erosion is much more likely to be affected by the level of ambition rather than the precise formula. An ambitious simple Swiss approach, however, might have a greater effect than other approaches. To some extent, improvement in the scope and operation of existing preference schemes, including simpler administration and rules of origin, could help offset some losses.

The eventual decision on the tariff-cutting formula could also have important implications for the developing countries' own obligations, but again the issue is much more a matter of ambition, not formula. The simple Swiss approach, most likely with dual coefficients, will tend to level tariffs across countries more than the ABI approach or its variations that take greater account of the diverse regimes of developing countries. Calculations of the effects of the various proposals on tariffs show that whichever approach is used, developing countries will be required to make deeper absolute cuts (except LDCs, which are expected to increase their binding coverage substantially but not to cut rates) and this will cast doubt on the value of the Doha provision for "less than full reciprocity" by developing countries.

While developing countries generally accept that trade liberalization is beneficial, at least in the long term, many are concerned about adjustment costs as well as potential losses from preference erosion and a decline in tariff-based revenues. Economic models do not produce reliable estimates of adjustment costs, losses due to preference erosion or revenue decline. Of course, allowing developing countries an extended period to implement commitments will facilitate adjustment to liberalization but will also delay the delivery of benefits to the sectors that might expect to expand. Countries highly dependent on tariff revenues will need time to restructure their tax systems and to find alternative domestic sources of revenue. Faster implementation by developed countries will create new export opportunities for those expected to gain from MFN liberalization, helping to generate a supply response and reducing potential balance of payment difficulties. However, it will mean that preference losses will come sooner rather than later.

Some developing countries are concerned that their own liberalization will mean forgoing the use of trade policies for industrial development, given that WTO rules preclude other second-best options. Paring away tariffs could also increase the use of anti-dumping and other such measures. Finally, if the countries liberalize too fast they might create a protectionist backlash that sets back long-term liberalization.

Success in implementing the eventual agreement on new commitments depends critically on developing countries being able to generate a supply response that takes advantage of market opportunities. To do this, many countries will need to build physical and institutional infrastructure, especially for transport. This need can be met only by substantial financial flows that go beyond the remit of the WTO. Complementary action is therefore needed to address this issue as well as the other costs of adjustment and provision of social safety nets – aid for trade.

The World Bank and the IMF have indicated that existing programmes, including the IMF's new Trade Integration Mechanism, are sufficient to solve problems likely to arise from implementing new WTO commitments. This willingness to address issues before the conclusion of negotiations fills a lacuna in the Uruguay Round package that embittered some developing countries. But for many highly indebted countries likely to be affected by the negotiations support by means of bilateral aid flows may be preferable. The G8 initiative on debt forgiveness should also be helpful.

Notes

* The chapter is based on work carried out over several years at UNCTAD with my colleagues Santiago Fernandez de Córdoba and David Vanzetti, with data support by Aki Kuwahara and Fabien Dumesnil.
1. See UNCTAD (2006a) and Milner (2006).
2. Mode 4 under the General Agreement on Trade in Services (GATS).
3. No overall target was fixed, unlike in some earlier rounds of negotiations in the GATT. For example, from the outset it was agreed that industrial tariffs would be cut by one third in the Kennedy Round, while in the Uruguay Round it was agreed that developed countries would cut tariffs by 36 per cent and developing countries by 24 per cent.
4. In WTO negotiations on trade in goods, members commit to "binding" tariffs and lowering already bound tariffs. This involves each member listing commitments in a schedule of concessions. Increasing such bound tariff rates requires renegotiating schedules under GATT Article XXVIII and offering other tariff reductions to principal suppliers.
5. "Zero for zero" refers to an agreement by a critical mass of key importers and exporters to eliminate duties on selected products, with zero rates then being made available to other participants in the negotiations under the most favoured nation (MFN) principle, but without requiring any commitment on their part. "Sectoral elimination", as discussed the Doha Work Programme, refers to agreement by all participants in negotiations to eliminate duties on selected products. Developing countries have argued that should such a modality be agreed, their participation should be voluntary. "Request and offer" refers to bilateral agreements on selected tariff rates that would apply to other participants in negotiations under the MFN principle.
6. Tariff peaks are undefined in the WTO, but are being interpreted as rates that exceed three times a member's national average rate. "International tariff peak" refers to any rate above 15 per cent. Tariff escalation refers to the practice of having higher rates on goods that are processed; thus raw materials (basic commodities, minerals) are often set at zero rates, intermediate goods (components, parts, other inputs to final production) at a higher rate and final goods, such as consumer goods, at the highest rate. This practice increases protection on the value added in processing, and makes it more difficult for exporting countries to sell more processed goods in a market characterized by tariff escalation.
7. For a discussion of some of the issues related to "policy space", see Messerlin (2006), Rodrik (1999) and UNCTAD (2006b).
8. These are discussed in Laird, de Córdoba and Vanzetti (2003).
9. Although not acknowledged, this was based on a proposal by Francois and Martin (2003).
10. This is based on the earlier EU and India proposals.
11. GTAP is the Global Trade Analysis Project, a modeling system and database stored at Purdue University. See http://www.gtap.agecon.purdue.edu/.

REFERENCES

Anderson, K., W. Martin and D. van der Mensbrugghe (2005) "Doha Merchandise Trade Reform and Developing Countries: What's at Stake?" mimeo, Washington, DC: World Bank.

de Córdoba, F. S., and D. Vanzetti (2006) "Now What? Searching for a Solution to the WTO Industrial Tariff Negotiations", in Laird and de Córdoba, eds, *Coping with Trade Reforms: A Developing Country Perspective on the WTO Industrial Tariff Negotiations*, London: Palgrave.

Fisher, B. (2006) "Preference Erosion, Government Revenues and Nontariff Trade Barriers", *World Economy* 29(10): 1377–1393.

Francois, J., and W. Martin (2003) "Formula Approaches for Market Access Negotiations", *World Economy* 26: 1–28.

Laird, S., and F. S. de Córdoba (2006) *Coping with Trade Reforms: A Developing Country Perspective on the WTO Industrial Tariff Negotiations*, London: Palgrave.

Laird, S., F. S. de Córdoba and D. Vanzetti (2003) "Market access proposals for non-agricultural products", in I. Mbirimi, B. Chilala and R. Grynberg, eds, *From Doha to Cancún: Delivering a Development Round*, Economic Paper 57, London: Commonwealth Secretariat.

Messerlin, P. (2006) "Enlarging the Vision for Trade Policy Space: Special and Differentiated Treatment and Infant Industry Issues", *World Economy* 29(10): 1395–1407.

Milner, C. (2006) "Making NAMA Work: Supporting Adjustment and Development", *World Economy* 29(10): 1409–1422.

Rama, M. (2003) "Globalization and Workers in Developing Countries", Policy Research Working Paper 2958, Washington, DC: World Bank.

Rodrik, D. (1999) *The New Global Economy and Developing Countries: Making Openness Work*, Washington DC: Overseas Development Council.

UNCTAD (2006a) *The Least Developed Country Report 2006: Lifting Productive Capacities*, Geneva: United Nations.

UNCTAD (2006b) *Trade and Development Report 2006: Global Partnership and National Policies for Development*, Geneva: United Nations.

World Bank (2006) *Economic Growth in the 1990s – Learning from a Decade of Reform*, Washington DC: World Bank.

5

Trade in services and policy priorities for developing countries

Gary P. Sampson

The General Agreement on Trade in Services (GATS) holds the potential to greatly expand trade in services and profoundly change international patterns of investment, production and consumption. The World Trade Organization (WTO) negotiations launched in 2000 to liberalize global trade in services have the potential to accelerate this process. After a slow start, and meagre progress, these negotiations have now been folded into the "suspended" Doha Development Agenda. The prospects for a speedy relaunching of the Doha negotiations, and therefore significant future liberalization of trade in services, look bleak at best.

Against this backdrop, it is perhaps timely to reflect on some of the broader considerations of policy relevance with respect to GATS. Should negotiations be re-launched, a precondition for their successful conclusion is for all countries to be convinced that it is in their interests to sign on to the outcome. Of the almost 150 countries needed to join the consensus, two-thirds are developing countries. It is crucial that not only the market access outcomes of the services negotiations, but also the usefulness of GATS for development purposes, are seen to be sufficiently positive by developing countries for them to accept the outcome.

Gaining access to markets is, of course, a plus for developing countries, but GATS offers more in terms of its potential role in economic development. However, linking the services sector to the broader goals of economic development is a relatively recent phenomenon. In fact, many famous growth economists, such as Allan Fisher, Walter Rostow and

Developing countries and the WTO: Policy approaches, Sampson and Chambers (eds),
United Nations University Press, 2008, ISBN 978-92-808-1153-7

Colin Clark, promoted theories where the process of development consisted of three main phases. First the pre-industrial phase followed by the industrial phase. As this stage, manufacturing plays the dominant role with a shift of production from agriculture to industry. The last stage was seen to be the post-industrial stage where the economy became a service economy. Viewed in this perspective, a well-functioning services sector was considered a *symptom* rather than a *source* of economic development.

The long-term value of GATS is that it raises the profile of the services sector as an important ingredient of economic development, and creates an analytical framework within which countries can engage in domestic regulatory reform. Autonomous liberalization can be pursued at the chosen speed, and reforms into domestic legislation can be eventually locked in through binding commitments at the multilateral level.

In what follows, I will argue that GATS has been constructed in such a way as to do just that. In other words, to permit developing countries to pursue their own development strategies and undertake commitments in line with their chosen speed of autonomous liberalization. As such, it provides an important tool that should be central to any regulatory reform and eventual trade liberalization. It is perhaps worth noting that this positive role for GATS, which reflects the vision of its founding fathers, is the antithesis of that held by a number of others. For some, GATS could "have devastating effects on the ability of governments to meet the needs of their poorest and most powerless citizens" (Oxfam, 2002: 224). This chapter addresses the question of whether this really is the case.

The outline of this chapter is as follows.

There is first a very brief commentary on some aspects of the original negotiation of GATS. The idea is certainly not to provide an historical overview of the creation of GATS – even though such an historical record is sorely needed. The purpose is rather to highlight the fact that developing countries were remarkably successful in negotiating an agreement where development is indeed an integral part of the agreement itself: not an "add on" as in the case of Part IV of the General Agreement on Tariffs and Trade (GATT). Characteristics of the agreement that have always been important for developing countries are highlighted in this section, as they are just as important today as they were at the time of their original negotiation.

This section is followed by a more recent overview of the negotiating process through to the current suspension of the Doha Development Agenda. The most interesting aspect of this phase is certainly not the disappointing trade-liberalizing results of the formal negotiations. What is interesting is the search for ways to liberalize trade in such diverse services activities when such disparate country interests are involved. Like many other traditional GATT processes and concepts, the request and offer process for liberalization of goods trade can not be simply transferred to trade in services.

This is followed by a number of policy-related considerations that were important for developing countries in the original negotiations and are perhaps even more important today. It is appropriate at this time to re-call the flexibilities provided in GATS for developing countries, and the manner in which the development-related concepts are useful for both autonomous reform and negotiated liberalization. The concluding chapter draws on the foregoing discussion to outline a number of policy conclusions.

Early history

Prior to, and during, the early years of the Uruguay Round, the scepticism of developing countries with respect to the advantages they could draw from a trade in services agreement remains legendary. History has proven that their early scepticism was well placed (see Sampson 1988: ch. 7).

In the period prior to the Uruguay Round, and during the Round itself, the options in terms of the envisaged outcome were varied. They included an expanded version of GATT with the texts of the various GATT articles modified to include references to services at various agreed places. This was resisted for a number of reasons. It was quickly apparent that many of the conventional GATT concepts, such as non-discrimination as both favoured nation treatment (MFN) and national treatment, could not be applied in their "raw form" to services trade. Furthermore, some GATT articles such as those on regional trade agreements, subsidies and safeguards would just not work for services trade. In addition, even after adjusting traditional GATT concepts to account for the special nature of trade in services, there was no guarantee that the application of these concepts would be to the benefit of developing countries.

Another option was an addendum to GATT along the lines of its Part IV, something that history had proven to be of limited usefulness to developing countries. It was rejected by developing countries. Other options included a conditional agreement with limited GATT membership along the lines of the Tokyo Round Codes or the best endeavour agreements in the OECD. A further option was to have a series of sector-specific agreements coupled with best endeavours statements of good intent.

From the outset of the Uruguay Round, developing countries insisted that the economic development of developing countries must be integrated into the text of the agreement itself, with full GATT membership of the Agreement, and without it being an addendum to GATT.

From an initial position of strong opposition, the passage of time resulted in developing countries' warming to the idea of a services agreement. There are a variety of reasons for this. First, there was a realization that the effective provision of infrastructural services – such as health, education, local communications and local transport – was indeed a priority for developing countries' own national economic development. A carefully negotiated and balanced agreement could assist in achieving this goal. Second, there was also a realization that many services – maritime transport, freight insurance, marketing, distribution and international finance – are vitally important in determining developing countries' export supply capacity of goods. More international competition could result in better-quality and less expensive services of this nature.

Third, there were services of direct interest to developing countries that were currently traded (exported and imported) or could be exported (or replace imports) if various trade barriers were removed; these include tourism, international transport and certain off-shore labour-intensive services. In a more general perspective, there was the orientation in a number of key developing countries toward more outward-oriented development strategies in both goods and services. Concessions could be obtained elsewhere as a result of liberalization that had already taken place in services (and the goods sectors) and where future liberalization could be important for the economy as a whole.

Fourth, if properly negotiated from a developing country perspective, there should be flexibility for them to open fewer sectors, liberalize fewer types of transactions, progressively extend market access in line with their development situation and, when making access to their markets available to foreign service suppliers, attach to such access conditions aimed at achieving the objectives of a greater integration of developing countries into the world trading system. This suited those countries pursuing autonomous liberalization at their own speed.

Finally, and most importantly, developing countries realized that, by negotiating effectively in an area in which they were not the *demandeurs*, they could achieve a paradigm different from GATT – development could be an integral part of whatever agreement emerged. They were correct in this respect.

Contrary to the accusations of some critics, developing countries, in large measure, secured precisely what they were looking for in the negotiations. There are many examples of this.

One relates to the notion of the *progressive* liberalization of trade in services. The wording was important for developing countries. They insisted on its inclusion as there was no desire for immediate liberalization through the adoption and application of legally binding, yet untried obligations. Many developing countries had not yet liberalized their own domestic services sectors. If national activities relating to banking, insurance, security trading, basic and enhanced telecommunications and public works were state monopolies, why open the market to foreign corporations in the absence of the proper domestic regulation and liberalization?

Thus, there was a formal recognition in GATS that given the asymmetries in the development of services regulations, there was a particular need for developing countries to have the appropriate regulations in place before considering domestic liberalization. In other words, liberalize domestically – or at least revise domestic regulations – before liberalizing internationally.

This meant that at the time of signing the Agreement, apart from the binding of some existing market access opportunities, few liberalization commitments were undertaken by developing countries.

Second, the GATS text aimed to achieve a more integrated role in world trade in services of developing countries. This was to be done through strengthening the capacity, efficiency and competitiveness of their own domestic services. GATS does not oblige – or even encourage – any country to privatize or deregulate its services sectors. Of course they can, and have, but most of this is quite independent of the existence of the GATS, and is most certainly not due to GATS obligations.

Finally, a real attraction of the Agreement for developing countries was that foreign service providers were not only obliged to respect domestic regulations (as were local companies) it provided them the possibility of imposing restrictions and limitations on certain aspects of the activities of foreign service providers. This meant that the control of foreign service providers was available through the use of scheduled and legally enforceable commitments. This option was not open under bilaterally negotiated deals with more powerful trading countries (or companies) where they might be pressured unduly. Importantly, non-respect of obligations on the part of foreign service providers is actionable under the WTO dispute settlement provisions.

More recent history

In its own Articles, GATS provides for future liberalizing negotiations. These were to begin "not later than five years from the date of entry into force of the WTO Agreement", that is, not later than the year 2000.[1] The logic of this rather unusual approach of providing for a "next round" of negotiations in the Agreement itself was linked to the fact that most of the Uruguay Round was devoted to creating an entirely new agreement where the intellectual underpinnings had to be developed from scratch. Little time was left for negotiating liberalization commitments. Additionally, as noted above, countries were hesitant to negotiate legally binding liberalization commitments when the commercial implication of their application was completely untried.

The collapse of the Seattle Ministerial Meeting in late 1999 did not prevent the negotiations from being launched in 2000. The Seattle draft Ministerial Declaration contained a widely supportive mandate for the services negotiations to proceed. It was broadly felt that a commitment to future negotiations was a means to ensure an opportunity to give content to what was essentially a framework agreement. The Agreement could be further developed and refined while deepening the liberalization commitments and promote the interests of all countries while securing an overall balance of rights and obligations. At the more practical level, it was also thought that with numerous technological advances transforming trade in services, new avenues of liberalization could be explored, and perhaps acknowledged, in the Agreement. The negotiators were certainly right in this respect.

However, the scope of the future negotiations was left unclear. While there was the possibility to be ambitious – with no sectors or modes of supply excluded – ideas differed as to the nature and degree of ambition. What was already clear was that the Uruguay Round had led to a wide array of unequal country and sector-specific commitments. There were wide differences regarding actual and prospective market access opportunities among sectors and/or countries. As a consequence, there was an opportunity to improve both the overall level and balance of specific commitments.

With disagreement as to the scope and nature of the negotiations, it was clear that negotiating guidelines were needed to advance the process by defining the objectives, modalities, time frame and the practical arrangements for organizing the work. However, as the overall climate had deteriorated in the period since the Seattle Ministerial Meeting, the Guidelines were long in coming. This delay was accentuated because of the very different and hotly disputed views on how to proceed. The debate surrounding this process is particularly instructive as it raised a number of fundamental questions about the uniqueness of negotiating the multilateral liberalization of services.

Some suggested that there should be commonly agreed methods of liberalization on a sectoral or cross-sectoral, or a modal or cross-modal basis.[2] There could be standardized lists of services products for a given sub-sector to be included in each Members' commitments; establishment of standardized minimum liberalization commitments on a sub-sectoral or on a modal basis (including the movement of natural persons); and exclusion of certain types of restrictions across the board. The idea of a "formula" technique was advanced, which would permit Members to make identical or equivalent levels of commitments with regard to certain modes or types of restrictions across the board, and thereby fulfil the objective of moving toward a liberalization target in a more structured manner.

Individual sectors were also advanced as priorities for liberalization. Some assigned priority to completing negotiations on maritime services, as there were only limited commitments without the MFN principle being applied. Air transport services were also identified as a priority, as the Annex on Air Transport Services leaves the sector with limited coverage in terms of both general obligations and specific commitments. There were also sectors that some governments thought needed to be revisited because of technical changes in the delivery of services (professional services), as well as sectors where commercial interests place a particular priority (environmental services, energy, educational and distribution services).

It was also unclear how to deal with MFN exemptions.[3] For both developed and developing countries, a number of sectors were characterized by preferential arrangements at the time of the negotiations. For example, all countries had preferential arrangements in their air transport sectors, a number of developing countries had preferential cargo-sharing arrangements for their maritime service sectors and some developed countries had preferential arrangements in their maritime and audiovisual sectors.

Throughout the Uruguay Round, developing countries had consistently and successfully argued that MFN must be an unconditional general obligation, rather than the subject of bilateral negotiation. This was perhaps the most single "make or break issue" for developing countries for the entire Uruguay round. Thus, to deal with existing preferential arrangements, it was agreed that exemptions could be taken either at the time of entry into force of the Agreement or at the time of accession to the WTO. The result was that more than 70 WTO members specified services activities in a list of MFN exemptions. These exemption lists are governed by conditions set out in a separate Annex to GATS that make clear that no new exemptions can be granted, at least not by this route, and that future requests for non-MFN treatment can be met only through WTO waiver procedures.[4]

It was not until March 2001 that the Services Council approved the two-page "Guidelines and Procedures for Negotiations on Trade in Services" (WTO 2001). There is some merit in outlining the content of the Guidelines as they remain the basis for future negotiations.

The Guidelines firstly confirm the objective of progressive liberalization; provide for appropriate flexibility for developing countries, with special priority to be given to the least-developed countries; make reference to the needs of small and medium-sized service suppliers; and undertake a commitment to respect the existing structure and principles of GATS (e.g., the hybrid approach to the scheduling of commitments). No sectors or modes of delivery are to be excluded; special attention is to be given to the export interests of developing countries; and there is to be the renegotiation of existing most favoured nation exemptions. Finally, the Guidelines confirm that current schedules are the starting point for the negotiations, and the request-offer is to be the main approach to liberalizing negotiations. Negotiating credit is to be given for anonymous liberalization according to agreed common criteria; and the Services Council is to evaluate the results of the negotiations for developing countries prior to their completion.

In other words, the Guidelines provided for broad and ambitious negotiations.

Doha Development Agenda

In view of these relatively detailed guidelines, the Doha Ministerial Declaration confined itself to endorsing them and integrating the services negotiations into the wider framework of the Doha Agenda. The Doha Declaration contains target dates for the circulation of initial requests (30 June 2002) and initial offers (31 March 2003) of specific commitments, and envisages all negotiations, which form part of a single undertaking, to be concluded not later than 1 January 2005. The Declaration recognizes that the work initiated in 2000 has been taken over by the wider Doha negotiations and reaffirms the importance of the Guidelines. The work has proceeded on two fronts: trade-liberalizing negotiations and the completion of outstanding work from the Uruguay Round relating to rules.

With respect to liberalization, GATS does not recommend or prescribe templates for undertaking commitments. Each Member is free to structure its commitments in line with its national policy objectives and constraints. There are no WTO documents that trace the initial requests exchanged between members. The early stage in the negotiating process is essentially bilateral and not subject to notification requirements. It is for individual members to decide who to approach, in what form, and what issues to raise under the relevant GATT provision, including MFN exemption.

What is sure, however, is that while developing economies have undertaken fewer commitments on average than other members, many of them have implemented sweeping reforms in recent years. Since such reforms have often been associated with profound institutional changes (e.g., the abolition of telecom, transport or insurance monopolies), and as they are irreversible from a domestic perspective, they are not easily drawn on as negotiating coin. Nevertheless, governments can seek credit under the modalities for the treatment of autonomous liberalization, which was adopted by the services Council in March 2003.

As far as rules are concerned, GATS provides for negotiations on three issues: emergency safeguards, government procurement and subsidies. With respect to safeguards, a country may currently modify or withdraw a specific commitment if it can show the Council for Trade in Services that the action is necessary, in spite of the normal rule that such commitments cannot be changed for three years. The question of the desirability and feasibility of traditional safeguard action is open to question, as there are considerable difficulties in determining the scope of action, the criteria for taking action (e.g., what constitutes serious injury) and its justification, as well as the temporary remedial procedures.

There is little doubt that subsidies can distort trade if foreign suppliers are not entitled to receive subsidies given to a competing domestic supplier. Many countries have, in fact, specifically excluded the possibility of granting subsidies to foreign suppliers by stating in their schedules that certain subsidies will not be available to foreign suppliers. GATS provides that adversely affected countries may request consultations that will be accorded sympathetic consideration. On government procurement, there is little advancement as there is disagreement on the scope of the negotiations coupled with the need to coordinate the work with processes elsewhere in the WTO.

The Cancun Ministerial Conference in early September 2003 marked a new setback in the progress of negotiations. The concluding statement merely reaffirmed the Doha Declaration is in decisions and committed members to implement them fully and faithfully. Reflecting the lack of political impetus, the request and offer process in services virtually ground to a halt. It was not until mid-2004 that the so-called July Package (the work program-decision adopted by the General Council on 1 August 2005), injected a new momentum into the negotiations.

The July 2004 package contains a target date of May 2005 of the submission of revised offers, and adopted a set of recommendations that members that have not submitted initial offers do so as soon as possible; ensure a high quality of offers, in particular in sectors and modes of export interest to developing countries, with special attention being given to least-developed countries; intensify efforts to conclude the rule-making negotiations; and provide targeted technical assistance to developing countries with a view to enabling them to participate effectively. In addition, the Council was mandated to review progress in the negotiations and provide a full report to the Trade Negotiating Committee, including possible recommendations to the purpose of the Hong Kong meeting in December 2005.

At the most recent of the WTO ministerial meetings, the Hong Kong Ministerial Declaration adopted Annex C of the Declaration, where ministers agreed to intensify the negotiations "with a view to expanding the sectoral and modal coverage of commitments and improving their quality".[5] In accordance with the Hong Kong outcome, countries started presenting their requests on various services sectors in February 2006. Plurilateral meetings to discuss these requests continued through to April 2006.

Between March 2003 and March 2004, 69 initial offers (counting the European Community as one) were submitted with 29 revised offers submitted by the end of January 2006. While there is disagreement on many fronts in the negotiations, there seems to be a consensus that the offers to date fall well below the expectations of all. To date, the request-and-offer process has only produced limited results: by the end of October 2005, only 69 Members had submitted offers, including 30 revised offers. In other words, 23 offers are outstanding, if least-developed countries (LDCs) are not counted. If LDCs are factored in, 54 offers would remain to be submitted.

Policy priorities

In the early years of GATT, the policies advocated by economists were clear. Developing countries depended heavily on commodity exports and, owing to the decline in commodity prices, coupled with low price and income elasticities, free trade would entail a continuing dependence on commodity exports. This dependence would mean perpetual poverty. Export pessimism was the name of the game.

To grow, countries needed to accumulate capital, and this could not be done with a workforce in agriculture with negative marginal returns. In such circumstances, capital could not be imported; the domestic production of manufactured goods was required. The policy prescription was clear. According to Hollis B. Chenery, Economic Adviser to the

President of the World Bank from 1970 to 1972 and later World Bank Vice President for Development Policy: "Industrialisation consists primarily in the substitution of domestic production of manufactured goods for imports" (Chenery 1956).

Services were not part of the development deal. As noted earlier times have changed. A viable services sector is now considered not as a result of development, but as a precondition for it. The negotiation of GATS has contributed greatly to this change in thinking and constitutes one of its principal successes. The following outlines a number of policy considerations that are important for developing countries in maximizing the benefits and flexibilities of GATS when undertaking domestic autonomous reform or negotiating for improved market access.

Obligations à la carte

GATS resembles other trade agreements relating to goods. It has a central set of rules coupled with commitments to liberalize or bind restrictions on trade. However, these similarities are in many ways quite superficial.[6] The word "trade" itself has a totally different meaning in terms of GATS compared with GATT, as "trade" in services can take place without any cross-border transaction taking place. However, perhaps the most notable difference comes with *non-discrimination* as embodied in national treatment and most-favoured nation treatment. This difference provides for considerable flexibility and potential advantages for developing countries when undertaking liberalization commitments.

National treatment is stated in very similar terms to those in GATT, but is limited to commitments listed in a country's schedule. The limitations specified in a schedule give them the same character as a GATT-bound tariff and represent the minimum treatment that may be given. Importantly, national treatment is a *negotiated* obligation; the limitations placed on it are important in terms of the maintenance of national autonomy. Furthermore, conditions can be placed on foreign corporations that are advantageous to the individual developing country (e.g., obligations to employ and train local technicians) and which become legally binding obligations inscribed in schedules.

Non-discrimination between supplying countries – most-favoured nation treatment – is specifically provided for in GATT as an over-arching general obligation. As noted above, in GATS there is the possibility for exemptions from the obligation when joining the Agreement. The importance of MFN is that it guarantees that liberalization will be extended to all members. Although it does not, by itself, require any particular degree of market openness, it does ensure unbiased competition among trading partners. It is certainly attractive for developing countries, which fought hard collectively in the Uruguay Round negotiations to have MFN as a compulsory and general obligation rather than negotiated for each service category.

In more general terms, GATS provides a great degree of flexibility for developing countries to pursue their own development paths. The policy space that they consider absent in other WTO agreements can be found in GATS. From this perspective, it is odd that the Agreement is savagely criticized by a number of developmental non-governmental organizations when developing countries see it as a major achievement of the Uruguay Round. It is perhaps interesting and insightful to speculate on why this is the case.

One contributing factor may be a perception that countries – particularly developing countries – are obligated to undertake more commitments when joining the Agreement than is the case. Another closely linked consideration may be that it is thought that the scope of application of the Agreement is broader than it actually is, with correspondingly fewer possibilities to make exceptions or to revoke earlier commitments. Another contributing factor could be that some consider the Agreement not to be development-oriented and not to have the support of developing countries. These considerations will be addressed at different times in the following paragraphs.

In fact, an advantage for developing countries – along with others – is that there is a high degree of autonomy in the negotiation of commitments. This comes from the fact that there are two broad sets of obligations in GATS.

The first comprises general obligations, which are compulsory and generic in coverage. They are compulsory in the sense that they apply to all WTO members and are non-negotiable. They are generic in the sense that that they apply to all measures covered by the Agreement. They set the floor in terms of the commitments undertaken when WTO members joined the Agreement – or join through the process of accession to the WTO. Like others closely associated with the process of negotiations and implementation of these agreements, I consider them to be non-onerous and sensible. In any event, they are considered to be neither contentious nor unreasonable for the signatory countries, and therefore are not under critical review within the WTO.

The second set of obligations is voluntary in the sense that they apply only to sectors and sub-sectors where governments have chosen to go beyond the compulsory and generic obligations mentioned above. If they have taken this option, it is because they consider it to be in their national interests.

With negotiated commitments, unlike the GATT, they are subject to limitations and conditions imposed by the importing country on foreign service providers. They are, in effect, "tailor-made" to meet the requirements of the importing country. This feature of the Agreement is particularly attractive to developing countries. As noted above, a government can legally register the conditions to be respected by the foreign service supplier. Furthermore, and of critical importance to developing countries, any service activity that is not inscribed in the schedule is subject only to the first set of obligations: the compulsory obligations that apply to all measures affecting trade in services.

Standards

The vast majority of measures that affect trade in services arise from domestic regulations. The potential problems in this area will not lessen with the passage of time. As the degree of sophistication of the nature and provision of services increases with technological advancement, so does the concern of the public with health, environment and safety. Consequently, the regulation of services trade and production will become increasingly complex. Considerations that are plaguing goods trade – such as what is the legitimate degree of regulation that is appropriate to meet nationally preferred standards when international standards are not adhered to – has now emerged in the area of trade in services. Nevertheless, notions such as "product and non-product related production processes", "like products" and all their concomitant problems threaten to pose no fewer challenges in services trade compared to goods trade.

There is, thus, a need for effective disciplines on the domestic regulation of services activities so as to ensure that they do not "constitute unnecessary barriers to trade in services". A balance, however, must be struck between such multilateral disciplines and the right of Members to have an adequate domestic regulatory framework to achieve legitimate objectives. GATS requires Members to "ensure that all measures of general application affecting trade in services are administered in a reasonable, objective and impartial manner" in sectors where they have undertaken specific commitments. The objective is to ensure a transparent and predictable regulatory environment, which can provide legal certainty and confidence to service suppliers, investors, users and consumers. It requires Members to develop horizontal disciplines in respect of "qualification requirements and procedures, technical standards and licensing requirements" so as to ensure that they "do not constitute unnecessary barriers to trade in services".

Some would argue that the principles relating to domestic regulation are presently too imprecise – specific disciplines in individual sectors will be needed, especially in sectors where particular regulatory constraints exist and effective access to foreign markets by services suppliers may in some sub-sectors require greater specificity in the general principles contained in GATS. Existing examples are the reference paper for the telecommunication services, as well as disciplines on accountancy services. A number of WTO Members are of the view that further disciplines of this kind should be envisaged for other sectors. For some, the argument continues that a horizontal approach to the professions that takes account also of profession-specific disciplines could be an effective way to proceed in the immediate future. Specific candidates mentioned in this respect include the legal, engineering, architecture and surveying professions. If progress in not made in this area, then attention will further shift to regional preferential arrangements.

Domestic regulation

Most countries strictly regulate many services activities, irrespective of whether they are supplied by local or foreign firms or by the government itself. A principal criticism of GATS is that the foreign provision of these services could constitute an encroachment on national sovereignty in developing countries and undermine domestic regulations. A number of points are important in this respect.

For those government services that are supplied on a commercial or competitive basis, the coverage of the activity means that only the compulsory obligations apply. Second, additional obligations are undertaken because the government chooses to do so. Third, and most importantly, if governments do admit foreign suppliers in these areas, these suppliers are obliged to operate in accordance with domestic regulations, and the restrictions and limitations written into the national legally binding schedules. These restrictions and limitations are transparent and are legally enforceable through the WTO dispute settlement system.

This is far superior to negotiating a foreign presence and the content of domestic regulations bilaterally with powerful transnational corporations. A further point is that there is nothing in the Agreement that requires – or even encourages – publicly provided services (e.g., health, education, public utilities) to be privatized. If governments make no specific commitments on these sectors – and undertake only the general obligations of the Agreement – they are free to maintain both public and private monopoly suppliers.

The reality is that governments have indeed undertaken commitments with respect to government services supplied on a commercial basis in the area of education and health services. They have not, however, engaged in a privatization of public healthcare or education systems. They most certainly have not compromised domestic regulations; indeed, they have enforced the same standards on foreign suppliers as on nationals for the protection of the public. As it is their right under GATS (see above), a number of governments have also imposed additional requirements on foreigners beyond those required of national service suppliers.

Trade or investment

In the early stages of the Uruguay Round negotiations, there were differing views about the dividing line between trade in services and investment in services. Developing countries had successfully opposed launching fully fledged negotiations on investment, and were sensitive to the risk of services negotiations delivering an investment agreement through the back door. If the Agreement were to encompass services provided through the establishment of foreign service providers, it would indeed be tantamount to creating a multilateral agreement on investment in services. On the other hand, if the agreement applied only to trade in the traditional sense of something crossing the border, then a vast and growing area of commercial activity in the services sectors would be outside the discipline of the agreement.

Over and above the concern over the coverage of the Agreement was the concern that a number of developed countries were insisting that the Agreement should establish not only a definition of trade in services to encompass a foreign presence, but also establish a *right* to invest in services activities in the importing country.

The concerns were met by agreeing that there are various "modes" for supplying services internationally, some of them being alternative means to reach the same end. It was also agreed that conditions and limitations could be placed on any foreign commercial presence (see above) or even that access could be denied in total. This ensured that investment would not be considered a "right" in the Agreement. In addition, horizontal limitations could be placed on all foreign services suppliers (e.g., through approval from an investment review body), which assured developing countries that investment could be regulated and directed to the required sectors.

Thus, the definition of trade in services was to be based on the means by which services were supplied internationally.[7] Four modes of supply were identified: cross-border movement of the service; consumption abroad of the service; the commercial presence in the consuming country of the service supplier; and the presence of natural persons in the importing country to supply the service.

Restrictive business practices

There may be different, and perfectly legitimate, motivations for the existence of monopoly suppliers. However, services supplied by monopolies often constitute inputs to other service activities: obvious examples are telecommunications, financial services and transport. GATS does not prohibit the maintenance of monopoly or exclusive rights to supply a service, but each member is required to ensure that any monopoly acts in a manner consistent with that member's obligations. For example, if a telecommunications monopoly allows interconnection to suppliers of value-added telecommunications, it should do so on the basis of MFN treatment.

One general obligation of GATS that has no GATT counterpart relates to anti-competitive practices of private enterprises. GATS explicitly recognizes the anti-competitive effects that "certain business practices of services suppliers" may have. This is a pioneering clause in a multilateral trade agreement and, under GATS, members agree to consult on such practices, when so requested by another member, and to exchange information with a view to eliminating them.

Legally binding in obligations

One of the most significant differences from GATT is that GATS provides for the increasing participation of developing countries but links this goal to the negotiation of legally binding specific commitments. One of the principal criticisms by developing countries is that most of the provisions of GATT, the Enabling Clause and other WTO Agreements are of a best-endeavour nature. This is not the case with the GATS Agreement. As noted above, when developing countries provide access to their markets for foreign service suppliers, they are free to attach conditions aimed at increasing their participation in trade in services.

The provisions relating to the increasing participation of developing countries are designed to improve the supply capacity of developing countries rather than afford preferential market access or exempt them from obligations. In fact, unlike in the Enabling Clause, no preferential market access is provided for. Nevertheless, as noted, in negotiating specific commitments, appropriate flexibility is provided for individual developing countries to open fewer sectors, liberalize fewer types of transactions, and progressively extend market access in line with their development situation.

Worker mobility

Eight Annexes are attached to GATS, along with eight Ministerial Decisions adopted in Marrakech on the same day that GATS was signed. There is also an Understanding on Financial Services. These are all important with respect to the GATS rules. Two of the most important and permanent Annexes are on MFN exemptions and the Movement of Natural Persons. The other permanent Annexes concern four specific sectors of trade in services: air transport; financial services; telecommunications; and maritime transport services.

The Annex on Movement of Natural Persons Supplying Services is of particular importance to developing countries. It deals with the temporary movement of natural persons who supply services in the territory of another member. It is made clear that the Agreement does not apply to measures regarding citizenship, residence or employment on a permanent basis, or to people who travel abroad looking for work. As a result, the Agreement applies only to the stay in a foreign country of natural persons supplying services.

The Annex also states that members may regulate the entry of natural persons into their territory and impose border controls, provided that such measures are not applied in such a manner as to nullify or impair the benefits accruing to any member under the terms of a specific commitment.

Movement of natural persons constitutes the fourth mode of supply. As a result, it does not constitute a sector *per se*. Most members of the WTO have covered movement of natural persons in the horizontal section of their schedule of specific commitments. At the end of the Uruguay Round, because developing countries were dissatisfied with the commitments made for this mode of delivery of services, in which they felt they had particular competitive strengths, it was agreed to resume negotiations after the end of the Uruguay Round with the aim of achieving higher commitments. The Decision on Negotiations on Movement of Natural Persons provided for an extended period of negotiations, stating their objectives and establishing a negotiating group.[8]

Proposals on mode 4 have included a call for the harmonization of categories of the type of service supplier used in scheduling commitments; more commitments on lower-skilled workers; the reduction of barriers involving such matters as nationality, residency and work permit requirements; tax treatment; wage parity requirements; and the duration of stay. The emergence of "off-shoring" activities in recent years has turned the spotlight on cross-border trade.

Policy conclusions

Developing countries were successful in making development an integral part of GATS. The most important policy challenge facing them now is how to best exploit the opportunities presented in the Agreement. This can be viewed from two perspectives.

The first is that GATS provides a framework within which developing countries can promote domestic policy reform. While it may seem unusual to turn to a multilateral agreement in order to consider the option to domestic reform, particularly when the agreement specifically states that national policy choices will not be circumscribed, this is indeed the case. This conclusion comes from looking at GATS in a broader historical context.

While it may now seem obvious that there are four modes of delivery; that the same service can be delivered through alternative modes of delivery; that granting national treatment brings different obligations compared to goods trade; that the production and consumption of services varies greatly across sectors; that regulations differ greatly for services and modes of delivery; that there are both horizontal and specific regulations; and so on, this certainly was not the case prior to the creation and implementation of GATS. From a macro perspective, the services sector was considered to be a bundle of activities that emitted little attention from a national policy or development perspective. GATS has changed that.

Within the analytical framework provided by GATS, developing countries should, at their own speed, pursue their domestic regulation and eventual liberalization of those services activities that would most benefit national development through international competition. The potential benefits that accrue to developing countries through the removal of trade restrictions and distortions and improved allocation of resources domestically are just as realizable in the case of services trade as they are in goods trade.

However, the pace of this autonomous liberalization depends very much on the individual country concerned and, in particular, whether or not the human and institutional capacity is in place to deal with the change. In this respect, differentiated treatment is appropriate for developing countries in terms of, for example, the period of transition available to implement the commitments undertaken. The notion of special and differential treatment applied in a generic fashion as in the past is even less applicable to trade in services than it has been to trade in goods.

On the market access front, as is formally recognized, developing countries should receive recognition for liberalization undertaken autonomously. This is formally recognized by governments, as is the fact that services sectors and modes of delivery of importance to developing countries should be a priority for market openings.

The Doha development agenda is suspended and whether or not it will ever be revised is not clear at this time in history. In broad measure, however, developing countries should not be waiting for the multilateral exchange of "concessions" to undertake domestic policy reform. GATS provides the framework within which to structure domestic reform, and here lies its true long-term value.

Notes

1. According to Article XIX of GATS, the negotiations in 2000 should aim to achieve progressively higher levels of liberalization; be directed to the reduction or elimination of the adverse effects on trade in services of measures as a means of providing effective market access; promote the interests of all participants on a mutually advantageous basis and secure an overall balance of rights and obligations; take into account national policy objectives and the level of development of individual Members, both overall and in individual sectors; and provide for appropriate flexibility for individual developing-country Members including measures taken by the latter aimed at achieving the objectives referred to in Article IV of GATS.
2. Modes of delivery are discussed below.
3. This relates to the fact that the most important general obligation is most-favoured nation (MFN) treatment, which is also a key obligation in GATT and other WTO agreements. It requires members to grant services and service suppliers of any other member the most favourable treatment granted to like services and service suppliers of any other country. It is discussed below.
4. Although some exemptions are subject to a stated time limit, some members have indicated that their intended duration was indefinite. For those that are not, the Annex provides that in principle they should not last longer than 10 years (that is, not beyond 2004), and that in any case they are subject to negotiation in future trade-liberalizing rounds.
5. The key aspects of Annex C are: best-endeavour modal and cross-cutting objectives for making new and improved market access commitments with appropriate flexibility for developing Members; intensification of negotiations on GATS rules; a mandate to develop disciplines on domestic regulations; intensification of the request-offer negotiations; specific regard to trade-related concerns of small economies; specific (and mandatory) provisions for least-developed countries; provision of technical assistance to developing and least-developed countries; and timelines for a second round of revised offers by 31 July 2006 and final draft schedules by 31 October 2006.
6. GATS consists of 29 complex Articles that elaborate the concepts, obligations and procedures on which the Agreement is based. There are also eight Annexes, which bring further specificity to sectoral considerations as well as the movement of persons, and in some instances modify the application of the concepts contained in the Agreement. Of nine additional Attachments, eight are Ministerial Decisions on a variety of subjects ranging from the environment to dispute-settlement procedures. There is also an Understanding on how some governments may wish to negotiate liberalization in financial services.
7. The first articulation of the architecture of GATS can be found in Sampson and Snape (1985).
8. WTO, *Decision on Negotiations on Movement of Natural Persons*, Geneva: WTO Secretariat, adopted by Ministers in Marrakech on 15 April 1994.

REFERENCES

Chenery, H. B. (1956) "The Role of Industrialisation Programmes in Development Programmes", in Â. N. Agarwala and S. P. Singh, eds, *The Economics of Under-Development*, Bombay: Oxford University Press, p. 463.

Oxfam (2002) *Rigged Rules and Double Standards: Trade, Globalization and the Fight against Poverty*, Oxford: Oxfam.

Sampson, G. P. (1988) "Developing Countries and the Liberalisation of Trade in Services", in J. Whalley, ed., *Rules, Power and Credibility*, Ontario: University of Western Ontario Press.

Sampson, G. P., and R. H. Snape (1985) "Identifying the Issues in Trade in Services", *World Economy*, 8(2).

WTO (2001) *Guidelines and Procedures for the Negotiations on Trade in Services: Adopted by the Special Session of the Council for Trade in Services on 28 March 2001*, S/L/93, Geneva: WTO, 29 March.

Part II
Legal flexibility

6

Special and differential treatment: The need for a different approach

Constantine Michalopoulos

Developing countries have argued since early in GATT's history that their development status requires that they be subject to different and more favourable trade rules than everybody else. This principle was accepted in GATT and later in the WTO, and has been enshrined as special and differential treatment (SDT) for developing countries. Another subgroup – the least-developed countries (LDCs) – is provided with even more favourable treatment.[1]

While the WTO agreements contain a very large number of provisions for SDT, developing countries have felt that they have not been properly implemented and that they need additional flexibility, more "policy space", so as to permit policies that are more conducive to their development. Also, to a significant extent, WTO rules reflect the interests of rich countries: they are less demanding about distortionary policies that are favoured by these countries, as, for example, in the use of agricultural subsidization, and the permissive approach that has historically been taken toward the use of import quotas on textile products – which in principle was prohibited by GATT rules. More recently, the inclusion of rules on the protection of intellectual property rights has led to perceptions that the WTO contract continues to be unbalanced.[2]

The Doha Ministerial Declaration reaffirmed the importance of SDT by stating that "provisions for special and differential treatment are an integral part of the WTO agreements". It called for a review of WTO SDT provisions with the objective of "strengthening them and making them more precise, effective and operational" (WTO 2001: para. 44).

Developing countries and the WTO: Policy approaches, Sampson and Chambers (eds), United Nations University Press, 2008, ISBN 978-92-808-1153-7

Despite extensive negotiations in the context of the Doha Round for over four years, very little consensus has developed on the whole SDT issue, although agreement has been reached on a few concrete steps in favour of LDCs.

There are big disagreements on both the scope and country coverage of SDT.[3] Many developing countries regard SDT provisions as meaningless, while many developed countries regard them as bad economics and outdated. The purpose of this chapter is to review the conceptual premises for SDT, analyse the main issues that have led to the current stalemate and come up with a series of practical recommendations for a new approach. The central objective would be to recast SDT in a way that would assist the development of low-income countries, be seen to do so by developing countries and be regarded as both "legitimate" and appropriate by developed country members.[4]

The conceptual premises for SDT

Several conceptual premises underlie the provision of SDT. The fundamental one is that developing countries are intrinsically disadvantaged in their participation in international trade, and therefore multilateral agreements involving them and developed countries must account for this weakness in specifying their rights and responsibilities. A related premise is that trade policies that maximize sustainable development in developing countries differ from those that do so in developed economies and hence that policy disciplines applying to developed economies should not apply to developing countries. The final premise is that it is in the interest of developed countries to assist developing countries in their fuller integration and participation in the international trading system.

Based on these premises the provisions introduced in the WTO agreements fall in two broad categories: positive actions by developed country members or international institutions and exceptions to the overall rules contained in the agreements that apply to developing countries with occasional additional exceptions for the LDCs (Michalopoulos 2001).

Developed countries have agreed to take three kinds of actions to support developing countries' participation in international trade:
- Provide preferential access to their markets, such as through the Generalized System of Preferences (GSP);
- Provide technical and other assistance to permit them to meet their WTO obligations and otherwise enhance the benefits developing countries derive from international trade; and
- Implement the overall agreements in ways that are beneficial or least damaging to the interests of developing countries and LDCs.

There are two fundamental ways in which developing countries and LDCs have accepted differential obligations under the WTO agreements. First, they enjoy freedom to undertake policies that limit access to their markets or support domestic producers or exporters in ways not allowed to other members. Examples include the special provisions for developing countries contained in Article XVIII of GATT, the general exemption from reciprocity in trade negotiations to reduce or remove tariffs and other barriers to trade, contained in the "Enabling Clause" and similar non-reciprocity provisions included in GATS Article XIX:2. Second, developing countries and LDCs get more time to meet obligations or commitments under the agreements.

Another way of looking at SDT is to distinguish between SDT provisions on the core WTO disciplines regarding preferential market access (provided by the developed countries) or tariff bindings and other "flexibilities" afforded to developing countries in the use of non-tariff barriers, tariffs or subsidies in trade policy and the SDT provisions that relate to the institutional capacity of developing countries to implement commitments. The case for SDT is much stronger for the second set of provisions than for the first (Hoekman et al. 2004). There are fundamental conceptual issues surrounding the first set of provisions, while the issues surrounding the second have to do more with which countries should receive SDT and for how long.

In the Doha Round, developing countries made a very large number of proposals for SDT. These proposals were split into two categories: generic proposals affecting the SDT concept in general and sector-specific special and differential provisions. The former were discussed in the WTO Committee on Trade and Development (CTD), traditionally a non-negotiating forum, and made little headway. The latter were discussed in the specific negotiating bodies, for example, on agriculture, non-agriculture market access (NAMA), and so on, and resulted in various degrees of consensus as discussed below.

SDT provisions

Preferential market access

The underlying premise for preferential treatment in market access relates to the importance for developing countries to diversify their exports into manufacturing and the difficulties that they may face in breaking into international markets for such products. Developed countries have provided tariff preferences to exports of manufactures from developing countries under the GSP and, within that context, for special treatment of the LDCs.

The evidence from the implementation of the GSP is that it has not been especially useful in promoting general integration of developing countries in the world trading system.[5] Many developing countries no longer benefit from the scheme either because they have graduated because they have been judged to be competitive or because they have access to deeper preferences based on regional or other preferential arrangements. Thus, the GSP does not hold promise as a long-term solution for developing countries' market access problems. However, there are cases of countries benefiting from the GSP that would be hurt from MFN liberalization undertaken in the context of a new Round. The discussions of this issue in the Doha Round have focused on two issues, on which no agreement was reached: (1) making the existing system work more effectively, for example, by simplifying the rules of origin, and (2) providing assistance to current beneficiaries that would lose markets as a consequence of multilateral liberalization following a new Round – an issue that is discussed in the following section.

Technical and other assistance

The WTO agreements contain numerous references to the desirability of developed country members and international institutions to provide technical assistance to developing countries and LDCs. The main objective of such assistance is the strengthening of the institutional capacity of developing and least-developed countries in a way that would enable them to meet the obligations they have assumed under the agreements. The main areas in which technical assistance is envisaged include TBT, SPS, Customs Valuation, Dispute Settlement and TRIPS.

The conceptual underpinning of these provisions is the emerging consensus that institutional constraints are of major significance in inhibiting the effective integration of poorer countries and LDCs in the multilateral trading system. Serious concerns have been raised regarding the high costs and affordability of implementing the Uruguay Round agreements (Finger and Shuler 2004). While it may be relatively easy to promulgate policies to liberalize trade, it is far more difficult to develop the capacity to take advantage of the opportunities international trade provides. Weaknesses in the human and physical infrastructure and institutions related to international trade are increasingly viewed as key impediments in developing countries' capacity to benefit from international trade.

The theoretical justification of aid for trade rests on the benefits that accrue to other countries (externalities) when one country takes actions that increase trade. All countries benefit when one country liberalizes (e.g., through a tariff reduction) or undertakes a trade related investment (e.g., that results in faster customs clearance). Benefits are increased when action is undertaken concurrently by many countries, as in multilateral WTO negotiations, which can be expected to generate global public goods (Michalopoulos 2006). However, the full benefits of reform or investment are not captured by the country itself, leading to potential underinvestment.

Thus, technical and other assistance by developed countries and international institutions (as well as longer transition periods – see below) have been recommended as means to address these problems and a number of international initiatives have been put in place. The one that has received the greatest attention has been the so-called Integrated Framework for Trade Related Assistance for the LDCs (IF), established in 1998, which involves a cooperative assistance effort of six agencies, the WTO, UNCTAD, the International Trade Center (ITC), the IMF and the World Bank. In the context of the Doha Round, both developed and developing countries voiced dissatisfaction with the way the IF was being implemented, and following the recommendations of a task force set up in late 2005 a new set of arrangements for an enhanced IF is in the process of being set under WTO leadership.

Despite the general promises for additional trade-related assistance by bilateral donors, developing countries have felt that the assistance provided so far has been inadequate to meet their needs. Following the Hong Kong Ministerial, in late 2005, another task force was set up, which came up with another set of recommendations – of a general nature which up to date have had no concrete follow up.

In parallel, and largely unconnected to these developments, discussions on trade facilitation had been making some progress as part of the Doha Round negotiations. The discussions were based on the premise that technical assistance and support for capacity building, including infrastructure development, will be addressed by developed country members, failing which implementation obligations of developing countries will be waived (WTO 2004).

The main questions that arise in this area of implementation of special and differential provisions are, which countries should get assistance, and what should be the links between the developing countries' WTO commitments and the provision of assistance to implement them?

Implementation of WTO provisions in a manner favourable to developing country members

The WTO agreements contain literally dozens of references in the preambles as well as in the substantive provisions of the various texts committing members to implement the agreements in ways that take into account the interests of developing and LDC. These references are mostly of a general nature, expressed in broad "best efforts" terminology; and not legally enforceable (Kessie 2000). They have been used very frequently by developed countries as a means of expressing their good intentions but have been of little material value to developing countries.

Exemptions from disciplines

While Article XVIII gives developing countries the freedom to grant tariff protection on infant industry grounds and apply quantitative restrictions for balance of payments purposes, there have been very few instances in which these provisions have been actually invoked. And there has been little discussion of the economic merits of the policies that underlie its provisions.

At the same time, consistent with the principle of non-reciprocity, many developing countries have not bound tariffs on their industrial products to the same extent as developed countries or have agreed to bind at substantially higher than applied levels.[6] In the Doha Round of negotiations, the principle of non-reciprocity was invoked by the developing countries in all aspects of the tariff-cutting negotiations (and elsewhere as well) and was not challenged by the developed countries. The main disagreement was over how much smaller developing country reductions will be.

In an effort to gain favour with the LDCs, the negotiations have already resulted in agreement by WTO members not to seek from LDCs to make any commitments to liberalize their trade regimes in the context of the Round (WTO 2005a: Annex F). This decision was taken for tactical reasons – so that the LDCs can feel that they have the "economic space" to pursue their individual trade policies, and not because it makes economic sense.

The agreement on agriculture also contains a variety of measures that exempt developing countries and, to even a greater extent, LDCs from disciplines and obligations that apply generally, and/or provides for longer timetables or more modest reductions in government support and subsidies than apply to other members. For example, investment subsidies or input subsidies to low income producers are exempted from the calculation of aggregate measures of support (AMS); reductions in export subsidies are either targeted to be lower or to occur over a longer period of time; and there are specific provisions regarding the operation of government stockholding programs aimed at enhancing food security as well as less-demanding minimum access provisions regarding primary agricultural products, which are the predominant staple in the traditional diet of a developing country. A number of developing countries have notified the WTO that they are implementing programs that take into account the specific exemptions contained in these provisions.

However, the agreement on agriculture as a whole is very lopsided in favour of developed-country interests, as it gives them extensive leeway to pursue trade-distorting measures using policies that they favour. In the Doha Round, developing countries pressed for SDT measures that would permit them to reduce tariffs by less than developed countries. They also pressed for the establishment of a category of "special products", which would be subject to smaller or no cuts based on food security concerns, as well as for the establishment of "Special Safeguard" provisions, which would apply only to them and which would aim to protect poor farmers from the adjustment costs resulting from import surges following trade liberalization. But there has been little discussion on the more economically meaningful discussions of providing SDT for poor farmers.

Developed countries agreed in principle on the main developing country demands but there is continuing disagreement over the scope of the "special product" exemptions, as some developing-country proposals would result in exempting such a large proportion of agricultural products as to make liberalization meaningless. Also the details of the "Special Safeguard" measures have not been agreed upon.

Exemptions from disciplines are also to be found in the Agreement on Subsidies and Countervailing measures: The agreement permits countries with per capita income of less than US$1000 and LDCs to maintain certain kinds of export subsidies that are otherwise prohibited; while for other developing countries the period over which subsidies can be provided is longer. Again, a number of developing countries have invoked these provisions in notifying the WTO that they maintain export subsidy programs. There has been little discussion of this issue in the Doha Round, although a number of developing countries have made proposals for increased flexibility in export subsidies.

Flexibility has thus emerged as the most widespread instrument of special and differential treatment. And it is the instrument that the developing countries have emphasized in their SDT proposals in the context of the Doha Agreement. A fundamental question regarding the flexibility afforded to developing countries in pursuing different policies is whether the latitude permitted, including, for example, regarding bindings, or the use of subsidies or non-tariff barriers results in policies that are more suitable to development.

Time extensions

The final way in which special and differential treatment is provided in the WTO is through the provision of extension in the time frame over which certain obligations under the agreements are to be implemented by developing and LDCs. Flexibility in transition times has been provided in practically all the WTO agreements, with the exception of the Agreement on Anti-Dumping Procedures and on Pre-shipment Inspection. Time extensions are provided for a variety of obligations assumed, especially under the TBT, SPS and TRIPS agreements, in Subsidies and Countervailing as well as in the Agreement on Agriculture, which permit developing countries to continue to subsidize exports for a period of time in a variety of ways prohibited for other members. In the majority of cases, flexibility takes the form of a slower rate of implementation of commitments agreed. For instance, the agreement on Subsidies and Countervailing measures allows for a transition period of eight years, while TRIPS allows for a transition period of five years. And a strong case can be made that these provisions regarding special and differential treatment to developing countries – unlike the provisions calling for developed-country actions, are legally enforceable (Kessie 2000).

The main issues that arise in the implementation of this aspect of special and differential treatment have to do with the realism of the time extensions and the cost it takes to build the institutional capacity needed for full implementation of the obligations undertaken in the agreements. The Uruguay Round negotiators did not consult in any systematic fashion with anybody involved in institution-building in developing countries about the transition periods agreed upon. In most cases, the time limits for the extensions have already passed and there is little evidence that countries have made sufficient progress in institution-building to permit them to implement their obligations fully.

As a consequence of these problems, one of the more urgent issues requiring systematic review by the WTO is the time limits set for full implementation of certain provisions of the agreements relative to the costs and time needed for building up the institutional capacity of countries to do so. A useful step was taken prior to the Hong Kong Ministerial to agree to extend for LDCs the transition period for the implementation of TRIPS until 2013 and for pharmaceuticals until 2016. Unfortunately, the decision affects only LDCs and does not cover other equally deserving low-income countries.

The special case of TRIPS

With the exception of differential time frames for implementation, TRIPS contains very few meaningful SDT provisions for developing countries. The same minimum standards and rules apply to all, although there is some national latitude in implementing the rules (Michalopoulos 2003). The agreement has been judged to provide very large benefits to developed countries whose firms hold the bulk of the patents protected by the agreement – and equivalent costs to developing countries. Some have even argued that the costs of TRIPS for developing countries as a group outweigh their benefits from the Uruguay Round (Finger and Wilson 2006).

One does not have to hold such extreme views about TRIPS in order to conclude that TRIPS is one area where meaningful SDT is needed. The events involving TRIPS and pharmaceuticals in developing countries is an important example of the need to revisit some Uruguay Round agreements on SDT. Under the TRIPS agreement, developing countries have the flexibility to reduce some patent system costs through compulsory licensing, in carefully delineated circumstances. Under Article 31, compulsory licensing permits governments to authorize the use of the subject matter of a patent by others if an effort has been made to obtain authorization from the patent holder on reasonable commercial terms and with reasonable application procedural protections. The condition is waived in cases of national emergency, extreme urgency or public non-commercial use. This flexibility was put to the test when it became apparent that developing countries needed to address the availability of drugs at affordable prices to deal with AIDS and other epidemics. Some actions on their part were opposed by the pharmaceutical industry because they violated TRIPS.

Following a great deal of public pressure on the pharmaceutical companies in developed countries that hold patents on HIV/AIDS drugs, WTO ministers agreed at Doha to a "Declaration on TRIPS and Public Health". It reasserted that under the compulsory licensing provisions of TRIPS each WTO member has the right to determine what constitutes a national emergency, and that public health crises relating to HIV/AIDS, TB, malaria and other epidemics can be a national emergency. But it became apparent that "one size does not fit all" because provisions for compulsory licensing are not meaningful for developing countries that do not have the capacity to produce the drugs domestically. Hence, the Declaration also instructed the Council of TRIPS to find a solution to this problem and report to the WTO General Council by the end of 2002.

An agreement was finally reached in 2003, under heavy public opinion pressure to settle the issue before the fifth WTO Ministerial Conference in Cancun. It did not limit the exception to certain diseases, but it did introduce requirements that go beyond those in TRIPS. This was originally set up as a waiver, until TRIPS was amended prior to the Hong Kong Ministerial.

Accession

There is no formal differentiation between developed and developing countries in the accession process. The Doha Declaration talks about "concluding accession proceedings as quickly as possible" and that the

WTO membership is "in particular committed to accelerating the accession of LDCs" (WTO 2001: para. 10).

There are two basic issues regarding accession. First, WTO members, unlike members of the international financial institutions (which are by and large the same governments – but represent different interests) do not see global benefits from universal WTO membership. As a result, unlike the international financial institutions, the WTO does little to help governments become members. The five or six professional staff of its accession division offer little beyond administration and general advice to the 25 to 30 countries in the accession process. The burden of meeting the requirements falls squarely on the acceding governments, aided in many cases by bilateral assistance agencies (not their trade ministry counterparts). Accession thus becomes a very long and difficult process, taking on average about five years, often longer.

The second issue is that each membership application is evaluated individually. There are no standards in terms of the commitments sought from new applicants. The outcome is that new members may commit to very different burdens, even though they may be at essentially the same level of development, and that new members frequently must take on more commitments than existing members at the same level of development – for example, regarding transition periods for implementing the agreements, or the use of certain instruments, such as subsidies.

To deal with some of these issues, the WTO adopted a decision that aims to provide guidelines regarding LDC accession (WTO 2002). These guidelines are quite general and they do not appear to have been followed in subsequent accession cases, although the importance of facilitating LDC accession has been ritually emphasized in subsequent Ministerial declarations including the latest in Hong Kong (WTO 2005b). Very little substantive change can be expected in the accession process under any of the scenarios for the conclusion of the Doha Round.

Assessment

There are two main problems with the present system of SDT. The first problem is that there is no consensus on whether developing countries should be subject to different trade rules, and in particular whether greater freedom from international disciplines on trade policies is good for development or poverty alleviation. Second, the system has encouraged a "pretend" culture in the WTO. The developing countries pretend that they are all the same, except for the LDCs. The developed countries pretend that they provide meaningful SDT to all, usually couched in the form of useless and unenforceable declarations of good intent. In practice, they provide meaningful SDT only for the LDCs, not necessarily because it is good for development but because LDCs are so small that they do not have a serious impact on their commercial interests – or to their "friends" in regional or bilateral agreements.[7] Underlying both problems is that the WTO is not a development institution but one in which trade policies formulated by trade ministers, primarily beholden to domestic producers, are negotiated. In the past, it has succeeded in liberalizing trade primarily because export interests seeking to expand market access have dominated import-competing industries seeking to raise profits through protection. There is a need for a different approach to SDT, else the future will continue to be cluttered by controversy on unfulfilled yet unenforceable commitments, while real problems constrain the effective integration of poorer developing countries in the world trading system.

Rules

Regarding different rules, first on market access, there is an emerging consensus that MFN liberalization would in the long run be most beneficial to all participants. There has been very little argumentation recently in favour of holding on to the preference margins offered by the GSP. And, clearly, developed countries are in no mood to provide preferential market access to their strong competitors among developing countries, including countries such as Brazil or India, China, Korea and Singapore – all developing countries under the self-selection principle of the WTO. On the other hand the developed countries have been prepared to offer preferential treatment to the LDCs. At the Hong Kong Ministerial there was agreement in principle to extend duty- and quota-free access to these countries' exports with minimal exceptions. The discussion has thus properly shifted on how to deal with the adjustment costs for preference erosion and, more generally, trade liberalization, which would adversely affect a number of countries, and what to do, if anything, about the rather substantial administrative costs of implementing preferences – up to 4 per cent of the export value according to some estimates (Hoekman 2006).

The bulk of the preference erosion costs will be faced by countries that are beneficiaries of EU preferences; and they will be smaller the larger the overall liberalization undertaken by all WTO members, including developing countries.[8] At the same time some countries are bound to face some costs. In addressing this issue one must distinguish among three kinds of adjustment costs: (1) balance of payments adjustment as a consequence of trade liberalization or preference erosion; (2) budgetary adjustment as a consequence of revenue loss due to trade liberalization; and (3) private adjustment costs to labourers, farmers or firms adversely affected by trade liberalization or preference erosion.[9] A case can be made that adjustment assistance to address balance of payments problems is already available under existing IMF facilities, which may help countries to address balance of payments problems that derive from their own trade liberalization or those of others (the Trade Integration Mechanism).[10] Similarly, budgetary shortfalls deriving from tariff reductions can best be addressed in the context of the overall budgetary envelope faced by different countries – which is supposed to be an ongoing concern of the international financial institutions.[11] But there is no credible source of trade-related assistance to address the third kind of adjustment: costs of dislocation primarily of labour and farmers as a consequence of increased imports or reduced exports. The size of these costs could be large, and affect the poor who can ill afford them because of the inadequacy of safety nets (Maur 2005). At the same time, it can be argued that, as preference erosion costs are primarily linked to individual country preferential schemes, these should be dealt with bilaterally or regionally. Still, the question remains as to whether a global aid for trade facility may not be needed which *inter alia* may be able to address the third kind of adjustment costs deriving from trade liberalization and which countries should be eligible to benefit from such a facility.

Extensive controversy continues regarding the other kinds of rules, which relate to the freedom of developing countries to restrict imports, not liberalize as much as developed countries, and/or subsidize exports, as this would be beneficial to their development. This is a very old controversy. The weight of academic opinion is that trade liberalization is beneficial to long-term development. But there are a lot of dissenting voices. And there are many examples of developing countries that have made important strides in expanding exports and integrating in world trade while maintaining substantial restrictions on imports to their domestic markets. A key aspect of their success may have been their capacity to design complex incentives that do not penalize exporters; a capacity that few of the poorest countries and LDCs possess.

In the WTO this issue has been resolved pragmatically: the LDCs have been essentially given a freedom to pursue whatever protective policies they wish – almost with no restraints, except perhaps in imposing quantitative restrictions, which, almost everybody agrees, have especially distortionary effects. As noted, they have been exempted from liberalizing anything in the Doha Round negotiations. This is primarily because these countries do not constitute important markets for developed countries' exports, not because it can be demonstrated that maintaining their current level of protection or absence of bindings is good for their development. Similarly, is it developmentally responsible to give LDCs total freedom to subsidize exports, as the current rules permit? Other developing countries are expected to liberalize, but not as much, in both agriculture and industry – again, not by reference to their development needs, but rather by reference to how important they are as potential markets.

In the longer term, this situation will foster a basic split in the WTO membership between the LDCs and all the other countries, with the LDCs having the freedom to pursue protective policies unconstrained by any multilateral commitments. The situation will become analogous to that which existed in GATT during several decades before the 1990's, which permitted developing countries in general to pursue trade policies unconstrained by multilateral commitments and which resulted in inhibiting their integration into the international trading system and hampering their overall development.

Thus, there is a lot of merit in establishing uniform rules with respect to basic WTO disciplines regarding, for example, that all tariffs should be bound, and that all quantitative restraints and all export subsidies should be eliminated and that no SDT be allowed for these disciplines. However, an equitable trading system also requires that the major opt-outs and exemptions that benefit interest groups in developed countries at the expense of developing countries be removed. Agricultural subsidy programs, tariff peaks and escalation that imply high rates of effective protection for developed country industries must be eliminated to establish a level playing field and maximize global public goods.

Country coverage

But one size does not fit all when it comes to implementing the many WTO agreements on SPS, TBT, TRIPS, Customs Valuation and the like, all of which involve "behind the border" policies that require significant institutional infrastructure for their implementation. The cost of establishing the institutional infrastructure needed to implement these agreements is substantial. And their priority in low-income developing countries is doubtful given other developmental needs. The SDT issue revolves around the need to recognize that one size does not fit all when it comes to regulatory disciplines and the "behind the border" policy agenda pursued in the WTO. Hence, there is a clear need for differentiation, in terms of the timing and reach of disciplines across countries. And there is also a need for assistance to countries that cannot meet their institutional capacity needs by themselves. But the need for assistance varies significantly among countries and requires addressing the politically thorny country-differentiation issue.

Country differentiation requires agreement on the criteria used to define eligibility for SDT. At the moment, the WTO recognizes only one sub-category of developing countries: the 50 LDCs, of which 32 are

WTO members. For the rest, vast differences in institutional capacity and degree of integration in world markets are ignored. Because of the principle of self selection, under WTO rules on SDT the treatment of all developing countries by developed countries is supposed to be the same: Singapore and the Republic of Korea are supposed to be treated the same way as Ghana and Saint Lucia; Argentina and Brazil the same as the Maldives and Mauritius. A policy is needed that more narrowly defines which countries are eligible for SDT.

Many problems of institutional capacity are common to LDCs and other low-income and small and vulnerable developing countries – roughly the G90 countries – with limited participation in international trade. These problems are not faced by more advanced developing countries. One approach would be to introduce per capita income and/or share of world trade indicators to differentiate developing countries in terms of transition periods, scope of implementation and access to assistance. In practice, SDT could be extended to this group of roughly 90 countries, including the LDCs but excluding the more advanced developing countries. Substantial differentiation exists regarding financial flows from all the international financial institutions and from the UNDP. In the World Bank, some developing countries get no assistance at all, others are eligible only for loans on hard terms, others for soft loans and still others for a mix. Why cannot the principle that has been accepted without serious difficulty on issues of finance – and, as noted earlier, in the subsidies agreement – not be acceptable more generally for SDT related to institutional capacity constraints and aid for trade?

Another approach would be to attempt to define SDT eligibility for different groups of developing countries separately for each WTO agreement (Kek and Low 2004). Still another suggestion would be to define SDT eligibility and graduation for each WTO member individually – as countries reach specific institutional thresholds they would presumably submit to greater disciplines, as is being considered under the trade facilitation agreement. Both approaches have merit, but may well be extremely difficult to implement in practice: imagine the monitoring requirements for following developments along one hundred-odd developing countries in implementing a dozen different WTO agreements. The experience regarding graduation from LDC status is instructive in this respect. The UN process that involves annual reviews of about half a dozen variables has been extremely politicized and has resulted in only two countries graduating in roughly 30 years.

An effort was made in the Doha Round to introduce some degree of differentiation that would extend SDT to all low-income countries in a number of agreements, including in the Aid for Trade initiative. This effort has largely failed, primarily because of opposition both from the more advanced developing countries and the LDCs. Yet, the only meaningful assistance commitments are likely to be made in the context of an IF limited to LDCs – the jury is still out on how meaningful these commitments will be because there are serious questions about the IF governance structure and LDC ownership.[12] The broader Aid for Trade initiative involves only vague promises of assistance and adherence to broad principles – with no money behind it.[13] This is because no aid agencies will commit concessional assistance funds to high income "developing" countries, some of which they view as fierce competitors.

It is clear that unless some differentiation is introduced among developing countries that would eliminate SDT for the more advanced and well integrated in the trading system, developed countries can be expected to continue to make commitments to developing countries in general which involve vague and unenforceable promises. They will make concrete commitments only to LDCs, which have a very small share of world trade. And they will rely on their own criteria – frequently politically motivated and non-transparent – in determining which countries to give more favourable treatment or market access.

Monitoring

A regular review of SDT implementation also needs to be mandated. The best way to do this is by utilizing the Trade Policy Review Mechanism (TPR). The Trade Policy Review Mechanism, introduced with much fanfare in the late 1980s as one of the major innovations of the Uruguay Round, has been receiving less and less attention. TPR meetings have been relegated to the smaller WTO meeting rooms with attendance primarily by lower-level staff. And the Secretariat, which prepares the Reviews, rarely presents critical remarks or recommendations for policy improvements.

A much more serious system of monitoring and evaluation of members' policies is needed that would include for developed countries and the larger and more developed of the developing countries a review of their policies and assistance efforts in the field of trade – as well as an assessment of the impact of their policies on other countries and the system as a whole. The focus of reviews for the poorer developing countries should be on the effects of their own policies on development, the constraints they face in further integrating into the trading system and priority assistance needs. Finance ministers have accepted a surveillance role for the IMF regarding the world financial system; they are prepared to have an international secretariat review their own policies and recommendations for change. What makes trade ministers so special or so sensitive that they should refuse a similar surveillance role for the WTO Secretariat?

Accession

To promote universal WTO membership on equitable terms, two kinds of actions are needed. First, the WTO needs to issue detailed guidelines regarding the commitments sought from acceding members – linked to their institutional capacity to implement them – and ensure that acceding members are not required to meet more onerous conditions in shorter time periods than existing members. Second, the capacity of the Secretariat to assist in the membership process needs to be greatly enhanced.

Recommendations

The first major recommendation on SDT is to reduce its scope. The key market benefits to developing countries would result if the Doha negotiations give priority to MFN liberalization of trade in goods and services in which developing countries have an actual or potential export interest. The focus should be on eliminating special opt-outs on commercial policy of dubious developmental value for both developed and developing countries. All tariffs should be bound by all countries at levels reasonably close to the currently applied ones. In this connection, the Doha Round commitment to the LDCs that they do not have to participate in the trade liberalization process is unfortunate, but pragmatically it is impossible to go back on it. It should be the last time that such a commitment is made.

The GSP system should be retained – basically because it would be politically impossible to drop it. But no effort should be made to expand it, modify it or make it more permanent. The benefits from such proposals are likely to be small and would continue to create a sense of dependency for "beneficiary" countries. The only substantive improvement should be to simplify and loosen the rules of origin that govern individual preference-giving schemes, so as to enable the intended beneficiaries to benefit from them.

But there may still be adjustment problems in individual countries, as a result of preference erosion of regional preferences and the GSP. The problem is likely to hit some of the poorer countries, where markets do not work well and safety nets are weak or non-existent. These should be addressed through essentially two approaches: trade related, such as the Special Safeguard Mechanism, which should be designed to address import surges that could especially affect poor farmers, and trade-related assistance measures as discussed below.

The second major recommendation on SDT is to recognize that one size does not fit all when it comes to regulatory disciplines and the "behind the border" policy agenda that is increasingly being pursued in the WTO, in such agreements as TRIPS, SPS, TBT, and Customs Valuation. Both the development priority and the capacity of the developing countries to meet their commitments in these agreements is very different. Hence, in these agreements there is a clear need for differentiation, in terms of the rules and the timing of implementation across countries.

Eligibility for SDT, including longer transition – or even full exemption from the rules, as well as assistance, should be limited to a group of countries that includes the LDCs and other low-income developing countries, roughly 90 countries in all, but excludes the more advanced developing countries. Per capita income and/or share of world trade indicators need to be introduced to differentiate among developing countries in terms of transition periods, scope of implementation and access to assistance, which would exclude more advanced developing countries.

In recognition of the problems that low-income developing countries face in meeting their commitments under the existing WTO agreements because of institutional capacity constraints, all these agreements, but in particular those involving TRIPS, SPS, TBT, and Customs Valuation, should be reviewed in order to determine whether low income developing countries and transition economies, essentially the G90, need additional time to implement them. The review should be undertaken systematically for each country and funded under a new aid for trade scheme.

Additionally, the TRIPS agreement requires further scrutiny because of its potential costs to developing countries. First, as envisaged under the Doha Round, it should be reviewed in terms of its consistency with other international agreements, under which the developing countries retain greater control of their intellectual property. Second, the agreement should be reviewed in order to find ways to operationalize some of the vague promises to extend technology transfer to developing countries in order to balance the costs they would incur under the agreement's patent provisions (for details, see Michalopoulos 2003).

The third major recommendation is that in order to deal with the institutional capacity constraints faced by the poorer developing countries a new fund for trade-related capacity building in developing countries should be established (the "World Trade Fund") that would address LDC requirements but also provide assistance to other needy countries.

This Fund would subsume the existing arrangements under the IF for LDCs but extend beyond the IF both in terms of scope of assistance and country coverage.

The objective of this new World Trade Fund (WTF) would be to promote the more effective integration of developing countries in the world trading system through the provision of predictable, reliable and additional technical and related financial assistance. The WTF would support strengthened institutional capacity in: (1) trade policy and regulation, design and implementation; (2) trade support services; (3) trade facilitation; and (4) trade adjustment. Funding in these areas would be provided for training and human resource development, diagnostic studies, expert advice and software but also for related hardware and some limited construction.

WTF beneficiaries would include LDCs as well as other low-income countries, and vulnerable small island economies. To safeguard LDC interests, two separate windows could be established: one for LDCs, and a separate one for non-LDCs. The latter may be set up in two different ways: either it could be designed to include developing countries based on eligibility criteria (e.g., per capita income, size); or it could be open in principle to funding requests from any developing country but managed under guidelines that give priority to funding assistance requests from low income and other vulnerable and needy countries.

There is also a need for greater policy coherence in addressing developing country concerns arising from the WTO negotiating process with the allocation of aid resources so that developing countries will be better able to meet commitments in the WTO's rules based system. One possible approach, which could be utilized in the first instance in connection with the trade facilitation negotiations, would be to develop procedures under which developing countries notify the WTO Secretariat and the Fund of TA requirements to meet specific obligations under the future agreement. The WTF, in collaboration with the governments, would then develop specific projects to address these problems. It is also important to develop within the WTO additional surveillance of developing country institutional capabilities as well as of developed country assistance efforts to provide trade-related assistance. One way of doing this is through an expanded role of the Trade Policy Review Mechanism.

Strengthening the TPR system can also contribute to increasing transparency and promote the integration of developing countries in the world trading system. The assessment of all country policies, developed as well as developing ones, should include an assessment of the effects of their trade and other policies on developing countries, especially the poorest and least well-integrated in the world trading system. The TPRs should also include an assessment of developed country programs of trade-related assistance to developing countries as well as other aspects of Special and Differential Treatment.

Finally, regarding accession of new Members, the WTO should issue new detailed guidelines regarding the commitments to be sought from acceding members that (1) are linked to their institutional capacity to implement them and (2) ensure that acceding members are not required to meet more onerous conditions and/or in shorter time periods than existing members.

This is a long agenda of things to do to make SDT more meaningful and effective as well as focus it more on countries that truly need it. The suspension of the Doha Round of negotiations gives the international community some time to reflect on how to integrate developing countries into the trading system more effectively. Some of these recommendations would be useful in bringing the Doha Round to a successful conclusion. Others are needed for the long term to make the WTO an institution that truly reflects the interests of all of its members.

Notes

1. There are 50 LDCs currently on the UN list, of which 32 are WTO members, while an additional eight are candidates for accession. The LDC designation is based on whether countries meet specific poverty and vulnerability criteria, though exceptions have been made targeted at individual countries, and only two countries have actually graduated from the list in over 30 years.
2. There is a long tradition in GATT/WTO of rules that are perceived to be "too difficult" to be only honored in the breach – e.g., the GATT Article XI ban on quantitative restrictions and disciplines on trade-distorting policies in agriculture, for which the US obtained a waiver in 1955. See Michalopoulos (2001) and Hoekman and Kostecki (2001) for further discussion and references to the literature.
3. For a succinct but comprehensive summary of the post-Doha SDT discussions in the WTO, see ICTSD (2003).
4. The analysis is based in part on previous work of the author to be found in Hoekman et al. (2004) and Michalopoulos (2001: ch. 3; 2006).
5. There is a huge literature on the subject. Some of the most recent analyses can be found in Hoekman (2006).
6. Following the Uruguay Round, all developing countries have bound all tariff lines for agricultural products; countries in Latin America have also bound practically all non-agricultural tariff lines. But many developing countries in Asia and Africa have left large segments of their non-agricultural tariff schedules unbound (Michalopoulos 2001).
7. See Michalopoulos (2001: ch. 10).
8. This is because wide and deep trade liberalization provides offsetting opportunities in other markets that may compensate in part or in full for the preference-erosion losses.
9. Note that private adjustment costs are likely to exceed social costs as trade reform may result in benefits that accrue, for example, to other workers or consumers that would have to be netted out; at the same time, adjustment needs are often attributed to imports, when the real cause is technological change.

10. Only three countries have used this facility so far.
11. Moreover, tariff reductions based on international negotiations are always phased in slowly over time and can be addressed by budgetary reforms that generate other sources of revenue. However, implementing tax reforms in low-income developing countries takes a long time; thus placing a premium on the pace and sequencing of trade reforms that affect the revenue stream.
12. See the Development Committee *Communique* of 18 September 2006 (WTO and IMF 2006).
13. WTO (2006). The Task Force's recommendation, however, was that a separate fund similar to the IF be set up for "IDA only", that is, poor developing countries.

REFERENCES

Finger, J. M., and P. Shuler (2004) "Implementing the Uruguay Round Commitments: The Development Challenge", in B. Hoekman and W. Martin, eds, *Developing Countries and the WTO: A Pro-Active Agenda*, Oxford: Blackwell, pp. 115–130.

Finger, J. M., and J. S. Wilson (2006) "Implementing a WTO Agreement on Trade Facilitation", Policy Research Working Paper No. 3971, Washington, DC: World Bank.

Hoekman, Bernard, and Michael Kostecki (2001) *The Political Economy of the World Trading System: From GATT to WTO*, 2nd ed., Cambridge: Cambridge University Press.

Hoekman, B., C. Michalopoulos and A. L. Winters (2004) "More Favorable and Differential Treatment of Developing Countries: Towards a New Approach in the WTO", Policy Research Paper No. 3107, Washington, DC: World Bank.

ICTSD (2003) "Midterm Review Reveals Development in Peril in Doha Round", *Bridges* 1(13), available from http://www.ictsd.org/monthly/archive.htm.

Kek, A., and P. Low (2004) "Special and Differential Treatment in the WTO: Why, When and How", Staff Working Paper No: ERSD 2004-03, Geneva: WTO.

Kessie, E. (2000) "Enforceability of the Legal Provisions Relating to Special and Differential Treatment under the WTO Agreements", paper presented at WTO Seminar on Special and Differential Treatment of Developing Countries, Geneva, 7 March.

Maur, J. C. (2005) "Coping with Trade Liberalization: Political Economy: Dimensions", mimeo, London: UK Department for International Development.

Michalopoulos, C. (2001) *Developing Countries in the WTO*, Houndmills and New York: Palgrave.

Michalopoulos, C. (2003) *Special and Differential Treatment of Developing Countries in TRIPS*, TRIPS Issues Paper No. 2, Geneva: Quaker United Nations Office.

Michalopoulos, C. (2006) "The WTO as an Institution: An Assessment", in Secretariat of the International Task Force on Public Goods, *Meeting Global Challenges: International Co-operation in the National Interest*, Stockholm: International Trade, pp. 59–110.

WTO (2001) Doha WTO Ministerial, "Ministerial Declaration", T/MIN(01)/ DEC/1.

WTO (2002) "Guidelines on LDC Accessions", WT/L/508.

WTO (2004) "Doha Work Programme", WT/L/579.

WTO (2005a) "The Future of the WTO: Addressing Institutional Challenges in the new Millennium", Report of the Consultative Board, Geneva: WTO.

WTO (2005b) Hong Kong Ministerial "Ministerial Declaration", MIN(05) DEC.

WTO (2006) "Recommendations of the Task Force on Aid for Trade", WT/AFT/ 1, July 27.

World Bank and International Monetary Fund (2006) *Development Committee: Communique*, Singapore Sept. 18, available from http://www.worldbank.org/ devcommittee.

7

Special and differential treatment for developing countries in the World Trade Organization

Manickan Supperamaniam

The concept of Special and Differential Treatment (SDT) for developing countries in the multilateral trading system dates back to the earliest years of the General Agreement on Tariffs and Trade (GATT). It is a fundamental element of the multilateral trading system (MTS).

The SDT concept was conceived in acknowledgement of the fact that developing countries are at very different stages of economic, financial and technological development and therefore have very different capacities as compared to developed countries in taking on multilateral commitments and obligations. It has therefore been accepted that special advantages and flexibilities must be given to developing countries so that they could adopt appropriate national policies to support their trade regimes. However, the form of favourable treatment for developing countries in terms of objectives and conditions in relation to international trade policy and rules and national development strategies has changed over time.

SDT provisions: Background

From the time of the first WTO Ministerial in Singapore onwards, the "implementation" agenda, which also includes an SDT element, has increasingly defined the terrain upon which developing-country participation in the trading system was to be debated. Most developing countries viewed implementation issues primarily as an expression of an imperative

Developing countries and the WTO: Policy approaches, Sampson and Chambers (eds),
United Nations University Press, 2008, ISBN 978-92-808-1153-7

to revisit the substantive content of various WTO agreements on the grounds that the rules did not adequately reflect the development needs and economic interests of developing countries. Implicit in the latter view was the conviction that developing countries had been pushed into their current commitments as a result of the "take it or leave it" approach characterized by the single undertaking.

During most of the GATT era, the concept of SDT was narrowly defined. Developing countries were not required to be involved in the gradual liberalization of trade through successive rounds of multilateral trade negotiations. They had the right to promote their exports through subsidies and to use tariffs and quantitative restrictions on imports to protect their balance of payments positions.

The SDT that has evolved since the inception of GATT includes preferential market access, a longer tariff phase-down period, flexibilities on implementing GATT/WTO disciplines and rules as well as offers by developed countries to provide technical assistance and capacity-building to facilitate implementation of GATT/WTO agreements.

However, under the Uruguay Round agreements the principle of SDT changed from one of providing a range of flexibilities and spaces for development policy based on economic criteria to one of time-limited derogations from the rules with more favourable treatment regarding tariff and subsidy reduction commitments and more generous thresholds in the application of market defense measures (e.g., countervailing and anti-dumping duties).

WTO agreements contain approximately 155 provisions on SDT aimed at enabling developing countries to avail themselves of the rights provided while observing their obligations. The experience of implementing the Uruguay Round agreements has shown that these SDT provisions have failed to even remotely achieve their objectives in terms of integrating developing countries into the multilateral trading system and improving their trading conditions. They have not effectively addressed the fundamental concerns and needs of developing countries, especially the inequities and imbalances of the rules-based trading system.

The reasons for these shortcomings were obvious. The SDT provisions largely only recognized the interests of developing countries in very general terms; or merely provided for a longer time frame for implementation; or at best provided for some national technical and financial assistance. The SDT provisions did not reflect the reality that the costs and benefits and implementation differ between developed and developing countries. Generally, the costs to developing countries in implementing the rules have been higher than their benefits, with the benefits going mainly to the developed countries. SDT in the form of a longer transition period and technical assistance would not be able to provide a solution to the lack of implementation capacity and supply side constraints.

Developing countries succeeded in putting SDT in the Doha agenda as an important component of the development dimension to correct the inequities and imbalances of the international trading system carried forward from the Uruguay Round agreements. So it was a kind of recognition of that imbalance, plus in order to get the developing countries on board for another round, that SDT was made very much the integral part of WTO agreements.

There are two key elements of the SDT provisions in the Doha Declaration. The Declaration directs that "all Special and Differential provisions shall be reviewed with the view to strengthening them and making them more precise, effective and operational".

In respect of this mandate, about 88 agreement-specific proposals have been submitted by developing countries for strengthening, making mandatory, going beyond the best-endeavour aspects and making them firm commitments. Developing countries have also forcefully articulated that these proposals are positively considered as they are aimed at providing them with improved market access opportunities, flexibility of rules and enhanced capacity-building programmes. They have further argued that a consideration of these proposals should not be subject to any conditionality of differentiation or graduation. Clearly, from the point of view of developing countries, there is no room for introducing the differentiation or graduation concept, beyond the LDC and the non-LDC differentiation that exists and which is accepted.

The discussion of these proposals has been somewhat desultory and no headway has so far been made despite intense negotiations and several extended deadlines. The proposals have elicited different kinds of responses from developed countries. One has been to question the utility of trying to make many SDT provisions mandatory. There is also an underlying unwillingness to contemplate the possibly of dispute-settlement proceedings applying in some of these cases. Furthermore, developed countries have argued that prior to evaluating the proposals, detailed discussions on the broader "principles and objectives" must occur. They generally view SDT as a means of integrating developing countries into the multilateral trading system and insist that the WTO must provide one set of rules for all members. Seemingly, they appear willing to consider some derogations for certain countries at lower levels of development provided criteria for eligibility are established to determine which members are eligible for which flexibilities.

The other aspect of the SDT Doha mandate relates to how SDT could be incorporated into the architecture of the WTO rules. Discussions on this aspect of the mandate have centred on cross-cutting issues including principles and objectives of SDT, the issue of eligibility, technical assistance and capacity building and universal or differentiated treatment.

There are two serious problems with the current WTO approach to SDT. First there is a fundamental flaw in the presumption that developing countries are equipped to take on obligations similar to developed countries that have reached higher levels of economic development. Thus the idea that developing countries should liberalize on the same basis as developed countries, albeit at a modest pace, ignore the real differences in adjustment capacity and in development needs. There are vast differences in competitiveness between and within developing countries and capacity to adjust at a sectoral level. In the rulemaking area, costs and benefits as well as implementation capacity differ between developing and developed countries.

Justification for enhanced SDT

The single undertaking and equal treatment resulting from the single tiered hierarchy of obligations have reinforced the need and relevance of SDT for developing countries given their differences in level of development and capacity to assume and implement obligations. The efforts by the WTO system to create a level playing field with the same rules had negatively impacted on the flexibilities available to developing countries in respect of domestic policymaking. Generally, under the Uruguay Round agreements, the importance of SDT was significantly diminished. In fact, there has been an erosion of the principles underpinning the SDT. For the majority of developing countries, the agreements composing the multilateral trading system have put them in a disadvantageous position by restricting them from evolving and implementing a range of policy measures designed to stimulate growth, industrial development and diversification of their economies.

There are strong reasons why favourable treatment for developing countries should be maintained and further enhanced in the WTO. One of the very clear arguments for SDT relates to a wide range of level playing field issues, whether it is in terms of size of economies, trade share, industrial capacity, poverty issues or the size and capacity of enterprises. Indeed, many are well aware of this kind of size imbalance.

Furthermore, the WTO also includes a whole host of agreements that constrain domestic policy choices that are proven to be necessary if they are to make strategic liberalization moves or strategic interventions in the economy in order to move it in the right direction. In such a situation,

SDT has a crucial role in giving them more flexibility and development space in respect of those agreements in the case of instruments and obligations.

Some have claimed that SDT will create a two-tier system of rights and obligations. Furthermore, there is the suspicion that SDT could be used for protectionist purposes as well as shielding developing countries from taking up their trade obligations. This need not necessary be so because SDT is essentially aimed at enabling developing countries who are slow to catch up as well as ensuring that they are not burdened with onerous obligations that stifle their trade capabilities. SDT should be looked at not as exceptions to the general rules but more importantly as a useful tool and dynamic instrument to enable beneficial integration of developing countries into the multilateral trading system.

The focus of the Doha work programme on development requires that efforts be made to mainstream development considerations into existing WTO rules and emerging disciplines. Potential problems will arise from the outcome of the Doha negotiations and other elements of the work programme in terms of the costs of current and emerging WTO agreements. These costs will vary between agreements and between WTO members with a particularly heavy burden on developing countries. This is because developing countries are the ones more often asked to be standard takers on multilateral trade norms whilst for developed countries it is just a question of formalizing multilaterally what they may be following nationally. The implementation of WTO agreements have shown that that implementation costs are high and require time, technical expertise and additional financing, otherwise such compliance can crowd out development priorities. In addition, there are also costs of adjustment to the real side of the economy, for instance, changes in trade, output and employment.

Thus, in approaching the objective of mainstreaming trade into development, trade rules and their application must contain built-in policy flexibility and development space in the form of effective and operational SDT in all areas so that developing countries are able to overcome their structural, institutional, human resources and entrepreneurial deficiencies and use trade as a genuine locomotive of growth and development. SDT for developing countries would help ensure that in articulating the synergies between trade and development, developing countries are not forced to implement multilateral trade agreements at the cost of their development priorities.

In view of the aforementioned reasons, it would be logical to draw the conclusion that until there is a situation where countries have equal capacities developing countries would need some kind of handicap in the form of policy space. SDT should therefore remain as an important tool for developing countries to advance their economic and development objectives within the ambit of the multilateral trading system. It is equally important that WTO members recognize the asymmetrical situation and find creative ways of effectively addressing the inherent deficiencies into specifically goal-oriented and legally enforceable SDT. An important policy response in this regard is to design and implement effective and operational SDT provisions that carve out areas of domestic policymaking for developing countries and reforming the Uruguay Round agreements to expand and strengthen the policy flexibilities.

Future approaches to SDT in the WTO

Generally, WTO members both developed and developing recognize that the concept of SDT is both an important and a relevant tool to facilitate developing countries, especially LDCs, to effectively integrate into the multilateral trading system, including benefiting from the opportunities. However, there are differing views on how the form and content of SDT should be approached within the body of WTO rules.

Some useful work has been done by several research organizations and development economists on the future approaches to SDT in the WTO. One economist has argued that a "one size fits all" approach to SDT may not be feasible in view of the heterogeneous nature of developing countries. He has argued for identification of indicators that would lead to grouping of countries with similar concerns and constraints for which a common set of SDT provisions would apply, yet differentiated treatment from others. Seemingly, the approach is premised on providing total flexibility to developing countries so long as other WTO members are not harmed. The difficulty that may be encountered will be on agreeing to the set of indicators and how they should be measured and monitored.

A second approach, while recognizing heterogeneity of developing countries, proposes identifying developing countries that share common characteristics with LDCs and others that could be grouped together with developed countries. Enhanced SDT flexibilities could then be accorded for an LDC-plus group characterized by broad criteria such as per capita or size. It has been argued by the proponents that such a crude differentiation would encompass all developing countries with similar implementation concerns across WTO agreements. Those developing countries not part of this group may also avail themselves of the same SDT rights on a case-by-case basis but subject to an appeals procedure.

A country-specific SDT approach has also been flagged whereby time-bound exemptions from specific agreements are provided for individual countries. The eligibility of the countries is to be determined on the basis of the costs and the capacity of the country to implement an agreement (implementation audits). It is proposed that the temporary exemption be also linked to the provision of technical assistance and capacity building. This implies categorization of countries and would be politically sensitive.

Yet another approach that has been proposed emphasizes the provision of policy space as the focus of SDT. This option is premised on the assumption that the implementation of resource-intensive agreements may not pass a cost-benefit analysis test in some countries. This policy space argument presupposes that developing countries assume all obligations in core areas, for example, market access, but be exempted from obligation in non-core areas, for example, regulatory issues. But exemptions sought are required to be supported by independent economic analysis. Non-compliance by developing countries would be subject to a more cooperative or "soft law" approach that identifies good practices under the purview of an independent oversight body.

Some have proposed a provision-specific approach that basically calls for identification of situations or circumstances that would require SDT policy interventions. In determining such situations, factors to be taken into account include market failure, including static or dynamic externalities, economies of scale and imperfect competition. In respect of this approach, it has been suggested that measurable criteria be developed that characterize those situations or circumstances that justify providing access to the SDT provisions for an appropriate period of time. This approach seemingly addresses the key concern of developing countries vis-à-vis differentiation as it does not a priori exclude countries that are eligible for SDT flexibilities. Agreeing on what constitutes the measurable criteria would pose a major challenge.

These options/approaches will inevitably receive mixed reactions. The approach will vary among developing countries and would very much be shaped by their respective development situations as well as their structure and composition of trade. Clearly for any approach contemplated to receive broad support, it must address the basic question of how the concept of SDT should be effectively operationalized to facilitate the diversification and development process of developing countries without negatively impacting on the multilateral rules-based system. Therefore, the appropriate approach that would lead to the strengthening of SDT would need to be carefully thought out.

The current impasse in the SDT negotiations stems from the polarization of WTO members around the eligibility of developing countries to SDT benefits and how to improve the development content of SDT. Constructive solutions aimed at overcoming the deadlock must respond to both of these sets of concerns.

Most developed countries appear concerned with issues of eligibility (including graduating countries away from flexibility once it is no longer required), ensuring compliance and integration of developing countries into the multilateral trading system. A large number of developing countries, however, take the position that SDT must be provided on a non-discriminating basis and sufficient flexibility in the rules must be maintained in order to allow exceptions from certain disciplines for development purposes.

The challenge facing policy makers is to strike a balance between the need to correct the imbalance and inequity perceived to be inherent in the multilateral trading system as it currently exists while maintaining the credibility of already concluded multilateral agreements under the WTO.

Seemingly, the way forward would be to find a middle ground approach that moves away from the polarized positions and provides a framework that incorporates the flexibilities and policy space sought by developing countries in the SDT while upholding the intrinsic value of the multilateral trading system.

In this context, a "one size fits all" approach to SDT would not effectively address the concerns and developmental interests of developing countries. Equally, an approach that provides SDT to only certain countries on the basis of agreed eligibility criteria will not be politically acceptable to a large number of developing countries. But what would be feasible and desirable is to consider an approach where enhanced SDT is provided on the basis of a clear set of criteria applicable to a limited number of specific circumstances/constraints most frequently encountered in pursuit of development goals. Such an approach would address the internal heterogeneity of development within all developing countries. It will also be a creative way of getting around the contentious issue of differentiations including graduation. More importantly, the form and content of SDT would be more focused and targeted.

This approach could be further developed to become a practical pro-development SDT framework/umbrella agreement in order to institutionalize and rationalize the adoption and application of SDT provisions. The framework should include provisions reflecting the objectives and principles of SDT for developing countries. It should also embody important elements such as the mandatory and legally binding nature of SDT, incorporation of development dimensions in all future agreements, evaluations of implementation costs in terms of financial, capacity building and technical assistance, establishing linkage of transition period to economic and social criteria, a safeguard mechanism escape clause for development purposes and a mechanism to review plans submitted by developed-country members for the purpose of implementing the SDT obligations.

Part III

Facing challenges

8

Making TRIPS work for developing countries

Graham Dutfield

Effective developing-country decision making concerning TRIPS, and international intellectual property (IP) rulemaking more generally, is hampered by a number of factors. The first is an inevitable consequence of these nations' enormous diversity in terms of economic circumstances. This diversity translates into quite disparate interests with respect to TRIPS. So while congruent negotiating positions across the developing world are possible, widely conflicting ones can arise too.

The second difficulty is that intellectual property rights are designed with certain assumptions as to what a protectable intellectual production should look like, and these categories are abundant in the developed world but much less so in most developing countries. In the latter nations, creativity may be common but cannot easily be described or communicated in ways that lend it to IP protection. According to one commentator (Boyle 1996: 125), "the author concept stands as a gate through which one must pass in order to acquire intellectual property rights. At the moment, this is a gate that tends disproportionately to favor the developed countries' contributions to world science and culture. Curare, batik, myths and the dance 'lambada' flow out of developing countries, unprotected by intellectual property rights, while Prozac, Levis, Grisham and the *movie Lambada!* flow in – protected by a suite of intellectual property laws, which in turn are backed by trade sanctions". One may question the basis for his argument since corporations and not individuals tend to own the most valuable rights, but the consequences he describes are accurate.

Developing countries and the WTO: Policy approaches, Sampson and Chambers (eds),
United Nations University Press, 2008, ISBN 978-92-808-1153-7

The third difficulty is that the sophisticated and aggressive intellectual property forum management and other political strategies employed by the United States and the European Union seem to undermine WTO multilateralism. Increasingly, developing countries are pressured outside the WTO forum to raise their IP standards well above those required by TRIPS to become what is commonly dubbed "TRIPS plus".

On the other hand, I would argue that consumers everywhere are affected by the phenomenon of IP overprotection. If correct, it is possible to envisage the emergence of powerful transnational alliances to counter this situation that could lead to greater balance in national and international IP rules. There is some evidence that such alliances are being formed and that developing-country negotiating stances in forums like the WTO and the World Intellectual Property Organization (WIPO) are being influenced by these informal coalitions consisting of diplomats, NGOs, "counter-experts" and some companies.

Intellectual property and the varied interests of developing countries

The current conventional wisdom is that the world's most successful nations are those best at producing, acquiring, deploying and controlling valuable knowledge. Knowledge, especially new knowledge unavailable to one's rivals, is key to international competitiveness and therefore to national prosperity. Those who accept such a view tend to assume, first, that knowledge-based economies are nowadays wealthier, almost by definition, than traditional or natural-resource–based ones. Second, that wealth-creating knowledge, of the kind that turns economies into knowledge-based ones, comes almost exclusively out of universities, corporate laboratories and film, music, art and design studios, and not out of such unlikely places as peasant farmers' fields and indigenous communities. Third, this transformation requires the availability of high US- or European-style standards of intellectual property protection and enforcement. In short, rich countries have such standards, poor countries do not. Therefore, to be like rich countries, poor countries must adopt these standards; the "magic of the marketplace" will presumably conjure up the rest.

Taking the first assumption, this is of course basically true. Nonetheless, reality defies lazy platitudes. While Singapore is a prosperous and increasingly creative economy (Chow et al. 2007), the similarly sized Qatar and Brunei are just plain rich. India, with Bollywood, its impressive and rapidly expanding software industry and its sizeable and growing biotechnological capacity in relation to its GNP, is mired in poverty that may take generations to eliminate. Of course, India cannot become a rich, oil-based economy when there is no oil to base its economy on. But most Indians work on the land, and the diffusion of state of the art knowledge and technologies is only one part of the whole solution to the problem of how to eke a decent income from agriculture.

Turning to the second assumption, statistics produced by international organizations like the UN Development Programme, WIPO and the World Bank suggest that most developing countries are not only failing to be innovative but actually have to improve their innovation climate dramatically before they can be competitive in high-technology fields, except perhaps as assemblers and exporters of high-tech goods invented elsewhere, like Costa Rica. Admittedly, our usual indicators of innovation, such as R&D spending, education statistics and patent counts do not tell the whole story and may in fact be misleading. But there appears clearly to be a massive innovation gap between the rich and poor worlds that is not going to be bridged for a long time except by a few elite countries, like China, India and Brazil.

But is such a negative and pessimistic view about developing countries entirely accurate? Is there really a massive knowledge and innovation gap between the rich and poor worlds? Confusingly, the best answer to both questions is "yes and no". The "yes" part is obvious. North America, Western Europe and East Asia have a massive lead over the rest of the world in virtually all of the usual social and economic indicators. But why is there a "no" in the answer at all? Because there is a cultural bias in how we use terms like "knowledge economy" and "knowledge worker" whose effect is to underestimate the presence and vital role of applied knowledge in all societies including those appearing to be the most backward and traditional.

Creativity is not the sole preserve of suited knowledge workers in glassy office blocks, professional artists and musicians and laboratory scientists. If necessity really is the mother of invention, you would surely expect to see most innovation where the needs are greatest. And no needs are greater than those of desperately poor people getting themselves and their families through each day alive and well. Whether we look at health or agriculture, we find that peasant communities are often able to draw upon a huge body of knowledge passed on through many generations (for examples see Dutfield 2005; Posey 1999). The same applies to hunters and gatherers. Local knowledge, technologies and traditional cultural expressions can be highly evolutionary, adaptive and even novel. In short, knowledge held within "traditional" societies can be new as well as old. We should not be surprised by this. Traditional knowledge has always had adaptive elements because the ability to adapt is one of the keys to survival in precarious environments.

So can we just assume, as we tend to do, that the world's knowledge and innovation "hotspots" are urban areas located almost exclusively in Europe, North America and East Asia? In fact, there are many other innovation hotspots, some in the most remote and isolated regions of the world. The problem is that few people recognize them as such, and few of those are in positions of real power or authority. Consequently, innumerable opportunities to harness local knowledge and innovation for trade and development are missed (see Gupta 2006).

Today's more positive view, which informs the work of many development workers, seriously challenges the idea that knowledge wealth necessarily goes hand in hand with material wealth, and that innovation cannot be common where there is mass poverty. What they point out also is that knowledge and creative people may be far less scarce than are the institutions to help convert knowledge into wealth for local people and for the benefit of the wider economy (Gupta 2006). Consequently, traditional knowledge and local innovations are being underutilized.

The third assumption that we come to is that achieving national prosperity and international competitiveness requires countries to make available high US- or European-style standards of IP protection and enforcement. Naturally, transnational corporations like governments to believe this. Indeed, corporate lobbying has largely been responsible for the barely accountable extension of patents, trademarks and copyright to completely new kinds of subject matter in recent decades. We can now patent microbes, plants and animals, even genes that have just been discovered. We can trademark the MGM lion's roar. The binary code behind software programs is classed as a copyrightable work of literature. Protection terms have been extended. The copyright term for authored works in Europe, the United States and many of their trade partners now continues for 70 years after the author's death.

But do developing countries really need to adopt such standards, as they increasingly have to, not so much because of TRIPS but as a result of new commitments arising from bilateral trade agreements? Arguably not. In fact, such standards may make them worse off. The historical record strongly suggests that many of today's economic leader countries were themselves "knowledge pirates" in the past, and benefited from being so (Ben-Atar 2004; Dutfield and Suthersanen 2005). As for the present, a good case could be made for arguing that we in the developed world are not becoming knowledge-*based* economies as quickly as we are becoming knowledge-*protected* economies, or even – and this is a bit more worrying – knowledge-*overprotected* ones, in which dominant industries maintain their market power by tying up their knowledge in complex bundles of legal rights and instruments such as patents, copyrights, trademarks and restrictive contracts and licensing agreements.

Such bundles of rights often cover just one product; a drug for example may be protected by a trademark, multiple patents, trade secrets and copyright on the instructions.

It is far less clear that the creativity and innovation coming out of laboratories and studios is increasing at a rate anywhere near as fast as the rapidly growing size of corporate IP portfolios. Worryingly, this level of protection may not only be a bad thing for consumers in terms of higher prices, but it may actually stifle far more innovation than it promotes. And things are getting worse. Every major company has to have an intellectual property management strategy, which usually entails the aggressive acquisition and enforcement of rights, because everybody else has one. Among the harmful consequences are increased prices and reduced access to knowledge.

Another trend to mention here is that public interest and pro-competitive limitations and exceptions to the rights in many parts of the world are being narrowed. That is a serious concern for developing countries seeking to acquire expensive life-saving drugs. Other likely negative effects include undue constraints on the reproduction and distribution of educational materials in countries where such materials are scarce, expensive and desperately needed.

What is now much less arguable than the consequences of these trends is that the incorporation of negotiations on IP standards of protection and enforcement, whose outcome was the TRIPS Agreement, was actively and aggressively promoted by developed-country governments including the European Community and industry associations and professional lobbyists.[1] The primary aim was to deal with at least three threats to the interests of large corporations and to the competitiveness of developed world economies, none of which was to enhance the development prospects of developing countries. These perceived threats were copyright piracy, unauthorized use of trademarks and unwelcome competition from generic drug firms able to take advantage of patent regimes' excluding drugs from protection. The underlying assumption, only partially correct, is that the interests of developed countries as represented by governments and the European Commission and those of transnational corporations headquartered in those nations, are congruent.

As a consequence of the huge stakes involved and of the way it came into being, TRIPS has always been controversial. For many critics, IP should never have been part of the Uruguay Round negotiations that led to the WTO's establishment. They say that IP is not trade-related, and should as a result be dealt with elsewhere. They certainly have good reason to question the need for the Uruguay Round to have covered intellectual property. Indeed, even some of those who were most enthusiastic about TRIPS have joined the sceptics, albeit for different reasons. For example, the very influential Bruce Lehman, a former head of the US Patent and Trademark Office, now claims in public that the United States would have been better off pushing for strict environmental and labour standards in the Uruguay Round instead of insisting with so much determination on an IP agreement.[2] But the critics are wrong to say that intellectual property is not trade-related. IP has always been inherently trade-related.

While we may accept as given that TRIPS was not intended to benefit developing countries,[3] it does not automatically follow that TRIPS cannot benefit them. I make this assertion not only because of the pro-development and social welfare language in several TRIPS articles, but for two other reasons. First, much of the language of TRIPS is "strategically vague". Consequently, it is subject to various plausible interpretations that may with imagination and vision translate into quite a lot of policymaking freedom. Second, developing countries are extremely widely differentiated in terms of scientific, industrial and technological capacities and market opportunities. Consequently, their interests are differentiated too. For the developing world generally, TRIPS is almost certainly a net loss, at least in the short term.[4] But for some developing countries, gains from implementing parts of TRIPS are definitely possible, especially in cases where certain industrial sectors are already fairly advanced. Of course it is not this simple. TRIPS was one of a whole package of agreements and so developing countries may have calculated that while TRIPS was a loss, they could identify net overall gains from the whole package of WTO agreements.

What developing countries are likely broadly to agree upon is that substantive harmonization of IP rights at the level of today's developed countries is very unlikely to be in any of their interests, in large part because it would close the door on past development strategies that worked. For example, in a comprehensive study of the evolution of the Japanese patent system, which shows that for almost all of its existence it was very much "TRIPS minus", Fisher (2004) is drawn to conclude that: "the meteoric rise from feudal serf to technological whiz-kid that the country has undergone in less than 150 years is little short of astounding, and poses the question of whether it could be repeated today. The homogenisation of patent law, the claim implicit in TRIPS that one size can, and indeed should, fit all, does not adequately correspond with the picture of Japan's evolution" (113).

Research by Kim (2003) on the experience of South Korea led him to find that "strong IPR [intellectual property rights] protection will hinder rather than facilitate technology transfer to and indigenous learning activities in the early stage of industrialisation when learning takes place through reverse engineering and duplicative imitation of mature foreign products". He also concluded that it is "only after countries have accumulated sufficient indigenous capabilities with extensive science and technology infrastructure to undertake creative imitation in the later stage that IPR protection becomes an important element in technology transfer and industrial activities" (5).

However, while all developing countries have good reason to oppose harmonization in favour of differentiation, this does not make their interests identical. Lall's (2003) research found ample evidence that "the need for IPRs varies with the level of development". Based in part on the work of Maskus (2000: 95–96), he went on to say:

> Many rich countries used weak IPR protection in their early stages of industrialisation to develop local technological bases, increasing protection as they approached the leaders. Econometric cross-section evidence suggests that there is an inverted-U shaped relationship between the strength of IPRs and income levels. The intensity of IPRs first falls with rising incomes, as countries move to slack IPRs to build local capabilities by copying, then rises as they engage in more innovative effort. The turning point is $7,750 per capita in 1985 prices ..., a fairly high level of income for the developing world. (Lall 2003: 11)

It is one thing to say that relatively advanced developing countries prefer, if given the opportunity denied to them by TRIPS, to weaken their IP rights in order to advance their capacities to innovate through imitation-derived technological learning, and then strengthen them later when they are more innovative. It is quite another thing to assume that such a policy works just because many governments have favoured it. Nonetheless, intuitively it makes much sense and there is a wealth of historical experience to back it up.

Competitive liberalization and the erosion of multilateralism

TRIPS may well be more harmful than beneficial for the developing world as a whole. Nonetheless, attempting to unify developing countries in a blanket opposition to all of its provisions is utterly unachievable. The interests are just too diverse, not just between countries but within them. For example, India tends to take a strong pro-copyright stance because of Bollywood, but is much more sceptical about patents, tending to side with most other developing countries. Besides, whatever the views of individual developing countries vis-à-vis TRIPS, the fact is that the central position of the Agreement in the international IP regime is under threat, as multilateralism itself is being circumvented and eroded. Until recently,

TRIPS seemed to be the most important element of the effort to pull up developing countries' IP standards of protection and enforcement to the level of the developed countries and to modernize IP protection so as to accommodate rapid advances in emerging fields like biotechnology and the digital technologies. But now, if recent trade deal-making and the views of people like Lehman are anything to go by, TRIPS may be outliving its purpose for those corporations that successfully lobbied for an IP agreement in the Uruguay Round and the governments that took up their demands. Why? First, because the WTO system of trade governance currently does not make it easy to achieve radical revision of existing agreements or, for that matter, consensus on the need for new ones. Second, developing countries have tended not to implement TRIPS with much enthusiasm, and enforcement measures continue to be inadequate from the view of the IP owners. Third, for the developed countries and transnational industry, other forms of trade diplomacy seem to further their interests more effectively.

What does transnational industry actually want? In the area of patents, the priority is global harmonization pitched at a level such that TRIPS is the floor, the absolute minimum that is acceptable. Moves are afoot at WIPO to go much further than TRIPS by intensifying substantive patent law harmonization in the interests of helping well-resourced companies to acquire geographically more extensive and secure protection of their inventions at minimized cost (Musungu and Dutfield 2003). Substantive harmonization is more than just making the patent systems of countries more like each other in terms of enforcement standards and administrative rules and procedures. It means that the actual substance of the patent standards will be exactly the same to the extent, for example, of having identical definitions of novelty, inventive step and industrial application. Given the rich countries' interests in harmonization, it is likely to result in common (and tightly drawn) rules governing exceptions to patent rights, and the erosion of freedoms to exclude from patentability types of subject matter or technological fields on public policy or national interest grounds.

Harmonization is important with copyright too, especially in such areas as term of protection and subject matter; for example, the developed countries are encouraging the developing countries to extend the term of copyright protection beyond that required by TRIPS to life of the author plus 70 years, as in Europe and the United States. But the situation is a little different. One reason is that the complex array of stakeholders[5] whose economic and moral interests are affected by copyright makes harmonization much more difficult to achieve. Another is that rapid technological developments have made the transnational copyright industries determined to achieve an international regime that is sufficiently dynamic

to respond speedily to the massive opportunities and vulnerabilities afforded by technological advances that (1) provide new means for copyright owners to disseminate their works to the public but that also (2)
threaten to undermine the control over markets in these works by enabling copiers to flood markets with unauthorized versions of these
works and by allowing potential consumers to copy them. Such "dynamic
responsiveness" cannot be achieved at the WTO, since, as we mentioned,
the WTO agreements have proved not to be susceptible to the substantial
periodic revisions that would be necessary to satisfy industry.

The TRIPS approach to achieving ever-higher IP protection levels is
being supplemented by an expanding menu of alternatives. These include
technical assistance, threats and intimidation, and "forum management"
including the use of WIPO and bilateral trade and investment agreements.

The provision of IP technical assistance by international organizations,
developed-country governmental agencies, IP offices and business and
law associations has become quite controversial. Such assistance often
seeks to promote standards of IP protection higher than those required
by TRIPS in order to protect the interests of providers and funders. Indeed, "industry experts have played a prominent role in IP-related technical assistance initiatives undertaken in the United States" (Matthews
and Munoz-Tellez 2006: 648).[6] Such assistance may involve training programmes, the dissemination of propaganda extolling the virtues of intellectual property and the harm caused by piracy and even the drafting of
legislation.

Sometimes rich countries are alleged to resort to intimidation and
threats of trade sanctions against poor countries they accuse of condon-
ing piracy or of having "inadequate" IP systems. The United States has
been particularly aggressive in this regard. Indeed, its government is required to take a tough stance against "offending" countries under the
country's domestic trade law.[7]

Forum management refers to a strategy sometimes referred to as
forum shifting (see Braithwaite and Drahos 2000). The former term is
more accurate and better accommodates the sophistication of US trade
and IP strategy, which can involve both the opening up of new forums
and the closing of old ones. Most countries seek to use it, but only the
powerful nations can practice it well. Weaker countries normally must
unite to have a chance of being good forum managers.

The idea behind the forum management concept is that where negotiations take place can make a big difference to their outcome, and is therefore a strategic matter. Achieving goals relating to certain issues can
involve the opening, closing and shifting of negotiating or jurisdictional
forums. For example, in the 1980s the United States opened up GATT

as another forum to pursue its IP-related interests. At the same time it kept the WIPO forum open to introduce "TRIPS-plus" standards through new conventions such as the WIPO Copyright Treaty, and the Substantive Patent Law Treaty currently under negotiation. On the other hand, while the United States is seeking to confine traditional knowledge (TK) to WIPO's Intergovernmental Committee on Intellectual Property and Genetic Resources, Traditional Knowledge and Folklore, several developing countries have insisted that TK also be covered by WIPO's Standing Committee on the Law of Patents, and in the TRIPS Council.

Perhaps the most significant new development in the field of IP forum management is the proliferation of bilateral and regional negotiations on trade and investment that have led to many developing countries' adopting heightened standards of IP protection through the resulting agreements. These bilateral and regional agreements have proved to be a useful way to get individual, or sometimes groups of, developing countries to introduce so-called "TRIPS plus" provisions that go beyond what TRIPS requires, such as:

(1) extending patents and copyright to new kinds of subject matter;
(2) eliminating or narrowing permitted exceptions including those still provided in US and European IP laws;
(3) extending protection terms;
(4) introducing new TRIPS-mandated IP rules earlier than the transition periods allowed by TRIPS; and
(5) ratifying new WIPO treaties containing TRIPS-plus measures.

In addition, they appear sometimes to require, at least implicitly, that developing-country parties drop certain IP-related demands the same countries are making in multilateral forums such as the TRIPS Council.

The United States and the European Community both use the bilateralism strategy, but the United States has been the more aggressive. Nonetheless, as an active and sophisticated IP forum manager, the US interest in bilateralism and regionalism does not mean abandoning the multilateral approach. In this case, forum management entails the proliferation of forums, keeping as many open at the same time as possible. According to the former United States Trade Representative, Robert Zoellick, US trade strategy is about not putting all of America's eggs in one basket:[8]

When the Bush Administration set out to revitalize America's trade agenda almost three years ago, we outlined our plans clearly and openly: We would pursue a strategy of "competitive liberalization" to advance free trade globally, regionally, and bilaterally.... At its most basic level, the competitive liberalization strategy simply means that America expands and strengthens its options. If free trade progress becomes stalled globally – where any one of 148 economies in the World Trade Organization has veto power – then we can move ahead regionally and bilaterally. If our hemispheric talks are progressing stage-by-stage, we can point to more ambitious possibilities through FTAs [free trade agreements] with individual countries and sub-regions. Having a strong bilateral or sub-regional option helps spur progress in the larger negotiations.

It is perhaps because of these developments that criticisms of TRIPS and WTO multilateralism seem to have become less shrill in the last few years. For many people there are far worse things going on in intellectual property diplomacy than anything that happens in the rooms and corridors of the WTO!

Implications for TRIPS negotiations

So far in this chapter we have raised some important issues relating to international IP rulemaking and the developing countries. We have also criticized certain trends in IP law, suggesting that they are harmful, or at least suboptimal, to developing countries and probably – and this is a highly significant point – to people everywhere. TRIPS deserves criticism for failing adequately to accommodate the freedom each WTO member should have, within reason, to design the IP rules that best serves its interests. However, imperfect as the WTO rulemaking and enforcement system undoubtedly is, developing countries should use the WTO regime to the maximum in order to achieve the necessary checks and balances so that the opportunities in TRIPS, and international trade more generally, can be exploited to their best advantage.

Achieving the necessary checks and balances should be about far more than opposing TRIPS-plus. For one thing, developing countries should have a positive agenda concerning IP rights; rather than just oppose developed country initiatives, they should be putting forward their own proposals based on assessments of how they can design IP rules to support domestic industry and the public interest. In any case, it is unrealistic to expect the WTO to shelter developing countries from TRIPS-plus pressures in other forums.

So are developing countries making the most of their opportunities in the WTO to pursue a positive pro-development IP agenda? And if not, what can they do? Without doubt, developing country WTO members have succeeded in resisting further tightening of the TRIPS rules and have had some small victories along the way by concentrating their efforts on a set of issues that a sufficient number of them deem important. On the other hand, other important matters are accorded insufficient attention.

Perhaps the issues in which developing countries have invested the most effort in terms of agenda setting and the submission of substantial proposals are public health and the review of Article 27.3(b), which has covered the exceptions to patentability in the field of biotechnology, the *sui generis* system for plant varieties and the relationship between TRIPS and the Convention on Biological Diversity. Traditional knowledge has also been discussed as part of this review. It is probably not coincidental that public health and Article 27.3(b) issues have been the focus of a great deal of NGO campaigning. In addition, some developing countries have actively debated the subject of geographical indications, which may arguably be useful means for traditional rural populations to generate wealth from products based on the application of their local knowledge, which is otherwise difficult to protect by patents. It is important here also to mention technology transfer and the transitional periods, neither of which is a particularly "sexy" issue for NGOs, but which are of special importance to the least-developed countries because of certain provisions in TRIPS that are specific to that category of poor countries.

Let us look more closely at the subjects of public health, Article 27.3(b), traditional knowledge, technology transfer to LDCs and the transition periods for the LDCs. The coverage of these subjects should provoke consideration of at least three key questions: (1) Are these the issues that developing countries should be focusing on? (2) Are positive results being achieved? And (3) are issues of greater strategic import for developing countries and for which prospects for success may be greater being overlooked?

Public health

At the November 2001 Doha Ministerial Conference, the WTO members adopted the Declaration on the TRIPS Agreement on Public Health. The Declaration was a response to concerns expressed by many developing countries that the patent-related obligations in the TRIPS Agreement and the fairly constrained limitations and exceptions to the rights formed a barrier to access to life-saving medicines due in large part to the effects that patent monopolies have on prices.

The Declaration could not have resulted without a great deal of developing country unity plus support from a few sympathetic developed countries, some powerful NGO actors and a small group of expert legal advisors who we might wish to refer to as "counter-experts". It opens by stating, "the TRIPS Agreement does not and should not prevent Members from taking measures to protect public health". Perhaps the most important paragraph is the fifth, which clarifies the freedoms all WTO members have with respect to compulsory licensing, their determination of what constitutes a national emergency or other circumstances of extreme urgency, and exhaustion of rights. Thus, the declaration reaffirms the right to use to the fullest the provisions in TRIPS allowing each member "to grant compulsory licenses and the freedom to determine the grounds upon which such licenses are granted". The declaration explicitly mentions that public health crises "relating to HIV/AIDS, tuberculosis, malaria and other epidemics, can represent a national emergency or other circumstances of extreme urgency".

One matter the declaration left unresolved is whether governments can only grant a compulsory license to a domestic manufacturer. Since TRIPS stipulates under Article 31(f) that unauthorized use of a patent shall be "predominantly for the supply of the domestic market", awarding a license to an overseas manufacturer would conflict with TRIPS since the use would be to supply a foreign market. This is an important issue because many poor countries lack the capacity to manufacture the HIV/AIDS treatments and would therefore need to import them from countries like India, an important supplier of relatively cheap generic drugs. To make the situation even more difficult, India is required by TRIPS to introduce product patents on drugs from 2005 and has recently complied. Normally patents prevent not just the unauthorized sale of protected products but also their manufacture. Therefore, even if a poor country granted a compulsory license to a generic firm in India or in any other foreign country, if the drug were protected by a patent in the generic firm's country too, the licensee would not actually be able to make the drug.

The obvious solution would be for the rules to be changed so that manufacture of the patented drug would not in such cases have to be predominantly for the supply of the domestic market. Paragraph six of the Declaration acknowledges this problem, instructing the TRIPS Council "to find an expeditious solution to this problem and to report to the General Council before the end of 2002". No solution was reached within this deadline, and it was only in August 2003 that one was agreed, the August 30 Decision (WTO 2003a).

The most important part of the August 30 Decision is paragraph two, which provides the terms under which a WTO member may export a pharmaceutical product under a compulsory license to a country with no or insufficient manufacturing capacity on the basis of a waiver of the condition in Article 31(f). These terms are fairly detailed, in part because the pharmaceutical industry was concerned that drugs manufactured under the waiver might be diverted to other markets.

On 6 December 2005, a more permanent solution was found when the WTO members agreed to amend TRIPS by adopting a protocol that supplements TRIPS with the insertion of an Article 31 *bis* and an annex. Together these have the effect of making Article 31(f) inapplicable in the case of an eligible exporting member supplying an eligible importing member with a drug under certain clearly defined terms (WTO 2005).

To date, no developing country has been able to take advantage of this rather complicated system. One wonders whether all of the considerable effort in devising and adopting it will lead to any substantial enhancement in access to medicines for the poor.

Despite so much attention being given to this issue, one very important matter concerning public health that has *not* been adequately debated in the TRIPS Council to the great cost of developing countries is that of test data exclusivity as provided in Article 39. For pharmaceutical companies whose drugs are soon to go off patent, the way that governments regulate third-party access to and use of clinical-trial and other test data can, at least in some cases, make a difference as to when a generic firm can enter the market with its equivalent product. Clearly the stakes are very high, especially for poor countries with large numbers of people unable to afford the drugs they need to stay alive.

Article 39.3 provides for the protection of test data in respect of pharmaceutical and agricultural chemical products that utilize new chemical entities. It must be protected against "unfair commercial use". Disclosure of such data is prohibited but may be allowed if necessary to protect the public or if legal protection measures against unfair commercial use are already in place. In justifying such provisions, Article 39.1 refers to Article 10 *bis* of the Paris Convention, according to which "any act of competition contrary to honest practices in industrial or commercial matters constitutes an act of unfair competition".

How countries may give effect to Article 39.3 is unclear but the vagueness of the language suggests that WTO members have a fair bit of leeway to interpret it as they see fit. Some of them have provided a period of exclusivity – typically at least five years – to the originator of the data during which drug regulators may not use the data to determine whether to approve the marketing of purportedly equivalent products, and generic firms may not use it in an attempt to convince regulators that their product is sufficiently "equivalent" to be marketable. Alternatively, the provision can be interpreted as not prohibiting regulators from doing this but merely as preventing generic producers from being able to acquire the data through dishonest commercial practices (UNCTAD-ICTSD 2005: 531).

In the case of test data protection, strategic vagueness has probably not served the developing countries well. In the absence of an agreed minimalist interpretation in the TRIPS Council, developing countries are being pressured to emulate the developed countries by implementing Article 39.3 in their national laws in the form of a limited period of data exclusivity. On account of industry lobbying, data exclusivity provisions frequently crop up in bilateral and regional free trade agreements where the United States is one of the parties. In some cases, they are bound to become a barrier to the market entry of generic drugs, thereby unduly and unnecessarily restricting price-lowering competition and limiting the freedoms of governments to do much about it.

Consider two recent free trade agreements, the 2004 US-Chile FTA and the 2005 US-Dominican Republic-Central America FTA (US-DR-CAFTA). The US-Chile FTA provides that generic companies are prohibited from marketing a new chemical entity-based drug on the basis of undisclosed clinical trial data submitted to the government as a condition of its approval. This prohibition is for at least five years after the approval date. In some cases this will hold up the marketing of the generic drug until some years after the expiry of any patent on the drug.

The US-DR-CAFTA differs somewhat, for example, in recognizing that some countries may approve a new drug on the basis of its prior approval in another country (e.g., the United States) without the company having to submit clinical trial data in those countries too. But, as with the US-Chile FTA, the prohibition on marketing the generic version is for at least five years from the date of approval of the original pharmaceutical product.

Such a provision applies even in cases where a generic firm is seeking to enter the national market before the original manufacturer, who may not be interested in supplying this particular market. Clearly, these requirements have the potential to stall the introduction of generics in cases where the patent has already expired *or where there was no patent in the first place*, and are not balanced by any language affirming the right of countries to respond to public health crises as they see fit.[9] This is despite the aforementioned clarification in the Declaration on the TRIPS Agreement and Public Health that "the TRIPS Agreement does not and should not prevent members from taking measures to protect public health".

Article 27.3(b) and traditional knowledge

In essence, Article 27.3(b) concerns exceptions to patentability in the area of biotechnology. It permits WTO members to exclude from patentability "plants and animals other than micro-organisms, and essentially biological processes for the production of plants or animals other than non-biological and microbiological processes. However, Members shall provide for the protection of plant varieties either by patents or by an effective *sui generis* system or by any combination thereof. The provisions of this subparagraph shall be reviewed four years after the date of entry into force of the WTO Agreement."

The review of the provisions of Article 27.3(b) began in 1999 and is ongoing. At Doha, ministers representing WTO members clarified their commitment to opening up negotiations on issues relating to Article 27.3(b) to include the relationship between the TRIPS Agreement and the Convention on Biological Diversity (CBD), and the protection of traditional knowledge and folklore. According to paragraph 19 of the Ministerial Declaration,

> We instruct the Council for TRIPS, in pursuing its work programme including under the review of Article 27.3(b), the review of the implementation of the TRIPS Agreement under Article 71.1 and the work foreseen pursuant to paragraph 12 of this Declaration, to examine, *inter alia*, the relationship between the TRIPS Agreement and the Convention on Biological Diversity, the protection of traditional knowledge and folklore, and other relevant new developments raised by Members pursuant to Article 71.1. In undertaking this work, the TRIPS Council shall be guided by the objectives and principles set out in Articles 7 and 8 of the TRIPS Agreement and shall take fully into account the development dimension.

The key challenge for developing countries is that many of them remain unclear about how to tailor their patent regulations to promote their interests in the acquisition, development and application of biotechnology, and therefore how best to exploit these flexibilities. In essence, two types of flexibility exist in Article 27.3(b). These are (1) the optional subject matter exceptions and (2) the possibility to define the terms in a variety of ways. Clearly, the language of this provision is complicated. But it is also subject to a wide range of interpretations, a situation that allows policy makers to implement TRIPS in a very large number of possible ways. Inevitably, developing-country WTO members vary in terms of where they should focus their energies, and where they would prefer these negotiations to lead.

The challenges that subsequently arise are threefold. The first is to identify all possible ways that Article 27.3(b) can be interpreted. The second is to identify the goals that governments wish to use their biotech-related patent rules to further. This must surely be based upon assessments of present biotech capacity of the country in question and of its future potential. The third challenge is for government policy makers on the basis of such an assessment, and a decision on the goals it wishes to pursue, to select from all of the possible interpretations the optimal patent rules available under Article 27.3(b).

Understandably, though, much of the discussion on Article 27.3(b) has focused on how best to address a wide range of moral, political and economic concerns about "patenting life" and "biopiracy" (to use two popular NGO slogans). Far less consideration has been paid to how developing countries can best take advantage of the subparagraph to further their development interests.

The CBD-TRIPS relationship and the protection of TK and folklore, both positive and defensive, are also being discussed in other forums. These include WIPO's Intergovernmental Committee on Intellectual Property and Genetic Resources, Traditional Knowledge and Folklore, and the Conference of the Parties to the CBD and its subsidiary working groups. Not surprisingly, similar debates and proposals come up in each of these forums. Some developed countries, most notably the United States, prefer to confine debate on IP and genetic resources, the CBD and traditional knowledge to WIPO's Intergovernmental Committee, and treat these as purely technical issues that can be resolved by modifying the implementation of existing norms rather than creating new ones.

One key developing-country demand that has come up in all the forums is that of disclosure of origin including prior informed consent. Many developing countries are counting on the WTO as the forum that can secure the incorporation of disclosure of origin in international patent law while accepting that more far-reaching norm-creating activities such as drafting a possible treaty on the protection of traditional knowledge should be left to WIPO.

"Disclosure of origin" has become a collective term for certain requirements to be incorporated into patent law. These requirements vary widely in terms of the weight and nature of the legal, administrative or informational burdens placed on patent applicants and owners. Accordingly, it is convenient to describe three types of disclosure requirement.

The first may be called "voluntary disclosure" and would encourage the disclosure of genetic resources and/or traditional knowledge relevant to an invention being patented. Its omission would not disqualify the patent application from being accepted, being granted or being subsequently enforced. In other words, non-compliance gives rise to no legal consequences.

The second version is "mandatory disclosure". Failure to disclose or dishonest disclosure would have one or some of the following consequences: the patent application would not be accepted; it would be rejected during the prosecution stage; if granted it would not be enforceable; or if granted it would be revoked with possible criminal sanctions for wrongdoers. The burden of compliance is placed on the patent applicants and the patent granting offices. The role of provider country governments would be to monitor compliance and take legal action in cases of alleged non-compliance.

The third version can be called "proof of legal acquisition". This would tie the patent system more closely to the CBD's access and benefit sharing (ABS) provisions, in particular to the ABS regimes operating in those countries directly providing the genetic resources and/or traditional knowledge. One way to implement this is to require patent applicants to submit with their application official documentation from provider countries proving that genetic resources and – where appropriate – associated TK were acquired in accordance with the ABS regulations including conformity with such obligations as prior informed consent, with the terms mutually agreed between providers and the recipients, and with the need to comply with CBD Article 8(j), which deals with the knowledge, innovations and practices of indigenous and local communities, and requires that benefits from their usage be shared with them.

In May 2006, Brazil, India, Pakistan, Peru, Thailand and Tanzania proposed in the WTO General Council that new text be incorporated into the TRIPS Agreement under Article 29, which deals with conditions on patent applicants. Paragraph 2 of the proposed Article 29 *bis* on disclosure of origin of biological resources and/or associated traditional knowledge would state the following:

> Where the subject matter of a patent application concerns, is derived from or developed with biological resources and/or associated traditional knowledge, Members shall require applicants to disclose the country providing the resources and/or associated traditional knowledge, from whom in the providing country they were obtained, and, as known after reasonable inquiry, the country of origin. Members shall also require that applicants provide information including evidence of compliance with the applicable legal requirements in the providing country for prior informed consent for access and fair and equitable benefit-sharing arising from the commercial or other utilization of such resources and/or associated traditional knowledge. (WTO 2006)

Clearly this issue is important to some developing countries. But should it be? It is an open question, but while developing countries understandably do not wish to be exploited, the measures proposed by those six countries are unlikely to work in practice without an effective and inexpensive monitoring system for cross-boundary genetic resource transfers. No such system is in operation yet. Besides, so much of the discussion on disclosure of origin seems to be about preventing so-called "biopiracy". Relatively little consideration has been given to encouraging collaborations with foreign institutions and scientists that can help developing countries to enhance their scientific and technological capacities in order to generate wealth from their biological resources.

Geographical indications

Geographical indications (GIs) are defined in the TRIPS Agreement as "indications which identify a good as originating in the territory of a Member, or a region or locality in that territory, where a given quality, reputation, or other characteristic of the good is essentially attributable to its geographical origin". GIs are similar in function to trademarks, the difference being that the former identifies a product with a particular territory, whereas the latter identifies a product with a company or brand.

WTO members are required to permit legal action enabling traders to prevent: (1) the designation or presentation of a good (such as a trademark) that suggests, in a manner that misleads the public, that the good in question originates in a geographical area other than the true place of origin; and (2) any use that constitutes unfair competition. Article 23 deals solely with wines and spirits, which are subject to additional protection. This evidences how far the European wine- and spirit-exporting countries were willing to go in pursuit of their economic interests with respect to such goods.

In November 2001, the WTO members attending the Doha Ministerial Conference agreed "to negotiate the establishment of a multilateral system of notification and registration of geographical indications for wines and spirits by the Fifth Session of the Ministerial Conference". With respect to the possible extension of the enhanced protection of geographical indications to products other than wines and spirits, it was agreed that issues related to this matter would be addressed in the Council for TRIPS, an indication of the lack of consensus.

Despite the fact that they are in TRIPS largely at the instigation of the European Commission, GIs have for several years been promoted as a concession to developing countries that they ought to take advantage of. Supposedly, they provide the means by which developing countries can use IP to protect categories of local rural knowledge that they possess in abundance. In particular, the European Union and the Swiss government are very keen to promote GIs worldwide by arguing that this part of TRIPS can potentially provide substantial gains for developing countries. This seems plausible when one considers that GIs are especially appropriate for the produce of small-scale producers and cultivators, and, it should be underlined here, not just for foods and beverages but also handicrafts and other hand-made items. As one scholar argues, when countries adopt GIs they implicitly accept "the underlying philosophy of the distinctiveness of local and regional products". Furthermore, "globalization of ... artisanally-based principles" inherent to geographical indications "counters the standardization of products which is normally considered the outcome of the internationalization of the agro-food industries [and] assists small family firms to resist the industrialization and corporatization of production" (Moran 1993).

GIs appear superficially to be a subject that developing countries should be able to adopt a unified stance on. Indeed, generally speaking, developing countries consider the additional protection extended to wines and spirits to typify the lack of balance in TRIPS. But after that, the consensus starts to break down.

Many developing countries are rich in traditional knowledge having applications in agriculture, food production and small-scale manufacturing. So GIs would appear to have real potential in terms of developing and exploiting lucrative markets for natural products including those manufactured by resource-poor farming communities. Such countries tend to favour the extension of the additional protection to cover all products, not just beverages. Are they right to be so pro-GI with respect to products they wish to export? Possibly they are, but caution should be exercised. GIs are useless without good standards of quality control and marketing, and up-to-date information on markets, including foreign ones, if the products are to be exported. At present the potential of geographical indications for developing countries is somewhat speculative because this type of IPR has been used only in a few countries outside Europe. Moreover, many GIs have quite small markets, and a relatively small number trade internationally.

Other developing countries do not have an abundance of TK and are key exporters of products that compete with well-established GI-protected goods coming from Europe. For those countries, GIs may be considered a threat and not an opportunity. Indeed, some such countries are understandably concerned that the present enthusiasm for GIs among Europeans is really about protectionism. For example, New World developing country wine-producer countries like Chile and Argentina and also South Africa are competitors with Europe, and tend to be unhappy about the privileged status of wines and spirits because this serves the interests of their Old World competitors. Many of the place names in these countries originated in Europe. Some developed countries, such as Australia, feel the same way.

In short, there can be no "developing country position" on GIs and it is futile to try to achieve one. But since the interests and negotiating positions of developed countries also differ sharply, these negotiations on GIs could end up in stalemate.

The least-developed countries

Under TRIPS, the least-developed countries (LDCs) were allowed until 1 January 2006 to apply the Agreement in full. However, they have managed to secure two extensions. The Doha Declaration on the TRIPS

Agreement and Public Health allowed LDCs to delay implementation of patent protection for pharmaceutical products and legal protection of undisclosed test data submitted as a condition of approving the marketing of pharmaceuticals until 1 January 2016. In November 2005, the TRIPS Council extended the deadline for fully implementing the rest of TRIPS by a further seven and a half years to 1 July 2013. Undoubtedly, these are achievements for LDCs, even if some of them have already implemented some or all of TRIPS.

As for technology transfer, the Ministerial Declaration expressed agreement on the establishment of a Working Group to examine "the relationship between trade and transfer of technology, and of any possible recommendations on steps that might be taken within the mandate of the WTO to increase flows of technology to developing countries". The Doha Decision on Implementation-related Issues and Concerns reaffirmed the mandatory nature of Article 66.2, according to which "developed country Members shall provide incentives to enterprises and institutions in their territories for the purpose of promoting and encouraging technology transfer to least-developed country Members in order to enable them to create a sound and viable technological base". The TRIPS Council was directed to establish "a mechanism for ensuring the monitoring and full implementation of the obligations in question".

Pursuant to this, in February 2003, the Council for TRIPS adopted a decision requiring the developed country WTO members to "submit annually reports on actions taken or planned in pursuance of their commitments under Article 66.2" (WTO 2003b). Such reports must provide the following information: (1) an overview of the incentives regime put in place to fulfil the obligations of Article 66.2, including any specific legislative, policy and regulatory framework; (2) identification of the type of incentive and the government agency or other entity making it available; (3) eligible enterprises and other institutions in the territory of the Member providing the incentives; and (4) any information available on the functioning in practice of these incentives.

It is hard to see such pressure on developed countries to comply with Article 66.2 going very far. The real difficulty is that technologies tend to be privately owned and governments are limited in terms of how far they are able and willing to intervene so as to assure they are transferred to the LDCs.

Conclusions and a proposal for more development-friendly IP rulemaking

Historical evidence shows that well-designed IP systems can benefit national economies just as poorly designed ones can harm them. But how does one go about designing and negotiating an appropriate IP system or fine-tuning an existing one? The economic and social impact of IP reform is very hard to predict reliably, especially in the long-term. This is particularly the case for developing countries. This is a real handicap in the present situation where countries are pressured to negotiate and implement new multilateral trade rules, bilateral or regional free trade or investment agreements, and to respond to powerful stakeholder groups – often foreign ones – demanding changes to national regimes that may not serve the interests of their citizens and other domestic stakeholders. Such difficulties in measuring impacts make it difficult for governments and their representatives to know what negotiating position to adopt on IP, how best to handle complex trade issue-linkage bargains, and how far they should accommodate the demands of international business interests clamouring for change to domestic IP rules.

As with other areas of business regulation, IP policymaking and negotiation position formation is, or at least should be, a matter for *national* decision making involving the collaboration of all *national* stakeholders, including owners, users and the public. Foreign interests should not be ignored but government business regulation is about what is good for the national economy and the country's citizens. Good policymaking cannot be based solely on the implementation of obligations accepted in multilateral treaties or regional or bilateral trade agreements. Unfortunately, policymaking often seems to be done in this way, which is to say that policy*taking* is the norm rather than policy*making*. What we have here are political and technical challenges.

Until recently, intellectual property was a subject for specialists, and was considered to have little if anything to do with, for example, biodiversity conservation, the rights of indigenous peoples and poor farmers in developing countries, human rights (except for author's moral rights) or spiritual values, or with the interests of consumers, patients or librarians to name just a few. Therefore, IP lawyers and commercial intellectual property user groups were the only ones assumed to have a legitimate interest in IP regulation and the only "experts" able to offer rational and objective technical advice to policy makers.

In recent years this state of affairs is being challenged by alternative voices. These are much more critical of the excessive influence of the rather closed network of IP experts and interest groups, and are more sceptical that stronger rights are in the best interests of the national population or the developing world. Several NGOs have actively sought to reverse the IP strengthening trends of recent years in the developed and developing worlds. They are highly skilled and motivated networkers disseminating information and organizing their campaigns through Web sites, newsletters, media and e-mail alerts, sign-on declarations and letters circulated on the Internet, parallel sessions to intergovernmental conferences and attention-seeking stunts.

NGOs and the counter-experts who advise them on the technicalities, and in some cases on the political strategy, provide both opportunities and threats for developing countries. The NGO-led access to medicines campaign is a case where these organizations and the counter-experts they recruited provided invaluable political *and* technical support for developing country WTO members. Efforts by the open source and access to knowledge movements to defend existing limitations and exceptions to IP rights and block the extension of IP rights to cover new types of production and subject matter are also proving to be useful for developing countries as they seek to transform WIPO into a more development-friendly organization, and tap into alternative technical assistance networks that help in conceiving better-balanced IP rules at home and more sophisticated position statements in international forums.

However, there is a danger when NGOs set the agenda and developing countries fall into line without sufficient reflection as to where their national interest really lies. Much of the discussion relating to the Article 27.3(b) review seems to exemplify the pitfalls. Arguably, the conduct more generally of many developing countries in the TRIPS Council over the years may also justify some anxiety about this. One cannot help but wonder if more attention should have been paid to other parts of TRIPS, including copyright, which for many developing countries is more important than patents and is a complex IP right that is extremely hard to design and regulate.

This article closes with a new approach that may contribute to better and more development-friendly IP negotiating and rulemaking outcomes whether at the WTO or elsewhere. It is based on a suggestion made by a group of developing countries at the first session of the Inter-sessional Intergovernmental Meeting on a Development Agenda for WIPO, which is that implementing pro-development principles and guidelines in WIPO might involve:

> undertaking independent, evidence-based "Development Impact Assessment" (DIA) to consider the possible implications of each norm-setting initiative for core sustainable development indicators such as innovation, access by the public to knowledge and products, job creation, poverty alleviation, equity, respect for cultural diversity, protection of biodiversity, health, and education, particularly in developing and least developed countries. (WIPO 2005)

To date, nothing has been done to consider how DIAs might work in practice. So let us briefly explore what might be the advantages of development impact assessments and how they could be conducted. As we will see, the WTO is one forum where they might be applied. One can immediately think of some positive strategic and practical results arising from their promotion and operationalization. First, making DIAs a requirement in terms of norm-setting would place a heavy burden of proof on those demanding strengthened IP protection to produce more convincing evidence of its necessity than they customarily offer.

Second, if conceived holistically, development impact assessments would broaden the investigation of the effects of IP reform far beyond narrow conceptions of economic efficiency such as Pareto optimality[10] or Kaldor-Hicks efficiency,[11] important as these may be, toward wider and deeper notions of development that incorporate human welfare and environmental sustainability. Consequently they could become an extremely valuable and appropriate analytical and decisionmaking tool for development.

As to what IP DIAs would look like, one can envisage them having at least two elements. The first is the assessment itself. The second is the on-going consultation process involving stakeholders and independent experts. The assessment would comprise determination of the *timing* of the DIA, its *objectives*, its *scope*, the *development indicators* to be selected and of what *data* to be generated for measuring performance levels and monitoring trends in respect of the indicators. The assessment would lay out the *benefits*, *costs* and *risks*, but would not be just descriptive and analytical. It would of necessity be prescriptive; it must feed into policy-making, otherwise it is pointless.

The timing of the DIA is very important. It could take place at the start of negotiations or during the drafting stages of a given proposal, reform or agreement. But ex post DIAs may also generate useful results, for example, in terms of taking advantage of the interpretative flexibilities in adopted agreements like TRIPS and of designing "damage limitation" responses and counterproposals.

The DIA could be very broad or reasonably narrow and would be determined by the following factors:

- The scale of the assessment
  One could envisage an ambitious DIA whose scale is sustainable development in all its aspects. But in many cases, this would be infeasible and unnecessary. Or it could deal with a specific development objective like one of the Millennium Development Goals or Targets. Alternatively, one could focus the DIA on a particular issue of current concern to developing countries, such as the extent to which access to knowledge, technology transfer or the achievement of food security would be, or are being, facilitated or hindered.
- The scope of the negotiation, proposal, reform or agreement
  The breadth could cover a whole agreement. This would be a huge task, especially with a complex and wide-ranging agreement like TRIPS and

if a broad range of development indicators were being considered. It could, on the other hand, be more modest in its aims, such as assessing an FTA, provisions being considered for a WTO Ministerial Declaration or trade round, or a specific legal reform or rule change such as disclosure of origin, extension of copyright term or introduction of five years' pharmaceutical test data protection.

- The number of development indicators
  A small number of indicators could be used, such as ones relating to the achievement of food security, or to universal access to medicines. On the other hand, one could select a range of indicators to cover a broader development issue (or issues), such as those that may be gleaned from the United Nations Development Programme Human Development Reports. Clearly, the number of indicators selected would largely depend on whether the focus of the DIA is development in its broadest sense or a specific development-related issue, or a development objective.
- The geographical or economic breadth to be covered
  The DIA could have a global scope or it could be confined to a national economy. Alternatively, it may be limited to a specific economic activity, business sector or type of product.
- The extent of accuracy desired
  One could envisage a thorough in-depth assessment. This may in some cases be expensive and time consuming. On the other hand, "quick and dirty" DIAs may still be worthwhile.

The consultation process should be multi-stakeholder and democratic, ensuring that all groups with an interest and expertise to offer including consumers and the poor have the opportunity to design, influence, monitor and review the process. If not, there is a real danger that the DIA could lack all legitimacy and be perceived as "rubber stamping" decisions already made. Also, without such an inclusive and open process, it will be much more difficult for governments to determine where exactly the national interest lies in respect to IP policymaking and negotiating.

Notes

1. According to Sell (2003), TRIPS is a case of twelve US corporations making public law for the world. This only makes sense if one takes it to mean that the active engagement of these firms was a necessary condition for there being a TRIPS Agreement, but not a sufficient one. Influential as they undoubtedly were, these corporations did not actually sit down and write the TRIPS Agreement themselves. Not only did divisions emerge

between Europe and the United States that required compromises, but developing countries were much more involved in the drafting than Sell and others give them credit for. As Watal (2001) explains, they achieved favourable language in ten of the 73 articles, albeit with the necessary support of a few developed countries.

2. For example at the 13th Fordham University conference on International Intellectual Property Law and Policy, New York, 31 March 2005.

3. Indeed, a strong case could be made for the claim that TRIPS was meant to harm developing countries. One of the ways that businesses persuaded the US government to take a proactive stance on IP in the GATT was to produce statistics showing how far developing country pirates and counterfeiters were free-riding on US innovation. Accordingly, and if correct, gains for US business from eliminating such free-riding would be equivalent to the losses for developing country businesses, consumers and economies that, thanks to TRIPS, would now have to pay for what previously they had acquired for free or very cheaply. There again, the piracy statistics presented by industry to the US government were not credible anyway.

4. According to the World Bank, "if TRIPS were fully implemented, rent transfers to major technology-creating countries – particularly the United States, Germany, and France – in the form of pharmaceutical patents, computer chip designs, and other intellectual property, would amount to more than $20 billion" (World Bank 2001). Stated baldly, and if the assumptions on which the research is based are reliable, this means that TRIPS represents a $20 billion-plus transfer of wealth from the technology-importing nations – many of which are developing countries – to the technology exporters – few if any of which are developing countries – that may or may not be outweighed by future gains.

5. These include authors, publishers, performers, film production companies, phonogram producers, Internet service providers and broadcasters.

6. In the United States, much of the technical assistance is targeted at the enforcement of rights, which in many developing countries are mostly owned by foreigners. Some of it is provided through the US Agency for International Development and is classed as overseas aid.

7. The 1988 Omnibus Trade and Competitiveness Act in its Special 301 provision requires the United States Trade Representative office annually to "identify those foreign countries that deny adequate and effective protection of intellectual property rights, or deny fair and equitable market access to United States persons that rely upon intellectual property protection".

8. Letter from Robert Zoellick to David Walker, Comptroller of the United States, 3 December 2003, available from http://www.ustr.gov/releases/2003/12/2003-12-03-letter-gao.pdf.

9. For a more detailed explanation of the data protection-related problems with US-DR-CAFTA, see Abbott (2004).

10. "If an economic system is Pareto efficient, then it is the case that no individual can be made better off without another being made worse off. It is commonly accepted that outcomes that are not Pareto efficient are to be avoided, and therefore Pareto efficiency is an important criterion for evaluating economic systems and political policies." Wikipedia, "Pareto Efficiency", available from http://en.wikipedia.org/wiki/Pareto_efficiency, accessed 9 November 2006.

11. "Using Kaldor-Hicks efficiency, a more efficient outcome can leave some people worse off. Thus, an outcome is more efficient if those that are made better off could in theory compensate those that are made worse off". Wikipedia, "Kaldor-Hicks Efficiency", available from http://en.wikipedia.org/wiki/Kaldor-Hicks_efficiency, accessed 9 November 2006.

REFERENCES

Abbott, F. (2004) "The Doha Declaration on the TRIPS Agreement and Public Health and the Contradictory Trend in Bilateral and Regional Free Trade Agreements", Occasional Paper no. 14, Geneva: Quaker United Nations Office.

Ben-Atar, D. S. (2004) *Trade Secrets: Intellectual Piracy and the Origins of American Industrial Power*, New Haven, Conn.: Yale University Press.

Boyle, J. (1996) *Shamans, Software, and Spleens: Law and the Construction of the Information Society*, Cambridge, Mass.: Harvard University Press.

Braithwaite, J., and P. Drahos (2000) *Global Business Regulation*, Cambridge: Cambridge University Press.

Chow, K. B., K. M. Leo and S. Leong (2007) "Singapore", in U. Suthersanen, G. Dutfield and K. B. Chow, eds, *Innovation without Patents: Harnessing the Creative Spirit in a Diverse World*, Cheltenham: Edward Elgar, pp. 73–118.

Dutfield, G. (2005) *Africa and the Economy of Tradition*, Paris: Fondation pour l'Innovation Politique.

Dutfield, G., and U. Suthersanen (2005) "Harmonisation or Differentiation in Intellectual Property Protection? The Lessons of History", *Prometheus* 23(2): 131–147.

Fisher, M. (2004) "Growth of the Japanese Patent System: A Lesson for Us All?" *Intellectual Property Quarterly* 22(1): 85–113.

Gupta, A. K. (2006) "From Sink to Source: The Honey Bee Network Documents Indigenous Knowledge and Innovations in India", *Innovations: Technology, Governance, Globalization*, Summer, 1(3): 49–66.

Kim, L. (2003) "Technology Transfer and Intellectual Property Rights: The Experience of Korea", in Issues Paper no. 2, UNCTAD-ICTSD Project on Intellectual Property Rights and Sustainable Development, Geneva: UNCTAD/ICTSD.

Lall, S. (2003) "Indicators of the Relative Importance of IPRs in Developing Countries", with Manuel Albaladejo, Issues Paper no. 3, UNCTAD-ICTSD Project on Intellectual Property Rights and Sustainable Development, Geneva: UNCTAD/ICTSD.

Maskus, K. E. (2000) *Intellectual Property Rights in the Global Economy*, Washington, DC: Institute for International Economics.

Matthews, D., and V. Munoz-Tellez (2006) "Bilateral Technical Assistance and TRIPS: The United States, Japan and the European Communities in Comparative Perspective", *Journal of World Intellectual Property* 9(6): 629–653.

Moran, W. (1993) "Rural Space as Intellectual Property", *Political Geography*, 12(3): 263–277.

Musungu, F. S., and G. Dutfield (2003) "Multilateral Agreement and a TRIPS Plus World: The World Intellectual Property Organization", TRIPS Issues Paper no. 3, Geneva: Quaker United Nations Office/Quaker International Affairs Programme.

Posey, D. A. (1999) *Cultural and Spiritual Values of Biodiversity*, Nairobi and London: United Nations Development Programme/IT Publications.

Sell, S. K. (2003) *Private Power, Public Law: The Globalization of Intellectual Property Rights*, Cambridge: Cambridge University Press.

UNCTAD-ICTSD (2005) *Resource Book on TRIPS & Development*, Cambridge: Cambridge University Press.

Watal, J. (2001) *Intellectual Property Rights in the WTO and Developing Countries*, New Delhi: Oxford University Press.

World Bank (2001) *Global Economic Prospects and the Developing Countries 2002: Making Trade Work for the World's Poor*, Washington, DC: World Bank.

World Intellectual Property Organization (2005) Inter-sessional Intergovernmental meeting on a development agenda for WIPO, "Proposal to establish a development agenda for WIPO: an elaboration of issues raised in document WO/GA/31/11. Document prepared by the Secretariat". IIM/1/4.

WTO (2003a) "Implementation of Paragraph 6 of the Doha Declaration on the TRIPS Agreement and Public Health: Decision of 30 August 2003", WT/L/540, Geneva.

WTO (2003b) "Implementation of Article 66.2 of the TRIPS Agreement: Decision of the Council for TRIPS of 19 February 2003", IP/C/28, Geneva.

WTO (2005) "Amendment of the TRIPS Agreement: Decision of 6 December 2005", WT/L/641, Geneva.

WTO (2006) "Doha Work Programme – The Outstanding Implementation Issue on the Relationship between the TRIPS Agreement and the Convention on Biological Diversity: Communication from Brazil, India, Pakistan, Peru, Thailand and Tanzania", General Council, Trade Negotiations Committee WT/GC/W/564 – TN/C/W/41, Geneva.

9

The development objectives of the WTO: State-centred versus human rights approaches

Ernst-Ulrich Petersmann

Ambivalence of the WTO objectives: Power politics in disguise

The Preamble to the Agreement Establishing the World Trade Organization (WTO) defines its objectives mainly in economic terms. Idealists therefore view the WTO as an instrument for promoting economic welfare through trade, non-discriminatory conditions of competition and efficient use of policy instruments. Realists counter that GATT and WTO rules and negotiations are no less used for justifying trade protection, trade discrimination and the redistribution of income for the benefit of rent-seeking interest groups. The 45 years of GATT and WTO cotton and textiles agreements discriminating against exports from less-developed countries (LDCs), and the lack of economic rationality of many WTO rules (e.g., on discriminatory anti-dumping measures, agricultural export subsidies) illustrate the ambivalence of the economic functions and political exceptions of GATT/WTO rules.

The reciprocity principle underlying the WTO objective of "reciprocal and mutually advantageous arrangements directed to the substantial reduction of tariffs and other barriers to trade" (Preamble WTO Agreement) is based more on political than on economic rationales. In the Doha Round negotiations, realists blame the lack of reciprocity (e.g., between the EU offer for agricultural market access, the US offer for agricultural domestic support, the offers by the 22 LDCs cooperating in the "G20" for industrial goods and services) as the major stumbling block

Developing countries and the WTO: Policy approaches, Sampson and Chambers (eds),
United Nations University Press, 2008, ISBN 978-92-808-1153-7

preventing a "grand bargain". Economists counter that the "balance of concessions" may exist only in the eyes of the negotiators; in terms of consumer welfare, the alleged "reciprocity advantages" may be smaller than the opportunity costs of delaying and risking the successful conclusion of the Doha negotiations. Some objectives in the Preamble of the WTO Agreement – such as recognition of the "need for positive efforts designed to ensure that developing countries, and especially the least developed among them, secure a share in the growth in international trade commensurate with the needs of their economic development" – reflect principles of distributive justice and solidarity. Similar objectives had already been accepted in Article XXXVI of GATT 1947, for example, "that individual and joint action is essential to further the development of the economies of less-developed contracting parties and to bring about a rapid advance in the standards of living in these countries". The still-marginal share of the least-developed among the LDCs (LLDCs) in world trade, and the widespread poverty of almost half the people living in LDCs on less than 2 US dollars per day, confirm that "member-driven trade governance" has failed, in far too many countries, to effectively protect consumer welfare, poverty reduction and other citizen interests.

The role of WTO law suffers from the same ambivalence as WTO politics. Idealists claim that "member-driven governance" serves the "public interest". Realists counter that consumer welfare, human rights and other constitutional safeguards of citizen interests are neither mentioned nor effectively protected in WTO law. WTO negotiations are driven by producer interests, bureaucratic and political interests; citizens, their human rights and consumer welfare are treated as marginal objects of benevolent governance, resulting in widespread alienation of citizens and democratic distrust vis-à-vis intergovernmental power politics in the WTO. When I joined the GATT Secretariat in 1981 as the first "legal officer" ever employed by GATT, most GATT officials and trade diplomats claimed that GATT should continue to operate "pragmatically" without a Legal Office and without participation of legal officers in GATT negotiations and dispute-settlement proceedings. It was only in 1983 that the European Community agreed to the establishment of a GATT Legal Office on the condition that its first director could only be an experienced trade diplomat without thorough legal training. As several GATT panel proceedings had found against the European Community's agricultural subsides and restrictions in the late 1970s and early 1980s, EC Trade Commissioner Willy de Clercq continued to claim that "GATT must never become a court". GATT Director-General Arthur Dunkel, recognizing the power-struggles by economists and diplomats opposed to sharing their powers with lawyers in GATT negotiations and dispute-settlement proceedings, kept the GATT Legal Office under his direct supervision and directly located next to the Director-General's office inside the GATT Secretariat. Yet, following several GATT dispute-settlement findings against US anti-dumping measures during the Uruguay Round, Dunkel gave in to the request by US Trade Representative Carla Hills to transfer responsibility for dispute-settlement challenges of anti-dumping, countervailing duty and safeguard restrictions from GATT's Legal Office to a "Rules Division" directed by bureaucrats eager to prevent independent legal advice. The continuing distrust vis-à-vis rule of law in international trade, as illustrated by the insistence of EC and US governments that domestic courts must not directly apply WTO law, illustrates that "member-driven" trade governance remains dominated by political, bureaucratic and protectionist self-interests without adequate safeguards for rule of law among private economic actors, general citizen interests and respect for human rights.

From "member-driven governance" to "democratic self-governance" in international economic law?

The "Westphalian system of international law among states" evolved as an "international law of coexistence" protecting state sovereignty, as well as an "international law of cooperation" based on intergovernmental agreements and organizations, without regard to the democratic legitimacy of governments and without effective safeguards of human rights. As emphasized by Kofi Annan in his final address as UN Secretary-General to world leaders assembled in the UN General Assembly on 19 September 2006, this state-centred international legal system has proven to be "unjust, discriminatory and irresponsible" because it has failed to effectively respond to the three global challenges to the United Nations: "to ensure that globalization would benefit the entire human race; to heal the disorder of the post–Cold War world, replacing it with a genuinely new world order of peace and freedom; and to protect the rights and dignity of individuals, particularly women, which were so widely trampled underfoot". According to Kofi Annan, these three challenges – "an unjust world economy, world disorder and widespread contempt for human rights and the rule of law" – entail divisions that "threaten the very notion of an international community, upon which the UN stands".[1] Citizens should hold "member-driven governance" accountable for these obvious "government failures" and "constitutional failures".

Rational individuals commit themselves to "constitutional principles" in order to reduce conflicts inside their own minds (e.g., between human passions and rationality) and in their social relations. All UN member states have adopted national constitutions and have committed governments to "universal respect for, and observance of, human rights and fundamental freedoms for all" (Article 55 UN Charter). Yet, just as UN law does not provide for effective legal and judicial remedies against the widespread violations of human rights, so does WTO law fail to effectively protect consumer welfare and the rights of private producers, investors, traders and consumers as the main actors in international trade. The more state-centred rules and "member-driven governance" fail to empower and protect citizens and their human rights effectively, the stronger becomes the need for "constitutionalizing" policymaking in the WTO, similar to the constitutional restraints in European economic law protecting citizens against abuses of trade policy powers by their own governments (Joerges and Petersmann 2006).

The ever larger number of more than 250 regional trade agreements (RTAs) concluded all over the world, and the increasing focus in international economic, environmental and human rights law on the legal and judicial protection of individual rights and of private international economic transactions, entail a dynamically evolving "integration law" aimed at promoting mutually beneficial cooperation not only among governments, but primarily among individuals and people. The more than 60 RTAs concluded after the failure of the 2003 WTO Ministerial Conference to advance the worldwide "Doha Development Round negotiations" illustrate that regional agreements are increasingly perceived not only as alternative fora for trade liberalization, but also for trade regulation and non-economic integration. The initiatives for transforming RTAs into, for instance, an ASEAN Community, a Southern African Community, Andean, Central and South American Economic Communities reflect the European experience that the success of regional trade liberalization and economic integration may depend on embedding it into a broader constitutional framework of "just rules" and "fair procedures" supported by citizens, business and other non-governmental constituencies.

The evolution of the international economic order into a "layered legal system" raises questions as to the relationships between the different private and public, national, regional and worldwide levels of law. In European integration law, governments were forced – by citizens, parliaments and courts – to integrate the different layers of private and public, national and intergovernmental economic law into a mutually coherent constitutional system "founded on the principles of liberty, democracy, respect for human rights and fundamental freedoms, and the rule of law, principles which are common to the Member States" (Article 6 EU). In contrast to this citizen-oriented focus of European economic law, the WTO Agreement and WTO bodies treat citizens and non-governmental organizations as mere objects of benevolent trade governance, without individual rights to hold their own governments accountable for their frequent violations of WTO rules. Also, parliaments in most WTO member countries and in the European Community do not effectively control intergovernmental negotiations and rulemaking in the WTO. Hence, the influence of rent-seeking interest groups on periodically elected politicians (e.g., in the US Congress, the European Community and many WTO member states) is disproportionately stronger than the legal and democratic accountability of trade diplomats for promoting general consumer welfare and protecting individual rights of private participants in international trade.

The universal recognition of *jus cogens* and of "inalienable" human rights as *erga omnes* obligations has made individuals legal subjects of international law with an "inalienable core" of human rights. Notably in Europe, the intergovernmental structures of international economic law are increasingly limited by human rights obligations and by supranational powers of international courts and institutions. WTO law has, likewise, hierarchical structures that assert legal supremacy not only vis-à-vis domestic laws (cf. Article XVI:4 WTO Agreement); they introduce vertical legal hierarchies and constitutional "checks and balances" also among the institutions and different levels of primary and secondary law of international organizations (cf. Articles IX, XVI:3 WTO Agreement). They increasingly limit regional agreements (cf. Articles XXIV GATT, V GATS), bilateral agreements (cf. Article 11 of the WTO Safeguards Agreement, the WTO Agreement on Textiles and Clothing) and unilateralism through multilateral legal and institutional restraints (e.g., in Articles 16, 17 and 23 DSU) with citizen-oriented functions for the protection of freedom, non-discrimination, rule of law and welfare-increasing cooperation among producers, investors, traders and consumers across national frontiers. Yet, as long as citizens have no effective legal and judicial remedies against the frequent violations of WTO obligations by their own governments, protectionist collusion all too often prevails. Citizens increasingly challenge the democratic legitimacy of this intergovernmental exclusion of citizen rights and general citizen interests in the WTO.

Representatives of international organizations, like the European Commission and WTO Director-General Pascal Lamy, emphasize the political advantages of empowering self-interested citizens and "cosmopolitan constituencies" in support of the collective supply of international "public goods" (like a rules-based trading system) that cannot be unilaterally produced by national governments. Citizens and lawyers increasingly reject the non-democratic view that UN law should be interpreted exclusively from the perspective of "sovereign equality of states" (Article 2 UN Charter) without equal regard to the legally binding UN commitments to "principles of justice" and "respect for human rights and for fundamental freedoms for all" (Articles 1, 55). Sociological and constitutional approaches to international law have emphasized long since that all legal rules and governmental organizations, including international law and intergovernmental organizations, derive their legitimacy from their instrumental function to protect individual rights and citizen interests. Members of the "policy-oriented approach" to international law, including the president of the International Court of Justice Rosalyn Higgins and the former president of the WTO Appellate Body Florentino Feliciano, rightly argue that international law must be perceived not only as a system of intergovernmental rules, but also as legal decision-making processes in which individuals, their parliamentary representatives and non-governmental organizations increasingly participate (e.g., by submitting "amicus curiae" submissions to WTO dispute settlement panels, convening regular inter-parliamentary conferences at WTO ministerial meetings since 1999; Higgins 1978; Reisman 2006).

The more individuals have rights and duties under international human rights law, humanitarian law and economic and social law, the more it becomes anachronistic for trade diplomats to exclude and alienate citizens – as the main actors in international trade and "democratic owners" of the WTO – from participation in the WTO legal system. Constitutional economics confirms that empowering self-interested citizens (like producers, investors, traders, consumers) by individual rights and obligations is the most effective incentive for mutually beneficial cooperation among citizens and for the decentralized limitation of "market failures", in the economy no less than in the polity (Petersmann 2006a). As virtually all WTO member states have adopted national constitutions and international obligations committing their respective governments to the protection of human rights and citizen interests, diplomats have no mandate to abuse their foreign policy powers by disenfranchising their own citizens through intergovernmental collusion. The UN Charter (e.g., Article 1) and the Vienna Convention on the Law of Treaties (e.g., its Preamble) require interpreting treaties and settling disputes "in conformity with the principles of justice and international law", including "universal respect for, and observance of, human rights and fundamental freedoms for all". As WTO rules must be interpreted "in accordance with customary rules of interpretation of public international law" (Article 3 DSU), lawyers and judges may reasonably argue that "the basic principles ... underlying this multilateral trading system" (in terms of the Preamble to the WTO Agreement and numerous other WTO provisions) include the universal human rights obligations of all WTO Members, as emphasized by UN human rights bodies (see the following section of this chapter). This contribution argues (in the next section of this chapter) that the hu-

man rights obligations of all WTO members should also guide the preferential treatment of LDCs in future "Doha Round" agreements and their
domestic implementation, notably in the more than one hundred less-
developed WTO member countries where large parts of the population
suffer from unnecessary poverty. The WTO development objectives
should be defined in terms of "human development" and individual
rights, and the rights and obligations of WTO Members should be differentiated in accordance with "principles of justice". This does *not* mean
transforming the WTO into a human rights organization. Yet, WTO
bodies should respond constructively to the increasing challenges by
human rights bodies, citizens and their representative institutions of "diplomatic trade governance", secretive rulemaking, disregard for human
rights in WTO deliberations, exclusion of citizens as legal subjects of
WTO law and bureaucratic distribution of "protection rents" without effective parliamentary control. For instance, WTO Members and WTO
bodies could acknowledge their existing human rights obligations and
pledge to cooperate with citizens and their representative institutions as
the democratic owners of the WTO and the main actors in international
trade relations (Petersmann 2006b).

The "human rights approach" to international trade advocated by the UN High Commissioner for Human Rights and the International Labour Organization

All WTO Members have obligations to respect, protect and promote human rights under the UN Charter, UN human rights conventions, other
human rights instruments (e.g., in national laws, regional human rights
conventions, ILO conventions) and general international law. The UN
Declarations on the "right to development" (see UN 1995: 322–324) define "development" in terms of enjoyment of human rights:

- "The right to development is an inalienable human right by virtue of
  which every human person and all peoples are entitled to participate
  in, contribute to, and enjoy economic, social, cultural and political development, in which all human rights and fundamental freedoms can be
  fully realized" (Article 1).
- "The human person is the central subject of development and should
  be the active participant and beneficiary of the right to development"
  (Article 2).
- "All human rights and fundamental freedoms are indivisible and interdependent; equal attention and urgent consideration should be given to
  the implementation, promotion and protection of civil, political, economic, social and cultural rights" (Article 6:2).

- "States should take steps to eliminate obstacles to development resulting from failure to observe civil and political rights, as well as economic, social and cultural rights" (Article 6:3).

The fulfilment of most human rights (e.g., to food, health, education) depends on access to scarce goods and services (e.g., drinking water, cheap
medicines, health and educational services). Also, enjoyment of civil and
political human rights (e.g., personal freedom, rule of law, access to justice, democratic self-government) requires economic resources (e.g., for
financing democratic and law-enforcement institutions). The widespread,
yet unnecessary poverty, health problems and legal insecurity (e.g.,
among the more than 1 billion people living on 1 US dollar a day or
less) bear witness to the fact that many UN member states and UN law
have so far failed to realize the UN objective of "universal respect for,
and observance of, human rights and fundamental freedoms for all" and
"creation of conditions of stability and well-being which are necessary for
peaceful and friendly relations among nations" (Article 55 UN Charter).
Even though international trade is essential for increasing the availability
and quality of scarce resources, UN human rights bodies have, until recently, neglected international trade law or, as in a report for the UN
Commission on Human Rights of 2001, discredited the WTO as "a veri-
table nightmare" for developing countries and women (ECOSOC, 2000:
para. 15).[2]

Human rights dimensions of WTO law: The reports by the UN High Commissioner of Human Rights

In response to the widespread criticism of the anti-market bias of such
"nightmare reports", the UN High Commissioner for Human Rights
(UNHCHR) has published more differentiated reports[3] analysing human
rights dimensions of the WTO Agreements on Trade-Related Intellectual
Property Rights (TRIPS), the Agreement on Agriculture, the General
Agreement on Trade in Services (GATS), international investment
agreements, non-discrimination in the context of globalization and the
impact of trade rules on the right of everyone to the enjoyment of the
highest attainable standard of physical and mental health. The reports
call for a "human rights approach to trade" which

(i)   sets the promotion and protection of human rights as objectives of trade
      liberalization, not exceptions;
(ii) examines the effect of trade liberalization on individuals and seeks to de-
      vise trade law and policy to take into account the rights of all individuals,
      in particular vulnerable individuals and groups;

(iii) emphasizes the role of the State in the process of liberalization – not only as negotiators of trade law and setters of trade policy, but also as the primary duty bearer of human rights;
(iv) seeks consistency between the progressive liberalization of trade and the progressive realization of human rights;
(v) requires a constant examination of the impact of trade liberalization on the enjoyment of human rights;
(vi) promotes international cooperation for the realization of human rights and freedoms in the context of trade liberalization.

The UNHCHR emphasizes that, because every WTO Member has ratified one or more UN human rights conventions and has human rights obligations also under general international law, human rights may be "relevant context" for the interpretation and application of WTO rules. According to the UNHCHR, the needed human rights approach to international trade must recognize as "entitlements the basic needs necessary to lead a life in dignity and ensure their protection in the processes of economic liberalization"; these entitlements cannot be "left subject to the whims of the market" (Petersmann 2004: 623). The UNHCHR differentiates between obligations to respect human rights (e.g., by refraining from interfering in the enjoyment of such rights), to protect human rights (e.g., by preventing violations of such rights by third parties) and to fulfil human rights (e.g., by taking appropriate legislative, administrative, budgetary, judicial and other measures toward the full realization of such rights). In contrast to the often one-sided focus in the human rights literature on the use of trade sanctions for promoting respect for human rights abroad, the UNHCHR reports analyse the human rights dimensions of trade liberalization, trade restrictions and other trade regulations in a broader perspective, emphasizing both potential synergies as well as potential conflicts between human rights and trade rules.

As enjoyment of human rights depends on availability, accessibility, acceptability and quality of traded goods and services, the relevance of WTO rules for the collective supply of "public goods" (like access to low-priced goods and services), for limitations of "market failures" (e.g., inadequate supply of public goods like essential medicines for poor people), and for protection and fulfilment of human rights is acknowledged and discussed. The reports underline that what are referred to – in numerous WTO provisions – as *rights* of WTO Members to regulate may be *duties* to regulate under human rights law (e.g., so as to protect and fulfil human rights of access to water, food, essential medicines, basic health care and education services at affordable prices). The UNHCHR suggests, *inter alia*,

- to recognize the promotion of human rights as an objective of the WTO;
- to encourage interpretations of WTO rules that are compatible with international human rights as progressively clarified, for example, in the "General Comments" adopted by UN human rights bodies;
- to carry out "human rights assessments" of WTO rules; and
- to develop intergovernmental protection of human rights so as to ensure that trade rules and policies promote the human rights and basic needs of all.

The 1998 ILO Declaration on Fundamental Principles and Rights at Work: The expanding scope of an "inalienable core" of basic rights

Human rights are increasingly acknowledged today in national constitutions as well as in the law of worldwide organizations (like the UN, the FAO, WHO, UNESCO) and regional economic integration agreements (like the EC Treaty, the 2000 Cotonou Agreement, the 2001 Quebec Ministerial Declaration on a Free Trade Area of the Americas) as international *erga omnes* obligations of states and intergovernmental organizations with an "inalienable" and "indivisible" *jus cogens* core. The 1996 WTO Declaration on core labour standards helped to reach consensus in the International Labour Organization (ILO) to adopt, on 18 June 1998, the Declaration on Fundamental Principles and Rights at Work, which recognizes

> that all Members, even if they have not ratified the Conventions in question, have an obligation, arising from the very fact of membership in the Organization, to respect, to promote and to realize, in good faith and in accordance with the Constitution, the principles concerning the fundamental rights which are the subject of those Conventions, namely: (a) freedom of association and the effective recognition of the right to collective bargaining; (b) the elimination of all forms of forced or compulsory labor; (c) the effective abolition of child labor; and (d) the elimination of discrimination in respect of employment and occupation. (ILO 1998: 7)

The ILO Declaration and other modern human rights instruments[4] confirm that – in addition to the longstanding prohibitions of genocide, slavery, apartheid and torture – there is an increasing core of additional human rights that must be respected as *erga omnes* obligations. Since the end of the cold war, this international *jus cogens* continues to expand, as recognized by international courts,[5] notwithstanding divergent views on the precise scope and definition of such "inalienable human rights". Human rights law evolves from a national and European into a worldwide "constitutional public order" limiting all governance powers and requiring the interpretation of international and national laws as a functional unity for promoting and protecting "human self-development" as defined by human rights.

Human rights instruments recognize that human rights need to be mutually balanced and implemented by democratic legislation, which may legitimately vary from country to country. International courts have elaborated legal "balancing principles" (like non-discrimination, necessity and proportionality of governmental limitations of freedom and other human rights); courts emphasize the need to respect the "margin of appreciation" that national parliaments may enjoy in their domestic legislation protecting and promoting human rights (Yourow 1996). As human rights also protect individual and democratic diversity, views on the interpretation of government obligations to respect, protect and fulfil human rights may legitimately differ among countries. In view of the limited mandate of international organizations, there are also diverging views on whether, and to what extent, international organizations should not only *respect* human rights, but also *protect* and *fulfil* human rights. Yet, such differences of view over the interpretation and legal protection of human rights do not change the fact that citizens have become subjects of international law and should no longer be treated by trade diplomats as mere objects of their trade management.

Liberal trade rules, like human rights, should focus on human self-development

The reports by the UNHCHR identify potential synergies between trade rules and human rights: "trade liberalization is generally a positive contributor to poverty alleviation – it allows people to exploit their productive potential, assists economic growth, curtails arbitrary policy interventions and helps to insulate against shocks" (UN 2002: para. 33). Also, intellectual property rights may act as incentives for innovation in the pharmaceutical industry and for the transfer of technology to less-developed countries. Yet, the UNHCHR emphasizes the potential conflicts between "existential" human rights and "instrumental" WTO rules (e.g., on protection of intellectual property rights and investor rights), for example, if trade rules lead to higher prices (e.g., of food, seeds, pharmaceutical products), cause unemployment or entail "market failures" in the supply of essential medicines for tropical diseases. According to the High Commissioner, the needed "human rights assessments" of trade rules and trade policies must focus on the rights and basic needs of vulnerable individuals and of the most disadvantaged communities, whose human rights risk being adversely affected most in the process of trade liberalization.

The macroeconomic objectives and state-centred rules of WTO law disregard human rights. The High Commissioner, therefore, emphasizes the need for using WTO rules (e.g., on special and differential treatment of developing countries), WTO safeguard clauses and WTO "exceptions" for actively promoting mutually coherent interpretations of WTO law and human rights so as to enhance "human development". The UNHCHR criticizes the lack of guidance and of monitoring mechanisms in WTO law for ensuring the taking into account of human rights. The reports do not, however, identify concrete conflicts between human rights and WTO law. In view of the citizen-oriented functions of WTO rules for enabling citizens to increase their welfare through mutually beneficial trade transactions, for enhancing the domestic use of efficient (e.g., non-discriminatory) policy instruments and for protecting the priority of non-economic values (as reflected in the numerous "public interest clauses" in WTO law), conflicts between the flexible WTO rules and human rights appear unlikely on the level of international principles.

Even if the WTO objective of "sustainable development" and the numerous WTO "exceptions" appear to offer enough policy space for taking into account universal and other human rights obligations of WTO Members, WTO law in no way ensures that human rights obligations are actually taken into account in the legislative and administrative implementation of WTO rules and in their judicial protection. WTO diplomats and WTO judges have a longstanding preference for avoiding human rights discourse in WTO bodies. More than 35 WTO Members (including the United States) have not ratified the UN Covenant on Economic, Social and Cultural Rights. In view of the narrow limitation of the "terms of reference" of WTO dispute settlement bodies to the "covered WTO agreements", it remains controversial in WTO law whether – in WTO dispute-settlement proceedings – the parties to the dispute may invoke human rights law not only as relevant context for the interpretation of WTO rules, but also directly for justifying departures from their WTO obligations (e.g., in the case of US trade sanctions in response to human rights violations in Myanmar).

Defining WTO development objectives, principles and rules in conformity with "principles of justice" and human rights obligations of WTO Members

The American legal philosopher R. Dworkin begins his recent book *Justice in Robes* with the story of US Supreme Court Justice Oliver Wendell Holmes, who, on his way to the court, was greeted by another lawyer:

"Do justice, Justice!" Holmes replied: "That's not my job" (Dworkin 2006: ch. 1). Similarly, WTO Members emphasize the limited terms of reference of WTO dispute-settlement panels "to examine, in the light of the relevant provisions in (... the covered agreement(s) cited by the parties to the dispute), the matter referred to the DSB ... and to make such findings as will assist the DSB in making the recommendations or in giving the rulings provided for in that/those agreement(s)" (Article 7 DSU). As WTO law includes no explicit reference to justice and human rights, should WTO Members, WTO judges and domestic courts apply WTO law without regard to justice, just as economists perceive trade law as a mere instrument for promoting economic welfare? Does the separation of the judicial power from the legislative and executive powers require that, as postulated by Montesquieu, decisions of international and national courts must always conform to the exact letter of the law as understood by the legislator? Does the frequent emphasis by governments on the "member-driven" character of WTO law, and the frequent recourse to the *Oxford English Dictionary* in the case-law of WTO panels and the Appellate Body, confirm the view that, also in WTO law, judges must apply the positive law literally without regard to whether the applicable rules lead to a just resolution of the dispute?

WTO law must be interpreted in conformity with "principles of justice"

Law, according to Lon Fuller, orders social life not only by "subjecting human conduct to the governance of rules"; law also aims at establishing a *just* order and procedures for the *fair* resolution of disputes (Fuller 1969: 96). This understanding of law as a struggle for just rules and fair procedures goes back to legal philosophy in Greek antiquity. Its application to international relations remains contested by power-oriented, "realist" politicians, political scientists and lobbyists. All UN member states have committed themselves in the UN Charter "to establish conditions under which justice and respect for the obligations arising from treaties and other sources of international law can be maintained" (Preamble). They have defined the purpose of the UN as, *inter alia*, "to bring about by peaceful means, and in conformity with the principles of justice and international law, adjustment or settlement of international disputes or situations which might lead to a breach of the peace" (Article 1, para. 1 UN Charter). All UN member states have also accepted membership in the International Court of Justice (ICJ) as "the principal judicial organ" of the UN for the peaceful settlement of international disputes (Article 92 UN Charter). The "principles of justice" recognized in UN law include access to legal and judicial remedies, notwithstanding acceptance of the ICJ's compulsory jurisdiction (pursuant to Article 36 of the ICJ

Statute) by only about one third of the 191 UN member states. Individual rights of access to justice, subject to procedural and substantive conditions, are also recognized in UN and regional human rights instruments as well as in other international agreements.

In the Vienna Convention on the Law of Treaties (VCLT), most WTO Members have explicitly affirmed "that disputes concerning treaties, like other international disputes, should be settled by peaceful means and in conformity with the principles of justice and international law", including "universal respect for, and observance of, human rights and fundamental freedoms for all" (Preamble VCLT). WTO law and its Dispute Settlement Understanding (DSU) regulate "the dispute settlement system of the WTO" (Article 3) as a multilevel system with compulsory jurisdiction for (quasi) judicial settlement of disputes at intergovernmental and domestic levels.

Yet, none of the more than 200 WTO dispute settlement reports has referred to "principles of justice", and most domestic courts (also in the European Community and the United States) tend to ignore WTO obligations and WTO dispute settlement rulings. This incoherence in the multilevel "judicial governance" of international trade disputes runs counter not only to the basic ideas of rule of law and rules-based, democratic governance, but also to the underlying economic rationale of the WTO objective of "providing security and predictability to the multilateral trading system" (Article 3 DSU): The economic value of investments, trade transactions and consumer welfare is reduced if producers, investors, traders and consumers can no longer rely on legal security. Many economists, since Adam Smith, rightly emphasize that economic efficiency requires rule of law and respect for justice (*ubi commercium, ibi jus*).[6] Lack of rule of law is one of the principal causes of corruption and waste of scarce resources; the Latin-American economist Hernando de Soto, for example, explains much of the economic poverty in Latin America by inadequate protection of property rights, which operates as disincentive for borrowing, investments and enjoyment of human rights (de Soto 2000). The WTO's disregard for the legal protection of individual rights (other than intellectual property rights and the "rights to trade" protected in the 2001 WTO Protocol on the Accession of China) reflects the inefficient and non-democratic nature of "member-driven WTO governance".

Public discourse about the justice of WTO rules may contribute to rendering WTO rules more effective and more democratic

Constitutional democracies and the 2004 Treaty Establishing a Constitution for Europe increasingly emphasize the need for supplementing "representative democracy" by "participatory democracy" and "deliberative democracy" so as to promote individual and democratic self-government based on rules to which rational citizens can consent. The WTO Agreement explicitly recognizes, in its Preamble, "basic principles and objectives ... underlying this multilateral trading system". Some of these principles are specified in WTO provisions, for instance in the GATT (e.g., Articles III.2, VII.1, X.3, XIII.5, XX (j), XXIX.6, XXXVI.9) and other WTO agreements on trade in goods (e.g., Article 7.1 Agreement on Customs Valuation, Article 9 Agreement on Rules of Origin), services (e.g., Article X GATS) and trade-related intellectual property rights (e.g., in the Preamble of the TRIPS Agreement, Articles 8 and 62.4). The WTO requirement of interpreting WTO law "in accordance with customary rules of interpretation of public international law" (Article 3.2 DSU) refers to interpretative principles (such as *lex specialis*, *lex posterior*, *lex superior*) aimed at mutually coherent interpretations, based on legal presumptions of lawful conduct of states, the systemic character of international law and the mutual coherence of international rules and principles. It would strengthen public support for the WTO legal system and the individual empowerment of citizens if WTO Members and WTO dispute settlement bodies would explicitly acknowledge that WTO law must be interpreted "in conformity with principles of justice" no less than all other international treaties.

The basic principle of freedom of trade can be justified by all "liberal" (i.e., liberty-based) theories of justice, such as
- utilitarian theories defining justice in terms of maximum satisfaction of individual preferences and consumer welfare;
- libertarian theories focusing on protection of individual liberty and property rights;
- egalitarian concepts defining justice more broadly in terms of equal human rights and democratic consent; and
- international theories of justice based on sovereign equality and effective empowerment of states to increase their national welfare through liberal trade.[7]

Hence, the diversity of libertarian, egalitarian or utilitarian value preferences should not affect recognition that the WTO guarantees of freedom, non-discrimination and rule of law – by enhancing individual liberty, non-discriminatory treatment, economic welfare and poverty reduction across frontiers – reflect, albeit imperfectly, basic principles of justice. In terms of the Aristotelian distinction between "general principles of justice" (like liberty, equality, fair procedures, promotion of general consumer welfare) and particular principles of justice requiring adjustments depending on particular circumstances (cf. Aristotle 1999), WTO rule-making and WTO dispute settlement procedures can also contribute to "corrective justice" and "reciprocal justice", just as the special, differential and non-reciprocal treatment of less-developed WTO Members in numerous WTO provisions may contribute to "distributive justice". Engaging in public discourse on the justice of WTO rules and rulemaking will reduce public distrust in the WTO and contribute to clarifying the "principles underlying this trading system".

Universal human rights as "principles of justice" and "balancing principles"

As every WTO Member has accepted obligations under international law to protect and promote human rights, the WTO system, like any domestic legal and political system, will be increasingly evaluated (e.g., by civil society) from the perspective of respect for human rights. It seems unlikely that the political WTO bodies will respond to the UN proposals to adopt a "human rights approach to trade". In view of the insertion of human rights clauses into ever more regional trade agreements among WTO Members, it may, however, only be a matter of time until WTO dispute settlement bodies will be requested by complainants or defendants to interpret WTO rules with due regard to the human rights obligations of the WTO Members concerned. Such human rights clauses have rarely been invoked, so far, and call for *non-discriminatory* regulations (e.g., of health risks, supply of public services) rather than for discriminatory trade restrictions. The case law of the European courts confirms that concerns of trade diplomats – that human rights arguments may render trade disputes less predictable – are unwarranted. The universal recognition of human rights illustrates that every legal system rests not only on rules but also on general principles promoting the overall coherence of rules. In examining the potential impact of human rights as "relevant context" for interpreting WTO rules, WTO dispute settlement bodies should distinguish the following three different kinds of trade regulations:[8]

- International trade measures for promotion of human rights *abroad* must respect the "sovereign equality of states," the legitimate diversity of their national human rights laws and the often harmful effects of trade restrictions on citizen welfare and the enjoyment of human rights. The increasing recourse to UN human rights law as "objective standard" for differentiating trade preferences for LDCs may entail future WTO disputes on whether such trade differentiation can be justified in terms of human rights.
- WTO disputes over import restrictions for protection of human rights *at home* – for instance, over the European Community's import restrictions on hormone-fed beef, asbestos and the US restrictions on gam-

bling services – illustrate that WTO rules grant importing countries broad regulatory discretion regarding restrictions of imported goods with potential risks for human welfare and human rights. As UN human rights conventions prescribe minimum standards that do not prevent WTO Members from accepting higher human rights standards in regional and national human rights laws, the WTO-consistency of import restrictions designed to protect the human rights of domestic citizens may be legitimately influenced by arguments based on regional and national human rights rather than only UN human rights law. WTO law recognizes that "public morality" and "public order" may legitimately vary from one community to the other.[9] Hence, WTO dispute-settlement bodies have to respect the legitimate "margin of appreciation" of the national authorities concerned to define "public morality", "public order" and human rights in conformity with national and regional democratic preferences.

- Non-discriminatory WTO rules regulating intellectual property rights, technical and health standards, competition, environmental and investment rules, public services, private access to financial assistance in the context of trade-facilitation, and the administration of a WTO Register for private geographical indications may give rise to legal challenges whether such WTO rules are themselves consistent with national constitutional rights. WTO rules and WTO dispute settlement proceedings should respect the legitimate diversity of "balancing principles", which national and international courts (like the EC Court and the European Court of Human Rights) apply in examining whether the regulation of economic freedoms and other economic rights are consistent with human rights. The balancing principles may differ in cases of WTO obligations protecting private rights of market participants, such as "rights to trade", procedural rights, property rights and judicial remedies.

A "human rights approach" to the Doha Development Round Agreements?

From a human rights and economic perspective, the main causes of the unnecessary poverty in so many WTO member countries lie at the national level of government policies and economic regulation. The state-centred focus of international law and the lack of effective safeguards for the protection of human rights contribute to the fact that so many governments abuse trade policy powers for their protectionist self-interests rather than for the promotion of consumer welfare, general citizen interests and poverty reduction. The "member-driven" Doha Round negotiations focus more on harmful trade policy practices in developed countries (like agricultural and cotton subsidies) than on limiting "policy

space" in LDCs. A human rights approach should design trade liberalization agreements as instruments for promoting consumer welfare and protecting economic and social rights, notably in non-democratic and poor
countries without effective human rights guarantees; governments calling
for distributive justice in the WTO should prove their own commitment
to justice as defined by human rights.

*Democratic trade governance in the interest of citizens and their human
rights*

The human right to democratic self-government requires, *inter alia*, that
governments should explain to their citizens the contribution of their economic policies to the promotion of human welfare and human rights. If
WTO Members claim preferential treatment in the WTO, they should
meet their burden of proving (e.g., in their periodical reports for the
WTO "Trade Policy Review Mechanism") how their trade restrictions
and other trade policy measures contribute to the human development
of their citizens. Development and human rights bodies should assist
in such "human rights assessments" and democratic review of national
trade policy measures. Such promotion of "deliberative democracy"
could contribute to reviewing welfare-reducing trade restrictions and
the alternative use of more efficient policy instruments, including
development-oriented reforms of WTO rules empowering not only producers, traders and investors but also consumers and workers exposed
to the adjustment costs of import competition. As all future WTO negotiations depend on consensus by LDCs and by democratic parliaments,
the necessary "development focus" of future agreements is more likely
to be approved if "development commitments" focus more credibly on
trade-related adjustment problems and protection of citizen interests
and human rights in LDCs.

Reciprocal justice focusing on social adjustment capacities in LDCs

Trade liberalization tends to promote the quantity, quality and diversity
of goods and services, competition and the efficient use of scarce resources. A general exemption of LDCs from the WTO's reciprocity
principle could therefore impede economic development in LDCs. Non-
reciprocity should depend on the adjustment problems and adjustment
capabilities in LDCs. As the UN defines the 49 LLDCs by their low
GDP, their "human resource weakness" and "economic vulnerability",
the 32 WTO Members with LLDC-status deserve exemption from reciprocal liberalization commitments. The European Community's offer of a
"Round for Free" for 58 additional LDCs from Africa, the Caribbean
and the Pacific was justified on similar grounds (e.g., their "small, weak
and vulnerable economies"). The "upper income developing countries"

cooperating in the "G20" group have made their market access commitments subject to various conditions aimed at enhancing their adjustment capabilities, such as additional export opportunities in agriculture, protection of food security and rural development in LDCs and liberalization of international movements of natural services suppliers. Since more than 70 per cent of poor people in LDCs live in rural areas, LDCs legitimately insist that their farmers must be protected against the trade distortions caused by the high agricultural protectionism in developed countries.

Distributive justice: Special and differential treatment (SDT) and "aid for trade"

Many of the "small, weak and vulnerable" WTO Members cooperating in the "G90" group emphasize the need for SDT for dealing with their special development challenges, such as preference erosion, dependence on commodities and food imports, rural development, food security and supply-side limitations. Increasing their export capabilities through "aid for trade" and non-reciprocal liberalization of import barriers (e.g., for cotton) in developed countries has been recognized as a crucial component of a future "Doha bargain". The 2001 Doha Declaration further recognizes that "technical cooperation and capacity building are core elements of the development dimension of the multilateral trading system", and "sustainably financed technical assistance and capacity building programmes have important roles to play".[10] The WTO General Council's "Framework Agreement" of July 2004 called more specifically for "developing countries and in particular least developed countries to be provided with enhanced Trade-Related Technical Assistance and capacity building to increase their effective participation in the negotiations, to facilitate their implementation of WTO rules and to enable them to adjust and diversify their economies" (WTO 2004). Yet, many of the 88 proposals by LDCs for making SDT provisions in the WTO Agreements more "precise, mandatory and operational" have remained controversial because their focus on "policy space" left their contribution to promotion of human development and human rights in LDCs doubtful.

Corrective justice empowering and protecting LDCs and their citizens in the WTO dispute-settlement system

The compulsory WTO dispute-settlement system has transformed the "GATT 1947 bicycle", driven by bi-level trade negotiations at home and intergovernmental levels, into a "WTO tricycle" driven also by an ever larger number of WTO dispute-settlement findings clarifying and progressively developing WTO rights and obligations. Over the past years, LDCs have become the main users of the WTO dispute-settlement system. Notably in the area of agricultural subsidies (such as EC subsidies for sugar, US subsidies for cotton), they have successfully used the WTO dispute settlement system also for improving their bargaining position in the Doha Round negotiations (Petersmann 2005b).

Just as protection of human rights depends on procedural guarantees of "access to justice" (in terms of both access to courts and effective remedies, including legal aid for the needy), so does the contribution of WTO law to "sustainable development" in LDCs also depend on effective access of LDCs to the WTO dispute-settlement system. WTO law promotes this access by two different kinds of SDT provisions: Provisions specifying how generally applicable principles should be implemented in cases involving LDCs (e.g., WTO provisions on composition of dispute settlement panels, determination of a "reasonable period" for implementing dispute settlement findings), and compensating the lack of financial and legal resources of LDCs in WTO dispute settlement proceedings (e.g., Article 27.2 DSU, the Advisory Center for WTO Law), have proven effective and need to be further extended. Procedural privileges exclusively available for LDCs only (cf. Articles 3.12, 21.2, 21.7 and 8 DSU) have, however, been invoked only reluctantly (Roessler 2004).

Effective use of the WTO dispute-settlement system by LDCs is closely linked to effective legal and judicial remedies at national levels, as illustrated by the private rights to initiate WTO dispute settlement proceedings pursuant to Section 301 of the US Trade Act and the corresponding EC Trade Barriers Regulation, which have enhanced "private-public partnerships" and available "legal resources" in WTO litigation. Proposals for introducing special WTO remedies for LDCs (such as financial damages and attorney's fee awards) remain controversial. The still-limited number of LDCs actively using the dispute settlement panel, appellate and arbitration procedures of the WTO illustrates the need for additional financial, technical and legal assistance and "capacity building" for the benefit of LDCs, which often lack a citizen-driven, transparent rule-of-law system limiting domestic and foreign power politics.

"Sustainable development" as individual empowerment and protection of human rights

Similar to the focus of human rights on empowering individuals and people and protecting their rights against domestic abuses by their own governments, WTO law should focus on empowering private economic actors and consumers by protecting their rights against welfare-reducing abuses of trade policy powers at national and international levels. In the 2001 Doha Declaration, WTO Members "recognize[d] the need for all our peoples to benefit from the increased opportunities and welfare gains that the multilateral trading system generates". This contribution has suggested that these citizen interests – in order to reduce poverty and the welfare-reducing protectionism of governments more effectively – must be legally protected more effectively by defining the WTO objective of "sustainable development" in terms of human rights and by empowering "WTO citizens" as legal subjects and democratic owners of the WTO legal system. This focus on empowerment of individuals is in line with the long emphasis by economists – from Adam Smith via Friedrich Hayek up to Nobel Prize-winning economist Amartya Sen – that market economies and economic welfare are mere instruments for enabling and promoting individual freedom as the ultimate goal of economic life and the most efficient means of realizing general welfare.[11] It also reflects the universal recognition – in UN human rights conventions – of "the inherent dignity and of the equal and inalienable rights of all members of the human family [as] the foundation of freedom, justice and peace in the world". As governments and WTO dispute settlement bodies are legally required to interpret international treaties "in conformity with principles of justice" as defined also by universal human rights, WTO Members should recognize for the world trading system what the World Bank has long since recognized for its development assistance: "Sustainable development is impossible without human rights", just as "advancement of an interconnected set of human rights is impossible without development" (World Bank 1998: 2) and without a mutually beneficial world trading system protecting individual rights to produce, invest, trade and consume on the basis of rule of law and respect for human rights. This does not mean transforming economic organizations into human rights organizations. Yet, European economic integration demonstrates that "integration law" can, and should, reinforce promotion of freedom, rule of law and peaceful international cooperation for the benefit of citizens.

Notes

1. The speech of Kofi Annan is reproduced in UN document GA/105000 of 19 September 2006.
2. Apart from a reference to patents and their possibly adverse effects on pharmaceutical prices (depending on the competition, patent and social laws of the countries concerned), the report nowhere identifies conflicts between WTO rules and human rights.
3. For a discussion of these reports (with references for the following quotations) see Petersmann (2004).
4. E.g., the 1989 UN Convention on the Rights of the Child (ratified by more than 190 states) and the 1993 Vienna Declaration of the UN World Conference on Human Rights, in which more than 170 UN member states recognized that "the universal nature of (human) rights and freedoms is beyond question" (para. 1).

5. See the broad interpretation of UN human rights as international *jus cogens*, and as constitutional limitation of intergovernmental powers also of UN bodies, by the EC Court of First Instance (2006) in Cases T-315/01 (*Kadi v Council and Commission*) and T-306/ 01 (*Yusuf v Council and Commission*), judgements of 21 September 2005, in: *Common Market Law Reports 2005*, at 1334.
6. The founding father of economics, Adam Smith, justified his "system of natural liberty" on considerations of both economic welfare and justice: "Justice is the main pillar that upholds the whole edifice. If it is removed, the immense fabric of human society ... must in a moment crumble into atoms" (Smith 2000).
7. For overviews of these theories see Garcia (2004), Petersmann (2006c) and Kapstein (2006).
8. For a detailed explanation see Petersmann (2006d).
9. See, e.g., the footnote to GATS Article XIV(a), which states, "The public order exception may be invoked only where a genuine and sufficiently serious threat is posed to one of the fundamental interests of society."
10. WT/MIN801)/DEC/W/1, paras. 2, 38.
11. See Sen (2002), e.g., chapter 17 on "markets and freedoms"; Hayek (1960), at 35: "Economic considerations are merely those by which we reconcile and adjust our different purposes, none of which, in the last resort, are economic (except those of the miser or the man for whom making money has become an end in itself)." On legal protection of "market freedoms" see: Petersmann (2005a).

REFERENCES

Aristotle (1999) *Nicomachean Ethics*, M. Ostwald, ed., book five, Englewood Cliffs, N.J.: Prentice Hall.

de Soto, H. (2000) *The Mystery of Capital: Why Capitalism Triumphs in the West and Fails Everywhere Else*, New York: Basic Books.

Dworkin, R. (2006) *Justice in Robes*, Cambridge, Mass.: Harvard University Press.

ECOSOC (2000) "Globalization and Its Impact on the Full Enjoyment of Human Rights", E/CN.4/Sub.2/2000/12, 15 June.

Fuller, L. L. (1969) *The Morality of Law*, New Haven, Conn.: Yale University Press.

Garcia, F. J. (2004) *Trade, Inequality and Justice: Toward a Liberal Theory of Just Trade*, New York: Transnational Publishers.

Hayek, F. A. (1960) *The Constitution of Liberty*, Chicago: University of Chicago Press.

Higgins, R. (1978) "Conceptual Thinking about the Individual in International Law", *New York Law School Review* 24: 11–29.

ILO (1998) "ILO Declaration on Fundamental Principles and Rights at Work", CIT/1998/PR20A, Geneva: ILO, 19 June.

Joerges, C., and Petersmann, E. U. (2006) *Constitutionalism, Multilevel Trade Governance and Social Regulation*, Oxford: Hart Publishing Press.

Kapstein, E. B. (2006) *Economic Justice in an Unfair World: Toward a Level Playing Field*, Princeton, N.J.: Princeton University Press.

Petersmann, E. U. (2004) "The Human Rights Approach Advocated by the UN High Commissioner for Human Rights and by the International Labour Organization: Is It Relevant for WTO Law and Policy?", *Journal of International Economic Law* 7(3): 605–627.

Petersmann (2005a) "Human Rights and International Trade Law", in T. Cottier, J. Pauwelyn and E. Bürgi Bonanomi, eds, *Human Rights and International Trade*, Oxford: Oxford University Press, pp. 29–94.

Petersmann, E. U. (2005b) "Strategic Use of WTO Dispute Settlement Proceedings for Advancing WTO Negotiations on Agriculture", in Petersmann, ed., *Developing Countries in the Doha Round*, Oxford: Oxford University Press, pp. 143–160.

Petersmann, E. U. (2006a) "Human Rights, Markets and Economic Welfare", in F. M. Abbott, C. Breining-Kaufmann and T. Cottier, eds, *International Trade and Human Rights: Foundations and Conceptual Issues*, Ann Arbor: University of Michigan Press, pp. 29–68.

Petersmann, E. U. (2006b) "Human Rights, Constitutionalism and the WTO: Challenges for WTO Jurisprudence and Civil Society", *Leiden Journal of International Law* 19: 633–667.

Petersmann, E. U. (2006c) "Theories of Justice, Human Rights and the Constitution of International Markets", in Symposium on the Emerging Transnational Constitution, *Loyola Law Review* 37: 407–460.

Petersmann, E. U. (2006d) "WTO Dispute Settlement Practice 1995–2005: Lessons from the Past and Future Challenges", in Y. Taniguchi, A. Yanovich and J. Bohanes, eds, *The WTO at Ten: Dispute Settlement, Multilateral Negotiations and Regional Integration*, Geneva: WTO, pp. 38–94.

Reisman, W. M. (2006) "A Judge's Judge: Justice Florentino P. Feliciano's Philosophy of the Judicial Function", in S. Charnovitz, D. Steger and P. van den Bossche, eds, *Law in the Service of Human Dignity: Essays in Honour of Florentino Feliciano*, Cambridge: Cambridge University Press, pp. 3–10.

Roessler, F. (2004) "Special and Differential Treatment of Developing Countries under the WTO Dispute Settlement System", in F. Ortino and E. U. Petersmann, eds, *The WTO Dispute Settlement System 1995–2003*, London: Kluwer Law International, pp. 87–90.

Sen, A. (2002) *Rationality and Freedom*, Cambridge, Mass.: Belknap Press.

Smith, A. (2000) *The Theory of Moral Sentiments*, New York: Prometheus Books.

UN (1995) *The United Nations and Human Rights 1945–1995*, Geneva: United Nations Publications.

UN (2002) "Globalization and Its Impact on the Full Enjoyment of Human Rights", E/CN.4/2002/54, Geneva, 15 January.

World Bank (1998) "Development and Human Rights: The Role of the World Bank", Washington, DC: World Bank.

WTO (2004) "Doha Work Programme – Decision Adopted by the General Council on 1 August 2004", WT/L/579, Geneva, 2 August.

Yourow, H. C. (1996) *The Margin of Appreciation Doctrine in the Dynamics of European Human Rights Jurisprudence*, Lieden: Brill.

10

A human rights approach to "sustainable development" within the World Trade Organization

Jens Pössel*

In the age of globalization, international integration and the rule-of-law, we are witnessing a rapid change in global society. The "Four Freedoms" address of US President F. D. Roosevelt in January 1941 envisaged a new, post-war international order that was to rest on four pillars, trade and finance on the one hand, and peace and human rights on the other. Based on this speech, the first two pillars were further developed at the Bretton Woods Conference in 1944, resulting in the predecessor of the World Trade Organization (WTO) – the General Agreement on Tariffs and Trade (GATT) of 1947; human rights and the establishment of a legal framework for a peaceful post-war order were left to the new United Nations. The shared goals of the legal instruments for both international trade and human rights find their expression in Article 28 of the Universal Declaration of Human Rights of 1948: "Everyone is entitled to a social and international order in which the rights and freedoms set forth in this Declaration can be fully realised".

Since then, trade and its rules have become increasingly more important within national and international economic activities. The multilateral rules-based trading system has made a significant contribution to world economic growth and stability over the past fifty years, with the volume of merchandise trade increasing 18-fold and the trade of manufactured goods increasing 43-fold between 1948 and 1998 (Sampson 2001: 16–17). Moreover, as of January 2007, 150 states were Member States to the WTO, founded in 1995, with another 29 accessions pend-

Developing countries and the WTO: Policy approaches, Sampson and Chambers (eds), United Nations University Press, 2008, ISBN 978-92-808-1153-7

ing.[1] The WTO has been given extensive authority within the field of international economic affairs, resulting in an increasing involvement of the organization in matters that do not merely focus on trade, but that may be affected by trade, such as sustainable development.

The interrelatedness of trade, development and human rights becomes ever more obvious from the consequences of open markets on labour in developed countries to the realization of work and environmental standards in developing countries, from the question of trade-restrictive measures to protect public health to barriers to full participation by developing countries in the international economic system (Robinson 2001: 210). WTO rules, although essentially aimed only at liberalization of trade, have a potential impact on almost all other sectors of society and law. From both an economic and a social perspective, stable and rules-based societies constitute a necessary condition for sustainable development, a well-functioning world economy and a multilateral trading system (Robinson 2001: 211). Sustainable development has become a regularly expressed term within multilateral treaties and trade negotiations. Besides its incorporation in the Preamble of the WTO Agreement, the Doha Development Agenda, launched in November 2001, represents probably the most prominent and crucial round of trade negotiations, emphasizing the commitment of WTO Member States to the objective of sustainable development.[2]

The purpose of this chapter is to explore the human rights dimension of the term "sustainable development". Sustainable development essentially consists of three different, interdependent pillars. These are economic development, social development and environmental protection. Environmental protection has played an important role within the context of international trade and sustainable development. Whilst recognizing the significance of environmental protection for the realization of sustainable development, this article will nevertheless focus on the two other pillars within the concept of sustainable development, economic and social development. Although the pillar of environmental protection surely has implications on the realization and enjoyment of human rights, which are worth exploring further, in the context of this chapter the pillars of economic and social development provide a useful basis to explore the human rights dimension of sustainable development within the multilateral trading system. Hence, the starting point of this research is the examination of the relationship between the WTO and sustainable development objectives. From the very first day, the multilateral trading system has been committed to raising the standards of living and ensuring full employment.[3] Besides, the term sustainable development is appearing more and more often on the international trade agenda. Regarding this relationship from the legal perspective, it seems clear that the achievement of sustainable development is one of the main objectives of the WTO.

The next step will focus on an examination of the term "development". To be able to elaborate a human rights approach to sustainable development within the WTO, it is vital to define "development" as such. The legal basis for the human rights approach to sustainable development is the Declaration on the Right to Development of 1986. Importantly, it is possible to reconcile the two different legal regimes of international trade and human rights through the elaboration of a human rights approach to sustainable development, because the notion of sustainable development is one of the key elements of the human right to development. Moreover, achieving sustainable development always goes hand in hand with the progressive realization of human rights.

After establishing this legal basis, it is then necessary to take the different pillars of sustainable development within the context of international trade and its impact on the enjoyment of the right to sustainable development, as well as other human rights crucial to the development process, into consideration. To finally establish a direct link between trade, sustainable development and human rights, four different human rights essential to the development process[4] will be put into the context of one of the pillars of sustainable development. These rights are the right to non-discrimination, the right to work, the right to food and the right to health, all of which can be directly affected by international trade. Moreover, their realization forms part of the economic or social development process.

The chapter will conclude that sustainable development, besides environmental protection, essentially means nothing else but the effective realization of particular human rights associated with the economic and social development process. The globalization of human rights and of economic integration law offers mutually beneficial synergies: protection and enjoyment of human rights depend also on economic resources and on integration law opening markets, reducing discrimination and enabling a welfare-increasing division of labour (Petersmann 2002: 621). As a corollary, economic, legal and political integration are also a function of human rights protecting personal autonomy, legal and social security, peaceful change, individual savings, investments, production and mutually beneficial transactions across frontiers. It is therefore vital for WTO Member States to consider the human rights dimension of their respective trade policies. Furthermore, sustainable development is a goal that needs to be accomplished both on the domestic and the global level. Especially the WTO as one of the major players in the field of global economic activities should therefore consider the human rights dimensions of their activities.

The right to "sustainable development"

The WTO and sustainable development

The transformation of the General Agreement on Tariffs and Trade (GATT) into the WTO in 1995 changed the multilateral trading system fundamentally, resulting in significant differences between the former and the new multilateral trade regime (Ross-Larson 2003: 33). The GATT system was primarily about negotiating market access for traded goods. But the WTO's extension into new substantive areas and intrusiveness into domestic policymaking, its "single-undertaking" mandate, the explicit linkage of trade with protection of investment and intellectual property rights and strict enforcement of disputes and cross-retaliation have extended its authorities into areas of domestic regulation, legislation, governance and policymaking. The WTO has become one of the key players in international economic relations, fostering economic development through trade liberalization and rules that govern trade. The parties to the founding agreement of the World Trade Organization determined themselves to preserve the basic principles and to further the objectives underlying the multilateral trading system.[5] The Marrakesh Agreement establishing the WTO is the umbrella agreement for the entire WTO system and has thus a special status. Its preamble is the most comprehensive statement of the objectives of the WTO system:

The Parties to this Agreement,

Recognizing that their relations in the field of trade and economic endeavour should be conducted with a view to raising standards of living, ensuring full employment and a large and steadily growing volume of real income and effective demand, and expanding the production of and trade in goods and services, while allowing for the optimal use of the world's resources in accordance with the objective of sustainable development, seeking both to protect and preserve the environment and to enhance the means for doing so in a manner consistent with their respective needs and concerns at different levels of economic development,

Recognizing further that there is need for positive efforts designed to ensure that developing countries, and especially the least developed among them, secure a share in the growth in international trade commensurate with the needs of their economic development,

Being desirous of contributing to these objectives by entering into reciprocal and mutually advantageous arrangements directed to the substantial reduction of tariffs and other barriers to trade and to the elimination of discriminatory treatment in international trade relations,

Resolved, therefore, to develop an integrated, more viable and durable multi-lateral trading system encompassing the General Agreement on Tariffs and Trade, the results of past trade liberalization efforts, and all of the results of the Uruguay Round of Multilateral Trade Negotiations,

Determined to preserve the basic principles and to further the objectives underlying this multilateral trading system.

It is necessary, pursuant to Article 31 of the Vienna Convention on the Law of Treaties (Vienna Convention), to interpret a treaty in accordance with the ordinary meaning to be given to the terms of the treaty in their context and in the light of its object and purpose. More precisely, Article 31(3)(c) of the Vienna Convention directs that in interpreting a treaty, account must be taken not only of the treaty itself (*in casu*, the WTO treaty) but also of "any relevant rules of international law applicable in the relations between the parties" (Pauwelyn 2001: 542–543) Moreover, customary international law applies generally to the economic relations between the WTO members, as long as the WTO treaties themselves do not contract out of it.[6] In their Ministerial Declaration of 15 April 1994, the Ministers concluding the Uruguay Round of Trade Negotiations affirm that the establishment of the World Trade Organization ushers in a new era of global economic cooperation, "reflecting the widespread desire to operate in a fairer and more open multilateral trading system for the benefit and welfare of their peoples".[7] Hence, one of the main objectives of the multilateral trading system is the enhancement of the people's well-being. The WTO thus exists as a means to an end (Jordan 2001: 244). That end is to enhance the welfare and living conditions of all, both on the national and the international level – for developed and developing countries alike. Essentially, it means nothing else than putting trade policy into a contextual relationship of overall national and international objectives, which include economic, social and environmental development targets. An emphasis on the commitment to the objective of sustainable development within the multilateral trading system has also been put in the Doha Declaration, reaffirming in relevant parts "the commitment to the objective of sustainable development" and the belief that "the aims of upholding and safeguarding an open and non-discriminatory multilateral trading system, and acting for the protection of the environment and the promotion of sustainable development can and must be mutually supportive". The notion of development has thus been given a central position in the aims and objectives of the World Trade Organization. One might even say that the WTO has headed toward becoming a World Trade and Sustainable Development Organization,[8] because the extended authorities that were given to the WTO are central to the development process (Ross-Larson 2003: 33). Liberalization of trade, as well as the rules governing trade, has become inseparably linked with economic development, preservation of the environment and improving social conditions (Sampson 2005: 2). It is therefore vital to consider the human rights dimension of sustainable development within the WTO, especially with regard to states' duties on the domestic and global level to promote sustainable development. By approaching the term "sustainable development" from a human rights perspective under consideration of the applicable rules of interpretation under the Vienna Convention, legal rights and obligations of WTO Member States may be clarified to a certain extent.

The UN Declaration on the Right to Development

The notion of development within a globalizing economic system emerged first in the 1960s and 1970s. The emergence of a numerically dominant group of developing countries in the international arena as a result of decolonization led to the elevation of economic development issues to the top of the international agenda in various fora (Alston 1991: 218). Initially, states sought to address these problems through attempting to reform the major international economic institutions, with only limited success, until the formation of the United Nations Conference on Trade and Development (UNCTAD) marked the point when wider issues of international economic relations were addressed within the international community of the United Nations (Orford 2001: 129). The Declaration on the Establishment of a New International Economic Order and the Charter of Rights and Duties of States were adopted by the UN General Assembly in 1974,[9] promoting a new economic environment based on equity, interdependence, common interest and cooperation of all states in order to ensure steadily accelerating economic and social development, thereby stressing that economic as well as political and other relations shall be governed by the principle of respect for human rights and international obligations.[10] It was against this background of a changing and contested international political order that the notion of a right to development emerged.[11] In 1981, the right to development was included in Article 22 of the African Charter on Human and People's Rights (Banjul Charter), stating, "All peoples shall have the right to their economic, social and cultural development with due regard to their freedom and identity and in the equal enjoyment of the common heritage of mankind"; furthermore, "States shall have the duty, individually or collectively, to ensure the exercise of the Right to Development". Subsequently, the right to development was enshrined in the 1986 Declaration on the Right to Development.[12]

Legal status of the right to development

Within the strict normative hierarchy of international law, declarations or resolutions, such as the Declaration on the Right to Development, do not have a legally binding status in international public law (they are described as *soft law*; Ipsen 1999: section 16, RN 21). Pursuant to Articles 10*ff.* of the UN Charter, they are only recommendations and do not form part of general sources of public international law. These recommendations may nevertheless lead to the formation of customary international law when States act extensively and uniformly in accordance with those recommendations. International customary law is defined in Article 38(1)(b) of the ICJ Statute as rules that emerge as evidence of a general practice accepted as law.[13] A rule can thus be defined as being customary international law if two conditions, a subjective one and an objective one, are fulfilled. The first, subjective one is the *opinio juris sive necessitate* of the States, while the second, objective one is the acting of the States in accordance to the rule.

There are some arguments in favour of the assumption that the right to development has become a secure part of the framework of international human rights law. As noted before, it was against the background of a changing and contested international political order that the notion of a right to development emerged. It has been argued that there is no source of the right to development in the international bill of rights and that it is not relevant, if it ever was, claiming that promoters of such a right were nothing more than well-meaning optimists (Donnelly 1985: 478). However, both the International Covenant on Civil and Political Rights (ICCPR) and the International Covenant on Economic, Social and Cultural Rights (ICESCR) recognize the right of all peoples to pursue their economic, social and cultural development.[14] Moreover, since the Right to Development has been enshrined in the 1986 Declaration it has frequently been affirmed within various contexts of international relations and law. The right to development has also become an increasingly important part of the United Nations human rights agenda. In 1993, the World Conference on Human Rights reaffirmed in its Article 10 the Right to Development as established in the 1986 Declaration as being a universal and inalienable right and an integral part of fundamental human rights.[15] The General Assembly (GA) of the United Nations recognized in their resolution on the right to development[16] the need to place all human rights at the top of the global agenda and, in this context, the right to development in particular (Orford 2001: 133). This resolution has been accompanied by efforts of the Secretary General to mainstream human rights within all UN activities, including those in the development area.[17] Besides the establishment of a UN Development Group (UNDG) whose aim is to coordinate development policies and decisionmaking, the right to development forms a central part of those reforms to UN development programmes and funds (ibid.: 134). Those reforms have included the establishment of a UNDG ad hoc working group on the right to development (ibid.: 135). There are a number of development policy commitments by the international community. Probably the most prominent of these commitments are the Millennium Development Goals (MDGs).[18] Within the international trade arena, the Doha Development Agenda forms part of these development policy commitments. Yet not only in the international arena have the efforts with regard to the right to development emerged – also on the national level has this right been recognized. In many countries the right to development has become part of national developmental policies. Countries like Uganda, Sweden and Bosnia and Herzegovina recently presented their experiences in mainstreaming the MDGs, an aspect of the right to development, in their national development policies.[19] South Africa is alive to the need to integrate the right to development in its development policy (ECOSOC 2004b: para. 27).

State practice is thus not only, but also, expressed at the national level. It is expressed at the regional and international level in different forums or forms, including the states' involvement in agreements with other states or in its policies, plans, budgetary allocations, authoritative judicial pronouncements and so on (ECOSOC 2004b: para. 43). The fact that states and international institutions and agencies are implementing the right to development points to the conclusion that the Declaration on the Right to Development enjoys a reasonable degree of acceptance in the practice of states. After all, one can thus say that the right to development has become part of international customary law, as States do confirm their *opinio juris sive necessitate* by acting extensively and uniformly in virtually all fields of international law according to the principles set out in the 1986 Declaration. Moreover, it applies to the economic relations of the WTO Members. There is no provision contracting out of this rule of customary international law. Indeed, by objecting the multilateral trading system to the purpose of sustainable development, the Member States explicitly confirm the developmental aspirations of the 1986 Declaration.

Definition of "development"

The 1986 Declaration promotes a relatively flexible but nevertheless people-centred approach to what is meant by "development". The Preamble states with respect to the meaning that it "is a comprehensive economic, social, cultural and political process which arises at the constant improvement of the well-being of the entire population and of all individuals on the basis of their active, free and meaningful participation in development and in the fair distribution of the benefits therefrom". This definition takes into consideration different processes that happen to take place within a developing society. Economic developments and social developments, as well as cultural and political developments, are the main pillars of development that shall lead to the constant improvement of the well-being of the whole society and the individual. Thus, development at the very least refers to the pursuit and attainment of some generally agreed high standard of human progress and well-being – mental, moral, spiritual, intellectual and physical (ECOSOC 2004b: para. 2). Since development takes place in the context of material resources or the material world and other natural forces of immaterial nature, there is necessarily an interrelatedness and interdependence between individual human progress and changes in the material conditions and the other natural forces of immaterial nature (ibid.: para. 3). These processes can only take place on the basis of active, free and meaningful participation, that is, the whole society and all individuals must exercise development collectively and individually, thereby determining the model of development, controlling the process of development and equally distributing the benefits of development. In addition, development refers to values, systems, processes and institutions of social and political governance (ibid.: para. 5). Importantly, the right to development as enshrined in the 1986 Declaration incorporates the notion of sustainable development – one of the objectives of the World Trade Organization (ibid.: summary). The definition given in the 1986 Declaration is thus a very clear and comprehensive statement on the term "development" and a useful umbrella that incorporates the various scopes of development without losing sight of the main purpose of development – the constant improvement of the well-being of the entire population and of all individuals – while at the same time being indeterminate insofar as it is necessary to define the scope of certain pillars of development, such as economic or social development, in greater detail.

Key elements of the right to development

From the legal perspective, there is no doubt that the right to development expressly identifies the rights holders – individuals and peoples as a collective. Article 2(1) clearly states that the right must not only accrue to the community or to the collective, but also to the individual human person: "The human person is the central subject of development". The General Assembly of the United Nations recognized and confirmed that the right to development is "an inalienable human right by virtue of which every human person and all peoples are entitled to participate in, contribute to, and enjoy economic, social, cultural and political development, in which all human rights and fundamental freedoms can be fully realized".[20]

Moreover, the right to development clearly determines those with responsibility or who have an obligation to contribute to and safeguard the right – states, individuals and all peoples. Article 2(3) of the Declaration stipulates, "States have the right and the duty to formulate appropriate national development policies that aim at the constant improvement of the well-being of the entire population and of all individuals, on the basis of their free and meaningful participation in development and in the fair distribution of the benefits resulting therefrom". This provision must be read in conjunction with Article 3, which provides that it is the primary responsibility of states to create national and international conditions that are in favour to the realization of the right to development, thereby requiring full respect for principles of international law. Article 6(3) of the Declaration reads, "States should take steps to eliminate obstacles to development resulting from failure to observe civil and political rights, as well as economic, social and cultural rights". States have the primary responsibility to promote the realization of these rights on the international level, as well as on the national level. Therefore, the state is to be seen as the agent of the community and the individual in particular, since "states should realize their rights and fulfil their duties in such a manner as to promote a new international economic order based on sovereign equality, interdependence, mutual interest and co-operation among all States, as well as to encourage the observance and realization of human rights".[21]

The right to development is a self-standing right (ECOSOC 2004b: summary). At the same time, it is a composite of all other internationally recognized rights and freedoms. The right to development involves the realization of human rights and fundamental freedoms, and implies the full realization of the right of peoples to self-determination.[22] The Declaration states furthermore that all human rights and fundamental freedoms are indivisible and interdependent, and that equal attention and urgent consideration should be given to the implementation, promotion and protection of civil, political, economic, social and cultural rights.[23] By recalling the provisions of the ICESCR and those of the ICCPR, the General Assembly links its declaration directly to international human rights treaties that most of the Member States to the WTO have signed or ratified. The ICESCR, as well as the ICCPR, emphasizes the right of all peoples to freely direct and strive for their economic, social and cultural development. Article 1(1) of the ICESCR and Article 1(1) of the ICCPR provide identically that "All peoples have the right to self-determination. By virtue of that right they freely determine their political status and freely pursue their economic, social and cultural development."

Further key elements of the right to development include the requirement of direct participation by the people in development, the right to peace and security and the right and principle of self-determination (ECOSOC 2004b: summary). In the context of international trade, the fair distribution of the benefits of development, as stipulated in Article 2(3) of the 1986 Declaration, is one of the most important key elements of the right to development. Besides, the notion of sustainable development is inherent to the Right to Development, and is crucial within the context of the WTO. By referring to economic and social development, the definition of "development" in the 1986 Declaration embraces two pillars of sustainable development. In pursuing the right to development, it is paramount to take into account local and global contexts that provide enabling or disabling environments.

Conclusion

The WTO as one of the major international economic institutions plays an important role in enhancing sustainable development. Development has been given a central position in the aims and objectives of the multilateral trading system due to the extended responsibilities that have been given to the WTO. The main fields of activity of the WTO, trade liberalization and the creation of rules governing trade, have become inextricably linked to different parts of development, such as economic and social development. The human rights dimension of development within the WTO becomes apparent when the 1986 Declaration is taken into consideration to fill the abstract term of "development" with essential meaning. The 1986 Declaration provides a useful legal definition of the term. Essentially, development in itself does not mean anything else than the progressive realization of universally recognized human rights. Importantly, the Right to Development has achieved the status of customary international law and has thus binding character for all WTO Member States. The subject of development is the individual and the community, whereas states are the agents of the rights-holders. Besides, the 1986 Declaration provides a legally binding link between development and core international human rights treaties, the ICCPR and the ICESCR. Human rights are therefore inextricably linked to development, whilst development is inseparably linked to trade. Importantly, the Right to Development incorporates the notion of sustainable development by incorporating two main pillars, economic and social development, into the definition of development. A human rights-based approach to sustainable development and international trade is therefore indispensable to achieve this development. Economic and social development must contribute to, and be part of, the realization of human rights set out in the 1986 Declaration, the ICCPR and the ICESCR. From this fundamental argument, the human rights dimension of the term "sustainable development" within the WTO can be elaborated further.

The multilateral trading system and the right to sustainable development

The notion of sustainable development is one of the key elements of the right to development. Moreover, the achievement of sustainable development is a formal goal of the World Trade Organization (Sampson 2005: viii), and has found its way into the Preamble of the founding international agreement of the multilateral trading system, the Marrakesh Agreement. The objective of sustainable development has been strongly reaffirmed in the Doha Declaration by stating the conviction that "the aims of upholding and safeguarding an open and non-discriminatory multilateral trading system, and acting for the protection of the environment and the promotion of sustainable development can and must be mutually supportive".[24] Acknowledging that the multilateral trading system has played a significant role in economic growth, development and employment throughout the past fifty years,[25] the multilateral trading system plays an important role in enhancing development at the economic, social and environmental level. In this context, it is of even greater importance to recognize and realize the right to development in its multidimensional aspects, taking a balanced, integrated and multidimensional approach to sustainable development within the WTO.

Definition of "sustainable development"

Many definitions of the term "sustainable development" have been introduced over the years. The most commonly cited definition comes from the report *Our Common Future*,[26] more commonly known as the "Brundtland Report", which states, "Sustainable development is development that meets the needs of the present without compromising the ability of future generations to meet their own needs".

This definition of sustainable development contains two key concepts: The concept of needs, in particular the essential needs of the world's poor, to which overriding priority should be given; and the idea of limitations imposed by the state of technology and social organization on the environment's ability to meet present and future needs.[27] Thus, sustainable development focuses on improving the quality of life for all of the Earth's citizens without increasing the use of natural resources beyond the capacity of the environment to supply them indefinitely.[28] It seeks to develop means of supporting economic growth while supporting biodiversity and relieving poverty without using up natural capital in the short term at the expense of long-term development.[29] It requires an understanding that inaction has consequences and that we must find innovative ways to change institutional structures and influence individual behaviour, that is, it means that we must take action and change policies at all levels, from the individual to the international.[30] Sustainable development policies encompass three general policy areas: economic, environmental and social. In support of this, several United Nations texts, most recently the 2005 World Summit Outcome Document, refer to the "interdependent and mutually reinforcing pillars" of sustainable development as economic development, social development and environmental protection (UNGA 2005), thereby emphasizing that "poverty eradication, changing unsustainable patterns of production and consumption and protecting and managing the natural resource base of economic and social development are overarching objectives of and essential requirements for sustainable development". The objective of sustainable development is to maximize the goals across all three systems, which can be seen as interlocked (Elliot 2006: 9).

These definitions need to be put in context to the definition of development under the 1986 Declaration. Sustainable development can then be seen as elaborating in more detail two main pillars of development, economic and social development, while at the same time emphasizing the need for environmental protection. All the given definitions of the term imply a human rights dimension of development. Poverty eradication or the fulfilment of the essential needs of the world's poor mean at the very least the realization of economic and social rights. Although environmental protection does surely have implications on human rights as well, and is a crucial and essential pillar of sustainable development as such, the elaboration of a human rights-based approach to sustainable development will focus on the two pillars of economic and social development within the context of sustainable development and the international trade system of the WTO.

Economic development

Different aspects of economic development have been emphasized in the context of sustainable development. While traditional economics is primarily concerned with the efficient, least-cost allocation of scarce productive resources and with the optimal growth of these resources over time so as to produce an ever-expanding range of goods and services, economic development has a greater scope – it can be defined as the development of economic wealth of countries or regions for the well-being of their inhabitants (Hoselitz 1995: 9). Besides dealing with the efficient allocation of existing scarce (or idle) productive resources and with their sustained growth over time, the economic development process needs to deal with legal and institutional adjustments that have to be made to give incentives for innovation and investment so as to develop an efficient production and distribution system for goods and services. Bearing in mind that all three pillars of sustainable development are closely interrelated, economic development can after all be defined as a sustainable increase in living standards that implies increased per capita income and better education and health, as well as environmental protection. Economies and economic systems must be viewed in this broad perspective, since economic development in times of rapidly growing global trade within the multilateral trading system forces many countries that have not picked up the pace of "developed" countries to perform a rapid process, which, if it is to take root in a society, must penetrate widely and deeply and hence affect the social structural and cultural facets of a society (ibid.: 17). In other words, economic development consists not merely of a change of production techniques, but also, in the last resort, in a reorientation of social norms and values. It is therefore obvious that economic development must be analysed within the context of the overall social and legal system of a country and within the international, global context as well.

International economic institutions, such as the IMF, the World Bank and the WTO, are the key agents of global economic development. Economic and investment liberalization is largely carried out multilaterally. The WTO is seen in this context as the deliverer of higher living standards, free markets and economic development to the benefit of those who participate in the system. Competition, growth and non-discrimination are promoted effects of the trading system. Economic development shall first and foremost take place by a share of growth in international trade, trade liberalization and reciprocal and mutually advantageous arrangements directed to the substantial reduction of tariffs and other barriers to trade and to the elimination of discriminatory treatment in international trade relations.[31] The promoted benefits of the WTO trading system are the raise in income through trade, the cuts of costs of living and stimulated economic growth, to name but a few. These benefits of the WTO trading system have direct implications upon economic development. Economic development in turn has direct implications on the fulfilment of human rights. Within this context, international trade can have massive impacts upon certain human rights that are in terms of the 1986 Declaration included in the definition of development. The focus of this examination will lie upon two relevant provisions of the ICESCR, since those are rights *de facto* affected by trade and economic development. On the one hand, the right to non-discrimination is of particular concern in the context of international trade and economic development. On the other, the right to work and the right to just and favourable conditions are equally important to economic development within the multilateral trading system. Nevertheless, the aim of this part of the thesis is not to identify all possible human rights that can be affected, that is, the examples given are not exhaustive, but rather to highlight those rights that are *de facto* affected.

The right to non-discrimination

Globalization has brought a new focus on discrimination. On the one hand, the lowering of borders and improvements in information technology associated with globalization have brought people, products and services closer together. At the same time, this means that a range of new options for cultural and commercial exchange and economic growth has opened up, but on the other hand the striking inequalities both within and between countries are more clearly demonstrated through globalization (ECOSOC 2004a: 4). The greater flow of people, services and products promoted by globalization has highlighted the need to understand and accommodate difference, diversity and inequality. The principle of non-discrimination is one of the fundamental principles of the international human rights system. Article 2 of the Universal Declaration of Human Rights (UDHR) states, "Everyone is entitled to all the rights and freedoms set forth in this Declaration, without distinction of any kind, such as race, colour, sex, language, religions, political or other opinion, national or social origin, property, birth or other status". Similarly, Article 2.2 of the ICESCR provides that "The States Parties to the present Covenant undertake to guarantee that the rights enunciated in the present Covenant will be exercised without discrimination of any kind as to race, colour, sex, language, religion, political or other opinion, national or social origin, property, birth or other status". While the ICESCR does not provide for a definition of the term in their statement of the principle, it is generally accepted that the principle of non-discrimination prohibits any distinction, exclusion, restriction or preference having the purpose or effect of impairing or nullifying the recognition, enjoyment or exercise by all persons, on an equal footing of all rights and freedoms.[32] This definition includes four noteworthy elements. Firstly, the primary concerns of the principle of non-discrimination are state laws, policies and practices, but it also applies to private actors; secondly, there are no final prohibited categories of discrimination, that is, they are open-ended; thirdly, there is no requirement to demonstrate discriminatory intention; and finally and of significant importance, the principle of non-discrimination applies to both *de jure* and *de facto* discrimination (ECOSOC 2004a: para. 11). It is important to note that not every differentiation of treatment will constitute discrimination, if the criteria of such differentiation are reasonable and objective and if the aim is to achieve a purpose that is legitimate under the Covenant.[33]

In international trade, the principle of non-discrimination is an important element of trade and investment treaties and one of the underlying doctrines of the WTO Agreements. It is based upon two core elements. The first one is the principle of most-favoured-nation (MFN) treatment, which requires each WTO Member State to grant to every other Member State the most favourable treatment that it grants to any other country with respect to the import and export of "like" goods, services and service suppliers. Article 1 of GATT states in this respect that "any advantage, favour, privilege or immunity granted by any Member to any product originating in or destined for any other country shall be accorded immediately and unconditionally to the like product originating in or destined for the territories of all other Members", whereas Article II of the General Agreement on Trade in Services states according to the MFN principles that "With respect to any measure covered by this Agreement, each Member shall accord immediately and unconditionally to services and service suppliers of any other Member treatment no less favourable than that it accords to like services and service suppliers of any other country". In relation to intellectual property protection, the WTO Agreement on Trade-Related Aspects of Intellectual Property Rights (the TRIPS Agreement), MFN treatment requires that any advantage, favour, privilege or immunity relating to intellectual property protection (IPP) that is granted by a WTO member to the nationals of any other country shall be accorded immediately and unconditionally to the nationals of all other WTO members.[34]

The second core element is the national treatment obligation of each Member State. The national treatment obligation concerns competition between national and foreign goods, services and service suppliers. It requires each WTO Member State to treat foreign goods, services and service suppliers no less favourably than "like" domestic goods, services and service suppliers once they have crossed the border and they are part of domestic commerce (ECOSOC 2004a: para. 9). The fundamental purpose of national treatment in relation to trade in goods is to avoid protectionism in the application of internal tax and regulatory measures. Some discriminatory measures are permitted under trade rules within the multilateral trading system as well. Such flexibilities include general exceptions and country-specific flexibilities.[35]

As with the human rights principle of non-discrimination, MFN treatment and national treatment protect against both *de jure* and *de facto*, as well as direct and indirect discrimination.[36] Furthermore, both justify differential treatment in some cases where formal equality might not achieve the purposes of the prohibition on discrimination.[37] Nonetheless, the goals of the two principles are in many ways quite different. While the human rights principle of non-discrimination is intrinsically linked with the principle of equality, the trade principle of non-discrimination is primarily directed toward reducing trade protectionism and improving international competitive conditions rather than achieving substantive equality (ECOSOC 2004a: para. 26).

Besides the application of the trade principle of non-discrimination and its exceptions, the application of the human rights principle of non-discrimination in international trade can have a downright positive effect on economic development. Respect for the principle of non-discrimination can be of particular importance for women, indigenous people and rural populations amongst other categories of individuals. With respect to gender equality, for example, women often face discriminatory circumstances. Women often have the role of caretakers of families and communities. In many societies they dominate caring roles such as nurses and nursing aides. This leads to different needs, for example, concerning health services, particularly with regard to reproductive rights (OHCHR 2003: 6). In relation to HIV/AIDS, women often face a disproportionate burden of caring for family members with HIV/AIDS and, very often, assume responsibility for children orphaned by AIDS, while at the same time access to medication for women can prevent mother-to-child transmission of HIV. Within rural populations, discrimination sometimes also exists against women. Specifically, women can suffer as a result of intra-household relations that lead to incomplete pooling of household resources between men and women (ECOSOC 2004a: 13). Besides, women are confronted with serious impediments in gaining access to credit and traditional gender biases can distance women from important development opportunities (UNCTAD 2002: 116).

Also, small farmers and the rural poor continue to suffer from inequality and discrimination, often resulting from explicit legal inequalities in status and entitlements, deeply rooted social distinctions and exclusions and the application of neutral policies – including trade rules and policies – to the products of farmers with different resources and capacities (ECOSOC 2004a: 13). Current estimates indicate that the rural poor outnumber the urban poor in most developing countries, at times by a factor of two, and rural poverty tends to be deeper than urban poverty, with the rural poor suffering from lower levels of access to basic services such as drinking water, health and sanitation services and primary education, all of which are human rights guaranteed for in the ICESCR. The income disparity between urban and rural areas is widening in many countries and the rural poor face enormous obstacles in breaking the poverty cycle (FAO 2002: 29). Market distortions due to market access barriers to the agricultural exports of developing countries and subsidized competition from developed countries can affect rural development in poorer countries by constraining agricultural growth and even reducing agricultural growth as small farm incomes are reduced by decreasing agricultural commodity prices (ibid.: 30). This leads to the assumption that the root cause of the massive crisis of small farming communities, of rural poverty and hunger in poor agricultural countries lies in the exposure of poorly equipped and unproductive small farming communities to competition from far more productive agricultural systems (ibid.: 16). Even the incidence of external shocks in the form of depressed prices and import surges due to the fact that agricultural trade is increasingly open can further undermine domestic production.[38]

These are important examples of the impact of international trade on the human right of non-discrimination, as set out in Article 2.2 of the ICESCR and the UDHR. Trade rules and policies have thus a key role to play in alleviating rural poverty and gender discrimination. Trade offers opportunities to promote growth and economic development, which, if managed by appropriate policies, could help reduce global inequalities, rural poverty and discriminatory practices that affect populations (ECOSOC 2002). On the other hand, trade rules that do not take into account the need to alleviate rural poverty can increase the vulnerability of rural populations to external price fluctuations, expose poorer farmers to competition for which they are ill-prepared and reduce crop diversity and subsistence farming by focusing disproportionately on export crops, finally blocking the process of economic development. Respect for the principle of non-discrimination is a fundamental means of promoting a more inclusive globalization that reduces inequalities within and between nations (ECOSOC 2004a: para. 51). Lower inequality, in turn, can increase efficiency and economic growth (World Bank 2001: 56). The principle of non-discrimination is therefore not only a justifiable goal in itself, but combating discrimination and promoting equality can have a positive influence upon the dynamics of economic growth and poverty reduction (ECOSOC 2004a: para. 51). Importantly, the principle of non-discrimination is inherent in all human rights. All other human rights can therefore also be seen in the context of non-discrimination.

The right to work

Over the past two decades most international economic agreements, such as the revitalization of the European integration through the single market project and the monetary union, the North American Free Trade Agreement (NAFTA), the creation of the WTO and the attempt to negotiate a Multilateral Agreement on Investment at the OECD, have been designed to liberalize economic activity (O'Brien and Williams 2004: 215). The deregulation of labour markets was an important element in economic liberalization during the 1980s. "Flexible" labour was seen as the key to attracting foreign investment and export growth, thus fostering economic development (Oxfam 2002). Meaningful trade liberalization should promote economic growth, employment and development for all, benefiting countries at all stages of development (UNGA 2005: para. 27). With regard to employment, the central objective of all national and international policies as well as national development strategies is to achieve the goals of full and productive employment and decent work for all, including women and young people, in the support of fair globalization (ibid.: para. 47). The full realization of this goal shall include policies and techniques to achieve steady economic, social and cultural development under conditions safeguarding fundamental political and economic freedoms to the individual.[39]

The right to work is enshrined in Article 6(1) of the ICESCR, which provides that "The States Parties to the present Covenant recognize the right to work, which includes the right of everyone to the opportunity to gain his living by work which he freely chooses or accepts, and will take appropriate steps to safeguard this right". The right to work is complemented by Article 7 of the ICESCR, recognizing "the right of everyone to the enjoyment of just and favourable conditions of work which ensure, in particular, remuneration which provides all workers, as a minimum, with fair wages and equal remuneration for work of equal value without distinction of any kind, in particular women being guaranteed conditions of work not inferior to those enjoyed by men, with equal pay for equal work; a decent living for themselves and their families in accordance with the provisions of the present Covenant; and safe and healthy working conditions". Articles 6 and 7 of the ICESCR are further supplemented by the right of everyone to form trade unions and join the trade union of his choice in Article 8 of the ICESCR.

Besides the inclusion of the principle of non-discrimination in these provisions, the provisions deal with other issues, such as the individual's freedom of choice concerning work, just and favourable working conditions; health and safety issues and unionization rights.

Wages are undoubtedly among the most important conditions of work and employment at the enterprise level. Being a cost for employers as well as the main source of income for workers, wages may be a potential source of conflict.[40] At the same time, wages can represent a major source of discrimination and deprivation if no decent floor is guaranteed to the workers.[41] On the economic side, wages represent an important part of labour costs and are an essential variable for enterprises' competitiveness.[42] Wages also constitute the most direct channel between economic development and household income. Trade theory predicts that by increasing demand for labour, export growth will increase the income of households with members working in export sectors, leading to economic development (Oxfam 2002: 80). Unfortunately, economic growth has, in some parts of the world, been weakly linked to employment creation and rising wages. In Latin America, for example, real minimum wages were lower in 1999 in 13 out of 18 countries than they had been in 1980 (ECLA 2000). This apparent anomaly of the intended and possible goal of economic growth resulted out of a weak association of growth both with employment and wages (Oxfam 2002: 81). In countries such as Brazil and Peru, real wages have fallen even during periods of economic growth (Dancourt 1999; ECLA 2001). Meanwhile, urban unemployment at the end of the 1990s was twice as high as at the start of the decade (Oxfam 2002: 81). Wages in many high-growth export industries are low not just by the standards of international comparison, but also in relation to national poverty lines. Women workers in the garment industry in Bangladesh, for example, earn around US$1.50 per day, which is marginally above the poverty index of the United Nations of US$1.00 per day. Not only in Bangladesh are these wages insufficient to maintain a reasonable standard of living, but also in other countries wages remain far below the possibility for the worker to earn a decent living for himself and his family.[43] In China, many factories are run by the army, and the country has an extensive system of forced-labour camps where the labour is unpaid (Jordan 2001: 248). In southern China alone, there are 153 million manufacturing workers powering an economy unencumbered by any independent voice demanding higher standards or fair wages. One of the most often found misinterpretations is that minimum wages shall enable the worker to provide himself for a decent living. It is rather the living wage that generates this effect.

One of the most crucial issues concerning the right to work is the equal remuneration for work of equal value according to Article 7(a)(i) of the ICESCR. The gendered division of labour leads to women working in highly labour-intensive sectors such as clothing, footwear and microelectronic assembly (O'Brien and Williams 2004: 210). Being a woman in the global economy entails a much greater chance of being poorer, working harder and under worse conditions than the average man. There are various examples of how women are incorporated into the global labour market, and how the right to work and to just and favourable conditions of work are being affected by international trade. Importantly, the improvement of these conditions has significant impact upon the economic development of societies and individuals. One major example, highlighting the relationship between international trade, economic development and the right to work and the enjoyment of just and favourable conditions of work shall be focused on in the following – the relationship between women and transnational corporations (TNCs) in developing countries. Women have increasingly been integrated into global production through labour in TNCs, especially in export processing zones (EPZs). EPZs are designated areas within a country that are designed to attract foreign investment by providing financial incentives or regulatory relief from national laws. On average, 80 per cent of the workforce in these zones is female (Jordan 2001: 248). Furthermore, women now account for about one third of manufacturing workers in developing countries (Oxfam 2002: 81). The reasons for this development are manifold. Arguments range from the assumption that women are chosen because they have smaller fingers and can do more intricate work at a faster pace, to the assumption that women are more skilled at dextrous work because of having developed skills such as sewing, interpreting this skill as a biological difference rather than a difference in skill, resulting in the argument that a biological difference need not be rewarded with higher pay (O'Brien and Williams 2004: 213). Other, more reasonable, arguments point to the assumption that women make up a large percentage of the workers in EPZs because they are thought to be more compliant to manager's demands, they have less of a history of unionization and are often willing to put up with very poor working conditions to support families. The outcomes of this incorporation of women into export-oriented work are contradictive. Working conditions vary widely in TNCs. They are often very difficult, wages are poor and unions are often prohibited, exposing workers to dangerous and unhealthy working conditions and threats of physical and sexual abuse (ICFTU 1996). On the other hand, working conditions within TNCs can be better than in local firms, providing opportunity to local women (O'Brien and Williams 2004: 213–214). These opportunities have the effect that local gender roles are challenged, giving women the chance to leave restrictive home environments and secure increased status and independence from the incomes that they earn in the factories, that is, providing the opportunity to accumulate some wealth and education.

These examples illustrate perfectly that the rights set out in Articles 6, 7 and 8 of the ICESCR are massively affected by trade and economic development. In order to be able to develop economically in the era of global financial capitalism, individuals in a society must work. This leads to the accumulation of wealth, if the work is remunerated fairly and nondiscriminatorily, and allows people to gain a decent living for themselves and their families. The forming of trade unions does not only lead to a higher organization and therefore to the ability to represent the needs and interests necessary for the achievement of economic development, it also has impacts on the pillar of social development within the developing society. States, in turn, need people that develop economically to obtain sustainable economic growth. The consideration of those human rights set out in the discussed articles of the ICESCR help to build an environment which, at first, makes economic development possible, and, secondly, makes it sustainable. Sustainable economic development that benefits individuals and groups of societies, as well as societies as a whole, must therefore take into consideration the human rights dimension of the right to work, just and equal conditions of work and the right to form trade unions for the objective of sustainable development.

Social development

The second pillar, social development, is another vital aspect of sustainable development. As people, we seek positive change for ourselves, our children and grandchildren; we must do it in ways that respect the right of all to do so. To do this we must learn constantly – about ourselves, our potential, our limitations, our relationships, our society, our environment, our world. The term "social development" refers to qualitative changes in the structure and functioning of a society that help society to better realize its aims and objectives (Cleveland et al. 1999: 152). The basic mechanism driving social change is increasing awareness leading to better organization. Life evolves by consciousness and consciousness in turn progresses by organization. When society senses new and better opportunities for progress it accordingly develops new forms of organization to exploit these new openings successfully. The new forms of organization are better able to harness the available social energies and skills and resources to use the opportunities to get the intended results. Society will inevitably change or develop during this process. The human and social aspects of sustainable development mean that solidarity, equity, partnership and cooperation are as crucial as scientific approaches to environmental protection.[44] There are two human rights in the context of social development that are likely to be affected by sustainable development, and can also themselves effect sustainable social development. At the same time, it must be noted that the examples highlighted in this article are not exhaustive. At the core of social rights within the international human rights treaty system is the right to an adequate standard of living (Breining-Kaufmann 2005: 360). This implies that everyone shall enjoy the necessary subsistence rights of adequate food and nutrition, clothing, housing and the necessary conditions of care. The second, equally important social right that will be discussed is the right to health. It implies that everyone shall have the right to the enjoyment of the highest attainable standard of physical and mental health.

The right to food

Food is a most essential good for every human being to survive and plays an important part in each society's culture and policies. It is a biological necessity, a cultural statement and also commerce, since technology has increased productivity and thus made trade in food products possible (ibid.: 341). In 2002, food accounted for approximately 7 per cent of all imported/exported merchandise goods (World Bank 2004). Trade liberalization is generally a positive contributor to poverty alleviation, allowing people to exploit their productive potential, assisting economic growth, curtailing arbitrary policy interventions and helping to insulate against shocks (Ben-David et al. 2000). At the same time, however, trade liberalization creates losers even in the long run and trade reforms can exacerbate poverty temporarily (ibid.: 13). In the field of agriculture, trade liberalization is often quoted as being essential to promote growth and reduce poverty in developing countries but at the same time it is one of the most controversial and complex issues within the WTO framework (Breining-Kaufmann 2005: 342). At the core of social rights within the international human rights treaty system is the right to an adequate standard of living (ibid.: 360). This implies that everyone shall enjoy the necessary subsistence rights of adequate food and nutrition, clothing, housing and the necessary conditions of care. Article 11(1) of the ICESCR states in this respect that "The States Parties ... recognise the right of everyone to an adequate standard of living for himself and his family, including adequate food.... The States Parties will take appropriate steps to ensure the realisation of this right, recognising to this effect the essential importance of international cooperation based on free consent". It can therefore be assumed that states will use all legislative, economic, social and political means necessary to achieve the full realization of this right, including market-based mechanisms. Indeed, the ICESCR specifically identifies the need to ensure that international trade promotes the right to food (ECOSOC 2002: 7). Article 11(2) of the ICESCR states in this respect that the "States Parties to the present Covenant, recognizing the fundamental right of everyone to be free from hunger, shall take, individually and through international cooperation, the measures, including specific programmes, which are needed, taking into account the problems of both food-importing and food-exporting countries, to ensure an equitable distribution of world food supplies in relation to need". The right to food is realized when everyone has physical and economic access at all times to adequate food or means for its procurement (ECOSOC 1999: para. 19). The core content of the right implies the availability of food in a quantity and quality sufficient to satisfy the dietary needs of individuals free from adverse substances; and the economic and physical accessibility of food in ways that are sustainable and that do not interfere with the enjoyment of other human rights (ibid.: paras 8, 12–13). The link between trade and the right to food has explicitly been drawn on the World Food Summit in 1996. Commitment four of the Plan of Action adopted during this summit aims at ensuring that food, agricultural trade and overall trade policies are conducive to fostering food security for all through a fair and market-oriented world trade system.[45] This commitment is supplemented by the responsibility to implement, monitor and follow-up on the adopted Plan of Action at all levels in cooperation with the international community.[46] These commitments have been reaffirmed in the Declaration of the World Food Summit: Five Years Later – International Alliance against Hunger.[47]

WTO-regulated areas that may cause problems concerning the right to food are the Agreement on Agriculture (AoA), the SPS Agreement, the Agreement on Textiles and Clothing and the TRIPS Agreement. The focus of this examination is not, however, to provide a detailed discussion about the impacts of the relevant agreements on the right to food. Rather, trade liberalization in agriculture and the right to food need to be brought into a general context with sustainable development, making clear that it is a right that deserves to be considered within the context of international trade. Increased levels of trade in agriculture can contribute to the enjoyment of the right to food by augmenting domestic supplies of food to meet consumption needs and by optimizing the use of world resources (ECOSOC 2002: 13). Yet, especially the liberalization of agricultural trade can have immense negative impacts on certain individuals and groups. Resulting out of liberalization of markets, competitive pressure results in a general trend toward the consolidation of farms (FAO 2000). On the one hand, this consolidation process has resulted in an increase in productivity. On the other hand, it has also led to the displacement and marginalization of farm labourers, creating hardship for small farmers and food-insecure populations (ibid.: 25). For many developing countries, key agricultural sectors that were vital for the economy in terms of food security, employment, economic development and poverty reduction were being seriously eroded given the inability to compete with cheap imports (Breining-Kaufmann 2005: 368; FAO 2000). In Sri Lanka, for example, tariff reductions and the associated increase in food imports have put pressure on the rural sector, including employment (ECOSOC 2002: 13). More than 300,000 people previously involved in the production and marketing of onions and potatoes were adversely affected by tariff reductions. Another example is Guyana, where increasing imports of fruit juices from larger producers have displaced much of domestic production, resulting in a growing dependency in this country on imported foods (FAO 2000). The same picture can be observed in Brazil, where the agricultural sector has been transformed as a result of the reform process, leading to an increase in farm sizes and herds improving with large-scale firms moving in to replace traditional cooperatives. Agriculture fulfils different roles in the development of every country. In the case of low-income countries, the agricultural sector plays an essential role in ensuring food security and alleviating poverty (ECOSOC 2002: 15). In these countries, the sector is still the major employer and a significant contributor to GDP, as well as an important source for foreign exchange and revenue. Besides, food consumption accounts for a significant share of expenditure for households in many developing countries. From the perspective of development, significant progress in promoting economic growth, reducing poverty and enhancing food security cannot be achieved in most cases without developing more fully the potential capacity of the agricultural sector and enhancing its contribution to overall economic development (FAO 2000). For developed countries, the agricultural sector is often less significant as an employer and contributor to GDP, and food consumption accounts for a relatively small and decreasing share of household income (ECOSOC 2002: 15). The market access commitments of those countries toward countries with a potential competitive advantage in agricultural sector remain, however, poor. The Doha Development Agenda focuses on special and differential treatment and on market access. While special and differential treatment programmes such as the European Union and the United States GSP schemes proved to be little effective, there is consensus that liberalization by wealthy states in agriculture would assist growth and development in poor countries (Oxfam 2002: 47–63). A study of tariff peaks shows that many of them apply to major agricultural food products, such as meat, sugar, milk, diary products and chocolate, as well as to tobacco and some alcoholic beverages, and fruits and vegetables – all of which are products in which developing countries enjoy a competitive advantage (OECD 2001: 74). Quite often, such measures are associated with tariff escalation by which the tariffs on unprocessed products or raw materials are disproportionately less than the tariffs on processed products, therefore making it very difficult for poor countries to increase their incomes by processing the raw materials they produce (Breining-Kaufmann 2005: 365). Generally, tariff reductions have not been extended to all products and across broad sectors. These measures have *de facto* implications on the possibility of certain groups and individuals to develop economically and socially, and consequently on the enjoyment of the right to food set out in Article 11(1) of the ICESCR as part of the right to an adequate standard of living. Acts that constitute a violation of the right to food include the adoption of legislation or policies that are manifestly incompatible with pre-existing legal obligations relating to the right to food, the failure to regulate activities of individuals or groups so as to prevent them from violating the right to food of others, and the failure of a state to take into account its international legal obligations regarding the right to food when entering into agreements with other states or with international organizations (ECOSOC 1999: para. 19).

Since most people in the developing world derive their livelihood from agriculture, the implementation of policies that obstruct agricultural rights is undesirable – if not a violation of international norms – in a world where 840 million people are currently suffering from hunger and the effects of hunger (Thurow 2003). The importance of agriculture is shown by empirical evidence. More than 92 per cent of the population of Burkina Faso, 76 per cent of the population of Kenya and 74 per cent of Senegal's population find employment in the agricultural sector (Cullet 2001). Especially in the countries of sub-Saharan Africa, where a large proportion of the agricultural activities consist of subsistence agriculture, there is necessarily a close connection between agriculture and the fulfilment of the food needs of individuals (Edwardson 2005: 386). The similarities between the legal approach that emphasizes the multi-fold obligations of states with regard to the right to food, and the acknowledgement of the multifunctionality of trade in agriculture in the Agreement on Agriculture (AoA) are striking (Breining-Kaufmann 2005: 372). Both put the right to food and the liberalization of agricultural trade in the broader context of development and enhancing general welfare. The realization of the right to food therefore strongly depends on the rural and agricultural development. Besides, the accessibility and availability of food does have strong implications on the social and economic development of people, since it is the most essential good for humankind.

The right to health

Health is a fundamental human right indispensable for the exercise of other human rights. Every human being is entitled to the enjoyment of the highest attainable standard of health conducive to living a life in dignity. Further, health of individuals has implications on its ability to develop his personality, and his economic and social rights in dignity. The right to health is solidly enshrined in international, regional and national human rights instruments. Article 12(1) of the ICESCR provides that "The States Parties to the present Covenant recognize the right of everyone to the enjoyment of the highest attainable standard of physical and mental health". The reference in Article 12(1) of the ICESCR to "the highest attainable standard of physical and mental health" is not confined to the right to health care (ECOSOC 2000). On the contrary, the drafting

history and the express wording of article 12(2) of the ICESCR acknowledge that the right to health embraces a wide range of socio-economic
factors that promote conditions in which people can lead a healthy life,
and extends to the underlying determinants of health, such as food and
nutrition, housing, access to safe and potable water and adequate sanitation, safe and healthy working conditions and a healthy environment. According to the Constitution of the WHO, to which all Member States to
the WTO are Parties as well, "Health is a state of complete physical,
mental and social well-being and not merely the absence of disease or in-
firmity".[48] The basic elements of the right are availability, accessibility,
acceptability and quality (ECOSOC 2000: para. 12). The concept of
availability connotes functioning public health care facilities, goods and
services including relevant programmes. The precise nature of these facilities, goods and services to be provided in fulfilling the state's obligations will, however, vary from state to state and depend on a variety of
factors, including the level of development (Musungu 2005: 302). The
concept of accessibility connotes a situation where there is equitable access and rational use of quality essential medicines (Scholtz 1999).

Yet, for millions of people throughout the world, the full enjoyment of
the right to health remains a distant goal. According to the most recent
figures from the World Health Organization, 1.7 million persons died
from tuberculosis in 2004, at the same time as 8.9 million new cases were
registered.[49] From 350 to 500 million human beings suffer from malaria,
of whom 1 million – mostly children – die each year (WHO figures, in
Özden 2006). AIDS killed more than 3 million persons in 2005.[50] These
three devastating illnesses are responsible for more than 6 million deaths
every year, the overwhelming majority of which occur in the South (Özden 2006: 3). In the 2005 World Summit Outcome, HIV/AIDS, malaria,
tuberculosis and other infectious diseases have been recognized as posing
severe risks for the entire world and serious challenges to the achievement of development goals (UNGA 2005: para. 57). At the same time,
the need for a sustained international response has been emphasized.

Within the WTO trading system, the Agreement on Trade-Related Aspects of Intellectual Property Rights (TRIPS) is of particular interest for
the right to health. It is not the aim however, to provide a detailed analysis of the relationship of the human right to health and the TRIPS Agreement, but considering one situation in which the right to health can be
directly affected by the TRIPS Agreement can help in elaborating the
human rights dimension that this particular agreement has upon the objective of sustainable development. Intellectual property laws, especially
patent rights, might to a certain extent limit the enjoyment of the right to
health. The grant of a patent over processes for the manufacture of medicines or with respect to medicines themselves as products has the effect
of giving the patent holder a monopoly over the use of the processes and

or the manufacture and sale of the medicines (Musungu 2005: 306). There are various justifications that are given for granting patents, but one clear effect of the granting is that the cost for the covered technology is set at an artificially high level. Indeed, the high prices for new medicines resulting from the mandatory requirements for patent protection under TRIPS in developing countries have seriously compromised the ability of communities, governments and other players in the health sector to manage infectious and other diseases effectively. The cost disparity has virtually guaranteed that most of the sick in these regions of the world have little or no access to the best available treatments, since in most of these countries up to 90 per cent of the costs of health care for the poor are out of pocket. High drug prices also mean that governments need to spend a disproportionate amount of money on medical supplies, leaving very little for other critical health needs such as infrastructure development and training. The ICESCR contains a commitment and a legal duty to address these conditions and to transform society into one where life is based on human dignity. Article 12(2) of the ICESCR states in this respect that "the steps to be taken by the States Parties to the present Covenant to achieve the full realization of this right shall include those necessary for ... the prevention, treatment and control of epidemic, endemic, occupational and other diseases". This provision needs to be read in conjunction with Article 2(1) of the ICESCR, which imposes the duty upon the State Parties to take steps individually and through international assistance and cooperation in order to achieve progressively the full realization of the rights set out in the Covenant, including the right to health. But for as long as these conditions continue to exist for any reason, including high prices resulting from patent protection, this aim will not be possible to be achieved.[51]

The strengthening of patent protection for pharmaceutical processes and products under TRIPS has, after all, had the effect of limiting the enjoyment of the right to health as set out in Article 12 of the ICESCR. The lack in accessibility of essential medicines for the treatment of diseases such as HIV/AIDS or malaria can have devastating effects on personal economic or social development. Furthermore, in some parts of the world it already has a catastrophic effect on economies of whole states. Especially in regions where HIV/AIDS and malaria play a crucial role in the well-being of whole societies, the absence of essential medicines to treat or prevent such diseases have dramatic consequences for the development of the overall society. People that are lacking access to the basic medicines because they are simply too expensive, although they do exist, are not able to participate effectively in economic growth. It is therefore essential that the right to health be taken into consideration, especially with regard to the TRIPS Agreement and access to essential medicines.

Conclusion

The human rights approach to sustainable development opens the way for an explicitly accepted international legal human rights framework of universally recognized norms and values into the objectives of the WTO. Trade liberalization within the multilateral trading system entails changes in societies and economies, creating new opportunities for improving and realizing human rights such as the right to work, the right to an adequate standard of living or the right to health. Furthermore, trade affects the realization of human rights in various ways. All the human rights examined in this chapter are particularly affected by international trade within the multilateral trading system. The result of this examination shows clearly that international trade has an accentuating and distorting effect on structural changes within opening societies. Although general economic theory suggests that the gains of opening markets to the global economy will outweigh the losses, resulting in an overall increase in welfare of countries, the problem remains in the uneven distribution of the benefits therefrom. The examples highlighted in this part of the paper give evidence that the losses are generally felt more by marginalized and vulnerable groups within a society. The fair and equal distribution of the benefits of development, and thus sustainable development, is, however, one of the key elements of the right to sustainable development. This principle is clearly set out in the 1986 Declaration. Being a part of customary international law, the right to development sets out not only a commitment but also a legal obligation of all States to ensure that socio-economic rights are not negatively affected in the name of sustainable development. States are obliged to cooperate on the global level to realize the objective of sustainable development, and thus the right to sustainable development in particular. Whilst acknowledging the fact that economic growth and trade liberalization can and should play a positive role for sustainable development, it is necessary to put the emphasis on the essential aim of sustainable development – the enhancement of the well-being of all peoples and individuals of the world's society, not only of a few. The human rights approach to sustainable development within the WTO therefore includes the effective realization of the right to development.

Concluding remarks

The WTO is, as it is often emphasized, a rules-based system. Nothing but the rule of law shall govern the multilateral trading system. Besides the International Monetary Fund (IMF) and the World Bank, the WTO is a key player in international economic relations. It has the potential to enhance sustainable development to a large extent. Trade rules and liberalization of markets have an immense impact upon the economic and social development of individuals, communities and societies. The WTO is an agent of promoting sustainable development, if not a World Trade and Sustainable Development Organization. Sustainable development is, according to the Preamble of the Marrakesh Agreement, one of the key objectives of the multilateral trading system. This objective has further become part of the Doha Development Agenda and is frequently reaffirmed within the international trade arena.

Sustainable development *per definitionem* implies a human rights dimension on both the economic and the social pillar of development.[52] The concept of needs, elaborated already in 1987, essentially those needs of the worlds poor – opposed to the needs of TNCs, free traders or exporters – contains a clear dimension of human rights. A human rights approach to sustainable development is therefore *per definitionem* necessary to achieve this objective. The 1986 Declaration on the Right to Development provides a useful starting point for this approach. It takes a well-balanced, integrated and multidimensional approach to development by incorporating all the different facets of human development. As a matter of fact, the right to development has become a universally recognized human right over the past 20 years. Essentially, economic, social, cultural or political development is human development, since humans are always the ones that carry out development. At all levels of development the three essential capabilities are for people to lead a healthy and long life, to be knowledgeable and to have access to resources needed for a decent standard of living (UNDP 2000: 36). The right to development entails therefore the overriding necessity of the realization of the human rights set out in the International Bill of Human Rights.[53] Importantly, by embodying economic and social development into the definition of development, the 1986 Declaration integrates the notion of sustainable development. The economic and the social pillars of sustainable development can therefore be defined as a detailed elaboration of economic and social development as contained in the definition of development in the 1986 Declaration. This inclusion of the notion of sustainable development means essentially that there is a human right to sustainable development that has to be realized on both the domestic and the global level. However, the global context in which sustainable development, and thus the realization of human rights, is being pursued is not particularly human rights-friendly (ECOSOC 2004b: para. 34). A climate of hegemony of the global capitalist neo-liberal economic system that reinforces the marginalization of Third World countries through debt burdens and unfair trade relations, amongst others, prevails. Development in poor countries suffers extremely from negative terms of international trade and investment (ibid.: para. 37). Rules and decisions made by official and non-official bodies and forums, such as the World Trade Organization, the G7+1 and the World Economic Forum, determine to a large extent the space within which "development" or "underdevelopment" – and thus the realization of human rights – may occur. The gaps between rich and poor are widening not only in developing, but also in developed countries as a result of financial capitalism. As a matter of fact, financial and virtually all material resources are accumulated in the hands of a few major players that dominate not only international markets and trade, but also trade negotiations at the WTO. This leads to massive human rights impacts on the people depending on financial or other material resources to fulfil at least their basic needs of existence. As it has been shown, the human rights principle of non-discrimination is often undermined in favour of trade liberalization. Globalization under the auspices of the WTO has massive impacts on the right to work and the right to form trade unions in certain parts of the world. These rights form undoubtedly a major part of economic development. Social development and the fulfilment of human rights such as the right to food and the right to health are equally much affected by international trade, not taking into consideration other human rights crucial to the development process.

It is important to emphasize again that the objective of sustainable development has become a legal obligation of every state and the international community. The Right to Development forms part of customary international law. The international community has accepted the right to development as a universal human right and has thus a legal obligation to enhance the realization of this right in all its facets. In their resolution on the World Summit Outcome, the General Assembly of the UN reaffirmed the commitment to a global partnership for development as set out in the Millennium Declaration,[54] the Monterey Consensus,[55] and the Johannesburg Plan of Implementation.[56] The commitment to shared responsibility has been emphasized in the Millennium Development Declaration, stressing that the responsibility for managing worldwide economic and social development must be shared among the nations of the world and should be exercised multilaterally.[57]

Coherent policies and interdisciplinary, comprehensive efforts at both the domestic and the global level can make a true difference. The multilateral trading system can be a powerful supporter in promoting the realization of sustainable development. The WTO has not been established to benefit only free traders, companies or exporters, but to provide a holistic framework regulating trade relations between states, leading to the improvement of the life of the world's citizens. Consequently, other interests such as non-trade values (human rights, environmental obligations, core labour standards and sustainable development objectives) need to be taken into consideration besides mere trade liberalization. It is ever more important to emphasize that a system that is enthusiastically praising the rule of law must obey the law itself. This requires the recognition of the human rights dimension of sustainable development. Policies can therefore no longer be driven only by the recognition of certain needs of people, but the need to realize that people have rights, that is, entitlements that entail legal obligations on the state and other relevant actors (ECOSOC 2004c). A united effort on all levels and within all national, regional and international institutions is essential to realize the promises frequently made at international policy meetings. The human rights-based approach to sustainable development helps to bridge the divide between two legal systems that have developed separately from each other for nearly sixty years: If the main objective of trade is to enhance the well-being of all people and sustainable development, it follows that human rights enhance the main objective of trade.

Notes

* This chapter was written as master's thesis (LL.M.) research paper at the University of Stellenbosch, South Africa. I am extremely grateful to Professor Mustaqeem de Gama, Professor Gary Sampson, Lina Westin and Christopher Smith for sharing their ideas and comments with me on this topic. The paper is dedicated to my son Joshua – the world is ours to explore.

1. An overview is available at http://www.wto.org/english/thewto_e/whatis_e/tif_e/org6_e.htm.

2. WTO Ministerial Declaration, *The Doha Declaration*, adopted at the fourth Ministerial Conference in Doha on 14 November 2001, WTO Doc. WT/MIN(01)/DEC/1, para. 6

3. The Preamble of the GATT 1947 states that "relations in the field of trade and economic endeavour should be conducted with a view to raising standards of living, ensuring full employment and a large and steadily growing volume of real income and effective demand".

4. The examples of human rights in the context of this article must be understood to be non-exhaustive, i.e., there may be various other human rights that may be affected by international trade but are not analysed here.

5. Preamble of the "Agreement Establishing the World Trade Organization", Marrakesh, 15 April 1994, available at http://www.wto.org/english/docs_e/legal_e/legal_e.htm.

6. WTO Panel Report (2000) *Korea-Measures Affecting Government Procurement*, WTO Doc. WT/DS163/R, para 7.96, 19 June.

7. Marrakesh Declaration, 15 April 1994.

8. Sampson (2005), at 2, further stating that "the WTO has gravitated towards becoming a World Trade and Sustainable Development Organization", which is "by design or by default a reality of the day".

9. Declaration on the Establishment of a New International Economic Order, adopted 1 May 1974, GA Res. 3201 (S-VI), A/RES/S6/3201, available at http://www.un-documents.net/s6r3201.htm; Charter of Rights and Duties of States, adopted 12 December 1974, GA Res. 3281, A/RES/40/182, available at http://www.un.org/documents/ga/res/40/a40r182.htm.

10. Chapter 1 (Fundamentals of International Economic Relations) of Charter on Rights and Duties of States.
11. Alston (1991), at 218–219. Eastern European States supported the right to development although that support was premised upon the assumption that large-scale aid was owed by colonizers rather than industrial powers generally. Western States supported the obligation to cooperate with respect to development, but did not acknowledge that there was any duty to do so, especially that there would be any requirements concerning a change in their own policies.
12. United Nations Resolution GA/41/128 of 4 December 1986, hereinafter 1986 Declaration.
13. The Statute of the International Court of Justice can be found at http://www.icj-cij.org/documents/index.php?p1=4&p2=2&p3=0, visited 2 May 2007.
14. Article 1.1 of the ICCPR and Article 1.1 of the ICESCR provide identically that "All peoples have the right to self-determination. By virtue of that right they freely determine their political status and freely pursue their economic, social and cultural development."
15. Article 10 *Vienna Declaration and Programme of Action*, adopted 12 July 1993 at World Conference on Human Rights, UN Doc. A/Conf.157/23.
16. United Nations General Assembly Resolution 52/136, adopted 12 December 1997, UN Doc. A/RES/52/136.
17. United Nations Secretary-General, *Report of the Secretary-General on Renewing the United Nations: A Programme for Reform*, UN Doc. A/51/950, issued on 14 July 1997, para. 78.
18. *United Nations Millennium Declaration*, adopted by the UN-GA on 18 September 2000, A/RES/55/2.
19. ECOSOC (2004b), para. 27; these presentations took place at a seminar on "Global Partnership for Development: High-Level Seminar on the Right to Development", Geneva 9–10 February 2004. It was mandated by Commission on Human Rights resolution 2003/83, adopted by the Commission at its fifty-ninth session.
20. Article 1.1 of the Declaration on the Right to Development.
21. Article 3(3) of the 1986 Declaration.
22. Article 1 of the 1986 Declaration.
23. Article 9(1) of the 1986 Declaration.
24. Ministerial Declaration of the World Trade Organization (Doha Declaration), adopted 14 November 2001, Doha, WT/MIN(01)/DEC/1, para. 6.
25. ibid., para. 1.
26. *Report of the World Commission on Environment and Development ("Our Common Future")*, adopted as decision 14/14 of the Governing Council of the UN Environment Programme on 16 June 1987, UN Doc. A/42/427, Annex.
27. Council of the UN Environment Programme, *"Our Common Future"*, at p. 43.
28. Introduction to Sustainable Development, issued by the International Institute for Sustainable Development, available at http://sdgateway.net/introsd/definitions.htm, visited on 21 April 2007.
29. ibid.
30. ibid.
31. See the Preamble of the Marrakesh-Agreement establishing the WTO.
32. UNHCHR Human Rights Committee, *General Comment No. 18 on Non-Discrimination*, adopted at its 37th session, in 1987, para. 7, available at http://www.unhchr.ch/tbs/doc.nsf/385c2add1632f4a8c12565a9004dc311/3888b0541f8501c9c12563ed004b8d0e?OpenDocument.
33. ECOSOC (2004a), para. 13; some differential treatment, as for example temporary special measures such as affirmative action, are justifiable under the principle of non-discrimination.
34. TRIPS Agreement, Article 4.

35. WTO Working Group on the Relationship between Trade and Investment, "Most-Favoured-Nation Treatment and National Treatment", Note by the secretariat (WT/WGTI/W/118), para. 19.
36. ibid.
37. ibid.
38. FAO, *"Some trade policy issues relating to trends in agricultural imports in the context of food security"*, Committee on Commodity Problems, Sixty-fourth session, Rome, 18–21 March 2003 (CCP 03/10).
39. Article 6(2) of the ICESCR.
40. International Labour Organization (ILO) on Working Conditions and Wages, available at http://www.ilo.org/global/Themes/Working_Conditions/Wages/lang–en/index.htm.
41. ibid.
42. ibid.
43. Research in Honduras and the Dominican Republic, for example, suggests that wages for workers in export industries are often insufficient to maintain reasonable standards of nutrition (Oxfam 2002: 81).
44. United Nations Educational, Social and Cultural Organization (UNESCO), *UN Decade for Education for Sustainable Development (2005–2014)*, available at http://portal.unesco.org/education/en/ev.php-URL_ID=23279&URL_DO=DO_TOPIC&URL_SECTION=201.html, visited 14 May 2007.
45. FAO, *Rome Declaration on World Food Security and Plan of Action of the World Food Summit (1996)*, available at http://www.fao.org/wfs/index_en.htm, visited 17 May 2007.
46. ibid., commitment Seven.
47. Declaration of the World Food Summit: Five Years Later, available at http://www.fao.org/DOCREP/MEETING/005/Y7106E/Y7106E09.htm, visited 17 May 2007.
48. WHO Constitution, preamble, para. 1, 2, adopted by the International Health Conference (New York) 19–22 July 1946, available at http://www.yale.edu/lawweb/avalon/decade/decad051.htm.
49. Press release, 22 March 2006; available at http://www.who.int/mediacentre/news/releases/2006/pr15/en/index.html.
50. UNAIDS annual report, available at http://www.unaids.org/epi/2005/doc/EPIupdate2005_pdf_en/Epi05_02_en.pdf.
51. Musungu (2005), at 306, referring to *Soobramoney v. Minister for Health* (Kwazulu Natal), paras 8, 12 BCLR 1696 (1997).
52. As noted before, this chapter does not focus on the pillar of environmental protection. The relevance of this pillar for human rights is nevertheless recognized.
53. The UDHR, the ICCPR and the ICESCR are together being regarded as the International Bill of Rights.
54. *United Nations Millennium Declaration*, adopted by UNGA on 18 September 2000, A/RES/55/2.
55. Monterrey Consensus of the International Conference on Financing for Development (*Report of the International Conference on Financing for Development, Monterrey, Mexico, 18–22 March 2002*) United Nations Publication, Sales No. E.02.II.A.7; ch. 1, resolution 1, annex.
56. Plan of Implementation of the World Summit on Sustainable Development (*Report of the World Summit on Sustainable Development, Johannesburg, South Africa, 26 August–4 September 2002*) United Nations publication, Sales No. E.03.II.A.1 and corrigendum; ch. 1, resolution 2, annex.
57. UNGA *Millennium Declaration*, Resolution adopted by the UN General Assembly on 18 September 2000, UN Doc A/RES/55/2, para. I.6.

REFERENCES

Alston, Philip (1991) "Revitalising United Nations Work on Human Rights and Development", 18 *Melbourne University Law Review*, 216.
Ben-David, Dan, Hakan Nordstrom and L. Alan Winters (2000) *Trade, Income Disparity and Poverty*, Special Study No. 5, Geneva: WTO.
Breining-Kaufmann, Christine (2005) "The Right to Food and Trade in Agriculture", in T. Cottier, J. Pauwelyn and E. Burgi, eds, *Human Rights and International Trade*, Oxford: Oxford University Press, pp. 341–381.
Cleveland, H., G. Jacobs, R. Macfarlane, R. van Harten and N. Asokan (1999) "Towards a Comprehensive Theory of Social Development", in *Human Choice*, Minneapolis, Minn.: World Academy of Art and Science.
Cullet, P. (2001) "Plant Variety Protection in Africa: Towards Compliance with the TRIPS Agreement", *Journal of African Law* 45: 97–122.
Dancourt, Oscar (1999) "Neoliberal Reforms and Macroeconomic Policy in Peru", *CEPAL Review* 67, New York: UN.
Donnelly, Jack (1985) "In Search of the Unicorn: The Jurisprudence and Politics of the Right to Development", 15 *California Western International Law Journal*, 473.
Edwardson, Shelley (2005) "Reconciling TRIPS and the Right to Food", in T. Cottier, J. Pauwelyn and E. Burgi, eds, *Human Rights and International Trade*, Oxford: Oxford University Press, pp. 382–390.
Elliot, Jennifer A. (2006) *An Introduction to Sustainable Development*, 3rd ed., London: Routledge.
Hoselitz, B. F. (1995) "Non-Economic Barriers to Economic Development", in S. Corbridge, ed., *Development Studies*, Oxford: Oxford University Press.
Ipsen, Knut (1999) *Völkerrecht*, 4th ed., Munich: Beck-Verlag.
Jordan, Bill (2001) "Building a WTO That Can Contribute Effectively to Economic and Social Development Worldwide", in G. Sampson, ed., *The Role of the WTO in Global Governance*, Tokyo: United Nations University Press.
Musungu, Sisule F. (2005) "The Right to Health, Intellectual Property, and Competition Principles", in T. Cottier, J. Pauwelyn and E. Burgi, eds, *Human Rights and International Trade*, Oxford: Oxford University Press, pp. 301–310.
O'Brien, Robert and Marc Williams (2004) *Global Political Economy – Evolution and Dynamics*, Hampshire: Palgrave Macmillan.
Orford, Anne (2001) "Globalization and the Right to Development", in P. Alston, ed., *People's Rights*, Oxford: Oxford University Press, pp. 127–184.
Özden, Melik (2006) *The Right to Health: A Fundamental Human Right Affirmed by the United Nations and Recognized in Regional Treaties and Numerous National Constitutions*, Geneva: Series of the Human Rights Programme of the Europe-Third World Centre (CETIM).
Pauwelyn, Joost (2001) "The Role of Public International Law in the WTO: How Far Can We Go?", 95 *American Journal of International Law*, 535.
Petersmann, Ernst-Ulrich (2002) "Time for a United Nations 'Global Compact' for Integrating Human Rights into the Law of Worldwide Organisations: Lessons from European Integration", 13 *European Journal of International Law*, 621–641.

Robinson, Mary (2001) "Making the Global Economy Work for Human Rights", in G. Sampson, ed., *The Role of the World Trade Organization in Global Governance*, Tokyo: United Nations University Press, pp. 209–222.

Ross-Larson, Bruce, ed. (2003) *Making Global Trade Work for the People*, London: United Nations Development Programme, Earthscan Publications.

Sampson, Gary, ed. (2001) *The Role of the World Trade Organization in Global Governance*, Tokyo: United Nations University Press.

Sampson, Gary (2005) *The WTO and Sustainable Development*, Tokyo: United Nations University Press.

Scholtz, M. (1999) "WHO's Role in Ensuring Access to Essential Drugs", in *WHO Drug Information*, vol. 13, Geneva: WHO.

Thurow, R. (2003) "Changing Course: Ravaged by Famine, Ethiopia Finally Gets Help From the Nile", *Wall Street Journal*, 26 November.

Official Documents

Economic Commission for Latin America (ECLA) (2000) *The Equity Gap: A Second Assessment*, Santiago.

ECLA (2001) *Social Panorama of Latin America 2000–2001*, Santiago.

UN Economic and Social Council (ECOSOC) (1999) *General Comment No. 12*, UN Doc. E/C.12/1999/5.

ECOSOC (2000) *The right to the highest attainable standard of health (article 12 of the International Covenant on Economic, Social and Cultural Rights)*, General Comment No. 14, adopted 11 May 2000, UN Doc E/C.12/2000/4.

ECOSOC (2002) *Globalization and its impact on the full enjoyment of human rights*, Commission on Human Rights, Report submitted by the High Commissioner, UN Doc. E/Cn.4/2002/54.

ECOSOC (2004a) *Economic, Social and Cultural Rights – Analytical Study of the High Commissioner for Human Rights on the Fundamental Principle of Non-Discrimination in the Context of Globalization*, Commission on Human Rights, UN Doc. E/CN.4/2004/40.

ECOSOC (2004b) *The Legal Nature of the Right to Development and Enhancement of Its Binding Nature*, Commission on Human Rights, UN Doc E/CN.4/Sub.2/2004/16.

ECOSOC (2004c) *Study on Policies for Development in a Globalizing World: What Can the Human Rights Approach Contribute?* Commission on Human Rights, adopted 7 June 2004, UN Doc. E/CN.4/Sub.2/2004/18.

FAO, Committee on Commodity Problems (2003) "Some trade policy issues relating to trends in agricultural imports in the context of food security", Committee on Commodity Problems, Sixty-fourth session, Rome, 18–21 March (CCP 03/10).

International Confederation of Free Trade Unions (ICFTU) (1996) *Behind the Wire: Anti-Union Repression in the Export Processing Zones*, Brussels.

International Conference on Financing for Development, Monterrey Consensus of the International Conference on Financing for Development (2002) *Report of the International Conference on Financing for Development, Monterrey, Mex-*

ico, 18–22 March, United Nations Publication, Sales No. E.02.II.A.7; ch. 1, resolution 1, annex.

Office of the High Commissioner on Human Rights (OHCHR) (2003) *Human Rights and Trade (Reader)*, presented at 5th WTO Ministerial Conference in Cancun, Mexico, 10–14 September.

Organization for Economic Cooperation and Development (OECD) (2001) *The Development Dimension of Trade*, Paris.

Oxfam International (2002) *Rigged Rules and Double Standards – Trade, Globalisation, and the Fight against Poverty*, Oxfam International.

UN Development Programme (UNDP) (2000) *Human Development Report 2000*, Oxford: Oxford University Press.

United Nations Commission on Trade and Development (UNCTAD) (2002) *The Least Developed Countries Report 2002: Escaping the Poverty Trap*, Geneva: UNCTAD, Geneva.

United Nations Educational, Social and Cultural Organization (UNESCO) *UN Decade for Education for Sustainable Development (2005–2014)*, available from http://portal.unesco.org/education/en/ev.php-URL_ID=23279&URL_DO=DO_TOPIC&URL_SECTION=201.html.

United Nations Food and Agriculture Organization (FAO) (2000) *Agriculture, Trade and Food Security Issues and Options in the WTO Negotiations from the Perspective of Developing Countries*, vol. 2, Country Case Studies, Commodities and Trade Division, Rome: FAO.

FAO (2002) *Rural Development: Some Issues in the Context of the WTO Negotiations on Agriculture*, Papers on Selected Issues Relating to the WTO Negotiations on Agriculture, Rome: FAO.

United Nations General Assembly (UNGA) (2005) *2005 World Summit Outcome*, GA-Resolution A/RES/60/1, adopted 24 October 2005.

World Bank (2001) *World Development Report 2000/2001: Attacking Poverty*, Oxford: Oxford University Press.

World Bank (2004) *World Development Indicators 2004: Food Export/Import as a Percent of Total Merchandise Trade*, Washington, DC: World Bank, available at http://www.worldbank.org/data/wdi2004/.

World Food Summit (1996) *Rome Declaration on World Food Security and Plan of Action of the World Food Summit (1996)*, available at http://www.fao.org/wfs/index_en.htm.

World Summit on Sustainable Development, Plan of Implementation of the World Summit on Sustainable Development (2002) *Report of the World Summit on Sustainable Development, Johannesburg, South Africa, 26 August–4 September*, United Nations publication, Sales No. E.03.II.A.1 and corrigendum; ch. 1, resolution 2, annex.

WTO Working Group on the Relationship between Trade and Investment, *Most-Favoured-Nation Treatment and National Treatment*, Note by the secretariat, WTO Doc. WT/WGTI/W/118.

11

Asymmetric integration: The role of regionalism

Ken Heydon*

The proliferation of regional trade agreements (RTAs) – both plurilateral and bilateral – increasingly involves agreements between countries at markedly different stages of development. In recognition of these differences, RTAs commonly contain special and differential-type provisions that seek to benefit the less advanced partner. However, while RTA provisions often go beyond those found in the WTO and while there may be lessons for the evolving debate on aid-for-trade, care is needed in seeking to draw on RTA experience. Of the two broad types of special and differential treatment (SDT), we appear to have one – flexibility in liberalization commitments – that is widely applied in regional agreements but of questionable value insofar as it weakens the commitment to market opening, and another – financial and technical assistance – that is seen as being broadly beneficial but that is implemented in regional accords at a level well below its potential. Moreover, even where developing countries may benefit from SDT-type provisions in RTAs, such benefit needs to be set against the negative aspects of regionalism, including increased transaction costs for business and pressure to address trade-related concerns such as core labour standards or protection of the environment. While regional agreements can complement the multilateral trading system they can never be a substitute for it. Complementarity would be fostered by donor support for regional efforts at capacity building and by a strengthened commitment, by all countries, to open markets and strengthened rules of trade.

Developing countries and the WTO: Policy approaches, Sampson and Chambers (eds),
United Nations University Press, 2008, ISBN 978-92-808-1153-7

The growth of regionalism

The number of preferential regional trade agreements (RTAs) has grown rapidly in recent years, with some 200 RTAs notified to the WTO in the last decade. Over a quarter of these notifications have been made since the failed WTO Ministerial Conference in Cancun in September 2003. Most importantly, the share of world trade accounted for by RTAs has also grown considerably, from 40 per cent to over half of global trade in the past five years (Crawford and Fiorentino 2005).

One of the striking features of the recent growth of regionalism is the extent to which Asian countries that had previously eschewed regional deals are now engaged in this process. This may be driven simply by a concern not to be left out. But this raises the question as to why they do not wish to be left out. One explanation is that preferential RTAs are seen, rightly or wrongly, by both government and business, as offering quicker gains in market access than can be achieved through the process of multilateral negotiation. This may be an important factor for business, as product cycles get shorter and multilateral negotiating cycles get longer; a fact underlined by the current impediments to progress under the Doha Development Agenda (DDA). The symbolism here has been quite striking. In the immediate aftermath of the failed Cancun Ministerial, the Mexican hosts sat down with their Japanese counterparts to negotiate a bilateral deal.

A recent illustration of how it may be possible, in particular areas, to make progress regionally arose in the RTA agreed on 9 September 2006 between Japan and the Philippines. The agreement contains provisions for Filipino workers – especially nurses – to pursue employment and training in Japan, thus marking progress under GATS Mode 4 (the movement of natural persons), one of the most troublesome areas of the Doha negotiations in trade in services.

Regional agreements also offer the opportunity to address issues that have been deliberately excluded from multilateral negotiations – notably two of the so-called Singapore Issues, investment and competition, which have been dropped from the DDA. Opportunities may also be taken to include provisions dealing with trade-related issues such as core labour standards or protection of the environment. Regional initiatives may also be seen as a way of helping promote domestic policy change – a factor often cited in the case of banking sector reform in Japan.

Regional deals offer the chance to select one's partners on political or strategic grounds. By way of illustration, Australia was favoured over New Zealand as a choice of partner by the United States because of the respective policies of these two countries in the Iraq war. China's pursuit of a preferential deal with ASEAN is motivated to a considerable extent by broad foreign policy considerations and a concern to foster a sense of mutual benefit.

It is sometimes suggested that the motivations for pursuing regional agreements differ between developed and developing countries, with the advanced industrialized countries seeking deep integration while developing countries look for market access gains. This is too stark a distinction. Developing countries have a stake, through institutional strengthening, in deeper integration, while the advanced industrialized countries also have market access interests.

Developed-country concerns about market access have been amply demonstrated by the emphasis placed by the United States on access conditions for its beef under the RTA recently negotiated with Colombia. As part of the RTA negotiations, Colombia agreed to drop all mad cow disease-related restrictions on imports from the United States. This is a significant concession. Some 20 countries have maintained bans on importing beef from the United States since December 2003 when a cow there was found to have bovine spongiform encephalopathy (BSE). Many other governments impose various restrictions on US beef, only opening their markets to specific types of meat from cows under 30 months of age.

For the European Union too, improved market access is a key motivation for the pursuit of regional agreements. The new trade policy strategy of the European Union announced in October 2006 prescribes seeking RTAs with countries and trade blocs based on "market potential (economic size and growth) and the level of protection against EU export interests".

Another striking feature of the growth of regionalism is the extent to which bilateral deals are becoming more common. Of the 184 RTAs currently in operation, no less than 141 are bilateral. Moreover, these bilateral arrangements are increasingly negotiated between countries that are not only geographically distant but also at markedly different stages of economic development, and hence with markedly different degrees of negotiating strength.

Preferential trading arrangements, whether bilateral or plurilateral, between economically disparate countries commonly seek to address the asymmetric nature of the integration process. In what follows, we will seek to examine whether there is a pattern to asymmetric integration among different types of agreement, how far the treatment of asymmetries goes beyond provisions for special and differential treatment (SDT) in the WTO and whether or not regional approaches to asymmetric integration are successful in meeting their objectives. Throughout the chapter, the term "asymmetric" will have two senses, referring both to the economic disparities among the members of regional agreements and to the differentiated treatment and obligations that such agreements might embody.

Dealing regionally with asymmetries: Is there a pattern?

There are two broad sets of SDT provisions embodied within RTAs: financial and technical assistance for lesser developed members, and flexibilities or reduced liberalization commitments for the less advanced.

Plurilateral agreements between developing countries (South-South plurilaterals) provide extensively for both types of SDT. We see this, for example, in the Latin American Integration Association (ALADI), the Southern Common Market (MERCOSUR), the Caribbean Community and Common Market (CARICOM), the Andean Community (AC), the South Asian Free Trade Area (SAFTA), the Pacific Island Countries Trade Agreement (PICTA), the Southern African Customs Union (SACU), the Common Market for Eastern and Southern Africa (COMESA) and the Economic Community of Central African States (ECCAS).

Agreements between developed and developing countries (North-South agreements) commonly provide for financial and technical assistance for the less developed partner(s). We see this in the plurilateral agreements embodied in the North American Free Trade Agreement (NAFTA), through the North American Development Bank; in the United States-Central American Free Trade Agreement (CAFTA); and in the Asia-Pacific Economic Cooperation framework (APEC). The provision of financial and technical assistance is also commonly found in North-South bilaterals such as Canada-Costa Rica, EU bilaterals with Chile, South Africa and Tunisia, and US bilaterals with Chile, Jordan and Morocco. For example, US-Chile (Art. 19.5) provides that the United States will assist Chile in reducing pollution from past mining practices.

The situation with respect to the provision of flexibilities or reduced liberalization commitments in North-South agreements is much more nuanced. This is evident when looking at the approach taken by the United States and by the European Union in their respective regional accords.

At first sight, there is a significant element of flexibility in agreements to which the United States is party. Unlike the European Union, the United States is not inclined to pursue regulatory harmonization in its agreements. It has thus been observed that the US-centred model places less importance on approximation or policy harmonization, as is reflected in the limited standards-harmonization working groups established under NAFTA (Woolcock 2003). Moreover, the recently negotiated CAFTA includes important SDT-type provisions, such as longer transition periods for developing members.

Before concluding, however, that the United States is actively engaged in promoting asymmetric commitments or that CAFTA might represent a model for future US agreements, some qualifications are in order. First, while there may be no formal pursuit of harmonization in NAFTA, the US model appears to assume that market factors will bring about equivalence, leading to de facto approximation to US regulatory norms and standards (Woolcock 2003). This would be borne out by the fact that the United States resisted asymmetric liberalization commitments in the negotiation of NAFTA. Second, the US commitment to reciprocity has been very clearly demonstrated in recent negotiations with the members of the Southern African Customs Union. SACU concerns that it lacked the institutional capacities to meet US expectations was met with the response that ways should be explored to strengthen the trade and investment relationship in the hope that SACU "could undertake the obligations of a US-style FTA in the future". In other words, the US preference appears to be to defer conclusion of an RTA rather than to dilute the reciprocal character of its agreements. In this light, the asymmetric elements of CAFTA might be seen as the product of particular economic, political and strategic factors.

Agreements to which the European Union is a party frequently contain SDT-type provisions. This is particularly apparent in the Europe Agreements (EAs) between the European Union and the Central and East European countries (CEECs). While the EAs require both the CEECs and the European Union gradually to liberalize trade in industrialized goods over a transition period, the European Union has undertaken to do so more rapidly than its EA partners. In the EU-Poland Association Agreement, there is a specific provision for asymmetry in the treatment of investment. While the European Union immediately offered national treatment with respect to establishment of Polish firms on its territory, Poland undertook only to liberalize establishment on a gradual basis (Feldmann 2003). Asymmetry is also found beyond the realm of the Europe Agreements. In the EU-Mexico Free Trade Agreement, though both parties agreed to refrain from making full use of the transition periods permitted under GATT Article XXIV, the agreement provides that all industrial goods originating in Mexico were to be duty free within less than three years, by 1 January 2003, while Mexico is to liberalize all industrial products only by 2007 (Reiter 2003). And in the economic partnership agreements (EPAs) being negotiated between the

European Union and the African, Caribbean and Pacific (ACP) countries, transition periods for the ACP partners of 25 years are being considered.

Again, however, qualifications are in order to any assumption that the European Union consistently applies asymmetric provisions in its regional agreements. Given the European Union's pursuit of harmonization, it can be characterized as a regional hegemon that obliges smaller neighbouring countries to adopt prevailing European regulatory norms. This is particularly the case with the Europe Agreements that seek to formalize the relationship between the European Union and the CEECs applying for membership of the Union and under which compliance with the *acquis communautaire* constitutes a *conditio sine qua non* for acceding to the European Union. As for the EPAs, they are founded essentially on the principle of reciprocity. The requirement for reciprocity, which has led to expressions of concern from some ACP countries, such as Fiji and Senegal, that it could overwhelm fragile economies, reflects the view of the European Commission that tariff preferences are "an eroding lifeline". In agreements with more distant countries, it may even be that where there is asymmetric treatment, it could be interpreted as favouring the developed partner. For example, in EU-Jordan, EU foreign direct investment (FDI) gets both Most-Favoured-Nation (MFN) treatment and National Treatment in Jordan, while Jordanian investment in the European Union receives only MFN. This raises the question, however, as to whether in talking about asymmetric treatment it is necessary to distinguish between the legal and economic effects of such treatment. In this particular case, asymmetric *legal* provisions that seem to favour EU investment in Jordan may, because of the benefits of inwards FDI, in fact serve the *economic* interests of Jordan. This in turn raises the broader question of whether asymmetric treatment that serves to limit liberalization commitments actually promotes national self-interest. This issue will be returned to later in the chapter.

The treatment of economic disparities in regional accords is clearly evolving, and the identification of patterns in that treatment would warrant more extensive research. But it may nevertheless be tentatively concluded that asymmetric obligations in regional trade agreements are more likely to be found:

• In agreements among developing countries;
• The stronger the goal of deeper integration; and
• The closer the geographic proximity of partners.

It has also been observed that much more experimentation with SDT provisions has taken place in RTAs than in existing multilateral accords (OECD 2005a).

Dealing regionally with asymmetries: WTO-plus?

In many respects, regional agreements go beyond WTO provisions (WTO 2001) in dealing with asymmetric integration – whether in determining eligibility, providing for asymmetric commitments or in fostering cooperation and technical or financial assistance. As we shall see though, WTO-*plus* does not necessarily mean *better*.

Determining eligibility

Many of the RTAs examined in this chapter embody a formal differentiation among members based on their respective levels of development. In doing so, some agreements employ non-economic criteria in determining eligibility for asymmetric obligations, consistent with a "situational" approach to SDT. This explicit categorization of members contrasts with WTO practice where there is not even a definition of "developing country" and where the question of "differentiating" between Members remains highly sensitive.

In Latin America:

- ALADI emphasizes flexibility and differential treatment as a guiding principle in the implementation of the Treaty. SDT in ALADI is structured on the basis of three categories of countries (Resolution 4): countries at a relatively less advanced stage of economic development, intermediate developed countries and other members. In addition, Uruguay is granted exceptional treatment more favourable than that accorded to the other intermediate developed countries. Chapter III of the Montevideo Treaty creates a system favouring countries at a relatively less advanced stage of economic development. This chapter provides that designated countries are to be provided conditions to support their participation in the integration process based on the principles of non-reciprocity and community cooperation. Actions favouring countries at a relatively less advanced stage are also implemented through so-called "regional scope" and "partial scope" agreements

- The Caribbean Community has traditionally maintained a two-part classification of member states according to the levels of development: members of the Organization of Eastern Caribbean States, Belize and Haiti are known as less-developed countries (LDCs), whereas the other members form the category of more-developed countries (MDCs). Since its outset, the concept of SDT has been firmly embedded in the Caribbean Community. The 1973 Treaty provided a framework of "special measures for less developed countries". These measures were elaborated in the special regime for less-developed countries of the original Treaty and modified in 1999 by "Protocol VII on Disadvantaged Countries, Regions and Sectors". To create the Caribbean Single Market and Economy (CSME), special measures assisting less-developed members are again at the centrepiece of the CARICOM integration movement. The revised regime takes into account not only differing levels of development in member countries, but also differing degrees of vulnerability to natural disasters and indebtedness.

- The Andean Community (AC), established by the Cartagena Agreement in 1969 and amended by its subsequent Decisions, creates a system for economic and social cooperation toward integration that aims, *inter alia*, to reduce existing differences in the levels of development among member states. The AC explicitly refers to SDT by providing in Article 3 that Bolivia and Ecuador will receive preferential treatment. It also declares the need to find solutions to the problems associated with Bolivia's condition as a landlocked county.

- Initially, there was a lack of explicit SDT in MERCOSUR, which has been attributed to the fact that the agreement was the by-product of a bilateral deal between Argentina and Brazil (Bouzas 2003). Subsequent implementing programmes, however, have specifically addressed asymmetric economic capacities and development levels across the membership in order to achieve a common market.

In the Asia-Pacific region:

- The enlargement of ASEAN between 1995 and 1999 made it necessary to consider the relatively low levels of development of the new members (Viet Nam, Lao PDR, Myanmar and Cambodia) and develop SDT measures for them.

- PICTA makes it clear that members should address the differing economic potentials and special development problems of some parties. To enable the provision of SDT, the Agreement establishes two special categories of parties including least-developed country and small island state. Negotiations for the agreement came to an understanding that least-developed countries and small island states may be integrated under differing conditions and transition periods than other parties.

- The APEC Osaka Declaration of 1995 affirmed "the long-term goal of free and open trade and investment no later than the year 2010 in the case of industrialized economies and the year 2020 in the case of developing economies", and this differing schedule provides the clearest example of SDT in the APEC regime. The declaration also called for flexibility in dealing with "the different levels of economic development among the APEC economies and the diverse circumstances in each economy".

In Africa:

- The COMESA Treaty, at Chapter 22, creates a cooperative mechanism for least-developed countries and economically depressed areas. Under this mechanism, the main areas for cooperation include development of infrastructure, industry, agriculture and services. To implement SDT, COMESA envisages identifying a group of countries designated as least-developed (Pearson 2004).
- ECCAS membership represents one of the poorest regions in the world. To implement the SDT provision, the Protocol on the Situation of Landlocked, Semi-Landlocked, Island, Part-Island and/or Least Advanced Countries creates four groups of membership; less-advanced countries, island and partial island countries, landlocked countries and semi-landlocked countries.

In the sections that follow, we will consider how, once these special country categories have been created, differential treatment is implemented.

Asymmetric liberalization commitments

Regional agreements contain extensive provisions for asymmetric liberalization commitments of the sort that are proving so hard to negotiate multilaterally in the framework of the DDA.

Product exceptions

Explicit flexibility is provided in several RTAs by permitting some products to be exempt from tariff reduction commitments. The MERCOSUR Trade Liberalization Programme allows for varying levels of exemptions from liberalization commitments (Argentina: 394 items, Brazil: 324, Paraguay: 439 and Uruguay: 960; Ann. 1/Art. 6). Similarly, ALADI permits more extensive exception lists for relatively less-developed countries, when compared to those for intermediate-developed countries, which are themselves beneficiaries of broader exemptions than are other members (Resolution 5/First). Under SAFTA, the contracting states are to mutually agree upon a ceiling for the number of products on the Sensitive Lists; within this context least-developed country members are to be accorded increased flexibility when requesting derogations (Art. 7.3).

Infant industry protection

Another type of flexibility arises that may be regarded as going beyond – or at least, implementing more comprehensively – the provisions of GATT Article XVIII, which permits members to derogate in order to protect infant industries. CARICOM contains provisions allowing for less-developed countries temporarily to suspend community origin treatment in order to promote industrial development (Art. 164). Under PICTA, a party may raise tariffs under certain conditions to protect developing industries. Notably, small island states and LDC members are allowed to apply this derogation for a period of up to 15 years while others are subject to a 10-year maximum (Art. 14.3). SACU provides that Botswana, Lesotho, Namibia and Swaziland (but not South Africa) may levy additional duties on goods imported into their areas to protect infant industries for a period of up to eight years (Art. 26).

Some North-South bilateral RTAs also provide protection for infant industries as an SDT instrument. Both the EU-South Africa and EU-Tunisia agreements include an SDT provision in relation to trade in agriculture identified as "transitional safeguard measures", which may be applied only by the developing members. Significantly, the measures may be applied for the express purpose of assisting "infant industries or sectors facing serious difficulties" caused by increased imports from the European Union. Duties applied under this provision may not exceed the lower of 20 per cent *ad valorem* or the MFN duty rate of the product and must maintain an element of preference for imports from the European Union.

Flexible treatment of subsidies

CARICOM contains interesting provisions allowing for the flexible use of subsidies. Member states with per capita GNP of less than US$1,000 may maintain subsidies contingent upon export performance, whereas other members may not (Art. 104.1.a). In addition, member states with a per capita GNP of less than US$1,000 were allowed to maintain subsidies contingent upon the use of domestic over imported inputs until 2003 (Art. 104.1.b).

Transitional time periods

Many agreements provide for the preferential application of transitional time periods. MERCOSUR allows Paraguay and Uruguay to have one additional year to complete the trade liberalization programme. The AC Treaty provides flexibilities whereby Bolivia and Ecuador have transition schedules that differ from those applying to Colombia, Peru and Venezuela (Art. 82 and A106). Under CAFTA, tariffs are to be phased-out according to specific schedules negotiated on a product- and country-specific basis. According to Annex 3.3, tariffs will be reduced within one of the following time frames: immediate, 5 years, 10 years, 15 years and 20 years. While tariffs will be reduced in equal annual instalments over the phase-out period, tariff reductions for specific products are back-loaded, with smaller cuts in the initial years and larger cuts in later years of the transition period. Central American producers received longer time periods for tariff phase-outs as well as a greater share of the back-loaded phase out periods than US producers (World Bank 2005).

The only aspect of NAFTA that can be portrayed as an unambiguous example of SDT is the special consideration given to Mexican products in the tariff phase-out schedules. The Mexican tariff on corn and dried lentils is being phased out over 15 years. For remaining goods, existing customs duties will be eliminated immediately or phased out at some point over a ten-year period.

SDT provisions in the ASEAN Free Trade Agreement (AFTA) are largely limited to the category of transitional time periods. The original Common Effective Preferential Tariff (CEPT) Scheme did not adopt SDT provisions, including transitional arrangements; yet transitional flexibility was made available when AFTA implemented tariff reduction by introducing two track programs (the fast track program and the normal track program) in 1994. With the enlargement of membership, AFTA needed more fine-tuned transitional SDT to ensure that the new members integrate into the ASEAN Free Trade Area. In the process of incorporating unprocessed agricultural products within the liberalization program, transitional flexibility was granted for the new members. For the original members, all such products are scheduled to be phased in by 1 January 2010. However, the new members are allowed flexibilities to complete the parallel phase-in process by dates ranging from 2013 to 2017 (Protocol on Sensitive Products). The AFTA-CEPT amended in 2003 contains different deadlines for eliminating import duties imposed on the inclusion lists: Brunei, Indonesia, Malaysia, Philippines, Singapore and Thailand are to eliminate import duties not later than 1 January 2010, while the new members by not later than 1 January 2015, with flexibility however allowed for import duties on some sensitive products to be eliminated not later than 1 January 2018 (Art. 4.C.).

Under SAFTA, non-LDC members and LDC members are provided with differing transition periods. During the first phase, indicated as 2006–2008, non-LDCs are to reduce existing tariff rates to 20 per cent and LDCs to 30 per cent (Art. 7.1.a & b). The subsequent phase of reducing tariffs to 0–5 per cent will be implemented over a five-year period by non-LDCs and a longer, eight-year period by LDCs (Art. 7.1.c & d). Sri Lanka is given one additional year, totalling six years, to complete the subsequent phase (Art. 7.1.c).

PICTA provides that small island states and least-developed countries will cut *ad valorem* tariffs on originating goods to zero by 2012 (other countries by 2010) (Ann. II.1 & 2). In reducing and eliminating specific tariffs or fixed tariffs on originating goods, small island states and least-developed countries begin implementation two years later (1 January 2004) and complete implementation two years later (1 January 2012) than do the other members (Ann. II.3 & 4). For tariffs on excepted imports, both groups of members face the same deadline (1 January 2016), but small islands and LDCs enjoy more gradual rates of reduction (Ann. IV).

The South African Development Community (SADC) Trade Protocol requires phased reductions and eventual elimination of import duties (Art. 4). The principle of applying asymmetric tariff reduction schedules was agreed within subsequent negotiations. Its tariff phase-down schedule groups member states into three categories, including developed countries (South Africa), developing countries (Zimbabwe, Mauritius) and LDCs (the remaining members), and provides differentiated completion dates ranging from 2005 for developed countries and 2007–2008 for developing countries to 2008–2012 for LDCs.

Advantageous rules of origin

A number of regional agreements provide lesser-developed members with advantageous rules of origin. They do so by lowering the threshold for the local value added requirement in order for goods to qualify for originating status. There is no parallel for this in WTO rules.

MERCOSUR provides Paraguay with more flexible rules of origin (50 per cent instead of the normal 60 per cent of regional value added requirement).

The AC provides that in adopting and establishing the special provisions or specific requirements of origin, the Commission and the General Secretariat will seek to ensure that they do not hinder Bolivia and Ecuador from deriving the benefits of the Agreement (Art. 102). In this connection, AC Decision 416 approved on 30 July 1997 provides that for manufactured goods to be considered originating, the cost, insurance and freight (CIF) value of non-native materials should not exceed 50 per cent of the value of the final product in the cases of Colombia, Venezuela and Peru, but this threshold is increased to 60 per cent in the cases of Bolivia and Ecuador (Decision 416).

The general rule for qualifying products for originating status within CARICOM is that the value of materials from outside the community cannot exceed 65 per cent of the cost of repair, renovation or improvement in cases where goods have undergone processing in more-developed countries. Lesser-developed CARICOM members benefit from a lifting of the corresponding figure to 80 per cent (Art. 84.2).

SAFTA provides that the threshold for determining originating status is raised by 10 per cent for products from LDC member states both in the case of rules concerning the determination of origin as well as the rules governing cumulation (Ann. III, 10).

Cooperating on issues beyond the Doha Agenda

Many RTAs directly address issues that WTO negotiations have put aside, like investment and competition, or where the WTO has difficulty in advancing, like the environment. And they do so on the basis of cooperation among participating countries at differing levels of development.

A number of North-South RTAs provide for cooperation with lesser-developed members within a framework of investment promotion (PAT-CRA, EU-Tunisia, EFTA-Mexico, US-Jordan). Though, as we have seen with EU-Jordan, the provisions may warrant close attention.

Technical assistance in competition policy also features in North-South agreements (Canada-Costa Rica, EU-Chile, EU-South Africa, EU-Mexico, Japan-Mexico) and so contributes to the development of a competition culture in the less-developed partner country.

In the case of the environment, cooperation is prevalent in RTAs between countries with different levels of development. This may be seen as recognition by contracting parties of the existence of asymmetries and correspondingly of, first, the need to mitigate or address potential negative environmental impacts arising from trade provisions, which are often greater in developing countries, and, second, the importance of building on economic cooperation through social and environmental collaboration. Such provisions are seen, for example, in EU-Chile, Canada-Costa Rica and in the RTAs negotiated in recent years by the United States, such as those with Singapore, Chile, Bahrain and Morocco, as well as in CAFTA.

Financial support mechanisms

There is a growing, if belated, realization that public acceptance of trade liberalization requires that efforts be made to help those who lose from market opening. Unlike the GATT/WTO, many RTAs provide for financial support mechanisms for precisely this purpose.

The AC includes the Latin American Reserve Fund as one of its main bodies (Art. 6). The Fund is the financial institution of the Andean system and its main purpose is to promote the integration process in the Andean region (Art. 45). Resources for projects are to be allocated in accordance with the objective of reducing existing asymmetries among the members through favourable policies toward Bolivia and Ecuador (Art. 118). The Fund has provided short-term financing aimed at crisis prevention and management. Its financing has played an important countercyclical role during periods of high volatility in the international environment. Its loans peaked in 1996 and 1999 and facilitated the rapid recovery of GDP growth in the Andean countries following two severe external shocks in those years (Machinea and Rozenwurcel 2004).

SAFTA members are encouraged to consider the application of direct measures to enhance sustainable exports from LDC members. SAFTA also supports the establishment of an appropriate mechanism to compensate LDCs for their loss of customs revenue. In particular, this compensating mechanism and its rules and regulations will be established prior to the entry into force of the trade liberalization program (Art. 11.e).

The 2002 SACU Agreement reforms the previous Revenue Sharing Formula and refurbishes the Common Revenue Pool financed by customs, excise and additional duties collected in the common customs area. Part 7 and its Annex I provide a revenue-sharing formula in which funds from the Pool are distributed among member states (Kirk and Stern 2003). The share accruing to each member state will be calculated from three distinct components: the customs, the excise and the development components. While the customs and excise components will be shared in accordance with a formula based on the value of intra-SACU imports collected and GDP, respectively, the development component operates in the form of development assistance. At the initial stage, 85 per cent of excise revenue will be distributed on the basis of the relative GDP of the five members, and 15 per cent will be distributed in such a way as to narrow the relative difference of GDP per capita among members (Art. 32, Protocol).

COMESA establishes a special fund to tackle the problems of underdeveloped areas and other disadvantages resulting from the integration process (Art. 150). This fund includes elements of compensation designed to assist members suffering from revenue shocks due to the introduction of the common external tariff (CET) and a component for financing development projects.

ECCAS establishes two separate funding systems; the Fund for Compensation for Loss of Revenue and the Community Cooperation and Development Fund. The former aims to compensate for revenue loss resulting from implementing intra-Community trade (Art. 39). In 2002, the Conference of heads of ECCAS states and governments adopted an autonomous financing mechanism that foresees that both funds will be financed by the establishment of a tax or a levy on member states (Decision No. 5, 2002).

Capacity building and technical assistance

Deficiencies in supply-side capacity have prevented many developing countries from taking full advantage of the opportunities of growth through trade. Many RTAs pursuing a single market or an economic union contain extensive provisions that the members should make efforts to develop industrial, agricultural and services capacities of their less-advanced partners. Indeed, in recent RTA negotiations, technical assistance and capacity building have been at the forefront of deliberations (OAS 2002).

Article 21 of ALADI supports the establishment of cooperation programs and actions in the fields of investment, financing and technology that are supportive of LDCs as a means of facilitating tariff cuts. To put these commitments into practice, Resolution 4 requires that the members negotiate special cooperation programs with each relatively less-advanced member. Such programs cover the following activities: market studies, project pre-feasibility and feasibility studies; promotion of multinational Latin American enterprises; technological and management cooperation; and joint actions concerning projects of common interest. Resolution 4 also provides that an Economic Promotion Unit for relatively less-developed countries shall be established within the secretariat to provide support required for full participation within the integration process. In addition, member countries are encouraged to provide land-locked countries with facilities to establish free zones, warehouses or ports and other administrative international transit facilities within their territories (Art. 23).

The industrial development programs of the AC give special consideration to the situations of Bolivia and Ecuador, so that they can develop production facilities in their territories. This approach is apparent within their modes of industrial integration (Art. 111). In addition, AC members have committed themselves to acting jointly to secure technical assistance and financing for the broader development needs of Bolivia and Ecuador, particularly for integration-related projects (Art. 118).

Article 157 of CARICOM provides that disadvantaged countries, regions and sectors should be given technical and financial assistance. Such assistance includes grants or access to low-cost financing, preparation of project proposals and improved access to technology and factory design. In addition, technical assistance may take the form of aid to establish national standards bodies, assistance to advance diversification programmes, legal expertise for fair competition and expert assistance in the preparation of dispute resolution (Art. 157). The revised Treaty provides for technical assistance in areas including micro- and small-scale economic enterprises, standards and technical regulations and negotiation for the conclusion of (trade) agreements (Art. 53, 67 & 230).

Capacity building and technical assistance constitute a core element of CAFTA. CAFTA identifies administration and trade facilitation and technical barriers to trade, as well as labour and environment as areas for capacity building (Art. 5.12, 7.8, 16.5 & 17.9). In particular, the

CAFTA Agreement establishes the Committee on Capacity Building, under which Central American countries outline their national capacity building strategies (Art. 19.4). As part of the CAFTA negotiations, national action plans for Costa Rica, El Salvador, Guatemala, Honduras and Nicaragua call for each of these countries to identify their trade capacity building needs.

The SAFTA text requires that special consideration be given to requests from least-developed members for technical assistance and cooperation arrangements. Such assistance and cooperation agreements are seen as a means of assisting the expansion of their trade with other contracting states and capacity to benefit from SAFTA. A list of possible areas for such technical assistance will be negotiated by the members and incorporated as an integral part of this agreement (Art. 11.d).

Chapter 22 of COMESA indicates a wide range of cooperation and assistance measures for least developed countries and economically depressed areas including infrastructure, industry, agriculture and services. Realization of this mandate hinges on members encouraging new investments, introducing new technologies, promoting special programs and projects and strengthening chambers of commerce and other relevant bodies (Art. 144). Transport and communications are given special emphasis under efforts at infrastructure development (Art. 145).

Approaches being taken at the regional level may help inform the evolving debate on aid-for-trade (AFT) in the WTO. For although aid-for-trade is not part of the Doha single undertaking, progress on AFT in the WTO is nevertheless linked to the attainment of improved market access under the DDA. Indeed, the perception that it may be possible in certain areas to make more progress regionally than multilaterally may be heightened by the fact that the AFT money pledged by the EU in a WTO framework (€2 billion pledged at the Hong Kong ministerial meeting) will most likely be spent in a regional framework, through Economic Partnership Agreements.

How effective is regional cooperation in addressing asymmetries?

How effective are SDT-type provisions in RTAs in practice? This section looks at provisions for financial assistance and technical cooperation. The next section will assess provisions for asymmetric liberalization commitments.

It is one thing to gather information on the nature of provisions embodied in regional agreements. It is quite another thing to assess how these provisions are implemented. Going beyond the legal provisions is important because one has the impression that these provisions are often not fully implemented. Very few of the South-South initiatives for direct financial assistance are fully operational.

- The CARICOM funding mechanism has yet to be realized. In May 2005, the CARICOM Council for Finance and Planning discussed a draft feasibility study and recommendations outlining modalities for setting up and operating the fund.
- Currently, SAFTA members are negotiating modalities for the operation of the proposed compensating mechanism and fund.
- The SACU Revenue Sharing Formula is still at the development stage.
- The Seventh COMESA Summit adopted the Protocol for the establishment of the Fund for Cooperation, Compensation and Development in May 2002, but its ratification has yet to be completed.
- Although ECCAS heads of state agreed in 2003 that they would transfer 0.4 per cent of import-duty revenue to the proposed funds by January 2004, the funding system is not yet operating due to the lack of administrative procedures.
- An SADC Regional Development Fund is still on the drawing board.

Similarly, in the field of technical assistance and capacity building more broadly, many South-South initiatives are clearly still to be realized – like the Economic Promotion Unit to be established under ALADI or the technical assistance to be provided under SAFTA – and more generally, there must be questions about the extent of assistance being extended.

South-South agreements, by definition, do not have an advanced member able to fund assistance. Moreover, the successful implementation of funding mechanisms faces two particular challenges: the need for the participating countries to agree on which of them should be net contributors and which should be net recipients and, secondly, the need for a pooling of national competencies in the design of regional aids (Bouzas, 2005). In the face of these challenges, there is likely to be a persisting gap between stated objectives and actual help provided on the ground.

North-South agreements, in contrast, have a greater potential for resource transfers among members. Even here, however, it cannot be assumed that this potential is being fully realized. For example, it has been suggested that NAFTA's North American Development Bank lacks an adequate mandate and funding (Hufbauer and Schott, 2005). And although, as noted earlier, regional agreements are likely to be the principal vehicle for aid-for-trade assistance, the question arises as to how much additionality is involved here and how much of the funding represents a diversion of money already pledged.

North-South cooperation, precisely because it involves a relationship of uneven strengths, cannot be assumed *a priori* to be always to the benefit of the weaker partner. Clearly there are examples of beneficial exchanges. One such example arises from a case study of the avocado trade between Mexico and the United States. Exports from Mexico, which are now burgeoning, were facilitated by cooperation between the US and Mexican regulatory agencies dealing with SPS measures. This cooperation was made possible by the institutional framework embodied in NAFTA. This is demonstrably a question of asymmetries because the cooperation was intended to overcome handicaps faced by small Mexican farmers. But the benefits, shared by US consumers, were reciprocal (OECD 2005b).

In other cases, however, where "cooperation" involves sensitive issues such as core labour standards, environmental protection or intellectual property rights, the pressure brought to bear by the stronger partner may warrant closer scrutiny. In this respect, WTO-*plus*, in a framework of asymmetric integration, does not necessarily mean *better*. For example, ongoing negotiation of a US-Thai RTA has prompted the observation that a provision sought by the United States (also found in other RTAs) that would restrict generic drug companies from using brand name test data to get marketing approval goes beyond commitments required of WTO Members in a way that could be seen as unduly constraining. The importance of the respective size of negotiating partners has been highlighted by the ongoing negotiation of a bilateral agreement between two major players – the European Union and India. In this case, India has succeeded in keeping core labour standards off the agenda.

It might be observed from this brief survey of the effectiveness of regional cooperation in dealing with asymmetries that the realization of benefits, particularly from South-South cooperation, is likely to depend on complementary efforts by other parties – notably, the regional development banks, the international financial institutions and the donor community at the national level. Such complementary efforts are being pursued systematically, for example, by the Andean Community (FTAA 2003). Two specific areas have been identified where significant benefits might be expected from external assistance: infrastructure investment and technological development, where extra-regional resources can stimulate the learning process; and the design and development of common policy frameworks in order to foster equivalent institutional approaches and capacities (Bouzas 2005). However, the paucity of data on the actual implementation of cooperative initiatives suggests that this topic would warrant much closer analysis, backed by more systematic reporting at the regional level.

How effective are asymmetric liberalization commitments?

It is broadly accepted that for all countries, and not least for developing countries, own-liberalization is an important element of the gains from trade (Heydon 2006).

- In agriculture, fully one half of developing country gains from the DDA are estimated to come from their own liberalization (Anderson and Martin 2006).
- In services, own-liberalization by developing countries yields particular benefits because of the relatively high level of developing country barriers, and because of the negative effects on downstream users of impediments to service inputs (Dihel 2005).
- In non-agricultural market access, while developing countries get a greater share of total welfare gains (89%) with differentiated coefficients that allow them to liberalize less (5% for industrialized countries, 30% for developing countries), their absolute gains are greater if a Swiss formula/5 per cent coefficient is applied to all countries, that is, if developing countries fully commit to the liberalization process (Lippoldt and Kowalski 2003).
- In trade facilitation, if developing countries commit to reform they are estimated to reap two-thirds of the gains on offer. If, however, they opt out of the reform process, developing country GDP drops by 3 per cent (Walkenhorst and Yasui 2003).

Provisions in RTAs that allow countries to delay market opening or to open selectively, may encourage them, eventually, to engage in liberalization efforts that they would otherwise avoid. It is more likely, however, that asymmetric commitments bestowing lower obligations on less developed members will simply cause them to forgo the full benefits of trade liberalization while locking them into activities that do not correspond to their true comparative advantage. This is the widely documented pitfall of special and differential treatment. And it applies no less at the regional level than it does multilaterally. Take Mexico in the framework of NAFTA as a counterfactual example. The absence of asymmetric liberalization commitments in favour of Mexico has not impeded the ability of Mexico to benefit from the accord. Indeed the substantial trade and investment benefits that Mexico has derived from NAFTA can be attributed in no small part to the fact that among the three participating countries it was in Mexico that the most extensive regulatory reform occurred.

In summary, of the two broad types of SDT, we appear to have one – flexibility in liberalization – that is widely applied in regional agreements but of questionable value insofar as it weakens the commitment to market opening, and another – financial and technical assistance – that is broadly beneficial but implemented in regional accords at a level well below its potential.

Re-asserting the primacy of multilateral liberalization

It has been observed that while regional deals can complement the multilateral trading system, they are not a substitute for it (Heydon, 2003). This applies equally to regional provisions dealing with asymmetries. Regional agreements may in certain prescribed areas advance more quickly than is possible multilaterally, but they can never substitute for non-discriminatory MFN liberalization and broad-based multilateral rulemaking. And as regional and bilateral initiatives advance, there is need for a careful examination that the "benefits" being offered – should they take the form of lesser liberalization commitments – are not contrary to the genuine interests of the beneficiary.

Even if it is assumed that there may be gains to relatively less-advanced countries from entering regional agreements that address asymmetries, these gains need to be weighed against the costs that membership of preferential arrangements is likely to entail. Prominent among these costs is the increased complexity facing businesses within member countries, not least because of proliferating rules of origin and product standards. Take Chile as an example. Chile is a member of some 15 agreements, is ratifying another three, and contemplating another three (with China, India and Panama). This gives a myriad of rules of origin and, because plurilateral deals usually involve individual negotiations with each member country, some 50 sets of arrangements to keep track of. This is the balance that has to be considered. Chile may gain some 50 opportunities to address asymmetric integration, but it risks a trading regime 50 times more complex than it might otherwise be.

Another potential risk of regional and bilateral deals for the weaker partner arises from the pressure, alluded to above, to undertake commitments in respect of trade-related issues such as core labour standards and the environment. To the extent that RTAs – whether in a hub and spokes or a bilateral configuration – are likely increasingly to involve partners at markedly different stages of development, there would be benefit in closer consultation among less-developed participants. This would not alter the underlying disparity in dependence, based on relative market size, but it would enable developing countries to share experience and pool expertise. It has further been suggested (Baldwin, 2006) that there may be a role here for the WTO, in setting up an economic analysis service, akin to the WTO Advisory Centre on WTO law, that could help weaker countries in the course of negotiating regional agreements. Even more important than helping facilitate regional initiatives, such a service might serve to demonstrate that the underlying interests of developing countries are more likely to be advanced through their full commitment to broad-based liberalization on a multilateral basis.

Note

* This chapter has been developed from a paper by the author and Hyung-Jong Lee, "The Treatment of Asymmetries in Regional Trade Agreements", presented by Ken Heydon at the Third CEPII-IDB Conference on the New Regionalism, Washington DC, 9–10 February 2006. The author wishes to acknowledge the input of Hyung-Jong Lee to this work.

REFERENCES

Anderson, K., and W. Martin (2006) *Agricultural Trade Reform and the Doha Development Agenda*, Washington, DC: World Bank.

Baldwin, R. (2006) "Multilateralising Regionalism: Spaghetti Bowls as Building Blocs on the Path to Global Free Trade", Discussion Paper No. 5775, London: Centre for Economic Policy Research.

Bouzas, R. (2003) "Mechanisms for Compensating the Asymmetrical Effects of Regional Integration and Globalization: Lessons from Latin America and the Caribbean", presented at the seminar "Confronting the Challenges of Regional Development in Latin America and the Caribbean", Milan, 22 March.

Bouzas, R. (2005) "Compensating Asymmetries in Regional Integration Agreements: Lessons from Mercosur", in P. Giordano, J. Meyer-Stamer and F. Lanzafame, eds, *Asymmetries in Regional Integration and Local Development*, Washington, DC: Inter-American Development Bank, pp. 85–112.

Crawford, J. A., and R. V. Fiorentino (2005) "The Changing Landscape of Regional Trade Agreements", Discussion Paper No. 8, Geneva: WTO.

Dihel, N. (2005) "The Impact of Services Barriers on Effective Rates of Protection in Agriculture and Manufacturing", *Enhancing the Performance of the Services Sector*, 2005(8): 127–130.

Feldmann, M. (2003) "EU-Poland Association Agreement", in G. P. Sampson and S. Woolcock, eds, *Regionalism, Multilateralism and Economic Integration: The Recent Experience*, Tokyo: United Nations University Press, pp. 35–61.

FTAA (2003) "Subregional Strategy for Strengthening the Trade-Related Capacities of FTAA Countries", FTAA.SME/INF/145, 9 October 2003.

Heydon, K. (2003) "Regionalism: A Complement, Not a Substitute", in *Regionalism and the Multilateral Trading System*, Paris: OECD, pp. 11–21.

Heydon, K. (2006) "Advancing the Doha Development Agenda", *Agenda* 13(2): 161–174.

Hufbauer, G. C., and J. J. Schott (2005) *NAFTA Revisited: Achievements and Challenges*, Washington, DC: Institute for International Economics.

Kirk, R., and M. Stern (2003) "The New Southern African Customs Union Agreement," Africa Region Working Paper No. 57, Washington, DC: World Bank.

Lippoldt, D., and P. Kowalski (2003) "The Doha Development Agenda: Welfare Gains from Further Multilateral Trade Liberalisation with Respect to Tariffs", TD/TC/WP(2003)10 Final, Paris: OECD.

Machinea, J. L., and G. Rozenwurcel (2004) "Macroeconomic Coordination in Latin America: Does It Have a Future?" presented at the seminar "Regional Financial Arrangements", New York, 14–15 July.

OAS (2002) "The OAS Contribution to Trade-Related Capacity Building in the Americas", Washington, DC: Organization of American States, 27 February.

OECD (2005a) "Special and Differential Treatment: Thinking Outside the Box", TD/TC/RD(2005)5, Paris: OECD.

OECD (2005b) *Trade and Structural Adjustment: Embracing Globalisation*, Paris: OECD.

Pearson, M. (2004) "Capacity Building – Regional Trade Policy and Trade Facilitation: Experiences of COMESA", presented OECD-DAC/WTO Meeting on Trade Capacity Building, Paris, 2–3 March 2004.

Reiter, J. (2003) "EU-Mexico Free Trade Agreement", in G. P. Sampson and S. Woolcock, eds, *Regionalism, Multilateralism and Economic Integration: The Recent Experience*, Tokyo: United Nations University Press, pp. 62–99.

Walkenhorst, P., and T. Yasui (2003) "Quantitative Assessment of the Benefits of Trade Facilitation", TD/TC/WP(2003)31 Final, Paris: OECD.

Woolcock, S. (2003) "Conclusions", in G. P. Sampson and S. Woolcock, eds, *Regionalism, Multilateralism and Economic Integration: The Recent Experience*, Tokyo: United Nations University Press, pp. 314–318.

World Bank (2005), *DR-CAFTA: Challenges and Opportunities for Central America*, Washington, DC: World Bank.

WTO (2001) "Implementation of Special and Differential Treatment Provisions in WTO Agreements and Decisions", WT/COMTD/W/77/Rev.1.

Agreements and Treaties

Agreement on South Asian Free Trade Area (SAFTA; available at http://www.saarc-sec.org/main.php?id=12&t=7.1).

Agreement on the Common Effective Preferential Tariff Scheme for the ASEAN Free Trade Area (available at: http://www.aseansec.org/12375.htm).

Andean Subregional Integration Agreement (Cartagena Agreement; available at http://www.comunidadandina.org/ingles/treaties/trea/ande_trie1.htm).

COMESA Treaty (available at http://www.comesa.int/comesa%20treaty/comesa%20treaty/Multi-language_content.2005-07-01.3414/en).

Dominican Republic – Central America and United States Free Trade Agreement (available at http://ustr.gov/assets/Trade_Agreements/Bilateral/CAFTA/CAFTA-DR_Final_Texts/asset_upload_file148_3916.pdf).

Montevideo Treaty: Instrument Establishing the Latin American Integration Association (ALADI; available at http://www.aladi.org/nsfaladi/textacdos.nsf/).

North American Free Trade Agreement (available at http://www.nafta-sec-alena.org/DefaultSite/index_e.aspx?DetailID=78).

Pacific Island Countries Trade Agreement (PICTA) (available at http://www.forumsec.org.fj/).

Revised Treaty of Chaguaramas Establishing the Caribbean Community including CARICOM Single Market and Economy (available at http://www.caricom.org/jsp/community/revised_treaty-text.pdf).

Southern African Customs Union (SACU) Agreement (available at http://www.tralac.org/scripts/content.php?id=961).

Southern Common Market (MERCOSUR) Agreement (Treaty of Asunción; available at http://www.itcilo.it/english/actrav/telearn/global/ilo/blokit/mercoa.htm).

Treaty Establishing the Economic Community of Central African Countries (available at http://www.iss.co.za/AF/RegOrg/unity_to_union/pdfs/eccas/eccastreaty.pdf).

Treaty of South Africa Development Community (available at http://www.sadc.int/index.php?action=a1001&page_id=declaration_and_treaty_of_sadc).

Membership of Plurilateral Bodies

Latin American Integration Association (ALADI): Argentina, Bolivia, Brazil, Chile, Colombia, Ecuador, Mexico, Paraguay, Peru, Uruguay, Venezuela.

Southern Common Market (MERCOSUR): Argentina, Brazil, Paraguay, Uruguay.

Caribbean Community and Common Market (CARICOM): Antigua and Barbuda, Bahamas, Belize, Dominican Republic, Grenada, Guyana, Haiti, Jamaica, Montserrat, St Kitts and Nevis, St Lucia and the Grenadines, Suriname, Trinidad and Tobago.

Andean Community (AC): Bolivia, Colombia, Ecuador, Peru, Venezuela.

Dominican Republic-Central American Free Trade Agreement (CAFTA): Costa Rica, Dominican Republic, El Salvador, Guatemala, Honduras, Nicaragua, United States.

ASEAN Free Trade Area (AFTA): Brunei, Cambodia, Indonesia, Lao PDR, Malaysia, Myanmar, Philippines, Singapore, Thailand, Vietnam.

South Asia Free Trade Area (SAFTA): Bangladesh, Bhutan, India, Maldives, Nepal, Pakistan, Sri Lanka.

Pacific Island Countries Trade Agreement (PICTA): Cook Islands, Fiji, Kiribati, Marshall Islands, Micronesia, Nauru, Niue, Palau, Papua New Guinea, Samoa, Solomon Islands, Tuvalu, Tonga, Vanuatu.

Southern African Customs Union (SACU): Botswana, Lesotho, Namibia, South Africa, Swaziland.

Southern African Development Community (SADC): Angola, Botswana, DR Congo, Lesotho, Malawi, Mauritius, Mozambique, Namibia, South Africa, Swaziland, Tanzania, Zambia, Zimbabwe.

Common Market for Eastern and Southern Africa (COMESA): Angola, Burundi, Comoros, DR Congo, Djibouti, Egypt, Eritrea, Ethiopia, Kenya, Libya, Madagascar, Malawi, Mauritius, Rwanda, Seychelles, Sudan, Swaziland, Uganda, Zambia, Zimbabwe.

Economic Community of Central African States (ECCAS): Angola, Burundi, Cameroon, Central Africa, Chad, DR Congo, Congo, Equatorial Guinea, Gabon, Rwanda, Sao Tome and Principe.

Part IV
Process

12

Developing countries and the reform of the WTO Dispute Settlement System: Expectations and realities

George Akpan

The Uruguay Round of trade negotiations produced many commendable results.[1] Apart from expanding the scope of matters to be addressed by the multilateral trading system from the limited confines of trade in goods to trade in services and intellectual property, among others, one major acclaimed achievement of that round was the introduction of an effective rule-based system for resolving trade disputes that may arise from the many agreements spawned by that round. Commentators have described the system of dispute resolution introduced by that round in superlative terms.[2] This is not misplaced when viewed against the background of what was in place under the old GATT system.

There is no doubt that the introduction of the Dispute Settlement Understanding (DSU) enhanced the legitimacy of the multilateral trading system. One only needs to look at the weaknesses of the previous GATT system to begin to appreciate the pace-setting innovations of the DSU in the settlement of trade disputes. The system gave voice to smaller and weaker nations to be able to bring powerful nations before an international tribunal to account for their alleged non-conformity with international trade rules.

Be that as it may, the DSU is a human institution. In spite of the encomiums poured on it, it is not a perfect institution. The evolution of the current system of dispute settlement benefited from the experiences garnered from the operation of the old GATT dispute settlement system. Change is essential and constant in every human institution. It was perhaps in recognition of this fact that the Members of the WTO as part of

Developing countries and the WTO: Policy approaches, Sampson and Chambers (eds),
United Nations University Press, 2008, ISBN 978-92-808-1153-7

the Marrakesh Declaration made a conscious decision to review the DSU by 1999.

This chapter takes a look at the workings and the participation of developing countries in the DSU. It examines the complaints made against it and the state of play in ongoing negotiations for its reform. The chapter is divided into six sections. The next section looks at how the system has fared since its introduction in 1995. That is followed by a section dealing with the proposed reforms and some of the proposals made, then a section that deals with the participation of developing countries in the DSU. The following section explores the state of play and the direction of the negotiations, and the final section draws conclusions. The overall objective of the chapter is to examine some of the proposed reforms on how to improve the system and point the direction that developing countries should follow to make the DSU more accessible and credible.

How the system has fared

The Uruguay Round provided Members an opportunity to take a comprehensive look at the workings of the system of resolution of trade disputes and to introduce measures to cure the so-called "birth defects" that hampered the effective working of the system. The reforms produced remarkable results that are widely acclaimed.

The reforms, while retaining some of the traditional features of the old GATT system, introduced innovations to the dispute settlement process. One of the reforms is the removal of the ability of the party against which a complaint is brought from blocking key stages of the dispute settlement process and frustrating the system. Besides, the process also introduced strict time limits for panels to follow. Importantly, they introduced the Appellate Body (AB) as the final arbiter in trade disputes. This ensures coherence and consistency of rulings and adds to the predictability of the system.

Additionally, the reform introduced an integrated system of dispute settlement and makes recourse to the system for settlement of all trade disputes mandatory for all members. It reduces reliance on the use of force of power to settle disputes and makes the force of argument and the rule of law essential features of the system. By so doing, the system seeks to ensure expeditious settlement of disputes devoid of power play, cure the long delays that characterized the old GATT system and restore legitimacy, credibility and effectiveness to the system of settlement of trade-related disputes.

More than ten years after the adoption of the DSU and the operation of the new dispute settlement system in the WTO, various assessments have been carried out on the operation of the system. Many commentators have examined aspects of the system. Some assessments have looked at the number of disputes handled by the system. Others have looked at the number of disputes effectively settled at various stages of the process while others have concentrated on the results achieved, the number of participants from developed and developing countries and even the least-developed countries. Most of the assessments have returned favourable verdicts on the operation of the system within the first decade of its operation. One commentator intimately connected with the system commented thus: "The WTO dispute settlement system is widely praised by its users, by academics, and by other WTO observers. True there are a few naysayers, but their criticism is generally not so much directed to the process as it is about particular rulings with which they disagree. Perhaps the clearest evidence that there is not much that needs improvement is the fact that the negotiations on clarification and improvements of the system, which have been ongoing since 1998, have not led to a single change in the *Understanding on Rules and Procedures Governing the Settlement of Disputes* (DSU)" (Hughes 2006: 193). Others commentators similarly have positive words for the operation of the system (Davey 2005: 13–14).

Indeed, the number of complaints brought before the DSU has been phenomenal. As of 9 October 2006, up to 350 complaints have been notified to the WTO. Out of this, developed country Members brought 212 complaints, representing 60 per cent of all disputes, 131 of which were against other developed countries while 81 were against developing countries. Developing countries' share of the disputes was 132 (37%), 78 of these were against developed countries as respondents while 54 were against developing countries as respondents. Six complaints were brought by both developed and developing countries against developed-country members as respondents (WTO 2006).[3] The overview of statistical data also reveals that 98 AB and Panel Reports have been adopted and 51 mutually agreed solutions were recorded since 1995. Other complaints were either abandoned or are at various stages of the process. From these records, it is not in doubt that the results of the changes brought about by the Uruguay Round have been impressive. However impressive statistics may be, it may not reveal much about the actual participants in the system. The issue is whether all members of the WTO that have interest in using the system have been able to do so to defend their trade interest. Although the above statistics show that developing countries have brought many of the complaints, it does not reveal the identities of those countries and the fact that the majority of developing-country Members have never made use of the system even though they may have reason to want to do so. The success of the system cannot therefore be complete when it does not cater to the legitimate interest of all members and, particularly, the weak within the organization. This issue is discussed later in this chapter.

The reform of the DSU

Change is constant in any human setting. One of the most abiding attributes of the human race is the urge to seek improvement to the human condition, including its institutions. The evolution of the DSU itself is a testimony to this fact. It was the experiences generated from the operation of the old GATT dispute settlement system that informed the innovations of the Uruguay Round. The quest for improvement of the DSU will continue as long as it forms part of the multilateral trading system. It is therefore not surprising that the architects of the system adopted a decision early to review it by 1 January 1999. Preparations for negotiations were begun in 1997, but actual negotiations started in 1998. Members made many proposals on how the system is to be reformed. However, not much progress could be made before the controversial EC-Banana dispute and the so-called sequencing problem overshadowed the negotiations.[4] The deadline was extended to 31 July 1999. By the new deadline, there was still controversy in many areas, which did not produce any agreement. The matter did not receive much attention until the Doha Ministerial Meeting. At Doha, Members agreed to put life back into the negotiations on the reform of the DSU. Paragraph 30 of the Doha Declaration states the commitment of members to this effect: "We agree to negotiations on improvements and clarifications of the Dispute Settlement Understanding. The negotiations should be based on the work done thus far as well as any additional proposals by members, and aim to agree on improvements and clarifications not later than May 2003, at which time we will take steps to ensure that the results enter into force as soon as possible thereafter".[5]

The Declaration gave additional impetus to the negotiations on the reform of the DSU and Special Sessions negotiations were held in the DSB in 2002. What was significant in the negotiations was the enthusiasm of members to participate in them. Members actively participated and made many proposals on how to reform the DSU. Even more surprising was the involvement of many developing-country Members who hardly make use of the system. They actively participated and made proposals. This was done in the expectation that the reform of the system will enhance the participation of developing-country Members. Members still could not conclude negotiations by the deadline of May 2003. But there was interest by members to continue further negotiations after this deadline. The deadline was further extended by one year till May 2004.

Further negotiations were restarted in October of 2003 after the failure of the Cancun meeting in September 2003. Even with the replacement of the Chairs of all the Negotiating Councils, including that of the DSU in March 2004, the process could not be completed despite the effort of the new Chair, Ambassador David Spencer of Australia. The deadline of May 2004 was also missed, as there was no agreement among members on the reforms of the DSU. In July 2004, the General Council, perhaps taking cognizance of the many failed deadlines, decided that negotiations on the reforms of the DSU should continue, but did not deem it fit to fix any timeline within which negotiations should be completed. At the Hong Kong Ministerial Meeting, members adopted a declaration noting the progress made in the Dispute Settlement Understanding negotiations and directed the Special Session to continue to work toward a "rapid conclusion of the negotiations".[6] After the Hong Ministerial Meeting, several meetings of the Special Session were held in 2006 under the new Chair, Ambassador Ronald Soto of Costa Rica. Members made modifications to their earlier proposals and sought informal meetings to achieve consensus on controversial issues.

Some proposals for reforms

This section examines some of the proposals made by Members. The emphasis is on how these proposals would affect developing-country Members, which have actively participated in the negotiations. Although many proposals have been made, only a few of these proposals will be examined in this section. Proposals presented can be divided into three broad categories, namely, proposals that have to do with institutions of the WTO dispute settlement; proposals that concern proceedings of the WTO dispute settlement and proposals that deal with systemic issues.[7]

Proposals on institutions of the WTO

Strong institutions underpin the effective functioning of any system of dispute settlement. This is not different with the WTO's DSU. One proposal that relates to institutions of the WTO dispute settlement deals with the creation of a system of permanent panellists similar to that of the AB. The present ad hoc system is a carry-over from the old GATT days. It is made up largely of government officials, the system is prone to delays and the quality of the reports may be compromised as the time and dedication required to produce quality reports may be lacking. The proposal makes sense when it is placed against the background that the

WTO dispute settlement system is increasingly used by members and this trend is likely to expand and that the nature of disputes has increased in sophistication and complexity faster than the present ad hoc system can cope with. The proposal by the EC envisages a permanent roster of panellists composed of 15 to 24 persons appointed by the DSB. The proposal makes it possible for two persons outside the roster to be appointed as panellists where the disputants agree at the time of the establishment of the panel, but the external persons must have expertise in the area of the dispute. However, the Chairmanship of the Panel is limited to the permanent members on the roster. The roster is to be representative of the broad membership of the WTO and panellists are to have a non-renewable term of six years.

Although this proposal has received little support among members, there is much to be said in support of the establishment of a permanent panel for the adjudication of trade disputes in the WTO. For one, the effective and satisfactory resolution of any dispute requires a proper assessment of the factual basis of the dispute and the making of appropriate findings based on them by people with the necessary experience and expertise. The reality is that at the moment, there are few such experienced panellists that can be called upon as ad hoc panellists. A system of permanent panellists would allow experienced persons to be recruited from outside the traditional market from which ad hoc panellists are recruited and this will enhance the effectiveness and legitimacy of the system. Besides, the present system draws from government officials with some experience in trade issues. Also, experience has shown that members are frequently unable to agree on panel compositions with the result that this leads to waste of valuable time and the Director General invariably appoints panellists. It would help the legitimacy of the system to establish a permanent system from where panellists could be drawn without raising questions about the neutrality of the WTO Secretariat.

From an efficiency point of view, a more professional panellist would increase the efficiency of the dispute settlement system. The fact that panellists are experienced means that less time would be required for the factual analysis and the examination of the legal issues involved in a dispute. A permanent roster also means that much time would be saved in the process of composing panels. The result would be a more professional panel that will reduce the overall time that is spent in the dispute settlement process and improve the efficiency of the system. However, not all members agree to the necessity of a permanent panel. Members with opposing views argue that a permanent panel will erode the authority and legitimacy of the system in that Members would be excluded from the process of panel composition that allows for flexibility and the appointment of persons who are more at home with the values of the WTO

(Bercero and Garzotti 2005). Another argument is that the appointment of permanent panel members would require increased stipends for the panellists and, besides, it may be difficult to find qualified persons from developing countries to be appointed as panellists.

Fundamentally, some members oppose the idea of a permanent panel as this is seen as a further judicialization of the WTO, which does not sit comfortably with them. Overall, there are strong views in support as there are against the introduction of a permanent panel. However, one cannot deny the gains that would result from the adoption of a permanent panel. Some of the arguments against the introduction of a permanent panel are not unsurmountable. The EC proposal is flexible enough to allow members to have a hand in the appointment of panellists. The lack of experienced panellists from developing countries may be exaggerated. The cost factor could be surmounted once Members agree on the adoption of a permanent panel. The challenge would be finding a balance between the judicialization of the system and those that favour the diplomatic approach.

Where should developing countries stand on this issue? Some developing countries are opposed to the idea of a permanent panel in the WTO. They feel that it will lead to increased judicialization of the system and remove the flexibility that they may have in negotiating solutions to meet their particular circumstances. One is not clear as to how this will happen. In fact, the author believes that the reform of the system along the lines proposed by the EC with some modifications should be supported by the developing countries, as it would better protect their interest.

First, the appointment of panellists would be representative of the broad membership of the WTO and appointed by the DSB. Developing countries could use the opportunity and their majority power to push for the appointment of panellists that will take account of the special situation of developing countries, rather than in the present system that may not allow persons from developing countries to sit as panellists. A permanent panel will mean that there will be less room for political manoeuvres in the appointment of panellists and this should work to the advantage of developing-country Members that lack the political clout and resources to engage developed countries in such manoeuvres.

Secondly, as part of the institutional reform, proposals have been made with respect to the reform of the Appellate Body. The proposal relates to flexibility in increasing the AB's membership to be able to cope with increased workload. The membership of the AB is presently set at seven and one proposal will see this number increased by the AB itself when the need arises. This proposal is meant to ensure the effectiveness of the AB. Considering the difficulty of negotiating reforms of the dispute settlement system, the AB, which is faced with the task of deciding matters on appeal, should be given the flexibility to increase its membership to meet increased workload subject to clear criteria to be worked out during the present negotiations so as to ensure that the work of the AB does not suffer as a result of inadequate manpower. Developing countries should support or make proposals that would ensure the effectiveness of the AB.

Proposals in respect of WTO proceedings

Many members have made proposals that are supposed to improve upon procedures in the current system. They range from proposals for during the consultation process to proposals for the actual proceedings before the WTO adjudicatory bodies.

With respect to proposals in the consultation process, some members have proposed that the period required for consultations should be reduced from the present 60 days to 30 days. This is to address the problem of delays and to speed up the settlement of disputes. Developing countries expect that the negotiations would be sensitive to their need to have extended consultations. This explains why developing countries are opposed to reducing the time for consultations, as they argue that they require sufficient time to consult and reach amicable solutions. It is contended that the disagreement in this respect is unnecessary. Some members may require faster time for consultations and 30 days may be sufficient for such consultations. Others may need a longer period to consult effectively. A solution that may be acceptable to Members could be to adopt a 30-day period for consultations with a proviso that where a request for consultation involves a developing country or LDC a period of 60 days would be required unless the parties agree otherwise. The proposals made by the European Community and Japan contain the condition that both parties must agree to the extension. However, the proposal by China is more in tune with the suggestion made here. This addresses the needs of members who require faster consultations and of those that require a longer period. Given the peculiarities and the difficulties that developing and LDCs face in the DSU, it is believed that this flexible proposal will be more in accord with the desire of these countries to have more time to consult.

Another proposal made with respect to consultations is the enhancement of third-party participation in the consultation process. The current rules do recognize that a Member with substantial trade interest can apply to the Member against which the request for consultation is made and to join in the process as a third party.[8] The objection to this is that it gives the respondent too much power and that it may lead to discrimination, as the respondent may object to the participation of a Member who may not support its position in the consultations. In practice, the consent of the respondent is difficult to obtain. Developing countries expect the current negotiations to make it easier for them to participate in consultations as third parties. Many proposals have been tabled in order to enhance third-party rights in the consultation process. One proposal is the recognition of an automatic right to join in consultations whenever a request for consultations is made by developing countries and LDCs.[9] Some members are opposed to this proposal on the simple ground that it will lead to extensive delays and frustrate the aim of the dispute settlement system, which is to settle disputes between the disputing parties. Another proposal is "an all or nothing approach" to remedy the situation. By this proposal, a Member to which the request for consultations is made must consider all the requests made by third parties and decide either to accept all or reject the entire requests to join in the consultations. This proposal received mixed reactions from Members. One objection to the proposal is that if all requests are lumped together and either accepted or rejected, it would be difficult to treat each request on its merit considering the requirement that third parties applying to join consultations should have a "substantial trade interest". The right of individual members to be isolated and treated on the merits of their case would be compromised if all applications are lumped together and either accepted or rejected. Besides, it would encourage the responding party to routinely reject all requests if it perceives that a particular request is not justified. It was in recognition of these objections that Hong Kong made an alternative proposal on the conditions under which non-disputing parties should be allowed to participate in consultations as third parties. The proposal tabled in April 2006 basically recognizes "a presumption of acceptance of all requests to join in consultations by third-country Members, unless the responding Member and complaining Member either decide jointly or separately to reject the request".[10]

Developing countries should support proposals that would allow for enhanced third party participation in the consultation process. As many developing-country Members hardly make use of the dispute settlement system, it is contended that participation in the consultation process would provide developing-country Members an opportunity to learn about substantive and systemic issues that may arise in consultations and thereby garner the necessary experience and confidence to participate in the system more effectively. There is, however, the need to maintain a balance between the right of third parties to participate in consultations and the interest of the immediate parties to the dispute to reach amicable and mutually acceptable solution to the dispute. Whereas the author subscribes to the presumption of the right of participation unless jointly rejected by the immediate parties, where the disclosure of confidential information will complicate the resolution of a dispute, the main parties should be able to restrict such information to themselves, at least for sometime. Also, third-party participation should not be allowed to delay the consultation process.

With respect to Panels, some Members have proposed that panels should be established more speedily than is presently the case in order to reduce the time for disputes. The proposal is to the effect that instead of establishing the panel by reverse consensus at the second meeting of the DSB at which the request appears on the agenda it should be established at the first meeting at which the request first appears as an item on the agenda.[11] However, developing countries oppose such a proposal as they argue that they will require more time. Again, there is no need for disagreement on this point as the establishment of a panel can be made flexible, allowing those who require immediate establishment of a panel to have it and developing countries that may have reasons to delay the establishment of a panel to retain the present system. The proposal by China that where disputes are brought against developing-country Members the establishment of a panel should be made at the second meeting of the DSB at which the issue appears as an agenda item if the developing country member so requests addresses the need for this flexibility.[12]

Some proposals deal with both the panel and the AB processes. There are proposals made to enable Members to exercise control over the dispute settlement proceedings. One proposal is that provisions should be included that would give the parties to the dispute, by mutual consent, the power to extend the fixed time frames in the DSU. This will affect both the panel and the AB processes. Although this will promote flexibility and allow members to control the proceedings, the fear is that giving members such power may unduly delay the effective adjudication of disputes and compromise the legitimacy of the system. It is, however, possible to allow for members' control and set a time limit beyond which the proceedings could not be extended.   _

With respect to the AB's review proceedings, the introduction of interim review and the extension of the appellate review proceedings from the current 60 days to 120 days are being proposed. Interim reviews may be necessary, for instance, to suspend the challenged measure where an affected Member suffers an economic injury as a result of the challenged measure until the final determination of its legality. However, serious doubt has been raised concerning the practicality of such a measure when one takes into consideration the complexity of the matter.[13] With respect to the extension of the time frame, although this may be sought to enhance Members' control of the system, it is contended that an extension of time frame should not be undertaken just for the sake of allowing Members the control of proceedings. So far, the AB has largely been consistent in discharging its responsibility within the time limit. If any extension is required, the AB should be given the power to decide whether it needs more time to do its work and not the Members. It is conceded that Members are the ultimate drivers of the system, but their role should not be allowed to interfere with the efficient functioning of the system.

A proposal has also been made that would allow for the introduction of a remand procedure. The problem arose in that the DSU does not make provision for the AB to remand or send back a case to the Panel for factual analysis. Sometimes, the AB may find that the factual analysis is inadequate to support a ruling. Since the AB does not have the power to assess the fact, it is expected that it should send the case to the original panel. But the AB has no such power under current rules. The reality is that no ruling is made with respect to the situation and injustice may be occasioned. Proposals have been made to remedy the situation. One proposal is that the rules should be amended to make it possible for the DSB to remand to the original panel the issues that the AB could not pronounce on. Another proposal is to invest the AB with the power to remand cases to the original panel.[14] Generally, there appears to be broad agreement on the need to allow for remand of cases to the original panel to cure the miscarriage of justice that may result from the present system. The question is whether the power should reside with the DSB or with the AB. For those who seek the control of the dispute settlement system by Members, leaving the power with the DSB will confer such control. However, if the intention is to speed up the dispute settlement process, giving authority to the AB appears reasonable to achieve this. Fundamentally, however, the duty of the AB is to clarify the provisions of the covered agreements and it needs adequate factual support to be able to discharge its function effectively. If power were given to Members to decide whether or not to request the case to be remanded, where a Member does not want to request such a remand, an opportunity would be lost to clarify the provisions of the covered agreement for the benefit of all members. It will also save time for remand power to reside with the AB. It is for these reasons that developing countries should support proposals that will allow the AB to retain the power to *suo moto* send the case back to the original panel and to take the benefit of such analysis into its final resolution of the case.

Another proposal relates to the resolution of the sequencing problem that first arose during the compliance phase of the US-EC Banana import regime dispute. Article 22 of the DSU provides that a victorious party can request authorization to retaliate within 30 days after a compliance period has ended if the respondent has not complied. Article 21.5 requires disagreement over adequacy of compliance measures to be decided, where possible, by the original panel and the report, which can be appealed against, is to be submitted within 30 days. The provisions of the two articles reveal a clear gap in the system. The DSU does not appear to integrate Article 21.5 into the processes that follow in article 22. The proposal is that a new Article 21 *bis* be introduced to deal with the matter. Here, a compliance panel that would be made up of the original panellists as presently exist would be given the power to determine the question whether there has been compliance or measures introduced are consistent with the WTO rules. Alongside this proposal is that article 22 of the DSU be amended so that a Member can only request retaliation authorization where a compliance panel has concluded that the offending Member has not brought its measures in compliance with WTO rules. Thus, unlike the current position, which is not clear whether the compliance panel will complete its work before authorization of retaliation, this proposal leaves no one in doubt that the request and approval of retaliation can only take place after the final determination of the question whether the action of the offending Member falls short of its obligation under the WTO rules. The combined effect of these proposals would be to lay to rest the sequencing controversy that arose in the Banana case and the proposal enjoys broad support among Members.

A proposal has also been made to reform retaliation as a weapon that members could have recourse to as a last resort to make the offending member comply with the rulings of the panel or AB. Whereas it is recognized that retaliation can be effective in making the offending Member retrace its steps in holding on to the offending measures, it has long been recognized that retaliation can and has only been effective when it involves developed countries with large economies. One writer argues, "Retaliation must be sufficiently high to induce enough long term losses in order to incite the defendant to conform its trade practice to WTO rules" (Besson and Mehdi 2004). For many developing countries with small market sizes and few items of trade, the possibility of a credible threat of retaliation is limited. Indeed, retaliation may work to their disadvantage. It has been argued that the nature of the sanctions as they presently exist may, apart from discouraging some countries from using the system, also influence the final outcome of a dispute (Mosoti n.d.: 14). To make retaliation more effective, some proposals have been made.

One proposal sponsored by the African Group and the LDC Group calls for the introduction of "collective retaliation". Collective retaliation recognizes that although the original dispute may have been between the immediate parties, the suspension of concessions or other obligations would be undertaken jointly by all Members, not just by the immediate complainant. This proposal has not received support from developed-country Members. However, there is much to be said in favour of collective retaliation. The ability of developed countries or countries with large economies to refuse to comply with the rulings of panels or the AB poses a serious threat to the multilateral trading system and to the collective interest of all members. The introduction of collective retaliation will dissuade Members who are disposed to flouting such rulings from doing so as the collective weight of Members will be brought to bear on the offending member. There are commentators who oppose the idea of collective retaliation because retaliation itself is a matter of last resort and is rarely used in practice (Bercero and Garzotti 2005). It needs to be pointed out that the retaliation that has not worked in practice has been mostly retaliation of one member against another member and because the interest of the offending party may not be particularly hurt by retaliation. It is contended that a different situation may ensue where the collective weight of all members of the WTO is brought to bear on one erring Member. The fact that collective retaliation is allowed would not mean that it would be deployed lightly. Indeed, it may not even be used at all. But there is the necessity for the collective membership to retain the possibility to come to defend the efficacy of the system they have laboriously put in place and the presence of the threat of collective sanction will be a real deterrent to would-be recalcitrant Members. Developing-country Members that have a disincentive in using the system because of the fear that, even if they succeed in a dispute, they lack sufficient capacity to mount credible retaliation against powerful Members except to their own hurt may be encouraged to use the system to defend their trade interest.[15]

An additional proposal to strengthen remedies in the DSU deals with financial compensation. In this respect, it would be recalled that the remedies envisaged by the DSU are prospective in nature. That is, they are meant to take effect in the future and not to take account of the injury or damage the offending trade measure may have caused a Member. The prospective nature of the remedy may encourage a Member to introduce a measure it knows to be inconsistent with WTO law with the full assurance that whenever the measure is declared illegal; all that it would be asked to do will be to withdraw the offending measure with the benefit of additional time to do so. A Member would therefore hide under the laxity of the rules to introduce protective measures that may have disastrous consequences for the economy of a fellow Member. The effect of this may be disastrous for developing countries with small economies and few trading options. In such a situation, the question has been raised whether it would not be expedient to impose financial compensation in favour of the Member who has suffered economic losses. The intention is to increase the cost of non-compliance and to make it unattractive for members who may contemplate this course of action. It is proposed that monetary compensation should be made compulsory in the event of non-implementation of a ruling by a Member. However, it has been argued that financial compensation may not be an easy option. Apart from the fact that legislative authorization may be needed in most cases for such payment to be effected, this may be difficult to get and may thus cause delay. Another objection is that it may provide an easy way out of compliance in easy cases. It is further argued that it may not be an efficient remedy to deal with a non-compliance issue, as it would amount to a form of subsidy (Bercero and Garzotti 2005).

The objections notwithstanding, there is justification for providing some form of financial compensation to a Member whose trade has been adversely affected by the inconsistent actions of another Member. In fact, this is the expectation of developing countries in these negotiations. The difficulty of getting legislative approval should not act as a barrier as the payment of the compensation will become an obligation of the offending member and act as a further pressure on the member to comply. Compensation is not meant to be the final solution to the problem of non-compliance but to provide a remedy until the non-compliant measure of the member is withdrawn or modified. It will therefore not excuse a member from meeting its obligation of complying with a ruling. Financial compensation in the context in which it is proposed would not amount to a subsidy. The payment is to be made as a remedy for the nullification or impairment of trade advantages suffered by a member. It would be in the interest of developing countries to support the proposal to introduce financial compensation.

Proposals on systemic issues

Many proposals on the table are systemic in nature. One of these proposals relates to the issue of transparency of the WTO dispute settlement system. The proposal is that panel hearings and those of the Appellate body should be open to the public. The United States proposed that submissions and statements to the adjudicatory bodies should be made public and that final reports should also be made available to members of the public once they have been released to Members. However, developing-country Members appear not favourably disposed to the issue of transparency in the dispute settlement system, contending that this is an issue for the developed-country Members to worry about. They further contend that the present practice, which affords meetings in private and confidentiality of submissions, will enable them to decide on sensitive issues without attracting much opposition from home.

The author believes that the introduction of transparency in the dispute resolution process will help, rather than harm the interest of developing countries, as it would enhance the legitimacy of the institution. One of the reasons for the bad publicity of the WTO in many developing countries is the perception that trade officials cut deals in secret without taking the interest of their citizens into account. If the system is made open and it becomes apparent that the secret deals that are talked about are highly exaggerated, it would help the credibility of the institution and developing countries to explain some of the decisions taken at trade negotiations to their citizens. Many judicial systems of developing countries are already well advanced in open proceedings. Also, proceedings before other international adjudicatory bodies are open. It becomes incomprehensible and raises suspicion in the minds of citizens why the WTO should track a different path.

Related to this is the opposition of developing countries to the issue of amicus curiae briefs. Left to some developing countries, the advances made so far in this area would be reversed and amicus curiae briefs would be prohibited in the WTO. It is, however, contended that it is important that panels and the AB have access to all the information they need to be able to write balanced reports. Some of the information may not be otherwise available to the panels and the AB. Amicus curiae briefs provide a source of information that may be needed for a balanced resolution of disputes. The involvement of NGOs and other interest groups in the dispute settlement process will further enhance the external transparency and legitimacy of the dispute settlement process and should be supported by developing countries. While recognizing the need to accommodate amicus curiae briefs, it must however be cautioned that this should not be allowed to delay the resolution of trade disputes between the parties. Clear guidelines should be worked out on the time and the amount of information that should be submitted so as not to impede the work of panels and the AB. What this view advocates is some form of balance between amicus curiae briefs and the effectiveness of the dispute settlement system.

There is also a proposal to strengthen the special and differential treatment (SDT) provisions of the DSU for developing-country Members. The present rules contain a provision that requires Members to give special attention to particular problems of developing countries during consultations. This may involve extending the time for consultations. Another provision with respect to SDT requires panels to give developing countries sufficient time to prepare and present their cases. At the implementation stage, the rules require that particular interest should be given to matters affecting the interest of developing-country Members with respect to the subject of the dispute. After ten years of practice, it has been recognized by developing-country Members that most of these present SDT provisions are merely hortatory in effect and lack practical utility. Commenting on the SDT provision in the context of the DSU, one writer noted that although SDT clauses have been mentioned in a few cases, in practice they are of limited value for these countries in defending or claiming their rights (Delich 2002: 73). Specific proposals have therefore been made to change the wordings of these provisions to make them enforceable. Many of the proposals on the table relate to the access of developing countries to the dispute settlement system, to which we now turn.

Participation of developing countries in the dispute settlement system

The participation of developing countries in the WTO dispute settlement system has received extensive comments in the literature. Many writers have praised the increased participation of developing countries in the system when compared to its predecessor, GATT, as a sign of the success of the system. Hughes (2006) notes that between 1995 and 2002 developing countries brought about half of all complaints, and about 41 per cent of those were directed against other developing countries (195). Also, the author referred to comments of Experts Consultative Group, which recognized "a much greater participation of developing countries than was the case in the GATT dispute settlement system.... Developing countries – even some poorest ... – are increasingly taking on the most powerful".[16] The above comments represent the general view about the participation of developing countries in the WTO dispute system.[17] While it cannot be faulted that there has been increased participation of developing counties in the WTO dispute settlement system when compared to the former GATT system, one needs to be careful not to fall prey to over-generalizations. Such claims may mask the fact that, in practice, the participation of developing countries in the current system has been limited to a few large developing-country Members. The majority of developing-country Members has not participated in any significant way in the WTO dispute settlement system. Indeed, many developing countries can at best be described as onlookers in the system. While it is true that some developing countries, like India, China, Argentina, Chile, Mexico, Thailand, Korea, Brazil and a few others, have made use of the system to defend their trade interests and also appeared as defendants, the hard and indisputable fact remains that Africa as a region, which has nearly one-third of the membership of the WTO – the single largest block in the organization – has only participated peripherally in the system.[18] This is in spite of the fact that the share of trade in terms of GDP is very significant for African countries. To close an eye to such conspicuous exclusion will be tantamount to supporting the view that the participation of these countries does not matter! It has been asserted that the lack of participation of developing countries is not because these countries do not have potential disputes, which could be submitted to the DSU (Mosoti n.d.: 14), but the difficulties they have in accessing the system.

The non-participation of developing countries in the dispute settlement process has implications for these countries. The WTO dispute settlement system is a new system, which is still evolving. Many substantive and procedural rules that will form the core body of jurisprudence are being developed by the system, which are used and will continue to be used for the resolution of trade disputes. The point is that those that contribute to the evolution of these rules are active participants in the system. The developing countries that are not participating cannot therefore influence the evolution of the jurisprudence spawned by the system and such rules may not take account of the special needs and peculiarities of these countries.[19] Secondly, while trade is seen as important to the development of many countries, the lack of participation of many developing countries in the dispute settlement system signals the lack of integration of these countries into the multilateral trading system. This, it is contended, may encourage such countries to seek solutions outside the trade agreements, which will further marginalize them. Thus, one commentator has cautioned, "As long as the weakest of the WTO Membership which comprises majority of countries ... remain virtually absent in the dispute settlement process in all senses, the success of the system must not be taken as absolute, even implicitly" (Mosoti n.d.: 3). What is clear is that the system could do with some reform that will enhance the participation of developing countries. While many reasons may account for the non-participation of many developing countries in the dispute settlement system, improvement of the DSU would facilitate the participation of developing countries in the system. In order to suggest improvements, it is necessary to identify some of the factors that impede the effective participation of developing countries in the dispute settlement system.

Many reasons have been advanced for the low participation of many developing countries in the WTO dispute settlement system. Shaffer (2006) has identified three primary challenges that affect the participation of developing countries in the WTO dispute system to include (1) lack of legal expertise in WTO law and the capacity to organize information concerning trade barriers and opportunities to challenge them, (2) financial constraints in hiring outside legal counsel and (3) fear of political and economic pressure from powerful members.[20]

Taking the legal cost of litigation before the adjudicatory bodies as a starting point, many writers recognize the huge expense and complexity involved in activating the dispute settlement as militating against participation. The point is made that the reforms of the Uruguay Round on the DSU increased the cost of settling disputes in the WTO.[21] The fact that powerful countries may no longer be able to block panel and AB rulings means that much investment is now devoted to legal preparation of cases (Busch and Reinhardt 2003: 721). It is further argued that this new development will be less burdensome to developed countries that routinely maintain large and dedicated professional staff. Even at that, because of the complexities of the cases, some developed countries have had cause to call on outside counsel to represent them at these bodies. However, developing countries traditionally lack such legal expertise and the present situation will only complicate the picture. Many of them cannot also afford to hire outside counsel to represent their interest because of the huge cost involved. The point is that in the present system, members with greater legal expertise or resources to pay for them have made better use of the system than poorer countries.

Developing countries expect that the present negotiations will lead to a reform of the system for them to be able to access the system more cheaply. In this connection, therefore, proposals have been tabled to remedy this situation. One proposal is to authorize a panel or the AB to award an amount as litigation costs to developing countries. This is to address the high cost involved in bringing claims under the DSU, which tend to dissuade many developing countries from using the system. The African Group has also proposed the establishment of a "WTO Fund on Dispute Settlement". The proposal is made in recognition of the high cost of accessing the system. It recognizes the fact that although the WTO Secretariat offers technical assistance at present to developing-country Members that may require assistance, such assistance can only be of a limited nature considering the staff strength of the WTO and the requirement for neutrality by Secretariat staff. Also, the Advisory Centre on WTO Law presently offers assistance to developing-country Members involved in WTO disputes and is doing a commendable job in this respect. But such assistance is not free, as Members have to join the body as well as pay a Membership fee and access the services at subsidized fees. The Proposal to set up a fund that will provide assistance to developing countries in accessing the dispute settlement system appears reasonable to bridge the gap that presently exists. Also, many proposals have been put forward in the academic literature all geared toward helping developing countries overcome this problem. Suggestions ranging from better engagement with the private sector, NGOs and consumer associations have been put forward.[22]

Besides, lack of expertise to take on the difficult and demanding task of challenging violation of trade rules has been recognized as a fundamental problem. This involves the ability "to perceive injuries to its trading prospects, identify who is responsible and mobilise resources to bring a legal claim or negotiate a favourable settlement" (Shaffer 2006). This means that developing-country Members require expertise and quality information even before actual claims are commenced, to be able to identify the infraction of trade rules and to decide whether it would be meaningful to pursue a legal claim or negotiate a settlement. In this direction, a proposal has been made to substantially increase capacity development funding for developing countries. These countries can also take advantage of capacity development funding outside of the WTO.

The author wishes to add that technical assistance for capacity development should be viewed as an interim measure to help developing countries develop the necessary expertise not only to access the WTO dispute system, but also to effectively engage in the multilateral system. On the long term, there is no substitute for developing countries building their own individual expertise to cope with the demands of effective participation in the system. This will involve not only the capacity to bring claims before the system but in training key personnel to be able to detect when their trade interest are being compromised by other Members. This is important, as it has been argued that better results may be achieved in the consultation stage if Members are better prepared than by waiting for the process to run its course (Busch and Reinhardt 2003: 721). Many suggestions have been made on how developing countries can develop their capacity (Shaffer 2006). One possible solution is for developing countries "to develop their own coordinative mechanisms to include private sector and civil society representatives. Capacity building endeavours generally will be most sustainable if they permeate broadly throughout institutions and societies" (ibid.).

The author believes that a long-term perspective should be taken of the problem and one possible solution to improve the capacity gap of developing countries would be to introduce WTO-relevant courses as part of the curricula of higher institutions of learning in developing countries. WTO law and the use of the dispute settlement mechanism could become core components of those courses. Presently, as part of its capacity development initiative, the United Nations University Institute of Advanced Studies in collaboration with the WTO and ITC organize training programmes on WTO and Sustainable Development for professors from universities in developing countries. The intention is to train professors on overarching issues underpinning the multilateral trading system. The idea is that targeting the trainers will enable them to take back the knowledge to their universities and to introduce international trade-relevant courses in their curricula. As the primary institution responsible for capacity development, universities are better placed to develop requisite expertise in this critical area for their countries. This initiative needs to be supported with better funding, expanded and further fine-tuned to make it more effective and result-oriented. Developing-country Members can also pool their resources by establishing specialized regional institutions to develop capacity in the area of international trade. The Trade Law Centre in South Africa, which was set up by Southern African countries, is a positive step in this direction.

The lack of effective participation of developing countries in the dispute settlement system can be attributed to the effect of extra-legal political pressures from powerful countries. It has been argued that the powerful can exploit political imbalances and dress them in non-power terms, with the result that the goal of objective trade-dispute resolution would be undermined. This point is particularly powerful when one notes that many developing countries rely on preferential trade agreements and aid from the powerful countries that are also Members of the WTO (Alavi 2007). Bringing claims against these "benevolent" countries may amount to biting the hand that feeds one and give rise to serious economic consequences. This is a difficult situation to be in and there are no easy solutions. But in the long term, developing countries need to develop their trading capacity to be able to break loose from the influence of these powerful countries.

Where do we go from here?

From 1998, when negotiations formally began, several deadlines have been missed in the negotiations. As things stand, there is no chance that the negotiations would be completed by the end of 2006 or any time soon thereafter. Although phrases like "final phase" are being used by Members in the negotiating sessions, the reality on the ground is that Members are still poles apart on many of the proposals on the table for negotiations, although informal negotiations especially within the Mexico Group are being intensified.

At negotiating sessions of the DSB, Members usually stress the importance of reforming the dispute settlement system in order to strengthen it. However, little progress is made in actual negotiations. Although there have been many proposals on the table on the reform of the system, there is broad agreement on only a few of them. The question is what is responsible for the difficulty in reaching agreement on the reform of the DSU and what are we to expect from these negotiations?

Many reasons have been advanced for the reluctance of members to move forward rapidly with the reform of the DSU. Part of the reason may well be the fact that Members generally view the current system as working well and therefore requiring no fundamental changes. Indeed, an expert report to the former Director-General, Supachai Panitchpakdi had only positive words for the working of the system and warned negotiators not to do any harm to it (WTO 2004: 49). This perhaps explains the absence of urgency and political will that has characterized negotiations on the reform of the system.

It has also been pointed out that the institutional conservatism of the WTO may well be a factor in the slow pace of negotiations. The argument is built on the fact that even agreeing to the DSU in the first place was a bold step at judicialization of the WTO and that many members of the WTO are risk-averse in taking steps that may be perceived as strengthening the "judicial" function of the WTO (Bercero and Garzotti 2005). Finally, it must not be forgotten that negotiations – any negotiations at the international arena – are usually complex and difficult. Some members, especially developing countries, may see the present negotiations as an opportunity to secure some advantages, which, with the benefit of experience of operating the system for many years, they feel would enhance their participation. Others may be unwilling to accede to such concessions so as not to weaken the system or lose some advantages they already enjoy. In either case, the choices before the parties are difficult and the investment of political capital is needed to reach accommodation and move the process forward, otherwise the negotiations may continue without any tangible results.

However, considering the fact that the system has been operational for more than a decade now, there are certain aspects of the DSU that should be reformed for the effective functioning of the system. Developing countries feel that this is an opportunity to reform the system to make it possible for them to access the system easily and cheaply. This accounts for the initial enthusiasm shown and the large number of proposals put forward by them. It appears, however, that the high expectations for a radical reform of the system may not materialize after all. Developed country members have shown reluctance in acceding to some of the proposals tabled by developing countries that will radically transform the system, and appear content with leaving the system as it is with minor, non-fundamental amendments. Many members are opposed to tinkering with the system in any fundamental way. Such members argue that the brief of the negotiators was limited to "improvements and clarifications" of the DSU and these do not envisage fundamental changes.

Developing countries must not lose heart but must continue to push for the reform of the system, the challenges notwithstanding. Developed countries must show sensitivity to the proposals of developing countries that will encourage participation in the DSU, recognizing that full participation of all Members would engender greater confidence and respect for multilateral trading agreements. The experience in ongoing negotiations suggests that in future, a different strategy may be required for the reform of the DSU. It may be more expedient to leave the task of effecting changes to the rules to the Ministerial Meeting or to the General Council of the WTO. These bodies could be empowered to issue authoritative Interpretive Notes to effect changes to the rules when required. This will allow necessary changes to be made timeously without subjecting the system to unending negotiations.

Conclusion

The chapter examined the current negotiations to reform the DSU. Importantly, it examines how the present system affects the participation of developing countries and how the reforms could be anchored to enhance developing countries' participation in the DSU. Although negotiations have lasted almost a decade and many proposals have been made, it is doubtful whether the end product will meet the expectations of developing countries. With the mindset by many developed-country members that the system is working well and the cliché "if it ain't broke don't fix it" the guiding mantra, it is doubtful if the negotiations would deliver fundamental changes to the system.

However, it ought to be realized that the WTO consists of many Members. Many developing countries joined the organization in the expectation that it would help them to address their development challenges through trade. To have a chance to achieve this aspiration, they need to be able to participate in the system effectively, including using the dispute settlement mechanism to defend their trade interest. The present system whereby only a few members can, and have used the system to defend their interest is not ideal. It is not suggested that the rules are formally biased against developing countries; the argument is that given the peculiarities of developing countries, the rules should be more flexible or specific arrangements should be introduced to facilitate the participation of developing countries in the multilateral trading system, including the DSU. If the credibility and effectiveness of the WTO are to be enhanced, a reform agenda that will make it easier for Members who cannot presently use the system to be able to do so should be promoted. The legitimacy and effectiveness of the multilateral trading system depend very much on the ability of its dispute settlement system to address the needs of all members and not only some of its members.

Notes

1. All the Agreements are contained in the Final Act embodying the results of the Uruguay Round of Multilateral Trade Negotiations.

2. Phrases that have been used to describe the DSU include "jewel in the crown" and "centrepiece of the WTO".

3. See, Update of WTO Dispute Settlement Cases, WT/DS/OV/28 issued by the WTO on 11 October 2006.

4. The dispute was basically about when authorization to retaliate, a procedure permitted under article 22 of the DSU, should take effect. The dispute was brought about because of a contradictory provision in article 21.5, which envisaged a compliance procedure to determine whether compliance was sufficient. The disputants were two major trading powers, the European Community and the United States. While the European Union argued that a member could only resort to retaliation after a panel on compliance or the AB has decided that the measures adopted were not sufficient to bring the offending measure into compliance with WTO obligation, the United States, on the other hand, contended that retaliation should take place once the reasonable period of time to comply had elapsed without waiting for any determination by a panel or the AB. In effect, the disagreement was caused by the drafting of the two articles, which did not seem to take account of the 90 days allowed for determination whether compliance was satisfactory.

5. WT/MIN(01)/DEC/1 20 November 2001.

6. Paragraph 34 of Hong Kong Ministerial Declaration, WT/MIN(05)/DEC, adopted on 18 December 2005.

7. This categorization follows that of Van den Bossche (2003). This classification is preferable as it allows a focused discussion of the issues.

8. Under Article XXII of GATT 1994, members can easily join consultation if the request is made to the DSB at the meeting during which a panel is established.

9. This proposal was made by the African Group.

10. Submission of Hong Kong TN/DS/M/32, 26 June 2006. Hong Kong argued that her proposal has the advantage of minimizing the risk of a responding Member rejecting a third-country Member depending on whether or not it was supporting its position in the dispute, while retaining flexibility of parties to retain control over the dispute settlement system.

11. This proposal is sponsored by Japan and the European Community.

12. This proposal is contained in the Communication from China (Revision), TN/DS/W/51/Rev.1, 13/03/2003. It must be recognized that WTO Members consist of countries at different stages of development. Flexibility is required in the rules that are being negotiated to capture the different needs of Members.

13. Bercero and Garzotti (2005), pp. 862–863. The authors raise serious doubt about the utility of interim review in the adjudicatory proceedings of the DSU.

14. This was the original proposal of Jordan as was contained in its Communication of 28 January 2003, TN/DS/43. Jordan was, however, to change its position in its later proposal, which accords more with the EC position. See later Communication from Jordan dated 19 May 2004 in TN/DS/W/56.

15. Another proposal with respect to strengthening retaliation is the proposal to sell the right of retaliation to interested Members. This proposal has been defended by a former Ambassador from Mexico as being possible to assist developing countries to participate effectively in the dispute settlements system. However, one is not sure whether this proposal is practical and whether there will be a market or willing buyers of the right to retaliate.

16. Hughes (2006), quoting the Report of the Consultative Board set up by the former Director General of WTO, Supachai Panitchpakdi.

17. In fact, a respected academic writer commented, "Indeed, it is striking to consider the evolution in the use of the WTO dispute settlement system by developing countries. In

the first five years of the system's existence, developing countries initiated by themselves roughly one-quarter of the consultation requests. In the five years from 2000 through 2004, developing countries initiated around 60% of the consultations request – more than doubling their relative share of initiations.... Thus, in the last few years developing countries have become more frequent users of the WTO dispute settlement, both in absolute and relative terms" (Davey 2005: 13–14).

18. It has been noted that as of January 2004, only two African countries, South Africa and Egypt, have ever had consultations requested at the DSU. South Africa has had two complaints brought against it, by India and Turkey – India on anti-dumping duties on import of some pharmaceuticals products from India, brought in 2003 and Turkey on Definitive Anti-Dumping Measures. In January 2004, the United States requested for consultations with Egypt on Measures Affecting Import of Textiles and Apparel Products. Nigeria participated as a third party in the US Shrimp Dispute and African countries participated as third parties as part of the ACP in the Banana dispute between the European Community and the United States and in the EC Sugar challenge. This signifies low level of participation by African countries.

19. Not all writers agree with this view (Kessie and Addo n.d.). The authors argue that they are not in agreement with this view. The arguments made by the authors include the fact that the objective of the dispute settlement system is not to create new legal principles that would define or regulate multilateral trade relationships between countries, but to assist the parties to find a solution to their dispute. They argue that panels and AB are not allowed to enlarge the provisions of the trade agreements, that members have largely jealously guarded their rights and the agreements and that there is no system of *stare decisis* in the DSU. These are very strong and attractive arguments. However, it may be observed that agreements made by members are not self-explanatory. That is why these adjudicatory bodies are set up to interpret them and this involves the panellists giving their views as to what they think the agreements provide. Their views are generally regarded as the "law" that would guide other members. Although it is true that there is no system of judicial precedent in the DSU and that a panel is not bound to follow the rulings of the AB or other panels, in practice panels routinely follow AB rulings and refer to other panel rulings. It is submitted that a panel will normally follow the rulings of AB and the AB will also follow its rulings unless there are strong reasons not to do so. This is how the legal principles are built up to guide the interpretation of trade agreements.

20. This corresponds to the views of many other academic writers on the issue. But the reasons advanced here are not exhaustive. The reasons for the low participation of many developing countries in the DSU may be more fundamental than those given here. For instance, it has been pointed out in the case of Africa that "there are several possible reasons why African countries have not been making use of the dispute settlement system of the WTO to enforce their rights and legitimate expectations. These include the share of African countries in world trade, which was estimated last year to be around 2 per cent by the WTO. With this low figure, it may be argued that it is not surprising that African countries are not making use of the dispute settlement system. They export mostly a few commodities and the priority for them is to remove supply-side constraints which have prevented them from increasing and diversifying their exports" (Kessie and Addo n.d.).

21. It has been suggested that it may cost up to US$500,000 to run a case from panel through the AB; this is a large amount for many developing countries.

22. Brown and Hoekman (2005). Shaffer (2006) discussed several strategies that should be adopted by developing countries to deal with this problem outside the WTO.

REFERENCES

Alavi, Amin (2007) "African Countries and the WTO's Dispute Settlement Mechanism", *Development Policy Review* 25(1): 25–42.

Bercero, Ignacio Garcia, and Paolo Garzotti (2005) "Why Have Negotiations to Improve WTO Dispute Settlement System Failed So Far and What Are the Underlying Issues?" *Journal of World Investment and Trade* 6: 847.

Besson, Fabien, and Racem Mehdi (2004) "Is WTO Dispute Settlement System Biased against Developing Countries? An Empirical Analysis", available from http://www.ecomod.net/conferences/ecomod2004/ecomod2004_papers/199.pdf, visited 3 January 2007.

Brown, Chad, and Bernard Hoekman (2005) "WTO Dispute Settlement and the Missing Developing Country Cases: Engaging the Private Sector", available from http://www.brookings.edu/views/Papers/200505bown.pdf, visited 5 January 2007.

Busch, March, and Eric Reinhardt (2003) "Developing Countries and General Agreement on Tariffs and Trade/WTO Trade Organization Dispute Settlement", *Journal of World Trade* 37(4): 719–735.

Davey, William J. (2005) "The WTO Dispute Settlement System: How Have Developing Countries Fared?", Illinois Public Law and Legal Theory Research Paper No. 05-17, Urbana-Champaign: University of Illinois College of Law, November 30.

Delich, Valentina (2002) "Developing Countries and the WTO Dispute Settlement System", in Bernard Hoekman, Aaditya Mattoo and Philip English, eds, *Development, Trade and the WTO – A Handbook*, Washington, DC: World Bank, pp. 71–80.

Hughes, Valerie (2006) "The WTO Dispute Settlement System – From Initiating Proceedings to Ensuring Implementation: What Needs Improvement?", in Giorgio Sacerdoti, Alan Yanovich and Jan Bohanes, eds, *The WTO at Ten: The Contributions of the Dispute Settlement System*, Cambridge: Cambridge University Press, pp. 193–234.

Kessie, Edwini, and Kofi Addo (unpublished) "African Countries and the WTO Negotiations on the Dispute Settlement Understanding", draft paper on file with the author.

Mosoti, Victor (unpublished) "Does Africa Need the WTO Dispute Settlement System?", draft position paper on file with the author.

Shaffer, Gregory (2006) "The Challenges of WTO Law: Strategies for Developing Country Adaptation", *World Trade Review* 5(2): 177–198.

Van den Bossche, Peter (2003) "The Doha Development Round Negotiations on the Dispute Settlement Understanding", paper presented at the WTO Conference New Agendas in the 21st Century at Taipei, 28–29 November.

WTO (2004) "The Future of the WTO: Addressing Institutional Challenges in the New Millennium", Report of a Consultative Board to the Director-General, Geneva: WTO.

13

WTO negotiations on trade facilitation – Lessons for the future? New perspectives for and from the developing world

Nora Neufeld

Slow start ... but catching up fast

The delivery was a difficult one. Eight years of preparation, four Ministerial Conferences and countless educational activities inside and outside the WTO were necessary for the Trade Facilitation negotiations to see the light of day. Last to be added to the Doha Round, the Facilitation agenda holds the record for the longest labour, making it one of the most "pre-negotiated" negotiating files of the DDA.

The reasons for the slow start were complex. In large part, they had their origin in an initial reluctance among many developing countries to engage in what they saw as a new issue in the context of an already ambitious multilateral Round. Against the background of limited resources and mixed experiences with the Uruguay results, the idea of committing to another – developed-country initiated – subject held little attraction to some. The parallel attempt to launch negotiations on three other Singapore issues[1] and a later call for their package treatment[2] represented another reason for restraint. Faced with the request to harness Trade Facilitation (TF) to three far more contentious subjects, a low-ambition scenario seemed the preferred way to go. Complications also had to do with the specific birth requirements of the Facilitation talks. Unlike other parts of the Doha agenda,[3] agreement on the modalities was a precondition for the go-ahead and had to be found before the actual negotiating phase could commence.

Developing countries and the WTO: Policy approaches, Sampson and Chambers (eds), United Nations University Press, 2008, ISBN 978-92-808-1153-7

And yet the baby not only made it into the WTO world but quickly re-couped the time lost by its delayed start – turning into one of the fastest-progressing parts of the Round and making headway on all fronts.

A large part of the Trade Facilitation story is about how developing countries went from being sceptics to becoming increasingly enthusiastic proponents, building crosscutting coalitions to advance the initiative, injecting new ideas and approaches, and rising above the ideological North-South battles that too often have characterized other aspects of the DDA. What triggered this turn-around? Why was it possible for a latecomer to turn into a frontrunner? And, most importantly, are there any lessons from the TF experience that can be applied to the broader WTO universe, especially at this uncertain moment in the Doha Round?

The story so far

Although the history of multilateral efforts to facilitate trade goes back to the very beginnings of GATT,[4] it was not until the post-Uruguay Round era that things started to take a more incisive turn. By the mid-1990s, momentum was building up to make it a subject of separate attention, culminating in the introduction of Facilitation as a "new" topic at the Singapore Ministerial. Prior to that, TF work had mostly taken place in the context of customs or other market access-related WTO bodies[5] as more or less directly targeted by-products of measures to eliminate bar-riers to trade. Singapore marked the beginning of a distinctive Trade Fa-cilitation track, but it would take another eight years for the process to evolve from initial exploratory engagements to full negotiating mode.[6] It was only in mid-2004 that resistance to rulemaking could finally be over-come, leading to the launch of TF talks under the July Package chapeau.

Key areas under negotiation

Over the course of this evolution, the scope and parameters of TF work changed. Conceptually, the negotiations were designed to expedite the movement, release and clearance of goods as a complement to parallel tariff-reduction efforts. Their essential purpose was to make commerce more efficient through the rationalization of procedures, documentation and information flows. While the cross-border orientation of the exercise implied a focus on the customs side, the negotiations clearly extended be-yond this area to the border clearance terrain.

At the same time, they did not include many of the broader TF aspects addressed in other fora. The reasons for this are of a political nature and reflect the results of a long-lasting process to gradually limit the scope. Starting from a comprehensive perspective that included the banking, payments and insurance domain, Members soon started to narrow their field of operation. It was developing nations in particular that sought this limitation. In light of the WTO's rulemaking and enforcement features,[7] many felt more comfortable with a restricted scope of operation that would put less demand on their implementation ability. As a result, Trade Facilitation work after 1998 essentially limited itself to the GATT Articles V, VIII and X domain.

Translated into technical – and more concrete – terms, the mandate limits the areas under negotiation to three main pillars: (1) Improvements/clarifications to Articles V, VIII and X of GATT and provisions on customs cooperation;[8] (2) technical assistance and capacity building; and (3) special and differential treatment (SDT). Additional work areas relate to needs and priorities identification and the addressing of concerns about cost implications.[9]

Progress made

Work picked up steam right from the start. Within one month of its establishment,[10] the Negotiating Group adopted a Work Plan (WTO 2004b) and schedule of meetings. First proposals were submitted soon thereafter. By the end of its first year, the Group had not only addressed a substantive amount of input from the whole spectrum of the Membership but had also entered a process of refinement and consolidation. Even more significantly, delegations managed to create a unique atmosphere of cooperation and dialogue that would become the trademark of the Group. Putting an end to more than seven years of controversial – and sometimes even adversarial – discussion, the TF Group became a forum for open exchange and collaboration. It was the only Negotiating Body that agreed on its Hong Kong outcome ahead of time (WTO 2005a),[11] allowing Ministers to endorse the text.

Work continued to advance in the aftermath of the Sixth Ministerial Conference. Members returned to the negotiating table without losing time over procedural matters and maintained their forward-looking approach. Sensitive questions such as the time of moving into drafting mode turned out to be unproblematic in their post-Hong Kong handling. And the feared slow-down on political grounds never materialized. The Group even continued to make progress when the problems in other areas of the Round became impossible to ignore and carried on working until the day of the suspension call.

By that time, Members had not only been able to narrow the questions under negotiation to a clearly defined universe of issues but had also advanced in designing its basic architecture. The GATT-related area became the most developed domain, accounting for most of the discussion time. More than 100 written proposals were tabled on how to improve and clarify Articles V, VIII and X, most of them already in text-based form. They represented the result of a Member-driven convergence exercise that saw both a merger of ideas and a first delineation of common ground. While not constituting agreed rules, they clearly defined the targeted universe of measures and paved the way for a final screening and fine-tuning stage.

Important advances were also made in the challenging SDT and technical assistance and capacity building (TACB) field. Initially an area that was lagging behind, Members were able to catch up on the implementation front, bringing work on the SDT and technical assistance pillars closer to that on the Articles' side. The tabling of two advanced, developing-country-sponsored proposals that – at least with respect to one of them – found support, and even co-sponsorship, of large parts of the developed world[12] marked clear progress. While nothing was yet agreed and substantial differences remained,[13] the contributions shared certain elements and identified areas of common ground. Both of them suggested a staged implementation scheme and both based themselves on individually targeted, tailor-made approaches as opposed to a one-size-fits-all philosophy. Their emphasis on capacity enhancement as opposed to opting out also revealed common ground. Importance was placed on putting every Member in a position to actually implement the envisaged measures, with the proposed structure[14] meant to play an enabling function in that regard. In doing so, those proposals marked a shift in philosophy. During the pre-negotiating years, many developing countries sought assurances that they would not be obliged to commit. This thinking was still predominant in the modalities determination phase, as reflected in many of the mandate's provisions. It gradually disappeared in the actual negotiating phase when it became replaced by an emphasis on obtaining implementation support. Now even LDCs focused on getting assistance to enter into commitments rather than on using their enshrined rights to stay out.

Arriving there was no small achievement. For both sponsor groups, it implied giving up earlier demands. For one alliance (calling themselves the "Core Group"[15]), it meant dispensing with demands for SDT and TACB offers being worked into each and every measure.[16] It also had to weaken its stance on the dispute settlement front. For the proponent Colorado Group Members[17] that sponsored the competing W/137 proposal (WTO 2006a), it implied acceptance of a system that would delay full implementation by a considerable amount of time and put a lot of pressure on the donors to provide the required support. Far from providing merely transition times coupled with some kind of – not closely defined – capacity assistance, developed countries would have to provide extensive aid as a quasi condition for implementation on the part of the developing world. They would also have to live with a system that endowed the recipients with much more flexibility to determine their own capabilities. Compared with the predominant – transition period-oriented – structure of the Uruguay Round Accords, this would clearly break new ground. The main remaining difference is how they approach the disciplines side. Here, the Core Group suggestion leaves ample flexibility to developing Members and places emphasis more on the assistance as opposed to the commitment side.

Little differences exist over the nature of the envisaged overall product. Initially a sensitive question (leading to the mandate being neutral on the matter[18]), with all developed and several developing countries wishing to see a clear reference to a new "Agreement" as the targeted end-result, there were also voices in the developing world that called for a less ambitious goal, opting for a mere amendment of the three GATT Articles instead (or at least to be open for both alternatives). The reactions to the question became significantly more relaxed during the subsequent negotiating phase. The decision to focus on the substance of the measures and postpone the decision on their formal setting showed positive results. With growing comfort on the content side also grew a willingness to consider the Agreement option. Fears about overly ambitious disciplines gradually disappeared. The Hong Kong Declaration, while still avoiding the "A-word", already spoke of the development of "multilateral commitments" as the envisaged final result. Post-Hong Kong contributions then openly advocated the Agreement option, including those from the Core Group (CG).

Progress was also made at the atmospheric level with the creation – and maintenance – of a constructive cooperation and discussion climate, which even survived the turbulent late July phase. Despite the looming suspension decision, the Negotiating Group (NG) still managed to support a Chair's progress report without any opposition (WTO 2006b). Practically all contributions were backed by broad Member-alliances of different levels of development, revealing support from developed and developing countries alike. While clearly remaining a work in progress – with additional contributions still on the way and existing ones yet to be refined and lifted across the consensus bar – the comprehensiveness and specificity of the proposals record the advancement of work.

Overall, the Trade Facilitation negotiations were well underway and moving ahead when caught by the suspension act. Having progressed from initial discussions to an advanced consolidation and refinement stage, the talks were in full swing at the time they were brought to a halt.

More importantly, the first two years of TF negotiations had shown that they could deliver substantive improvements to the current trading regime. They produced a promising set of proposed rules that would not only significantly expedite the movement, release and clearance of goods – thereby substantively reducing trade transaction costs – but also create new trading opportunities and generate funding support. What was on the table when the Round was suspended was no less than a framework for completing an important part of the trade liberalization puzzle by eliminating many of the remaining barriers in the non-tariff field – rules that would represent a new dimension in Facilitation endeavours by simplifying import/export formalities, reducing related fees and allowing for effective transit of goods; all this without compromising on the need for flexible approaches and special support for the developing world, which actively contributed to the existing body of proposals and gave the negotiations considerable support. In other words, rules that would be effectively implemented and significantly change trading realities on the ground.

From sceptics to believers: The key role of the developing world

None of this would have been possible without the support of developing countries, which played a particular – and in many ways unique – role. Contrary to how some of them perceived the issue in the pre-negotiating phase, the developing membership came to take a very forward-looking stance, participating intensively in the negotiations and accounting for much of the positive tone.

Main interests

Interests of the developing Membership differ. They also underwent several changes and enlarged in scope. While any attempt to talk of a "developing-country" role runs the risk of oversimplifying individual positions, one can roughly distinguish three main groups with similar views.

The first consisted of the relatively more developed, proponent countries that had advocated an ambitious TF Agreement since Singapore.[19] Their interests were mainly of an offensive nature, seeking enforceable commitments on the transparency enhancement and import/export simplification side. While their individual concerns varied, they tended to be little different from those of the developed world.[20]

The second group covered the economically less advanced and/or less liberalization-oriented spectrum of the developing Membership, which tended to be sceptical of new commitments and often took a more defensive stance. During the preparatory phase of TF work, this grouping was home to the more pronounced opponents of negotiations on the subject. Traditionally, their interests were largely limited to the technical assistance and SDT field, where they pressed for maximizing support. Concerned about their lack of resources, they called for concrete offers to enhance their implementation capacities without restraining their political manoeuvring space[21] – allowing them to largely commit as they saw fit.[22]

It was only later in the process that these countries also discovered offensive interests. Landlocked developing Members were the first to see the TF negotiations as a means of alleviating the serious disadvantages inherent in their geographic setting. Already engaged in UN transit initiatives, they lobbied for an inclusion of Article V matters in the negotiating exercise.[23] Their lack of access to the sea – and the related economic costs[24] – was so significant a handicap[25] that even LDCs were soon advocating binding measures in this field, overcoming years of reservations against such commitments. Proposals by Rwanda[26] – jointly submitted with Mongolia, Switzerland and Paraguay – were the most prominent examples of this development. Even Cuba came to call for binding measures on the basis of Article V, discovering the talks as a means to address what it saw as a longstanding discrimination issue.[27]

Uganda followed with a call for the elimination of all consularization requirements,[28] pointing to the many disadvantages caused by this practice. This proposal was particularly noteworthy as it illustrated the relevance of Trade Facilitation for small and medium-sized enterprises (SMEs) and explained a key rationale for getting LDCs on board. According to the Ugandan delegation, small traders often had to pay up to US$80 per page to have their export papers legalized, with the overall costs per container frequently amounting to US$480 in the legalization procedure alone,[29] enough to drive – or keep – SMEs off the global market. Little wonder that Uganda came to see Trade Facilitation as "one of the areas with potential for utmost gains in the Doha Development Round".[30]

Yet another contribution worth mentioning came from the Dominican Republic.[31] Under the heading "Reinforcing the ethical conduct of staff and the integrity of customs administrations", the proposal calls for several measures on the anti-corruption front.[32]

A third grouping consisted of a number of large and economically relatively advanced developing countries that recently discovered an increased interest in Facilitation work. Some of them initially belonged to the sceptics' camp until two to three years ago. A typical feature of those actors is that they did not exclusively approach the issue from their own domestic perspective but sought to play a broader, intermediary role within the developing world.

India became particularly active in promoting offensive interests. Apart from the area of customs cooperation, whose addition to the mandate was largely the result of Delhi's initiative, the Indian delegation sought binding commitments on a wide range of issues.[33]

China focussed on transparency enhancement measures and a range of initiatives to simplify and expedite import/export formalities.[34] It also engaged in developing the technical assistance and enforcement side.

A common – continued – interest of all three groupings lay in the implementation domain. For many developing countries, a satisfactory outcome on SDT issues remained the litmus test of the success of the TF negotiations and the utility of the WTO as an institution supportive of development. Unsatisfied with what their developed partners initially had to offer, they took the lead in developing the first substantive proposals on this pillar. Both textual proposals currently on the table had their origins in initiatives of the developing world.[35]

Constructive group representation and growing emancipation

Another positive force was the way in which developing countries participated in the process, both within groups and on an individual basis.

Group representation became focussed and more offensive in tone. In addition to the regular alliances established across the whole spectrum of WTO work (African, ACP, CARICOM or LDC Group[36]), a new coalition was formed with an operation field in the TF area alone.[37] Initially consisting of little more than a handful of regular Members,[38] the Core Group (CG) had its heyday in mid-2004 when exercising noticeable influence in shaping the final negotiating terms. Under Malaysia's chairmanship, the CG established itself as an influential player that could – and had to – be worked with in the Facilitation arena. It showed a good hand in balancing ambition with flexibility and managed to enforce key demands while remaining constructive in tone and showing ability to compromise. The Group played a deserving role in managing to bring the most sceptical Members, which still harboured reservations vis-à-vis the negotiating perspective, into more conciliate waters where they gave up opposition against negotiations in favour of seeking to shape its terms.

Malaysia's leadership continued to exercise a positive influence on bridge-building initiatives and won such a trusted position that its ambassador was elected to become the first chair of the TF Negotiating Group.[39] His appointment showed that his success was not limited to gaining the full support of the developing world (which in itself already represented a remarkable accomplishment, given that this required finding a common line for countries with such diverse backgrounds and interests as India, Cuba, Tanzania or Bangladesh[40]), but that his reputation was good enough to also make him acceptable for the industrialized Membership.[41]

The role of the Core Group shifted during the subsequent negotiating phase. Faced with new challenges and a changed landscape where no player still opposed the Facilitation talks, the Group started its negotiating engagement with an insistence on a strict limitation of work on the three GATT Articles as the scope for possible commitments,[42] and by pressing for parallel advances in the areas of needs assessment and cost analysis.[43] Under the new chairmanship of the Philippines, emphasis was also placed on improving SDT offers in a more specific way. A similar complaint was expressed on the support side, accompanied by attempts to give Annex D's provisions an extensive interpretation so as to also cover financial aid.[44] Furthermore, the Group sought to revive the dispute settlement[45] and binding rules questions (WTO 2005i: 6) – both of which had already been raised, and addressed – in agreeing on the negotiating terms. It was also the Core Group who frequently stressed the linkage of advances on Facilitation with progress in other parts of the Round.[46]

Later Group initiatives focussed on shaping the outcome of the Hong Kong Ministerial. Here, the alliance pressed for an operationalization of SDT and TACB commitments and urged caution against an immediate move into drafting mode. Calls were also made for a "unification of proposals" (WTO 2006n: para. 49) in an attempt to cut down the perceived excess of input to more digestible limits. Post-Hong Kong engagement increasingly focussed on implementation matters, with the CG first reacting to the Latin American proposal before working on its own alternative.

While a common submission was not presented until the end of the second negotiating year (WTO 2006h), the Core Group kept issuing common statements and assumed a coordinating role behind the scenes. Although this did not keep individual Members from equally speaking in their personal capacity and individual positions differed,[47] the Group played a moderating role in bringing its more commitment-reluctant Members to middle-ground terrain and by finding a common denominator with positions of their more offensive partners.

In addition to this constructive role at the group level, there was also a positive engagement on an individual basis. Here, one could observe a trend of increased engagement in substantive – and mature – form, both in an addition to Group initiatives and as an exclusive means of participation. In some cases,[48] this extended to previously inactive Members.

What's so special about Trade Facilitation?

What made Trade Facilitation such a special case? Why did developing countries come on board, transcending the North-South divide that has limited progress in so many other parts of the Doha Round? And how come the negotiations worked so well?

Success, it seems, had many fathers. Apart from the general aspect of TF being politically less charged than other issues, one can find a number of reasons on the economic, political and procedural side. Additional factors have their origin in the nature of the subject, new approaches applied in determining the negotiating modalities and the NG's special way of operation. But most importantly, it is the result of the constructive role played by developing countries in the process.

The economic argument

Recognition had spread of the benefits of Trade Facilitation and its direct link to economic growth.[49] There was rising awareness of new trade patterns – and related obstacles – requiring increased attention and a crosscutting approach. Governments started to see the cutback on red tape as a necessary complement of liberalization efforts and essential for reaping the full benefits of a new Round. With earlier negotiations having brought down tariff levels to an all-time low and traditional trade barriers gradually fallen away, the focus shifted to the remaining obstacles on the non-tariff side. New patterns of production and distribution and the demands of just-in-time delivery made the addressing of those less visible – but very tangible – barricades an even more important call. Aware of investment decisions to critically depend on the ability to quickly move goods across borders and faced with the fact that the costs from red tape often exceed the ones from the tariff domain,[50] governments started to hear their traders' call for action on that front. No longer looking at Facilitation as the mere "plumbing" of trade policy, they came to see its advancement as a macro-economic issue and a core element of a country's external competitiveness strategy. The nature of the exercise as an attempt to reduce dead-weight costs that are of nobody's benefit and do not require trade-offs on the revenue side further facilitated the undertaking.[51] It added to an overall sense of the price of non-activity in this area simply being too high.

The development argument

This also gave Facilitation a compelling development rationale. Trade Facilitation was increasingly believed to have the potential to make global liberalization a tool for development by allowing for enhanced participation in international trade,[52] lower trade transaction costs, strengthen a country's tax and revenue base[53] and ensure better resource allocation. Positive development implications are equally expected from providing a predictable and non-discriminatory system that will attract additional support by offering an instrument to lock in reforms, secure the necessary political will and ensure that ongoing Facilitation efforts are geared toward the same direction.

Shifts in perception

Another – closely related – factor that facilitated the pro-negotiation choice and added to its rapid advancement was of an atmospheric nature. Earlier ideological quarrels over the need for multilateral Facilitation disciplines and a global rules-based system as a whole had increasingly given way to more pragmatic and result-oriented ways of looking at the issues at stake. The Washington consensus had been gradually replaced by a Monterrey-based line of thinking, seeking to promote a trade liberalization model that centres on poverty eradication and the bridging of gaps in development. The question of how to mainstream trade into the development agenda became a key concern for globalization endeavours.

The mandate – breaking new ground

Additional reasons for the go-ahead were more of a down-to-earth character. For many developing countries, willingness to embark on a rule-making exercise was essentially a reflection of their comfort with the agreed reference terms. For them, the negotiating mandate held the key to their willingness to embark on the negotiating adventure.

Having taken months – if not years[54] – to negotiate, the modalities set out in Annex D did much to create genuine readiness to move into negotiating mode. The contents of the mandate went a long way toward addressing the concerns of the developing world. Special emphasis was placed on technical assistance and the issue of SDT, often breaking new ground.

This is particularly evident in the area of SDT. Not only does the mandate call for such treatment to be an integral part of the negotiations and having to go beyond the transition periods known from the past,[55] it also creates a linkage between obligations and capabilities, relating "extent and the timing of entering into commitments ... to the implementation capacities of developing and least-developed Members".[56] The latter group is given even greater flexibility to commit as they see fit, holding that they "will only be required to undertake commitments consistent with their individual development, financial and trade needs or their administrative and institutional capabilities".[57] Assurances are equally given on the financial implications side, making addressing cost concerns an integral part of the negotiations and guaranteeing that developing and least-developed countries "would not be obliged to undertake investments in infrastructure projects beyond their means".[58]

New terrain was also embarked on in the technical assistance and capacity building (TACB) field. Elevated to an additional negotiating objective,[59] one finds Annex D to record the developed countries' commitment to provide support both during the negotiations and after their conclusion. For the first time, reference is made to the area of infrastructure,[60] recognizing the possibility of required support to also extend to this domain. Paragraph 6 further makes a link between the provision of such assistance and implementation obligations, ensuring that in certain cases[61] "where required support and assistance for ... infrastructure is not forthcoming, and where a developing or least-developed country continues to lack the necessary capacity, implementation will not be required".[62]

The mandate also includes several areas of particular interest to the developing world. Work on needs and priority assessment, cost analysis and assistance benchmarking were added at their request.[63]

Less (immediately) apparent, but equally relevant, were Annex D's delineations on the scope side. By largely limiting the negotiations' coverage to a well-defined area of GATT,[64] the mandate kept the level playing field within manageable limits, easing fears about the rulemaking exercise having the potential of going too far. In doing so, Annex D marked the end of an eight-year discussion on the proper outer boundaries, settling for the limited scope demanded by most developing nations against the initial wish of the developed world to stake off the territory more broadly.[65]

The comfort level and identification with the mandate also had to do with the way it was created. For the first time in the Trade Facilitation history, developing countries played a very active role, succeeding in significantly shaping the terms. Much of Annex D's language represents the merger of an earlier Chair's draft[66] with a proposal[67] by the Core Group. This text is directly responsible for most of the negotiating modalities on the issues of TACB and SDT.[68] It also marked the start of increased intra-developing country cooperation that gave some of the less active Members a louder voice.

Extensive preparation

The Trade Facilitation negotiations were one of the best-prepared areas of the Round. They could base themselves on – and benefit from – almost a decade of preparatory work when they finally took off. Most of the proposals had already been suggested in the pre-negotiating phase, allowing Members to draw on their earlier discussions without having to reinvent the wheel.

Special mode of operation

Many of the advances were enabled by the NG's special way of operation. A Work Plan adopted at the very beginning of the negotiations encapsulates the shared sense of a need for a balanced advancement, insisting on the discussions being Member-driven in their orientation and limiting the Chair's role in favour of a bottom-up approach. Agreement on a parallel addressing all elements of the mandate with no judgement on priority (and continued initiatives on the part of the Chair to see this understanding enforced) further helped the process, added to the creation of a spirit of partnership and cooperation and did much to break up earlier lines of disagreement.

Emphasis was further placed on a gradual approach. Despite its delayed beginning, and related extra baggage with respect to time, efforts were made not to rush matters. Even the most ambitious proponents exercised (self-)restraint. Their willingness to lower the envisaged level of ambition at certain stages in the negotiations[69] allowed for better prospects in the long-term. Instead of pressing ahead with ambitious demands, they responded to calls for preceding educational work. Substantive proposals were not submitted until several months into the negotiating calendar. And even then, they were soft in tone, seeking to persuade rather than impose, taking it slowly. Caution and accommodation were also displayed in the topic choice, starting with the little controversial transparency issues before working themselves up to more sensitive terrain. When approaching the Hong Kong Ministerial, there was no insistence on earlier calls for an explicit reference to an "Agreement" as the envisaged goal of the negotiations and no persistence on the Hong Kong text to already list its main elements.

At the same time, the special pressure created by the latecomer role helped instil a sense of need to focus. What initially seemed like a handicap turned out to be a useful reminder of there not being any time to waste.

Much effort was also made on the outreach and advance information front, leading to a considerable number of co-sponsorships, which became the rule rather than the exception. Transparency was also given a key role. Despite occasional calls for small group activities, meetings of the TF NG continued to be open-ended. While initial – even further reaching – demands of one delegation for all meetings to be formal and each Member having the right to participate even in informal consultations[70] was not generally acceptable, the Facilitation talks became known for their inclusive nature, rejecting all calls for operation in small groups. Even when approaching the Hong Kong Ministerial, efforts were made not to depart from the inclusive mode. Informal group consultations were kept to the minimum and reported on to the plenary forum, with the Chair insisting on there not being any kind of drafting group.

A large part of the credit also goes to the skilful chairmanship of Ambassador Muhammad Noor, whose careful handling of the TF file did much to advance affairs. In a situation where many developing countries based their willingness to explore new avenues on a sense of trust in the mission's goal and direction, his inclusive, open-minded way of conducting business and the obvious lack of any hidden agenda proved to be invaluable.

Engagement by the developing world

Participation and partnerships

Never before had developing – and even least-developed – countries engaged so actively in multilateral Facilitation work, (co-)sponsoring more than two thirds of all proposals and contributing to the shaping of many more. And never had there been such a readiness to engage in – sometimes hitherto unknown – alliances. There was an unparalleled engagement on all fronts, with decisions on alliances no longer being largely determined by a common level of development. Contrary to what could be observed during the pre-negotiations period where contributions from the developing world were largely limited to input from a handful of liberal – and relatively more developed – economies that were active supporters of an ambitious Trade Facilitation result (Chile, Colombia, Costa Rica, Hong Kong China, Paraguay, Singapore and so on), participation and sponsoring now extended to the less- and even least-developed world, with several of its Members assuming a pro-active role. For the first time, one could see developing and least-developed countries teaming up with developed nations in advocating binding measures. Joint proposals by Mongolia, Paraguay, Rwanda and Switzerland (WTO 2005d), Uganda and the United States (WTO 2005e; 2006f; 2006g) or Mongolia, Norway, South Africa and Switzerland (WTO 2006o) are only the most prominent examples of this trend. Equally significant are the developments in the substantive areas addressed. Unlike the early Facilitation days where input by (non-proponent) developing countries mostly limited itself to the technical assistance and SDT domain, and often was of a defensive nature, many developing – and even least-developed – countries now display offensive interests that exceed the implementation realm. The landlocked developing-countries' call for improved transit rights, Uganda's quest for the elimination of consularization or the integrity enhancement proposal of the Dominican Republic are only some of the examples of this development.

Interest promotion

New tendencies could also be detected in the way developing countries asserted their interests, showing considerable success in getting their developed counterparts to support their claims.

This is particularly noticeable in the SDT domain, where developing and least-developed Members managed to drive and shape the debate. It was their proposals that kept up the pressure for deliverables and lifted the bar for the minimum threshold in that regard. Initial suggestions from the developed world remained fairly vague.[71] Some of them simply quoted the relevant provisions of the mandate,[72] and almost all were limited to longer transition offers.[73] A proposal by the European Communities (WTO 2005t) came closest to anticipating later – more specific – SDT suggestions by advocating a staged approach that does not focus on a country's level of development as the sole criterion for granting favourable treatment, but promotes a measure-specific system instead. The contribution envisages a staged scenario in which certain general commitments would see immediate implementation, while others qualified for temporary exemption, with targeted assistance being provided during the transition time to allow for a later putting into force. An even more far-reaching approach by Switzerland that antedates many of the later SDT proposals was only floated verbally.[74]

The prevailing imprecision of S&D offers in those first generation proposals was generally explained by a perceived impossibility to be more specific on the SDT side before the substantive disciplines had been specified.[75] It largely continued throughout the subsequent consolidation phase where submissions sought to identify common elements of earlier suggestions on a given matter. Most of those second generation proposals did not add much specificity. In some cases, SDT contributions became even more general in presenting the issue as an "element requiring further discussion" rather than proposing specific offers.[76] The set of measures largely remained the same, ranging from the still predominant transition periods to progressive implementation and – in a few limited cases – best-endeavour (WTO 2005v; 2005w) suggestions. It was not until a group of – initially only Latin American – developing-country Members presented a substantive, across-the-board proposal (WTO 2006r) that the situation began to change. The proposition elevated the implementation debate to a new stage. It became a reference point for all subsequent SDT contributions.

While Switzerland – and to a certain extent also the European Communities – played some kind of a mentor role in having been the first to table certain ideas, it was a group of developing countries that took the lead in promoting them and that further developed their features. And the impact of the developing and LDC Membership on the SDT pillar did not stop there. A second text proposal for an implementation mechanism was presented soon thereafter.[77] Sponsored exclusively by developing and least-developed economies,[78] the suggestion takes up many of the other proposals' features while strengthening the assistance elements. More room is also given to the flexibilities side, placing less of an onus on the developing world to commit to substantive disciplines. While both submissions represent work in progress and agreement on any of its elements is yet to be obtained, one can already see their influence on the SDT – and related technical assistance – debate. Future contributions will inevitably be measured against the standards set therein, with it likely to be hard for anybody to undercut their offers on the SDT side. Compared to the earlier suggestions of the developing world, the co-sponsorship of major industrial nations of the much more far-reaching W/137 (WTO 2006a) proposal already marks a significant achievement in itself.

Developing and least-developed countries also had a good hand in obtaining support for their offensive demands. They obtained positive response to many of their GATT-related proposals with most of them even finding co-sponsors on the developed-country side.[79]

Nature of the subject

Finally – and this may seem paradoxical – the success of the TF negotiations also has to do with the technical, "non-sexy" nature of the subject that enabled Members to focus on the substance, which was relatively uncontroversial and allowed the politics to be low key. For most countries, Trade Facilitation is not a make-or-break matter. It does not lend itself to emotional debates and headline coverage. And the targeted gains do not have to be achieved at somebody else's expense. As a result, Members were able to address the issue on its own merits, without much heckling from the outside world. In some ways, the apparent unattractiveness of the subject therefore added to it becoming one of the bright spots in this Round.

Broader implications?

Some of the ingredients of the Trade Facilitation success may merit exploration for their potential to guide other negotiations. Certain factors stand out as being of broader applicability.

Extensive and inclusive preparations are one example. Although more a de facto reality than a conscious choice, the advancing of important groundwork to the pre-negotiations stage turned out to deliver advantageous results. As difficult – and painful – as it seemed at times to clarify the scope of the negotiations and to obtain agreement on its parameters before setting sail, the strategy showed clear returns. Long preparations at the technical level allowed the NG to base itself on previous work. More than half of the negotiating proposals had already been presented in similar form in the pre-negotiating phase, enabling a more informed discussion during the actual negotiations stage. Equally – if not even more – important was the developing countries' genuine comfort level with the modalities. Without that, the TF talks never would have been able to advance so quickly.

Obtaining this consensus required concessions in the SDT and TACB domains, with the proponents accepting terms they had considered to be no-go terrain before. This is especially the case for the agreed linkage between a country's capacity and obligation to implement, placing emphasis – and onus – on the creation of enhanced capabilities as opposed to mere temporary carve-outs. It also implied opting for flexible, individually targeted solutions of a hitherto unknown scope. Far from simply stipulating group-basis SDT offers for the developing and least-developed camps, the TF negotiations opted for tailor-made approaches that involved each country in the determination – and enhancement – process of its respective capacity. Doing so helped developing countries to see the development dimension of the talks, with several of them expressly recognizing the NG's way of incorporating this aspect into its work to "pave new ground" with the potential to constitute a "pattern for other aspects of WTO negotiations in the future".[80]

The emphasis on a Member-driven, inclusive mode of operation – that extended well beyond the mere lip-service sphere – could be another candidate. While the TF talks have not yet reached the final drafting stage where requirements for advancement may be different, it is no exaggeration to say that the TF NG exemplified efforts to maximize transparency and inclusiveness, rejecting calls for small drafting bodies and focussing on an open-ended exchange. Opting for a gradual – and parallel – way of addressing all elements of the mandate could also be mentioned here. For many developing countries, the constant focus on

SDT and technical assistance matters did much to maintain their comfort level.

Not pursuing a hard line on milestones (such as of the question of when to move into drafting mode) in favour of a flexible adjustment according to the needs of the situation proved beneficial as well. So did the explicit effort to focus first on the least controversial issues – to find common ground – and then build up from there. Postponing sensitive format questions, such as the shape of the outcome (Agreement versus amendment), and giving priority to the content side might equally have positive implications beyond the mere Facilitation domain.

As much as any effort to transpose lessons from one negotiating area to another has its obvious limitations, the TF negotiations may have set an example – perhaps even a standard – in those respects that will be hard to dismiss. At a minimum, the TF terms will serve as a reference point for future multilateral projects. Developed countries may find it hard to retroactively lower the threshold for rulemaking exercises yet to come. In some ways, it may even hold part of the answer on how to ensure a functioning multilateral negotiations machinery without dispensing with the consensus principle.

In some respect, the TF negotiations could also be seen as having pioneered a more integrated approach to trade liberalization. A focus that does not limit itself to looking at the elimination of trade distorting measures per se, but extends its perspective to their way of implementation. An emphasis on the *how* as opposed to the mere *what*. Trade Facilitation is emblematic for this manner of looking at trade policy and market expansion. It recognizes that much of a measure's success depends on the way it is put into practice, and that even the best initiative is bound to fail if not complemented with genuine concern for meaningful implementation. And it acknowledges that the devil is in the detail, and that there is not much point in calling for prompt publication (as Article X does) or the elimination of all unnecessary delays and restrictions (as required by Article V) without giving some thought to the means of implementation and their feasibility on the ground. Much of what has been proposed as an improvement to GATT Articles V, VIII and X was already an objective for the drafters of those provisions 60 years ago. The fact that we are still struggling with some of the problems they sought to address is only partly the result of shortcomings in the rules themselves. Some of the difficulties stem from a failure to embed the rules in a broader real world context that acknowledges the need for practicability verification and spirit (as opposed to letter)-based interpretation.

As such, Trade Facilitation is also about changed mentalities. No measure will have a real impact without a switch from mere enforcement mode to one of creating an enabling environment conducive for trade. And nothing will work without the political will to give real meaning to provisions that will otherwise remain a dead-letter creation. Tariff reductions might be implementable on a mere paragraph compliance basis. But for trade facilitation to work, more is required. The WTO negotiations on the subject seek to capture these additional aspects. In doing so, they may also pioneer a new way of looking at the multilateral trading system and its negotiating component as a whole.

Final thoughts

Remaining challenges

The obvious progress in the TF negotiations should not hide the fact that problems remain and need to be addressed. Substantive advances in discussing detailed proposals do not equal agreement on final outcomes. Further refinement and consensus-building work would even be required among the proponents to bridge differences over design and content of individual measures. The same goes for the implementation side, where substantive divergences remain. The current progress on the basic architecture is a necessary, but not a sufficient, condition for agreement on its final elements. Views especially differ on the appropriate support-commitment ratio, where concerns about costs and financing arrangements persist.[81] The precise applicability of dispute settlement procedures also continues to be an issue for some developing countries, as does the institutional settings of a possible capacity building verification and coordination mechanism. Furthermore, one can still find isolated fears over a perceived import orientation of the TF talks. Some developing countries fear their outcome to facilitate imports without delivering equivalent export opportunities into developed markets – resulting, for example, from non-compliance with industrial standards.[82]

And there are also wider systemic challenges – especially as regards the positioning within the Single Undertaking, related risks of hostage taking and the overall fate of the Round. They are especially noticeable for relatively unproblematic – and yet, often lower-priority – issues like Trade Facilitation, as could be observed with the July suspension call. Progress in its own area offered no protection against the general shutdown, even though its causes were entirely unrelated to the Facilitation front. And with the issue not representing a make-or-break domain, it would require extra efforts to make the case for a future on a stand-alone basis. Even a quick resumption within the framework of the Doha Round would involve special challenges due to heightened time constraints. Any breakthroughs in key areas (such as agriculture or NAMA) could then lead to strong pressure to wrap up in no time.[83]

At the same time, there is no doubt that the TF NG managed to move into the suspension phase on a positive note and would be well-positioned to quickly resume work. There is also clear and wide recognition of the need for the TF mission to be completed. Members repeatedly expressed their wish for the time-out to be nothing but a temporary one.[84] Whether that will translate into unanimous willingness to resume the Trade Facilitation negotiations – as part of a general recommencement scenario or on a separate basis – is still an open question. An across-the-board resumption would require Members' willingness to move on key areas of the Round (such as agriculture and NAMA) without there being much of a link to their stance on the TF side. The decision to enact the suspension mode was as unrelated to the state-of-play in Facilitation as a call for its termination would be.

A restart of the TF talks as part of a package of issues detracted – or always having been excluded[85] – from the Single Undertaking could be another option. While a related proposal (Mandelson 2006) presented by the European Communities immediately – and perhaps somewhat prematurely – after the suspension ruling was not universally accepted, the long-term perspectives for such a set-up are yet to be seen. A third scenario, the permanent freeze of the TF talks, seems rather improbable, given the broad support for the talks and the progress already made.

What is at stake?

Failure to conclude the TF negotiations would mean failure to realize their trade enhancement and cost-reduction potential – a failure to deliver on the very promises that led to the initiation of the Doha Development Round in the first place. It would not only destroy a decade of intense work with tangible advances, but also put an end to what many see as a new way of constructive cooperation between the developed and developing world. It would be a missed chance to improve rules that reflect the trading realities of the 1940s more than those of today's globalized world, and to revert to the days of opaque transaction requirements and major difficulties to get goods across borders. Without those negotiations, traders will remain at the mercy of governments when seeking predictability and minimum due process rights, with no assurances that changes in administration will not lead to a rescinding of reforms. It would throw the trading community back into an environment of multiple – and sometimes contradictory – recommendations that have no teeth and no guarantee of ever being put in place. They would have to settle for the pre-negotiations environment of cumbersome and non-transparent rules where compliance costs often exceed expenses on the tariff side. A reality, where small and medium-sized enterprises – which as a whole account for up to 60 per cent of GDP creation in many parts of the developing world – are not active players in international trade, and where inefficiencies in the border clearance and transit area impair export competitiveness and function as roadblocks to integration into the global economy.

Without those negotiations, there would be no mechanism to ensure that current facilitation reforms are geared toward the same direction and locked in to stay – essential to secure donor support and capable of making a real difference to the development prospects of much of the WTO world.

While domestic, bilateral and regional initiatives can complement each other and interact in a mutually reinforcing way, they are no substitute for multilateral TF efforts, as they risk creating inconsistencies that further increase the problems they seek to address. It is hardly possible to think about such piecemeal scenarios without considering the related risks of a further nationalization of a system that, by definition, requires a cross-border approach (not to mention the risk of a further weakening of the global economic system as a whole, which has already come under strain).

As economic independence deepens, traders need harmonized rules that avoid duplication of work. They also need modern rules that are there to stay. Moving from the current system of edentulous recommendations and outdated rules to one that lives up to the demands of today's trading reality is an imperative of the modern business world. It would not only secure the full benefits of the liberalization mission of the WTO, but also further the objectives that led to its creation in the first place.

The loss would be particularly ironic given that TF has made such striking progress – against initial odds – turning into one of the most promising areas of the Doha Round. It has pioneered new approaches and new ways of looking at traditional trade problems and provided clear and tangible evidence of the capacities of developing and developed players to find a common cause.

Some of the factors behind the Trade Facilitation success story may be of broader applicability. This could be the case for its careful preparation, the effort placed in arriving at negotiating modalities that have the genuine support of the whole Membership and the readiness to walk the extra mile in the area of SDT. It might also apply to the focus on country-specific solutions beyond the traditional group-oriented approach. Equally significant was the handling on the internal operation side, placing emphasis on gradual, balanced forms of advancement. Member-driven nature, inclusiveness, soft lines on milestones and flexible adjustment of ambition also had their role to play.

On a broader level, the TF negotiations support a trend in liberalization efforts toward a more integrated approach, extending the focus beyond the content of a measure to include its implementation mode. In recognizing the effectiveness of an initiative to critically depend on its ground-level applicability and the resulting need for holistic solutions, the TF talks could be seen as exemplary for a new way of looking at sustainable trade reform.

While the time and form of resuming Trade Facilitation work is yet to be seen, there is no doubt about the importance of this mission, which promises to ensure that today's trade is not governed by yesterday's rules.

Notes

1. The reference is one to (1) the relationship between trade and investment, (2) the interaction between trade and competition policy and (3) transparency in government procurement. Their common name stems from the Singapore Ministerial that led to them being added to the WTO's agenda.
2. Such demands were, inter alia, made by the European Communities and Japan. They were subsequently given up with all Members agreeing on the launch of negotiations in the Trade Facilitation area alone. The other three Singapore issues were decided "not [to] form part of the Work Programme" with there therefore being "no work towards negotiations on any of these issues ... within the WTO during the Doha Round". Decision adopted by the General Council on 1 August 2004 (WTO 2004a: 1g).
3. Examples include the agriculture and NAMA talks. One should, however, not overlook the different meaning – and, consequently, different implications – of the "modalities" term. In the Trade Facilitation area, consensus on the modalities implied nothing but an understanding on the general framework of – and a starting point for – future work, whereas it would represent a major breakthrough in the agriculture and NAMA talks, bringing them close to their finishing line. Originating from other areas of the Round, this Doha heritage was a bit of a misnomer in that it often gave rise to confusion.
4. In many ways, Trade Facilitation was nothing but a new name for an engagement as old as the institution itself. After all, the whole WTO is about facilitating trade.
5. Examples include the Committees on Customs Valuation, Rules of Origin or Import Licensing.
6. For a detailed history of the discussions on the scope of WTO work on Trade Facilitation and the early pre-negotiating phase, see Neufeld (2006).
7. At the same time, it was precisely those characteristics that led to the issue being added to the WTO's agenda in light of the special value added. If it were not for the WTO's enforcement mechanism, one could have left work to the other international organizations engaged in the process such as the WCO or several UN bodies.
8. The detailed reference is one to provisions for effective cooperation between customs or any other appropriate authorities on trade facilitation and customs compliance issues.
9. Annex D, section 4.

10. Other Negotiating bodies had required significantly more time for similar action. The NAMA Group, for instance, needed half a year to agree on a programme of meetings.
11. This report of the NG to the Trade Negotiations Committee was then taken up at the Hong Kong Ministerial Conference with Ministers endorsing its recommendations.
12. TN/TF/W/137 (WTO 2006a) is currently sponsored by Armenia, Canada, Chile, China, Dominican Republic, Ecuador, the European Community, Georgia, Guatemala, Honduras, Japan, Kyrgyz Republic, Mexico, Moldova, Nicaragua, Pakistan, Paraguay, Peru, Sri Lanka, Switzerland and Uruguay.
13. This is especially the case with respect to the requirements for committing to new disciplines.
14. Any commitment to apply a certain measure is preceded by – and conditional on – a capacity assessment, notification of detected needs, the development of capacity enhancement plans and some form of capacity acquisition verification system.
15. This developing-country grouping represents one of the two main non-geographically determined groupings in the Trade Facilitation arena. It currently comprises 21 Members: Bangladesh, Botswana, Cuba, Egypt, India, Indonesia, Jamaica, Kenya, Malaysia, Mauritius, Namibia, Nepal, Nigeria, Philippines, Rwanda, Tanzania, Trinidad & Tobago, Uganda, Venezuela, Zambia and Zimbabwe.
16. Such calls were repeatedly made in the first phase of the negotiations. See, for instance, the Core Group's statement as reflected in TN/TF/M/3, section 35 (WTO 2005b).
17. This group unites Members that advocated TF negotiations since Singapore. It includes practically all developed nations as well as a number of developing ones. The somewhat mundane background behind the naming relates to a picture of Colorado in the Geneva US Trade Representative office where the Group first met.
18. Footnote 1 to Annex D stresses that its terms are "without prejudice to the possible format of the final result of the negotiations and would allow consideration of various forms of outcomes".
19. Chile, Costa Rica, Singapore, Korea or Hong Kong China were the most prominent representatives of this grouping.
20. Proposals submitted by these Members address all areas of the negotiations' coverage. Suggestions ranged from measures to enhance publication and availability of information and increased consultation/communication mechanisms between border clearance parties to the reduction and simplification of import/export-related fees and formalities.
21. An initial submission by the African Group further insists that "The right to select policy options and exercise policy flexibility granted in favour of developing and least-developed countries must remain sacrosanct" (WTO 2005c).
22. This was also where their engagement started off. First submissions urged a tight limitation of possible disciplines to the three GATT Articles while seeking to improve the deliverables on the TACB side. All contributions from these Members called for the identification of their needs and priorities, and stressed the importance of assessing the suggested measures' costs.
23. Reflected not only in the listing of Article V but also in the negotiating mandate's reference to one of the objectives being the movement of goods, "including goods in transit" (Annex D, paragraph 1).
24. They are most directly felt as a negative impact on transport costs and related disadvantages for market access and economic growth. For landlocked developing countries, transport costs tend to be twice as high as they are for coastal states and often absorb a significant portion of their export earnings.
25. Their disadvantage is in fact a double one: they are vulnerable on the grounds of their own limitations and on account of their dependency on those of at least one other tran-

sit country, whose administrative, infrastructural and institutional framework is often just as weak.

26. TN/TF/W/39 (WTO 2005d) and W/119 (WTO 2006c). The suggestions were later merged with a paper by Armenia, the European Community, the Kyrgyz Republic, Macedonia and Moldova and circulated as W/133 (WTO 2006d).

27. A commitment is sought according to which "Members shall not apply discriminatory measures to goods in transit, or to vessels or other means of transport of other Members, for non-commercial reasons" without that excluding "the right to resort to the exceptions already laid down in WTO Agreements, for valid reasons and provided that the measure concerned does not constitute a disguised restriction on international trade" TN/TF/W/127 (WTO 2006e). Cuba was the first Member to present a text-based proposal.

28. TN/TF/W/22 (WTO 2005e), W/86 (WTO 2006f) and W/104 (WTO 2006g). In particular, Uganda seeks to obtain a commitment for all Members not to "require a consular transaction, including any related fee or charge, in connection with the importation of any good." TN/TF/W/104 (WTO 2006g: para. 2). All proposals were co-sponsored by the United States.

29. TN/TF/M/4 (WTO 2005f: para. 29). The figure does not include other export fees.

30. Ibid.

31. TN/TF/W/60 (WTO 2005g).

32. In particular, it is suggested to (1) establish a code of conduct in the customs services, spelling out the rights and obligations of the public servants; (2) introduce computerized systems to reduce (or eliminate) the discretion exercised by officials and employees with respect to basic customs decisions; (3) establish a system of penalties, to be directly incorporated in the country's customs legislation with offences by customs officials being considered as criminal acts; and (4) establish coordination and control mechanisms between customs administrations and the organizations involved in devising ethics policies in customs services. Calls are further made for technical assistance to create and build up a country's national capacity to prevent and control customs offences.

33. Examples include measures in the areas of import/export documentation requirements, border procedures, authorized trader and risk management schemes. The specific focus of those proposals is that they are to be designed and applied uniformly within all members of a customs union. India also advocated proposals aimed at establishing specific appeal mechanisms within such unions (for details, see W/122 (WTO 2006h: section V)) and at improving uniformity and traders' rights with respect to import alerts, detention and test procedures. Interestingly, these proposals comprise the measures most stretching Annex D's scope, triggering questions about the mandate's coverage even from the developed world.

34. Examples include proposals to accept commercially available information and copies of documents, reduce import/export-related formalities and documentation requirements and allow for post-clearance audit.

35. One – W/142 (WTO 2006h) – is exclusively developing- and least-developed-country sponsored, while the other – W/137 (WTO 2006a) – also attracted developed-country support.

36. Those groupings, which had been heavily engaged in coordination work on the Singapore issues as a whole, continue to play a role in current negotiating work. Both the ACP and African Group issued common statements and circulated written submissions on behalf of their Members. See, for instance, TN/TF/W/33 (WTO 2005c) and W/56 (WTO 2005h) for the African Group and – JOB(04)/102 (WTO 2004c) – and TN/TF/W/73 (WTO 2005i) for the ACP Group.

37. A forerunner grouping had already been formed in the immediate post-Doha days when like-minded countries teamed up for a common position on the Singapore issues. In some ways, the Core Group – which initially also addressed other Singapore issues – represents a Trade Facilitation-oriented offshoot of this Informal Group of developing countries.
38. Egypt, India, Indonesia, Jamaica, Kenya, Malaysia, Nigeria, the Philippines, Tanzania and Trinidad and Tobago were most active in the Trade Facilitation context. The Group later grew to include other developing and least-developed countries such as Bangladesh, Botswana, Cuba, Mauritius, Namibia, Nepal, Rwanda, Uganda, Venezuela, Zambia and Zimbabwe. China initially engaged in the Group but later decided to discontinue its participation.
39. Given his background as the head of the non-proponent Facilitation camp, Muhammad Noor's election was no small achievement.
40. For many of the least-developed Core Group members, which relied heavily on Group representation in the advocacy of their interests, agreement to launch negotiations was also a reflection of the trust placed in Malaysia's guidance on the matter.
41. And this despite their initial preference for a more pronounced negotiating supporter in the driver's seat. Much of the credit for Malaysia's positive role in winning developing-country support for agreeing on the negotiating modalities also goes to Mohamed Zain, who frequently stepped in for his heavily occupied ambassador and whose skilful balancing of ambition with pragmatism (of seeking the maximum outcome for his clientele while remaining within the limits of the feasible) won him respect on all sides.
42. See, for instance, the inventions by the Philippines on behalf of the Core Group as reflected in TN/TF/M/1 (WTO 2004d), M/2 (WTO 2004e: para. 184), M/3 (WTO 2005i: para. 33), M/4 (WTO 2005j), M/5 (WTO 2005k: para. 148) or M/7 (WTO 2005l: para. 7). Several proposed measures were questioned as going beyond the Articles' domain (See JOB(05)/64 or JOB(05)/159). Ironically, it later was Core Group Members (especially India) who proposed measures outside the realm of the three GATT provisions. See, for example, the Indian proposals TN/TF/W/77 (WTO 2006j), TN/TF/W/78 (WTO 2006k), TN/TF/W/101 (WTO 2006l) and TN/TF/W/102 (WTO 2006m).
43. See TN/TF/M/2 (WTO 2004e: para. 189).
44. A request for the inclusion of financial support had already been made in the CG's modalities proposal (JOB(04)/101, §5) without that being acceptable to the rest of the Membership. As a result, the final text of the mandate does not contain any express reference to "financial" support.
45. Calls for an addressing of "the applicability or non-applicability" of the DSU had already been made in the Core Group's draft modalities (JOB(04)/101). This had, however, been rejected by other Members with the consequence of the final mandate not containing any reference to dispute settlement procedures (and therefore an implicit assumption of their applicability).
46. See, for instance, the Group's statements in TN/TF/M/3 (WTO 2005i: para. 36).
47. The Group's implementation proposal even contains a written disclaimer to that end.
48. Examples include Djibouti, Jordan, Lesotho, St. Kitts and Nevis, the Solomon Islands, Trinidad and Tobago and Tunisia.
49. For a quantification of those benefits, see OECD (2005). The study shows a positive impact of trade facilitation on trade flows, government revenue and foreign direct investment. The OECD also showed that already a 1 per cent (of an estimated overall potential of up to 15 per cent) reduction of trade transaction costs for goods will bring annual gains of about US$40 billion on a world basis with most of those gains benefiting developing countries in relative terms (OECD 2003). World Bank research showed similar results.

50. According to a recent World Bank study, each day a product gets delayed in transit reduces trade by at least 1 per cent (Djankov et al. 2006). Against the background of average export and clearance times remaining at considerable levels (exports are still held up for an average of 34 days in South Asia and 29 days in Eastern Europe and Central Asia by delays in complying with trade-related regulations, while traders in Sub-Saharan Africa have to settle for an average of 47 1/2 days to get their goods from factory to ship; World Bank 2006), one can easily assess the dimension of the problem. And by far the largest per share of these delays are due to administrative hurdles (75 per cent in the case of Sub-Sahara's factory-to-ship time).

51. What remained were concerns about the financing side, leading to extensive provisions on TACB.

52. This is especially relevant for SMEs. For them, complicated and non-transparent import/export procedures often amount to prohibitive barriers to international trade.

53. Countries have shown to more than double their customs revenue after implementing comprehensive customs reform programmes (OECD 2005).

54. The calculation varies depending on what to consider the starting point. Much of the preparatory work already took place ahead of the 2003 Cancun Ministerial Conference.

55. "Members recognize that this [SDT] principle should extend beyond the granting of traditional transition periods for implementing commitments." Annex D of the July Package, paragraph 2.

56. Ibid.

57. Annex D of the July Package, paragraph 3.

58. Annex D, paragraph 2.

59. "Negotiations shall also aim at enhancing technical assistance and support for capacity building in this area." Annex D, paragraph 1.

60. All attempts to include even a general reference to "infrastructure" had been rejected as a no-go area by large parts of the developed world before.

61. The Annex refers to "certain commitments whose implementation would require support for infrastructure development on the part of some Members" and makes sure that "in these limited cases, developed-country Members will make every effort to ensure support and assistance directly related to the nature and scope of the commitments in order to allow implementation" (paragraph 6).

62. Annex D, paragraph 6.

63. For details, see paragraph 4 of Annex D.

64. There is one main addition: India succeeded in adjoining the development of "provisions for effective cooperation between customs or any other appropriate authorities on trade facilitation and customs compliance issues" as an additional aim of the negotiations. Annex D, paragraph 1.

65. For a detailed history of the discussions on the scope of WTO work on Trade Facilitation and the early pre-negotiating phase, see Neufeld (2006).

66. JOB(04)/96.

67. JOB(04)/101.

68. Paragraphs 3, 4, 8 and 9 of Annex D are largely based on the Core Group's draft.

69. This was especially the case at the very beginning of the negotiations and when approaching the Hong Kong Ministerial Conference.

70. See Tanzania's intervention at the first Negotiating Group meeting – TN/TF/M/1 (WTO 2004d: para. 12). Tanzania also wanted that "all decisions taken by the Negotiating Group in connection with the negotiations should be by explicit consensus" (WTO 2004d).

71. Typical examples for SDT suggestions contained in those first-generation proposals were references to the need to "take fully into account the principle of special and differential

treatment in the results of the negotiations and to make such treatment precise, effective and operational" – TN/TF/W/35 (WTO 2005m) – or suggestions that "If the proposed requirement would be inherently more burdensome for developing countries than for other Members, special and differential treatment to mitigate or manage such burdens would need to be considered" – TN/TF/W/24 (WTO 2005n). Some of them would at least contain some initial ideas of how that should materialize ["Special and differential treatment provisions reflecting the specific circumstances of individual Members could be incorporated within commitments, for example through provisions for progressive implementation." – TN/TF/W/20 (WTO 2005o)].

72. See, for instance, TN/TF/W/39 (WTO 2005d).
73. See, for instance, TN/TF/W/7 (WTO 2005p), W/8 (WTO 2005q), W/26 (WTO 2005r) and W/32 (WTO 2005s). Little more than 10 per cent of all first generation proposals suggested more than the granting of transition periods.
74. TN/TF/M/5 (WTO 2005k: para. 124). Part of the reasons for the decision to abolish the original idea of presenting an immediate written follow-up related to negative – informal – feedback from some developed Members.
75. See, for instance Canada's statement as reflected in TN/TF/M/8 (WTO 2005u: para. 81). Similar comments were even made by some developing countries such as Bolivia – TN/TF/M/4 (WTO 2005f: para. 154) – and Mexico – TN/TF/M/7 (WTO 2005l: para. 221).
76. See, for instance, proposals TN/TF/W/100 (WTO 2006p), W/101 (WTO 2006l) and W/102 (WTO 2006m). See also TN/TF/W/112 (WTO 2006q) and W/119 (WTO 2006c).
77. JOB(06)/230 later circulated as TN/TF/W/142 (WTO 2006h).
78. Bangladesh, Botswana, Cuba, Egypt, India, Indonesia, Jamaica, Kenya, Malaysia, Mauritius, Namibia, Nepal, Nigeria, the Philippines, Rwanda, Tanzania, Trinidad and Tobago, Uganda, Venezuela, Zambia and Zimbabwe.
79. See for instance the reaction to Uganda's proposal to eliminate consularization (WTO 2005f) or Rwanda's, Mongolia's and Paraguay's suggestions to improve free transit of goods – TN/TF/M/14 (WTO 2006s).
80. "Trade facilitation is an important component of ensuring the development dimension of the Round. Given the progress made so far, the NG is paving new ground on how to ensure that this dimension was incorporated in the negotiations which could be a pattern for other aspects of WTO negotiations in the future". Statement by the Philippines on behalf of the Core Group – TN/TF/M/10 (WTO 2005x: para. 88).
81. The sponsors of the Core Group proposal consider the alternative W/137 (WTO 2006a) proposal not to go far enough in that regard, while other developed countries did not sign on to W/137 on the grounds of it already going too far.
82. See, for instance, the views expressed by Pakistan's ambassador on the perspective of the developing world (please see Achmad (2006: x)).
83. Differences in process as a result from different requirements of substance have challenged the TF negotiations right from the start. Despite different starting positions (2 1/2 years delay, but already existent modalities in TF while they are yet to found in the AG and NAMA talks), divergent requirements (TF needing "words, not numbers", as remarked by Pakistan's ambassador), disparities in the negotiating dynamics (agreement on modalities marked nothing but a starting point in Facilitation while they would imply the near end in the AG and NAMA talks) and huge differences in political evaluation (AG and NAMA representing the heart of the Doha Round and holding the key for progress on other fronts while progress on TF does not have the potential to positively influence the AG agenda) the demands of the Single Undertaking imply a same finishing line.
84. See, for instance, the statements made by delegations at the last meeting of the NG as reflected in TN/TF/M/15 (WTO 2006t).
85. This would especially be the case for the Aid-for-Trade area.

REFERENCES

Achmad, Manzoor (2006) "Trade Facilitation Negotiations – How to Move Forward? A Perspective from Developing Countries", paper presented at the meeting of the Global Facilitation Partnership (GFP), Washington, DC, October. Available from: http://www.gfptt.org/uploadedEditorImages/00000323.pdf.

Djankov, Simeon, Caroline Freund and Cong S. Pham (2006) *Trading on Time*, Washington, DC: World Bank.

Mandelson, P. (2006) "We Need to Look Ahead and To Rebuild", Transcript of his remarks on his return from Geneva following the suspension of the WTO Doha negotiations, Brussels, 25 July. Available from: http://ec.europa.eu/commission_barroso/mandelson/speeches_articles/sppm110_en.htm.

Neufeld, N. (2006) "Trade Facilitation Negotiations in the Context of the Doha Round – The Role of the European Union", in G. Trondl and R. Hofmann, eds, *The European Union and the WTO Doha Round*, Baden-Baden: Nomos Verlagsgesellscha.

OECD (2003) *Quantitative Assessment of the Benefits of Trade Facilitation*, TD/TC/WP(2003)31/FINAL.

OECD (2005) *The Economic Impact of Trade Facilitation*, OECD Trade Policy Working Paper No. 21, 12 October, TD/TC/WP(2005)12/FINAL.

World Bank (2006) *Doing Business 2007*, Washington, DC: World Bank.

WTO (2004a) "Doha Work Programme – Decision Adopted by the General Council on 1 August 2004", WT/L/579, Geneva.

WTO (2004b) "Negotiating Group on Trade Facilitation, Work plan and schedule of meetings", 16 November, TN/TF/1, Geneva.

WTO (2004c) "Doha Work Programme, Draft General Council Decision," JOB(04)/96 of 16 July 2004 and Rev. 1 of 30 July 2004, Geneva.

WTO (2004d) "Negotiating Group on Trade Facilitation, Minutes of the Meeting", 12 October, TN/TF/M/1, Geneva.

WTO (2004e) "Negotiating Group on Trade Facilitation, Minutes of the Meeting", 22–23 November, TN/TF/M/2, Geneva.

WTO (2005a) "Negotiating Group on Trade Facilitation, Report to the Trade Negotiations Committee", 21 November, TN/TF/3, Geneva.

WTO (2005b) "Negotiating Group on Trade Facilitation", Minutes of the Meeting of 7 and 9 March, TN/TF/M/3, Geneva.

WTO (2005c) "Negotiating Group on Trade Facilitation – Communication from the African Group – Trade Facilitation", 28 April, TN/TF/W/33, Geneva.

WTO (2005d) "Negotiating Group on Trade Facilitation – Communication from Paraguay, Rwanda and Switzerland – Trade Facilitation: Improvement of Elements Related to Transit", 2 May, TN/TF/W/39, Geneva.

WTO (2005e) "Negotiating Group on Trade Facilitation – Communication from Uganda and the United States – Consularization – Proposal by Uganda and the United States", 21 March, TN/TF/W/22, Geneva.

WTO (2005f) "Negotiating Group on Trade Facilitation", Minutes of the Meeting of 22–24 March 2005, TN/TF/M/4, Geneva.

WTO (2005g) "Negotiating Group on Trade Facilitation – Communication from the Dominican Republic – Proposal by the Dominican Republic on Reinforcing

the Ethical Conduct of Staff and the Integrity of Customs Administrations",
8 August, TN/TF/W/60, Geneva.

WTO (2005h) "Negotiating Group on Trade Facilitation – Communication from
the African Group – Operationalizing Technical Assistance and Capacity
Building in Trade Facilitation", 22 July, TN/TF/W/56, Geneva.

WTO (2005i) "Negotiating Group on Trade Facilitation – Communication from
Mauritius on behalf of the ACP Group – Issues in the negotiations on trade facilitation and the importance of promoting development objectives through
technical assistance and capacity-building", 10 November, TN/TF/W/73, Geneva.

WTO (2005i) "Negotiating Group on Trade Facilitation – Summary Minutes of
the Meeting", held on 7 and 9 February, TN/TF/M/3, Geneva.

WTO (2005j) "Negotiating Group on Trade Facilitation – Summary Minutes
of the Meeting", held on 22–24 March 2005, TN/TF/M/4, Geneva.

WTO (2005k) "Negotiating Group on Trade Facilitation – Summary Minutes of
the Meeting", held on 2–3 May, TN/TF/M/5, Geneva.

WTO (2005l) "Negotiating Group on Trade Facilitation – Summary Minutes of
the Meeting", held on 25–26 July, TN/TF/M/7, Geneva.

WTO (2005m) "Negotiating Group on Trade Facilitation – Communication from
the European Communities – Freedom of Transit", 29 April, TN/TF/W/35,
Geneva.

WTO (2005n) "Negotiating Group on Trade Facilitation – Communication from
New Zealand – Proposals to Clarify and Improve Articles VIII and X", 21
March, TN/TF/W/24, Geneva.

WTO (2005o) "Negotiating Group on Trade Facilitation – Communication from
Canada – Possible Commitments on Border Agency Coordination – A Proposal by Canada", 18 March, TN/TF/W/20, Geneva.

WTO (2005p) "Negotiating Group on Trade Facilitation – Communication from
Korea – Clarification of Article X of the GATT: Publication and Availability of
Information and Prior Commenting Period on Core Measures", 27 January,
TN/TF/W/7, Geneva.

WTO (2005q) "Negotiating Group on Trade Facilitation – Communication from
Japan, Mongolia, and the Separate Customs Territory of Taiwan, Penghu, Kin-
men and Matsu – Trade Facilitation: Proposals to Clarify and Improve GATT
Article X", 28 January, TN/TF/W/8, Geneva.

WTO (2005r) "Negotiating Group on Trade Facilitation – Communication from
the People's Republic of China – Proposal on Clarification and Improvement
of GATT Article X", 21 March, TN/TF/W/26, Geneva.

WTO (2005s) "Negotiating Group on Trade Facilitation – Communication From
Hong Kong, China – Proposal for Improving GATT Article X", 28 April, TN/
TF/W/32, Geneva.

WTO (2005t) "Negotiating Group on Trade Facilitation – Communication from
the European Communities – Improvements to GATT Article VIII on Formalities and Requirements Connected with Importation and Exportation and
Related Proposals on Special and Differential Treatment and Technical Assistance", 9 June, TN/TF/W/46, Geneva.

WTO (2005u) "Negotiating Group on Trade Facilitation – Summary Minutes of the Meeting" held on 19–20 September, TN/TF/M/8, Geneva.

WTO (2005v) "Negotiating Group on Trade Facilitation – Communication from Singapore – Procedural Elements for Advance Rulings", 2 May, TN/TF/W/38, Geneva.

WTO (2005w) "Negotiating Group on Trade Facilitation – Communication from Singapore – GATT Article V (Freedom of Transit)", 9 June, TN/TF/W/47, Geneva.

WTO (2005x) "Negotiating Group on Trade Facilitation – Summary Minutes of the Meeting" held on 24–25 October, TN/TF/M/10, Geneva.

WTO (2006a) "Implementation Mechanism of Trade Facilitation Commitments Including Key Elements for technical assistance, Communication from Armenia, Chile, China, Dominican Republic, Ecuador, the European Communities, Georgia, Guatemala, Honduras, Japan, Kyrgyz Republic, Mexico, Moldova, Nicaragua, Pakistan, Paraguay, Sri Lanka, Switzerland and Uruguay", 21 July, TN/TF/W/137, Geneva.

WTO (2006b) "Negotiating Group on Trade Facilitation, Report by the Chairman of the Negotiating Group on the State of Play in the Negotiations", 27 July, TN/TF/4, Geneva.

WTO (2006c) "Negotiating Group on Trade Facilitation – Communication from Mongolia, Paraguay, Rwanda, and Switzerland – Trade Facilitation: Improvement of Elements Related to Transit", 7 June, TN/TF/W/119, Geneva.

WTO (2006d) "Negotiating Group on Trade Facilitation – Communication from Armenia, the European Communities, the Former Yugoslav Republic of Macedonia, the Kyrgyz Republic, Mongolia, Paraguay, the Republic of Moldova, Rwanda, and Switzerland", 10 July, TN/TF/W/133, Geneva.

WTO (2006e) "Negotiating Group on Trade Facilitation – Communication from Cuba – Improvement and Clarification of Article V of the GATT: Strengthening of the Principles of Non-Discrimination and Most-Favoured-Nation Treatment", 6 July, TN/TF/W/127, Geneva.

WTO (2006f) "Negotiating Group on Trade Facilitation – Communication from Uganda and the United States – Consularization", 4 April, TN/TF/W/86, Geneva.

WTO (2006g) "Negotiating Group on Trade Facilitation – Communication from Uganda and the United States – Consularization", 11 May, TN/TF/W/104, Geneva.

WTO (2006h) "Negotiating Group on Trade Facilitation – Communication from India – Proposal on GATT Article X", 4 July, TN/TF/W/122, Geneva.

WTO (2006i) "Negotiating Group on Trade Facilitation – Communication from the Core Group of Developing Countries on Trade Facilitation – Proposal on Implementation Mechanism for Special and Differential Treatment (S&D) and Technical Assistance and Capacity Building (TACB) Support", 31 July, TN/TF/W/142, Geneva.

WTO (2006j) "Negotiating Group on Trade Facilitation – Communication from India – Proposal on GATT Article VIII", 10 February, TN/TF/W/77, Geneva.

WTO (2006k) "Negotiating Group on Trade Facilitation – Communication from India – Proposals on GATT Article X", 13 February, TN/TF/W/78, Geneva.

WTO (2006l) "Negotiating Group on Trade Facilitation – Communication from the European Communities, Japan, Korea, Mongolia, and the Separate Customs Territory of Taiwan, Penghu, Kinmen and Matsu – Proposal on Release Time of Goods", 10 May, TN/TF/W/101, Geneva.

WTO (2006m) "Negotiating Group on Trade Facilitation – Communication from Costa Rica, the European Communities, Japan, Korea, Mongolia, New Zealand, Singapore, and Switzerland – Proposal on Prior Publication and Consultation", 10 May, TN/TF/W/102, Geneva.

WTO (2006n) "Negotiating Group on Trade Facilitation – Summary Minutes of the Meeting" held on 15–16 February 2006, TN/TF/M/12, Geneva.

WTO (2006o) "Negotiating Group on Trade Facilitation – Communication from Mongolia, Norway, South Africa, and Switzerland – The Use of International Standards", 7 July, TN/TF/W/131, Geneva.

WTO (2006p) "Negotiating Group on Trade Facilitation – Communication from Chile, the European Communities, Japan, Korea, Mongolia, and Singapore – Proposal on the Introduction of Single Window/One-Time Submission", 10 May, TN/TF/W/100, Geneva.

WTO (2006q) "Negotiating Group on Trade Facilitation – Communication from Hong Kong China, Korea, and Switzerland – Acceptance of Commercially Available Information and of Copies (H.L.F.)", 6 June, TN/TF/W/112, Geneva.

WTO (2006r) "Negotiating Group on Trade Facilitation – Communication from Chile, Dominican Republic, Ecuador, Guatemala, Honduras, Mexico, Nicaragua, Paraguay and Uruguay – Special and Differential Treatment: Application and Inter-Relationship with Commitments Arising from the Negotiations on Trade Facilitation", 3 April, TN/TF/W/81, Geneva.

WTO (2006s) "Negotiating Group on Trade Facilitation – Summary Minutes of the Meeting" held on 6–7 June, TN/TF/M/14, Geneva.

WTO (2006t) "Negotiating Group on Trade Facilitation – Summary Minutes of the Meeting" held on 24–26 July, TN/TF/M/15, Geneva.

Index

311